body and nation

AMERICAN ENCOUNTERS/GLOBAL INTERACTIONS
A series edited by Gilbert M. Joseph and Emily S. Rosenberg

This series aims to stimulate critical perspectives and fresh interpretive frameworks for scholarship on the history of the imposing global presence of the United States. Its primary concerns include the deployment and contestation of power, the construction and deconstruction of cultural and political borders, the fluid meanings of intercultural encounters, and the complex interplay between the global and the local. *American Encounters* seeks to strengthen dialogue and collaboration between historians of U.S. international relations and area studies specialists.

The series encourages scholarship based on multiarchival historical research. At the same time, it supports a recognition of the representational character of all stories about the past and promotes critical inquiry into issues of subjectivity and narrative. In the process, *American Encounters* strives to understand the context in which meanings related to nations, cultures, and political economy are continually produced, challenged, and reshaped.

body and nation

THE GLOBAL REALM OF U.S. BODY POLITICS IN THE TWENTIETH CENTURY

Edited by Emily S. Rosenberg
& Shanon Fitzpatrick

Duke University Press
Durham and London
2014

© 2014 Duke University Press
All rights reserved

Printed in the United States of America on acid-free paper ∞
Text designed by Chris Crochetière, BW&A Books, Inc.
Typeset in Quadraat by BW&A Books, Inc.

Library of Congress Cataloging-in-Publication Data
Body and nation : the global realm of U.S. body politics in the twentieth
century / edited by Emily S. Rosenberg and Shanon Fitzpatrick.
pages cm—(American encounters/global interactions)
Includes bibliographical references and index.
ISBN 978-0-8223-5675-2 (pbk : alk. paper)
ISBN 978-0-8223-5664-6 (cloth: alk. paper)
1. Human body—Political aspects—United States. 2. United States—
Politics and government—20th century. 3. United States—Foreign
relations—20th century. I. Rosenberg, Emily S., 1944– II. Fitzpatrick,
Shanon. III. Series: American encounters/global interactions.
E743.B614 2014
327.73009′04—dc23
2014005678

Cover art: Dichotomy (detail), Gil Bruvel. Stainless steel. Courtesy of the artist.

Dedicated to
Norman Rosenberg
and
Ruthann and Christopher Meyer

contents

introduction

EMILY S. ROSENBERG AND SHANON FITZPATRICK

Bodies attract and disgust; they are the most frequent objects of personal thoughts, desires, and actions. Moreover the anthropomorphic analogy contained in the term *body politic,* an analogy that has run throughout Western political and social traditions, most famously to Plato, illustrates the larger political and social meanings of bodies. *Body and Nation: The Global Realm of U.S. Body Politics in the Twentieth Century* brings together scholarship on the body with historical research on U.S. international and transnational relationships. It interrogates the connections among the body, the nation, and the world in twentieth-century U.S. history.

For the past thirty years theoretical investigations centering on the body, a topic once considered relevant largely to the biological sciences, have influenced most disciplines in the humanities and social sciences.[1] Foucault's exploration of biopolitics and biopower initially propelled interdisciplinary investigations of the disciplining and regulation of social groups and individuals.[2] Subsequent theoretical and historical studies have deepened our understanding of how the meanings and markings of bodies have come to be culturally constituted. The work of Joan Scott, Judith Butler, Anne Fausto-Sterling, and others, for example, explored how attributes of bodies (both individual and social) take shape in relation to particular circumstances that create a materiality emanating from reiterated cultural performances.[3] Scholars have also assessed the body's relationship to issues of personal identity, conceptions of social order, war making, modes of production and consumption, and norms of physical and social health.

The idea that bodily characteristics are heavily freighted with values and meanings and that these significations are often linked to arrangements within political and social spheres remain underdeveloped in the histories of America's relations with the rest of the world.[4] This collection—which presents bodies as complex, fluctuating, and interrelated sites of meaning production and as loci at which relations of power are constructed, enforced, and resisted—offers new insights for international and transnational historians interested in the workings of power. At the same time, the archival research, attention to diverse state and nonstate actors, and multisite analyses of these essays help create historically grounded portraits of the transnational and transactional dimensions of biopolitics.

Employing work in American studies and in U.S. international and transnational history, this collection both builds on and adds to existing multidisciplinary investigations by analyzing how constructions of physical bodies have intertwined with projections of a U.S. national body and by examining the relational meanings of both. The essays ask such questions as the following: In what ways have particular bodies been marked as belonging to, representative of, excluded from, or enemies of the nation? How do individual and national bodies coproduce meanings and provide signification for each other? How have relationships between the body and the nation changed over the course of a roughly hundred-year period marked by massive population flows, brutal wars, economic and media globalization, the ascendency of consumer cultures, and dramatic reconfigurations of personal and political identities?

Spanning the late nineteenth to the early twenty-first centuries, this volume is set within a conjuncture of several historical developments: multiple migrations of people, efforts to constitute (and oppose) strong national states and empires, a general shift from physical to cultural views of racial and ethnic difference, rapid growth of globalized mass media, and paroxysms of violence and warfare. These transnational historical developments, which occurred during a period in which the United States transformed into an imperial superpower with far-reaching economic, military, and cultural influence, provide a crucial backdrop to the individual studies. They help shape, along with the corpus of multidisciplinary theoretical scholarship on the body, the guiding themes of this collection.

The Essays

In engaging the ever-changing and ever-contested politics of body and nation, these essays have several main objectives. One is to encourage conversations between scholars identifying primarily with American studies and those identifying as historians of U.S. international relations or "the United States and the world." Another is to identify significant themes in U.S. body politics in global perspective through archival research that examines particular historical moments and representations. The goal is to open up investigative terrain, suggest new interdisciplinary links, and invite others to rethink the changing constructions of bodies and nations over the past century. Because the essays are arranged in roughly chronological order, it will be helpful first to summarize briefly the focus of each and then to elaborate three major connective threads that run through this volume.

The opening essay by Paul A. Kramer explores debates about the U.S. military's regulation of prostitution during the Philippine-American War. This very public controversy illuminated competing definitions of the U.S. empire as a moral, physical, and institutional body. In addition to providing a lens onto broader debates about colonialism and its racial and gendered implications for the United States, Kramer identifies how controversies over the inspection of "foreign" bodies became a specific way of conducting the much larger debate over the impact that overseas empire might have on the national body politic.

Janet Davis takes the concerns about the importance of healthy bodies to healthy nations in a different direction. Extending her earlier study of the American circus, she shows how the mutually constitutive relationship between the turn-of-the-century railroad circus, child's play, and the body helped articulate national identity at home as well as America's exceptionalist mission on the world stage. Davis illustrates how circus promoters promised that their activities would turn children and poor immigrant populations into productive and fit citizens of America; how militaries and circuses learned tactics of mobility from each other; and how circuses taught the racial taxonomies that bolstered turn-of-the-century imperialism.

The connection between fit bodies and fit nations threads through Annessa C. Stagner's essay, which addresses how "shell-shocked" soldiers came to symbolize the nation during and immediately after the Great War. After comparing European and American shell-shock discourse and treatment, Stagner illustrates how the interrelated realms of medicine, psychology, and popular culture helped Americans construct a recuperative vision of a healthy international system led by the United States.

Shanon Fitzpatrick's essay picks up the theme of globalizing media. She examines how the American physical culturalist and magazine mega-entrepreneur Bernarr Macfadden popularized and circulated images of strong, modern bodies around the world during the early years of the twentieth century. In an era marked by competing nationalisms and a flourishing eugenics movement, Macfadden's globally popular periodicals encouraged a transnational physical culture movement and a body-centric media culture marked by an ethos of self-transformation. This ethos spoke to new immigrants in the United States as well as to others who sought to hone strong, modern bodies and powerful, modern nations.

The ways immigrant diasporas and transnational mass culture combined to produce increasingly fluid and porous national and racial categories find further development in Shirley Jennifer Lim's essay on the Chinese American film star Anna May Wong. Focused on the late 1930s, Lim's multisite study places Wong's image within the development of a "transnational racial modernity" that was increasingly identified with American mass culture. In her careful staging of cosmopolitan hybridity, Wong evoked fascination with racial and national difference; at the same time, her career demonstrated how the slippages between these categories could be enacted as modern.

President Franklin D. Roosevelt's body during the Great Depression and World War II is the subject of the next essay, by Frank Costigliola. Costigliola explains how FDR, in both the national and international political arenas, skillfully cultivated a flexible self-presentation in which his physical impairments were projected as expertise, strength, charisma, and charm. Focusing on issues of disability, manliness, and gender performativity, Costigliola explores the discursive relationship between iconic male bodies and powerful nations.

Quite another take on issues of gender at war emerges in Brenda Gayle Plummer's analysis of "brown babies," the offspring of German women and African American soldiers during World War II. On both sides of the Atlantic, controversies about race, gender, and nation circulated around the portrayal and the fate of these babies. Plummer's analysis of these controversies shows how issues connected to brown babies illuminate policies related to both the reconstruction of postwar Europe and the transition toward defining a more inclusive citizenship in the United States.

Natalia Molina's essay provides a complement to the theme of race and nationalism. Focusing on three wartime periods (World War I, World War II, and post-9/11), she examines the role of "medicalized nativism" in the history of Mexican immigration to the United States. In addition to tracing the production of cultural representations of Mexicans as threats to the health of the U.S. national social body, Molina also calls attention to the ways disease and public health discourse have operated to define who was "foreign" to the nation.

Turning to the era of the early Cold War, Emily S. Rosenberg's essay on the "American Look" examines a trope that presented America in the shape of a fashionable, attractive young woman. Initially advanced to market American leadership in fashion design, the American Look became useful in post–World War II appeals to homecoming veterans, in export promotion, and in anticommunist propaganda offensives. Although the early Cold War is often portrayed as the time of a masculinized arms race, the American Look provided a complementary discourse that asserted American power by emphasizing attraction—youth, style, and modernity—rather than force and fear.

Continuing the discussion of iconic Cold War bodies in projections of foreign policy, Mary Ting Yi Lui examines the Korean American diver Sammy Lee's role as a U.S. goodwill ambassador. Focusing on Lee's 1954 tour through Asia, Lui teases out the various meanings ascribed to the Olympic champion's performances in different geographic and political contexts. Even as Lee could embody American discourses of postwar racial liberalism, representations of his athletic body were also easily wedded to narratives of decolonization and nation-building in Southeast Asia.

If the American Look and an Olympic champion had been used in campaigns to persuade the world to follow a U.S. model, tactics of war—particularly lethal air wars waged from on high in areas of civilian population—sought to compel it. Marilyn B. Young's essay explores the consequences of "body count" as a metric of success in wars. Used, though seldom noticed, during the Korean War, body count became the primary statistical way of assessing progress in defeating the enemy during the Vietnam War. In asking "Whose bodies count?" Young shows how techniques to raise body count shaped both the ferocity of that war and the toxic environment that Americans left (and largely ignored) in its aftermath.

The fate of a group of people constructed as enemies and pollutants within the nation provides the context of Kristina Shull's study of the Mariel Cuban refugees of 1980. In tracing the detention and processing of "unwanted" bodies during a perceived "mass immigration emer-

gency," Shull identifies the exercises of inclusion and exclusion that reinforced President Reagan's discourse of revitalized nationalism. While
some refugees were rendered acceptable additions to the national body
through cultural training and sponsorship, Shull emphasizes that "excludables" became nearly invisible through a new security apparatus of
immigration detention and private prison contracting.

The subject of privatized immigration detention facilities in the
United States provides an apt transition to this volume's epilogue,
"When the Body Disappears." Reflecting upon our themes of body and
nation, we consider the lack of historical visibility accorded to othered
bodies whose fates might challenge America's discourse of special benevolence. Examining the relative invisibility of atomic victims after
1945, the silences surrounding America's covert wars since the 1950s,
and the unknowns related to torture, rendition, drone strikes, and biosecurity over the past decade, we suggest that, just as visible bodies help
constitute the nation (and vice versa), less visible bodies and "asymmetric visibility" have helped to hide (and thus perpetuate) the exclusions
and violence of security regimes.

Rather than advance a single interpretive frame for the body and
nation connection, the essays in this collection suggest a variety of
themes. We have generally divided these themes, each of which thread
through many of the essays, into three categories: population migration and mixing, national security discourse, and mass-mediated cultural circulations.

Defining Bodies and National Affiliations in an Era of Empire and Global Migrations

U.S. imperial ambitions, together with the great population flows of the
late nineteenth and twentieth century, mixed people across continents
and thereby challenged boundaries of all kinds. Demographic shifts
created new borderlands, frontiers, and diasporas, generating ever-new
configurations of "bodies in contact" and national imaginaries.[5] In
this context of global migrations and U.S. political, economic, and cultural expansion, the relationship between body and nation was neither
static nor uncontested. Our collection illuminates how the meanings of
new contacts fostered through imperialism and migration were played
out by and played on individual bodies.[6] It also examines how transnational population flows variously shaped, challenged, and redefined
discourses of national embodiment.[7]

In keeping with a larger corpus of scholarship on immigration and state-building, several essays in this volume identify various techniques of exclusion, regulation, and containment deployed by the modern American state in order to manage the instabilities of population migration and delineate the nation.[8] From the nineteenth century on, consolidating national states throughout the world became intensely preoccupied with regulating and shaping the bodies of inhabitants (and hence the national body) in ways that would facilitate governance, promote the growth of commerce and national influence, and forge dominant majoritarian views of an optimal citizen. Kramer's treatment of prostitution in the Philippines, Plummer's study of "brown babies," and Molina's and Shull's essays on immigration control demonstrate how efforts to sort people into those who belonged and who did not often centered on regulating border-crossing bodies. In many instances, perceived threats to public health and national security, often identified with the bodies of racialized others, provided rationales for the exclusion of certain people from the national body. National exclusion became a marker of racial difference, and racial difference simultaneously became a justification for national exclusion. Essays in our volume ask how "nation" was invoked to justify containing and isolating boundary-crossing bodies, and how these processes also mark people who are constituted as foreign, alien, and perhaps even beyond humanity.

In bringing so many people and cultures into contact with one another, the processes of imperialism and migration did not just bolster classificatory and disciplinary regimes; they also fostered the production of new forms of knowledge about the human body that worked to sustain, undermine, and recast prevailing conceptions of the American body politic. In the time period covered in this volume, nineteenth-century preoccupations with anthropometry and race persisted but slowly gave way both to genetic science, which stressed the superficiality of physical differences such as skin color, and to cultural anthropology, which emphasized the cultural rather than racial construction of difference.[9] Racial segregation, antimiscegenation laws, immigrant quotas, restricted enfranchisement, and eugenics existed alongside ideologies of self-improvement, social betterment campaigns, and calls for "pluralism," "multiculturalism," and expanded civil rights. Over the course of the twentieth century, biologically rooted views of identity increasingly competed with new forms of scientific knowledge that bolstered claims that "proper" citizens were culturally made, not biologically born. By framing the body as an especially contested site for national definition, our volume demonstrates how traditions of incorporation, remolding, and mixture existed alongside and competed with regimes of exclusion and containment to shape both domestic body politics and international policies.

In the United States, as in many other parts of the world, the so-called physical fitness of individuals emerged as an important mark of American citizenship and of a strong nation.[10] Essays in our volume explore how state-building and bodybuilding became related processes in efforts to define and secure national boundaries of various kinds in the face of population flux. Kramer's analysis of the regulation of prostitution in the Philippines and Davis's exploration of the railroad circus emphasize two very different ways in which linked concerns over the physical and moral fitness of individual bodies served to bolster discourses of imperial nationalism. As the popularity of sports and exercise grew over the twentieth century, fit bodies became an increasingly strong component of nationalism and a standard measurement for national prominence around the globe.[11] The studies by Stagner, Fitzpatrick, Costigliola, Rosenberg, and Lui explore transnational processes through which personal health, beauty, athleticism, and physical mobility became signifiers of U.S. national virtue on the world stage.

What role did race, along with other forms of perceived bodily difference, play in defining American national identity and determining markers of national inclusion and exclusion? With their focus on both the physical and performative qualities exhibited by a range of historical actors, the essays in this volume carefully historicize and contextualize this question.[12] Exclusion certainly was often racialized, but certain figures embodied contested—and changing—interactions between discourses of nationhood and race. Imperialism and global migrations contributed to the rise of a diverse range of entertainers and media personalities who fostered varying narratives of national embodiment: circus performers (Davis's essay), physical culturalists (Fitzpatrick's essay), the movie star Anna May Wong (Lim's essay), and the Olympic diver Sammy Lee (Lui's essay) became iconic Americans precisely because they were, in many ways, liminal figures who invited others to cross borders and perform their own self-constructed—and eminently changeable—identities. Similarly, contested public debates over the fate of "brown babies" (Plummer's essay) and the place of immigrants in American society (Molina's and Shull's essays) highlight what Plummer refers to as the "ideological slippages" that attended attempts to define national inclusion and exclusion via essentialized notions of race.

Outsider Bodies and the Discourse of National Security

The insider/outsider and fit/unfit divides that shaped definitions of the national body became powerful elements in national security discourse, especially during times of political and economic strife. Because the symbolism around bodies emerges especially strongly in war, it is not surprising that many of our essays focus on periods of wartime. Indeed all of our essays, although illuminating a wide variety of contexts, show that representational practices surrounding bodies have remained at the very center of national security discourse and of calculations of strategic assets and liabilities.

The ways certain bodies became synecdochic for the nation during various twentieth-century conflicts is a connective thread that runs throughout this volume. Read together, the essays by Davis, Stagner, Costigliola, Rosenberg, and Lui build upon and also revise existing scholarship that emphasizes the close links between masculinity, nationhood, and national security and war.[13] Stagner and Costigliola trace how, at key moments, "disabled" male bodies (shell-shocked soldiers and a physically impaired president) were reconstituted as symbols of U.S. strength and leadership via the transnational realms of psychiatric medicine and diplomacy. The studies by Davis, Rosenberg, and Lui highlight how the bodies of children, women, and "ethnic" Americans could become "strategic assets" in intra- and international negotiations of power. In exploring how wars became sites for elevating particular formations of embodied nationalism, many of the essays draw attention to the wartime policing of boundaries of gender, sexuality, race, and morality. Kramer's and Plummer's studies of cases in which U.S. soldiers formed sexual encounters with women in occupied territories show how wartime "domains of the intimate" produced quite public regulatory regimes that aimed, in the name of national security, to reassert threatened racial and gendered hierarchies.[14]

How to delineate enemies and mold and destroy bodies became a particularly urgent matter of public policy in wartime, and the exigencies of the twentieth century's various national security emergencies thus gave rise to an array of tactics. Bodies may be ostracized, punished, tortured, killed—and all of these treatments represent a continuum for dealing with "outsider" bodies. Such treatments aimed not simply to deliver stress and harm to individuals but to create some kind of pedagogical ritual through which to warn and discipline other potential transgressors.[15] The various disciplinary treatments of outsiders, set within an often transnational and extranational geography of borderlands, inspection sites, detention centers, and war zones, constitute focal points of *Body and Nation*, as illustrated in the essays by Kramer, Molina, Young, and Shull.

During the wars that erupted from nationalistic rivalries and accompanied empire-building—from the War of 1898 through the Iraq War of 2003 and after—the American state (like other major powers) used new media to demonize enemies and new technologies to boost capacities to kill them. Young's examination of body count as the primary medium and strategic metric for gauging military success illustrates the impact of ever more deadly and remote weaponry on civilian casualties of war. She considers the question of what happens when certain bodies are grouped as such threats to the nation (and even to "humanity") that their lives (and deaths) become faceless statistics beyond the reach of law and morality. Her themes resonate with contemporary debates over rendition, torture, and drone technology in the security state of the early twenty-first century. These recent issues are taken up at greater length in the epilogue, which considers the question of the historical visibility of enemy or alien bodies.[16]

Nation, Bodies, and Modernity in U.S. Transnational Popular Culture

The United States, of course, was never simply a national state that sought to count, discipline, restrict, rearrange, rehabilitate, supervise, and bring victory to its citizenry. It was also home to the growth of a distinctive popular culture that celebrated the beauty, athleticism, and mobility of individuals and promoted a widely attractive consumerist ethos of self-improvement. A "body-centric" popular culture increasingly drew from the nation's demographic diversity and then attained global appeal during an age of expanding mass-media circulations. The relationship among bodies, nation, images of modernity, and transnational mass-mediated culture constitutes the third major theme of our volume.[17]

Many of our essays explore how American media circulations fostered political imaginaries centered on representations of the human body. American media enterprises, for example, seemed to promote ethnonationalism—that is, nationalism based on singular ethnic identities. Forms of popular culture, including circuses, magazines, movies, and news outlets, often presented exclusionary definitions of what constituted an "American" body by celebrating certain model citizens while marginalizing, demonizing, or simply ignoring racial minorities, the "disabled," radicals, and the "unfit." Yet because American mass culture was built by a diverse group of people and consumed by global audiences, it also constructed the cultural pastiche that constituted American life and the nation's multiethnic social body.[18] American nationalism was, after all, always simultaneously a transnationalism.[19] Furthermore, as media reached across oceans and continents, meanings became increasingly shaped and reshaped within this transnational circulation.[20]

The essays in this collection thus suggest that America's twentieth-century transnational media, though it often projected imagery that helped to solidify categories of race, ethnicity, gender, fitness and (dis)ability, and nation, simultaneously worked to mix and disrupt these very same categories. Several of the studies explore how mass-mediated representations of American bodies helped to associate the United States with a "look" of modernity increasingly characterized by motion, hybridity, and performance rather than by stasis, race, and essence. Davis's work on the American railway circus and Stagner's on popular representations of soldiers illustrate how U.S. transnational media circulations projected embodied narratives of American strength and resiliency. Fitzpatrick's exploration of "cosmopolitan primitivism" in the publishing empire of Bernarr Macfadden and Lim's study of Anna May Wong's "transnational racial modernity" shed light on America's global circulation of what were widely perceived to be attractive and flexible "modern" figures. During World War II and the Cold War, as Costigliola, Rosenberg, and Lui demonstrate, such bodies became central symbols in foreign relations discourse.

At the center of America's transnational media circulations was the emergence of the omnipresent modern consumer body—a highly mobile, often urban, and increasingly multiethnic, multiracial, and multigendered figure. The "modern body"—male and female—had a distinctive style that rendered it a frame for adornment. In Jean Baudrillard's words, the human body became not just a site of consumerism but became itself "the finest consumer object."[21] Essays in our volume explore how America's transnationally circulating media presented modern bodies as ever unfinished objects: they could be adorned in some fashion, or the sculpting of a seemingly unadorned body that was finely honed through physical culture could become its own special adornment. In marrying mobility and consumption, America's transnational media circulations helped associate the United States with, as Rosenberg outlines, "a compelling modernity" that could seduce as well as destroy.

Our essays suggest the very diverse ways bodies coded as both American and modern became defined in terms of their mobility: their ability to travel, participate in sports, move up in the world, slide into multiple social roles, design a highly mobile air war that rained destruction on people-in-place, or conquer immobilizing conditions such as paralysis and shell shock. Marilyn Lake and Henry Reynolds have succinctly written, "Modernity meant mobility."[22] To be static or place-bound was to be on the wrong side of the future. This wedding of modernity and mobility, accentuated in this age of global migrations, rapid media, and travel (with attendant restrictions on these kinds of mobility), manifests itself throughout our collection. In America's increasingly global circulations of body-centric mass culture, images of mobile, modern bodies inextricably intertwined with messages about U.S. national power.

The theme of media circulation, so important to emerging understandings of transnational flows in history, highlights the global body politics of America's celebrity-driven, consumerist commercial culture that exalted self-fashioning, self-improvement, and mobility. As one of America's most important exports to the world during the twentieth century, body-centric transnational media circulations constructed influential images of the American body politic and also helped to broker changing relationships between the United States and the world.

These three general areas of inquiry—population migration and mixing, national security discourse, and mass-mediated cultural circulations— are necessarily overlapping and even mutually constitutive. Global migrations of people, for example, can be instigated by wars and conflicts, shaped by mass-media representations of citizens and nations, and given political and historical meanings through popular culture. Similarly war making in the twentieth century has been predicated on the mass-mobilization of people, and media are frequently honed to project certain messages about national and enemy bodies. Moreover both migrations and wars have significantly influenced the channels through which body-centric American popular culture has circulated. Our essays, taken together, present specific historical examples of such interrelationships and show how the nexus between ever-changing meanings of bodies and nations can deepen critical historical understandings of international and transnational relations.

Notes

1. An overview of the so-called bodily turn can be gleaned from the useful and highly diverse essays found in Fraser and Greco, *The Body*; Blakemore and Jennett, *The Oxford Companion to the Body*; Johnston, *The American Body in Context*.

2. See Foucault, *Discipline and Punish* and *The History of Sexuality*. Foucault's insights about power and the body have informed a broad range of scholarship across many disciplines. Examples with particular relevance to our volume include Stoler, *Race and the Education of Desire*; Burchell, Gordon, and Miller, *The Foucault Effect*; Rail and Harvey, "Body at Work." Attempts to reevaluate Foucault's conception of biopolitics and biopower in light of new technologies, evolving theories about the body, and international and transnational geopolitical affairs include Jones and Porter, *Reassessing Foucault*; Clough and Willse, *Beyond Biopolitics*; Debrix and Barder, *Beyond Biopolitics*; Dillon and Reid, *The Liberal Way of War*; Melossi, "Michel Foucault and the Obsolescent State"; Fraser, "From Discipline to Flexibilization?"; Kelly, "International Biopolitics."

3. See Scott, "Experience"; Butler, *Gender Trouble* and *Bodies That Matter*; Diprose and Ferrell, *Cartographies*; Fausto-Sterling, *Sexing the Body*.

4. *Body and Nation* builds on an array of studies that have examined "body politics" within a multitude of specific national contexts. In addition to the U.S. body and nation scholarship outlined in the notes of the individual essays in this volume (which we have generally not repeated in this introduction), some examples include de Baecque, *The Body Politic*; Mangan, *Superman Supreme*; Ross, *Naked Germany*; Morris, *Marrow of the Nation*; Crombie, *Body Culture*; Ong and Peletz, *Bewitching Women, Pious Men*. Important discussions of the body politics of "global America" in earlier historical periods can be found in Brown, *Foul Bodies* and "The Anglo-Algonquian Gender Frontier"; Morgan, *Laboring Women*; Sweet, *Bodies Politic*.

5. For "bodies in contact," see Ballantyne and Burton, *Bodies in Contact*. The classic text on the construction of nationalism and imagined communities is Anderson, *Imagined Communities*.

6. On the "politics of intimacy" and bringing issues of postcolonial analysis and scholarship on the body into U.S. history, see especially Stoler, *Haunted by Empire*. Other relevant works include Kaplan, *The Anarchy of Empire in the Making of U.S. Culture*; Renda, *Taking Haiti*; Lipman, *Guantánamo*; Jacobs, *White Mother to a Dark Race*.

7. On immigration history as transnational and foreign relations history, see Gabaccia and Ruiz, eds., *American Dreaming, Global Realities*; Gabaccia, *Foreign Relations*; Zolberg, *A Nation by Design*.

8. Influential analyses of how modern states have gained and exercised power by managing and marking human bodies include Scott, *Seeing Like a State*; Mitchell, *Rule of Experts*; Anderson, *Legible Bodies*. On the United States,

see Briggs, *Reproducing Empire*; Greene, *The Canal Builders*; and essays in Go and Foster, *The American Colonial State in the Philippines*; Campbell, Guterl, and Lee, *Race, Nation, and Empire in American History*; McCoy and Scarano, *The Colonial Crucible*. Works that place both the U.S. state and nonstate actors in a transnational context with implications for body politics include Connelly, *Fatal Misconception*; Ngai, *Impossible Subjects*; Cullather, *The Hungry World*; Latham, *The Right Kind of Revolution*.

9. See Gross, *What Blood Won't Tell*. The essays in Goodman, Heath, and Lindee, *Genetic Nature/Culture* investigate the relationship between anthropology and genetic science across a broad range of contexts. For the fluidity of ideologies of race in the U.S. imperial context, see Kramer, *The Blood of Government*.

10. Nielsen, *A Disability History of the United States* offers an important historical perspective on the categories of ability and fitness in the United States. On American history viewed through the lens of disability studies, also see Longmore and Umansky, *The New Disability History*.

11. In addition to the many works cited in the essays, examples include Keys, *Globalizing Sport*; Jacob, *Working Out Egypt*; Guthrie-Shimizu, *Transpacific Field of Dreams*.

12. Cherniavsky, *Incorporations* provides a provocative context for viewing meanings of race in the context of its relationship to the global and imperial spread of capital.

13. See Nagel, "Masculinities and Nations." Influential studies that investigate the gendered body politics of war and nationhood include Enloe, *Bananas, Beaches, and Bases*; Hoganson, *Fighting for American Manhood*; Bederman, *Manliness and Civilization*; Shibusawa, *America's Geisha Ally*.

14. On "domains of the intimate," see Stoler, "Tense and Tender Ties: The Politics of Comparison in North American and (Post) Colonial Studies" in *Haunted by Empire*, 23–70. The essays in Hansen and Stepputat, *Sovereign Bodies* investigate how sovereignty is constructed within states through acts of violence enacted on bodies.

15. Scarry, *The Body in Pain*; McCoy, *A Question of Torture*.

16. The conclusion of Pitt, *Body, Nation, and Narrative in the Americas* focuses on issues of bodies that are "disappeared." Casper and Moore, *Missing Bodies* reflects on the hypervisibility and invisibility of bodies in American culture.

17. On mass media, globalization, and modernity, see Appadurai, *Modernity at Large*.

18. The relationship between America's multicultural population and the development of modern mass media is explored in Mizruchi, *The Rise of Multicultural America*; Rogin, *Blackface, White Noise*; Ross, *Working-Class Hollywood*; Pells, *Modernist America*.

19. On America as a transnation, see especially Tyrrell, *Transnational Nation*. For a historical perspective on this topic, see Randolph Bourne, "Trans-National America," *Atlantic Monthly*, July 1916, 86–87.

20. On such circulations, see especially Weinbaum et al., *The Modern Girl around the World*; Miller et al., *Global Hollywood*. Important discussions of U.S. mass media, international audiences, and the limitations of so-called cultural imperialism can also be found in Rydell and Kroes, *Buffalo Bill in Bologna*; Stokes and Maltby, *Hollywood Abroad*; de Grazia, *Irresistible Empire*; Kitamura, *Screening Enlightenment*. U.S. media culture and globalization at the end of the twentieth century is given further attention in the epilogue of this volume. For a useful primer on the academic field of media reception studies, consult Staiger, *Media Reception Studies*.

21. Baudrillard, *The Consumer Society*, 129.

22. Lake and Reynolds, *Drawing the Global Colour Line*, 23. The historical and discursive links between mobility and modernity are also addressed in Creswell, *On the Move*; Pratt, *Imperial Eyes*; Canzler, Kaufmann, and Kesselring, *Tracing Mobilities*; Sternheimer, *Celebrity Culture and the American Dream*.

one

Colonial Crossings
Prostitution, Disease, and the Boundaries
of Empire during the Philippine-American War

PAUL A. KRAMER

Major Owen Sweet was in trouble. The prostitutes from Japan had
been both a necessary evil and a pragmatic good, he explained to his
superiors; in any case, they had been dictated by unfortunate circum-
stance. Four months into the United States' war against the Philippine
Republic, the 23rd Infantry had taken control of Jolo, in the southern
islands, from Spanish forces, and his troops had quickly succumbed to
what he called "the lax moral conditions incident to the Philippines and
Oriental countries generally." A "personal" investigation had exposed
a veritable festival of vice: gambling houses, grog shops, saloons, and
"several resorts of prostitution" inhabited by Chinese, Japanese, and
Filipino "immoral women." Sweet feared that a spark might fly out of
this chaotic mix that could touch off a second, Muslim-American conflict that the U.S. military could not afford. By his own account, he had
sought to impose order on this moral unruliness, a "system of attrition"
consisting of raids and closures and the expulsion of nearly all local sex
workers.[1] But Sweet had been called to task for not going far enough. He
had allowed about thirty Japanese prostitutes to remain in Jolo, where
he mandated their regular, compulsory venereal inspection to protect
American soldiers from disease; in the process he had given explicit

government sanction to the "social evil." In Jolo, as elsewhere, it turned out that moral empire and military-hygienic empire could not easily be squared, and Sweet had chosen.

His choice had been controversial, and that controversy can illuminate both its particular moment and the cultural history of U.S. global power more broadly. At base it was about bodies: the bodies of Asian women and U.S. soldiers in the Philippines, on the one hand, and the "body" of U.S. empire, on the other. This second kind of body was strictly metaphorical. Or was it? As Americans in the metropole learned that U.S. military authorities like Sweet had been regulating commercial sex in the interest of venereal control—a policy successfully barred from the United States by "social purity" reformers to that point almost without exception—many made sense of this disclosure by linking together the two types of bodies: the meanings of colonialism for the American "body politic" could be read from the fortunes of U.S. soldiers' bodies in the Philippines. Particularly in the hands of colonialism's skeptics and critics, regulated prostitution in the Philippines came to symbolize colonialism's nefarious impact on the metropole: a medical technique aimed at preventing contagion, it would promote other, and perhaps more sinister, "contaminations."

While reformers agreed that something stank at the intersection of military occupation, commercialized sex, and its medical regulation, they tracked the smell to diverging roots. Was the problem that the U.S. military in the Philippines was sanctioning prostitution (as social purity campaigners maintained), or that its efforts were attached to and symbolic of an illegitimate invasion (as anticolonialists argued)? Was the problem racial in that it conceded to and sanitized colonial "miscegenation," or that it undermined national exceptionalist pretensions by rendering the United States more "European"? Or was the problem merely that regulated prostitution in the Philippines was visible, raising questions about America's moral image in the world?

The U.S. military-colonial regulation of prostitution threatened to sunder two related sets of imagined barriers. The first insulated the United States from Europe; for American social purity reformers, the regulation of prostitution was—along with imperialism, statism, and sexual license—closely associated with European societies. Not for nothing was it known as the "continental system." The sudden revelation that U.S. military authorities in the Philippines were, for the first time, also practicing regulation on a large scale prompted fears about the weakening of American moral exceptionalism. The second barrier shielded metropole from colony; coupled to American hopes for the stabilizing export of U.S. institutions to the new colonies were anxieties about the unanticipated and unwelcome "reflex actions" that might flow the other way, blowbacks that could include corrupting venereal disease, immoral methods for controlling it, and race-mixing.[2] Along both axes, regulated prostitution represented a dangerous colonial crossing that broke through the protective enclosures that Americans had hoped to raise around themselves, even as they ventured out into "the world."

Approached in this way, the history of U.S. military invasion, prostitution, and venereal disease control during the Philippine-American War provides one window onto the cultural history of U.S. imperial boundaries: of how Americans marked the place where the United States ended and the rest of the world began and how they made sense of their inability to completely control the processes that flowed across that elusive line. To talk about the bodies of U.S. soldiers and the hazards that sapped their force and purity was also to talk about the "body" of U.S. empire at a moment when that body's limits, constitution, and vulnerabilities were being hotly disputed. The rhetorical presence of Filipinos' bodies as sources of threat—and absence when it came to questions of sexual violence and vulnerability to disease—also said much about that imperial body's contours and occlusions. This examination of the body politics of empire, then, illuminates a history both of U.S. military-imperial disease control in a colonial setting and of the way that gendered and racialized fears of sexual contagion expressed and gave shape to deeper anxieties about the permeability of a globalizing United States.[3]

By the time Sweet sat down to defend himself, the coerced medical inspection of female sex workers had become a core element of municipal policy, sanitary strategy, and moral reform throughout the globe. First developed in continental Europe, its most varied projections were in the British Empire, where the Contagious Diseases Acts (CD Acts) empowered police officers in select districts to arrest prostitutes, subject them to venereal examination, and incarcerate the infected in "lock hospitals." Wherever practiced, regulated prostitution employed a double standard by not requiring the inspection and arrest of men. In its institutional imagination, women's bodies unleashed infection to which men were vulnerable but which they somehow did not transmit either to women or to each other.[4]

As regulation spread, so too did movements aimed at its abolition, especially in the Anglo-American world. As Ian Tyrrell has shown, these efforts brought together evangelical Christians, feminists, and suffragists who assaulted the state's toleration of vice for distinct and overlapping reasons. As regulation moved on imperial channels, organizations such as the World Woman's Christian Temperance Union (wwcTU) and International Federation for the Abolition of the State Regulation of Vice mobilized an Anglo-American, and self-consciously "Anglo-Saxon," constituency to oppose it. The high point of Anglo-American cooperation along these lines was reached when two Americans played a key role in scandalizing India's CD Acts, which were abolished eleven years after their repeal in the British metropole. In this cooperation, however, the Americans did not tire of pointing out that, apart from a few notable—and fleeting—municipal experiments, as in St. Louis, the United States had managed to remain "pure" of regulated vice.[5]

The U.S. military occupation of Manila in August 1898 permitted another, secondary occupation: what one startled commentator called a "cosmopolitan harlotry" entered the city from innumerable ports of call, chasing presumed sexual demand.[6] The largest numbers of prostitutes from abroad were Japanese, their numbers multiplying by nearly fifteen times during the first six years of the occupation. But more shocking to U.S. military authorities were prostitutes of European descent, including Russians, Austrians, Italians, Spaniards, Australians, and Americans.[7] The vast majority of Manila's sex workers, however, were Filipinas, many of them displaced from the countryside by rising rents, export agriculture, or Spanish repression and coerced into prostitution.[8]

The inspection regime was instituted in the context of a perceived medical crisis. By October there were three hundred U.S. soldiers in the hospital for venereal disease, specifically syphilis and gonorrhea, and fifty operations had been conducted. Without reserve troops, and fearing that disease might leave military efforts "seriously crippled," Provost Marshall General Robert Hughes felt compelled to "jealously guard the man behind the gun." The problem was that while the military Board of Health and police had made "strenuous efforts" to keep out foreign prostitutes, it was nearly impossible to locate "native females of bad character" and "prevent communication between them and our soldiers." For a peseta, a "native" brought "the female" to "any designated locality" to meet a client, a transaction preventable only by "making prisoners of the females."[9]

Some medical officers lamented these encounters in their own right, apart from an explicit disease context; many believed Filipinos to be

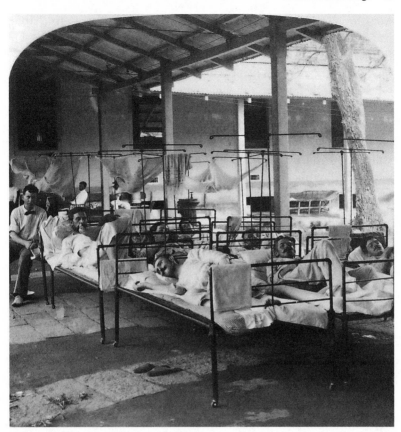

Figure 1.1. "Stricken with fever—more deadly than Filipino bullets—1st Reserve, Hospital, Manila, Philippine Islands," ca. 1900. William Johnson, a correspondent for a prohibitionist newspaper, reported being told by a doctor that one-sixth of the soldiers on the sick list—over three thousand cases—were infected with venereal disease. Courtesy of Library of Congress, Prints and Photographs Division.

inherently diseased (venereally and otherwise), making miscegenation both the sign and trigger of physical and moral "degeneration" among white American soldiers. For some, contracting venereal disease and sex with "native women" constituted related forms of bodily treason, the potential denial of one's physical constitution to the state.

In assembling their regulatory system, U.S. military-medical officers traveled a path of least resistance, continuing and modifying local practices initiated by Spain. A system had been put into effect in Manila by Spanish authorities in the late 1880s; a decade later, just prior to the collapse of Spanish rule, it enforced the mandatory registration of brothels and the inspection, incarceration, and treatment of infected women.[10] The U.S. regime drew on this Spanish framework (including its funding by compulsory fees and penalties paid by sex workers), but there were also differences: examinations now took place weekly rather than biweekly, and U.S. inspectors were not ordered to counsel prostitutes against their trade (although some would do so on their own). In a relatively straightforward case of what I have elsewhere called transimperial borrowing, U.S. officials self-consciously inherited and adapted policies from the very empire they were deposing rather than imported policy models from neighboring empires, U.S. colonies, or the U.S. metropole.[11] While "the regulations of Honolulu and St. Louis on prostitution" were on file, army surgeon and board member Charles Lynch noted, "no changes were deemed necessary in the methods pursued."[12]

By November 1898, just under three months into the occupation, the Bureau of Municipal Inspection, as it was called, was well under construction. The board also established a "womans [sic] hospital" for prostitutes found to be diseased in a wing of the San Lazaro leper hospital and turned a former vaccination center into an "office of inspection," where women free of venereal disease were given certificates and from which infected women were taken to the hospital by the police. Manila's police force was tasked with visiting "every known house of prostitution" at least once a week to check certificates and, in the case of a lapse in inspection, to close it "until every inmate has been properly examined."[13]

As elsewhere, the system's first principle was the female prostitute as the perpetual and exclusive source of contagion. In colonial contexts this assumption was often intertwined with racialized medical theories that cast colonized peoples as reservoirs of dangerous tropical disease.[14] The U.S. Army's inspections in the Philippines were, at first, no different, with heightened concern for the health of its soldiers unaccompanied by mandatory systems to inspect them. Such inspections were thought to be (as indeed they were) intrusive, humiliating, demoralizing, and dishonoring; sex workers apparently had no such honor to lose.

Over the next two and a half years the inspection program became more systematized and intensive. It incorporated some functions formerly exercised by the police, employing a "native physician (Spanish)" to visit brothels, hiring a "lay inspector" as his assistant, and replacing weekly certificates with "inspection books."[15] The fee for exams was set at $1 Mexican if performed at the hospital, twice that if done in brothels; fees were placed on a racial sliding scale, doubled for white women. The exams themselves cost an estimated 47 cents per woman. Between mid-1899 and early 1901 the Bureau turned an impressive 23 percent profit.[16]

In early March 1901 the examination system was reorganized and placed under the Board of Health, a complex agency charged with numerous sanitary and health-related tasks. This reassignment may have been undertaken in response to erupting scandal. It may also have been related to broader public health concerns; when bubonic plague struck Manila in January 1900, the board had inspected all brothels, "as it was believed that plague might spread from such foci." Whatever the rationale, the new system was whiter in personnel. The board hired an American physician "who does the work of the two former native physicians," assigning him an American orderly and lay inspector, both "excellent men."[17]

The new regime was also more forceful. Just two months into the shift, it was incarcerating 86 percent more women than previously; it had registered 115 percent more. It aspired half-heartedly to broaden its coverage to include soldiers and teamsters employed by the quartermaster, "among whom there is much venereal disease." It also enlisted the help of church women who spoke Spanish or Tagalog, and who were "not afraid of moral contamination from these prostitutes," to attempt to set the women on the true path. (For Lynch, Filipinas were especially reformable, having sunk to prostitution "through necessity" and not, as with American, European, and Japanese women, as a matter of hardcore professionalism.)[18]

Inspectors, however, ran into myriad problems of enforcement as sex workers resisted medical inspection. In an attempt to "dissociate their minds from the idea that the hospital is a prison," the institution began to offer treatment for women's "other complaints"; while few women initially availed themselves, military hygienists remained confident that they would, "as there is no other place where they can obtain good treatment."[19] The biggest challenges involved identification. First, how were U.S. medical authorities to recognize a brothel? The imposition of inspection fees meant that new, uninspected brothels would likely proliferate on the outskirts of surveyed districts; bribery virtually assured they would spring up inside the system itself. In May 1900 Dr. Ira Brown, president of the Board of Health, suggested that a strictly bounded red-light district be formed, in which only prostitutes could reside and to which they would be confined; such women could not be allowed to "mingle with outside society." This would help respectable Manila residents insulate themselves from vice and prospective clients clearly identify brothels. In the latter category, some men "suffering from acute alcoholism" had mistakenly "entered respectable houses located near those occupied by prostitutes."[20]

The thorniest predicaments of identification occurred, however, when it came to individuals. While U.S. military-medical authorities tended to depict the "vicious woman" as an unchanging type, they also knew that the category of "prostitute" phased off uneasily into the general population. When faced with an insufficient number of sex workers, Brown noted with dismay, "the enterprising women send out to a neighbor and ask her to come in and help out"; this enlistee was "not regularly in the business," escaped inspection, and, it was believed, spread disease.[21] But it was also challenging to identify even those women who were formally registered. For over a year certificates and inspection books had carried only names and identification numbers. But just as they often avoided surveillance and its costs, Manila's sex workers soon developed a vigorous trade in up-to-date, disease-free inspection documents. It is unclear exactly how the exchange functioned, but subterfuges were met with a technological response. In 1900 inspectors were ordered to photograph individual women and place one copy of their photograph on an index card for reference and another on their inspection book "so that one woman cannot substitute examination or book for another."[22]

While its most elaborate manifestation was in Manila, smaller-scale efforts at regulation were also undertaken in provincial cities, a process enabled by the decentralized nature of the U.S. command. The extent of these practices remains hard to assess, but the case of Jolo, where we began, suggests their variable and contextual character, operating as they did with a wide range of resources and subject to diverse political pressures. In Jolo, Sweet had aimed at the "elimination" of "native women" who were, as one second lieutenant put it, "according to common report almost universally affected with venereal disease."[23] But other sex workers were more or less invited in. Major E. B. Pratt recalled that shortly after the U.S. occupation, he was informed that "some Japanese women (prostitutes)" then in North Borneo wished to land at Jolo. After "considering the subject carefully," Pratt had permitted them entry. When they settled on "one of the principal streets," however, he directed them to relocate "near the outskirts in the vicinity of the walls"; they subsequently moved into four houses, one of them designated as a hospital, on a "back street" of the city.[24]

While both Pratt and Sweet later denied the charge of "licensing," the Jolo brothels were in many ways projects of state. Patrols stationed near them were ordered to segregate them racially, "to allow no persons but soldiers to enter the premises."[25] U.S. soldiers were prohibited from entering the brothel during inspections, if they were found diseased, or after the playing of taps, "except by written pass signed by the Company commander."[26] The brothels were also inspected once a month. The Japanese women were forbidden "to advertise themselves by parading in the streets," made to submit to weekly medical inspection by a U.S. Army surgeon, and, if found diseased, confined to the hospital.[27] Some American observers saw the system as a success because of its virtual invisibility. One lieutenant marveled that "any lady could have lived there the whole time" of the U.S. occupation and "never have known that such places existed."[28] When disorder broke out, it was due to the U.S. soldiers, "fighting and breaking furniture," stealing from the women and assaulting them.[29]

The decision to let the Japanese prostitutes into Jolo had been driven in large measure by military concerns, specifically by a sense of the urgent need to direct U.S. soldiers' sexual aggressions away from the surrounding Muslim population. According to Captain C. E. Hampton, "The report was by Sulu women that some of the soldiers had made improper advances to them."[30] This was an extremely flammable situation, as the 23rd Infantry was charged precisely with preventing a local outbreak of hostilities that might drain U.S. forces away from the ongoing struggle against the Philippine Republic. Furthermore, as Hampton discovered through an "intimate investigation," prostitution was "practically unknown" in Jolo, and any "interference, however slight," with Muslim women would be "resented in the hottest and most savage manner."[31] In this light the admission and inspection of the Japanese prostitutes was credited with having prevented not only the spread of venereal disease but the start of another war. The "toleration" of the brothels had, according to one captain, "not only promoted the health and contentment of the enlisted men" but "avoided unfortunate complications" with Muslims outside the walled town, where "our men would undoubtedly have gone in violation of orders."[32]

While U.S. military-medical authorities did not worry themselves over the fact, the Philippine-American War accelerated the spread of venereal disease in the rural Filipino population throughout the archipelago. While Americans generally assumed that U.S. forces had acquired disease only from their sexual encounters in the Islands, army doctors themselves conceded that large numbers of troops had left North America infected. According to Ken De Bevoise, seventeen out of every one thousand candidates for enlistment had been rejected on these grounds; venereal disease rates had risen during training as brothels sprang up around U.S. bases. While women in the Philippines would be incarcerated when identified with symptoms of venereal disease, soldiers found infected at the Presidio in San Francisco had been given medicine and returned to duty. An army official who traveled with one of the first regiments to depart, in mid-1898, reported that 480 of the unit's approximately 1,300 men had been "registered for venereal disease" prior to their departure.[33]

This rate rose again following the landing of U.S. troops in Manila. And the rapid dispersal of U.S. soldiers into the Philippine countryside after 1900, given the accompanying destruction of rural resources and massive dislocation and starvation of Filipinos that ensued, provided ideal conditions for the explosive spread of venereal disease. Guerrilla war meant close social contact between U.S. soldiers and Filipinos in garrisoned towns. Survival strategies among uprooted rural families in the Philippines included sending daughters to towns and cities in search of work. By shattering material livelihoods, the U.S. invasion not only generated demand for sexual laborers but spurred their supply. In larger towns, brothels were established to serve U.S. garrisons, becoming dense in disease vectors. In smaller centers "a transient class of native women" traveled "from one post to another."[34] Few Americans registered the possibility that Filipinas might contract disease from U.S. soldiers, although Major F. A. Meacham of the Manila Board of Health observed in mid-1901 that syphilis was "spreading among the native population of these islands," with results that he believed would tragically repeat "the history of this disease among primitive peoples."[35]

The Manila inspection system apparently went entirely undetected in the metropolitan United States for its first two years of operation, a sign of the army's care in masking it, the logistical difficulties of trans-Pacific communication, and, possibly, the success of U.S. Army censorship. What made this inattention surprising was the growing presence of Protestant missionaries in the Islands. They had, according to the missionary Charles Briggs, "long looked wistfully toward Manila"—the seat of overseas Spanish Catholicism—and "prayed the more earnestly that the everlasting doors might be lifted up there and let the King of Glory come in." The American victory at Manila Bay had been read as "a summons to enter the field"; by mid-1901 six denominations had divided the archipelago into "comity zones."[36] Given their zeal, it was striking that the missionaries allowed "regulated vice" to make headway; they may have possessed limited information as newcomers, or perhaps state-sanctioned prostitution failed to stand out against such an immense canvas of sin.

Nonetheless it may well have been a local missionary who tipped off reform journalists, setting loose the avalanche that followed. On June 27, 1900, William B. Johnson, a correspondent for the Chicago New Voice, a prohibition newspaper, filed a heated, sensationalist report, the details of which echoed, with further distortion, through the social purity, suffrage, and anticolonialist presses over the next two years.[37] The piece began ominously, with Johnson's visit to Manila's First Reserve Hospital, where a head surgeon had anonymously informed him of over three thousand cases of venereal disease among soldiers, about one-sixth of those on the sick list. An American editor took Johnson to the cemetery at Malate, where, he said, more of "our boys" had been sent "through bad women and drink than through the bullets of the Filipinos." Behind these stark realities stood a governmental machinery of vice. Through "newspapermen, police reports and officials," Johnson had learned there were about two hundred "licensed houses of prostitution" in the city, containing about six hundred prostitutes "under direct control of the military authorities, who represent American 'Christian' civilization here." While inflammatory in tone, Johnson accurately described the examination and incarceration system. When he asked why hospitalized women were "compelled to pay their way," he had been told that it was "'official business'" and of "'no concern to the public.'"

As would other reformers, Johnson depicted regulation, along with the sexual markets he saw flourishing under its protection, as both Europeanizing and Orientalizing, both cartographies evoking despotism and license. And so he found it particularly disturbing how "thoroughly American" the "whole situation" had become. The red-light district of Sampaloc was a "concrete revel of 'American civilization'"; there was hardly a brothel that was not "decorated with American flags," an adornment he had observed both "inside and out." To emphasize his point about the "official" character of Manila prostitution, Johnson included in his exposé two photographs he had taken at two separate sites, each captioned "Licensed House of Prostitution in Sampalog [sic] District, Manila." The boldface message that accompanied these descriptions—"Who Will Haul this Flag Down?"—was a deliberate provocation. Proponents of colonialism were at that same moment accusing anticolonialists of desiring to "haul down the flag" in the Philippines: the withdrawal of imperial prestige, honor, masculinity, and sovereignty. Johnson's ironic commentary threw this flag patriotism back on itself: the "flag" of empire had come with another, more sordid one.

Following this exposure, the problem of "regulated vice" in the Philippines was taken up by an eclectic array of reformers. Details from the Johnson report—cited, plagiarized, paraphrased, and reproduced with varying degrees of accuracy—soon appeared beneath indignant headlines in the social purity, suffrage, and anticolonialist presses. Each of these groups had its own agenda to advance and coalition to build; accordingly each took up the issue differently, prioritizing and linking in divergent ways questions of war, militarism, empire, prostitution, immorality, disease, and racial purity. Ultimately the combined force of their criticisms compelled the War Department and U.S. Army to reform—although not, as we will see, to eliminate—the system.

First and foremost among the critics were social purity reformers defined by their decades-long struggle against "regulated vice." Organizations like the American Purity Alliance (APA) and Woman's Christian Temperance Union (WCTU) circulated the Johnson report and mobilized petitions and letter-writing campaigns. Their critiques were consistent with earlier drives against "regulated vice" in Europe and its colonies, which centered on what might be called an erotic theory of the state: the "social evil" was enabled and encouraged by the state's protection, linking "license" (as state sanction) to "license" (as unregulated sexual expression). The state's approval of vice, in other words, denied individuals the character-building privilege of repressing themselves.

Even prior to Johnson's revelations, American purity reformers had viewed the acquisition of U.S. colonies in the Caribbean Pacific and Asia through the lens of European (and especially British) empire, darkly prophesying that the United States, once exceptional, would soon immerse itself in the fouling waters of both vice and its European-style regulation. Two months into the invasion, Dr. O. Edward Janney, future APA president, wrote, "We may be reasonably sure that the same problems as to the morality of the soldiers and the degradation of womanhood will stare us in the face as disturb the English people in reference to their army in India."[38] That same month Mariana W. Chapman wrote, "It will be a shameful record for our army to make, if we repeat East Indian conditions in relation to the native women. . . . The Filipinos may combine for us all the unfortunate situations in which Great Britain has found herself in India and Hong Kong."[39]

If one thing distinguished American purity reformers from their British counterparts, it was that they saw "empire" as a departure for the United States, which in turn encouraged them to cast "regulated vice" as the odious spawn of a fledgling colonialism. This formula crossed earlier social purity logic with republican antimilitarism: colonies meant standing armies, standing armies meant prostitutes, and prostitutes meant officers' attempts to regulate "vice" in the interests of disease control. As one American clergyman wrote of Barbados, "Social and sexual demoralization is one of the conditions incident to militarism."[40] This approach relied upon a geography of moral restraint: the farther armies were projected from the metropole, the farther they were from "restraining home influences" that were the proper, nonstate means for regulating vice. "The social evil and other iniquities find congenial environment," wrote Sergeant Oscar Fowler, just back from Manila, "in an atmosphere of a militarism existing far from the seat of the home government."[41]

While social purity reformers on occasion expressed concern for the morality—still less frequently, for the health—of colonized peoples, they were most preoccupied with imperial soldiers and the society to which they would return. Aaron Powell, the APA president, feared that "some of the soldiers and sailors, without moral restraint, and contaminated in their new environment," would arrive home and "in turn also contaminate our home population."[42] On another occasion he quoted Lord George Hamilton, secretary of state for India, who opposed regulation for its "domestic" implications, medical and nonmedical. Under regulation, Hamilton had warned, British soldiers returned to the metropole "bringing with them the debasing sentiments and habits acquired during their Indian training" and "infecting our industrial communities with a moral pestilence more destructive of the national stamina" than venereal disease itself.[43]

From this angle, "regulated vice" in the colonies not only promoted the spread of disease outward from the colonies but was itself a kind of "contagion." In the Philippine context, it was thought to move in two different but related directions. The first ran from Europe to the United States; if regulation was a natural offshoot of militarism, it was also (as was militarism itself) closely associated with Europeans. For this reason, adopting it meant endangering the virtuous "body" of the exceptional American nation. But the contagion of regulation also oozed from colony to metropole. Social purity advocates feared that the colonies would wedge open the United States for regulation more generally. A September 1900 APA memorial sent to President McKinley emphasized the risk of the "enactment of a similar regulation system by State Legislatures, incited by the example of the [national] government."[44]

While American social purity reformers saw Europe as a source of corruption, they also turned to British precedents for inspiration. Alongside the successful repeal of the British CD Acts in both the metropole and India, they enlisted the stern April 1898 order by Lord Wolseley, commander in chief of the British Army, instructing his officers that the proper way to prevent their soldiers from becoming "permanently disfigured and incapacitated" by sinful living was to lecture them on the "disastrous effects of giving way to habits of intemperance and immorality."[45] Wolseley noticeably failed to mention the regulation of prostitution and was therefore seen to oppose it. Unsurprisingly social purity activists forwarded Wolseley's order to the War Department; here their understandings of sex, morality, and the state were being voiced by the commander of the world's most powerful army.

Although social purity advocates most ardently claimed "regulated vice" as their concern, it was also taken up in a secondary way by the suffragists with whom they were closely allied. It was a commonplace of social purity thinking that woman suffrage was critical to the defeat of regulation. When it came to colonialism, woman suffragists were divided, according to Kristin Hoganson. Like their British feminist counterparts, some saw in empire an opportunity to assert white women's political power over and above that of racialized colonial subjects. Others, far fewer in number, made common cause with the Philippine struggle for independence and condemned patriarchy as "domestic imperialism." Potential alliances between suffragists and anticolonialists were undercut not only by suffragists' imperial hopes but by anticolonialists' patriarchal prerogatives: while some anticolonialists supported woman suffrage, most criticized colonial empire on explicitly masculinist grounds of national "honor."[46] Like the attacks of social purity reformers, those of suffragists stressed that colonial regulation was the predictable result of an all-male electorate. Also similar to social purity activists, theirs was a global politics that was uncommitted on the question of colonialism "itself"; whether regulation was incidental to colonialism or an essential feature of it, the elimination of "regulated vice" under women's influence would enhance the U.S. moral empire.

Concerns such as these prompted the National American Woman Suffrage Association (NAWSA) to pass a resolution, "adopted by a unanimous vote" and submitted to McKinley, in the wake of Johnson's exposé. It "earnestly protested" the introduction of what it called the "European system of State regulation of vice" into Manila on three grounds: it was "contrary to good morals," appearing to give "official sanction" to vice before "both our soldiers and the natives"; it applied a double standard by failing to mandate venereal exams for "vicious men"; and it was ineffective and currently being abandoned elsewhere. "The United States should not adopt a method that Europe is discarding," it read, nor "introduce in our foreign dependencies a system that would not be tolerated at home."[47] The following February, the Mississippi Woman Suffrage Association submitted its own five-point resolution to the president. While sharing NAWSA's preoccupations with moral messages and double standards, it also called regulation "an insult to womanhood" and expressed concern that it "breeds a moral and physical degeneration that will avenge itself upon our American society when these soldiers shall have been recalled to their native country."[48]

Anticolonialists (or "anti-imperialists," in the terms of the day) also turned "regulated vice" to their own purposes, although less consistently than either social purity reformers or suffragists. Anticolonialist argumentation was as wide-ranging as the strange political bedfellows—liberal Republicans, white supremacist Democrats, organized labor—it brought into alliance. Among their other concerns, anticolonialists condemned the impact of "militarism" on republican institutions and the risk of "mongrelization" that colonialism posed to the U.S. body politic. Many of these fears hinged on notions of "corruption": the decay of republican virtue before imperial tyranny and arrogance; the sinister influence of "trusts" in pressing for overseas conquests; the scams promoted by distant, "carpet-bagging" officials in the new colonies; the degradation of individual white bodies through miscegenation and of a collective, national white body through potential colonial immigration and labor competition.[49] As reports of high sickness rates among U.S. soldiers surfaced in the United States, disease proved an irresistible metaphor that condensed and concretized these various images of corruption. One before-and-after cartoon showed Uncle Sam prior to "his wish for expansion" in a condition of robust "Prosperity," overlooking smoke-belching factories; afterward he is figured as an invalid, confined to looking out a window at closed industrial plants, ill and emasculated.[50]

It was through these broader discourses of disease as "corruption" that concerns with "regulated vice" entered anticolonialist polemic. The most vivid example was Edward Atkinson's 1899 pamphlet "The Hell of War and Its Penalties," which took on the topic of colonial venereal disease with a specificity and indelicacy unknown in the social purity press.[51] Atkinson approached his theme, as did others, through the British imperial experience. According to an "English gentleman"

Atkinson had met, half of British troops in Hong Kong were infected, and while there might be a cure, "this disease works corruption of the blood to the third and fourth generation, ending in degeneracy." The moral and medical lessons for the United States, then deploying its own forces in Asia, were clear enough. Notably Atkinson made no mention of either prostitution or its regulation as modes of disease transfer; colonialism and venereal contagion were, on their own, inseparable processes of bodily and political decay.

The state's first response to spiraling accusation was denial. With apparently sincere bewilderment, War Department officials barraged with correspondence and petitions responded that they had no knowledge of the regulation program. In October 1900, for example, the acting secretary of war informed the WCTU's president, "So far as this Department is advised no such conditions obtain as set forth in your letter." He also promised that General Arthur MacArthur had been instructed "to investigate the subject fully, and to make full report on the subject matter of your resolutions."[52] The War Department found itself particularly vulnerable to criticism of this kind as officials sought the passage of the Army Reorganization Bill's command and staff reforms. Secretary of War Elihu Root complained to William Howard Taft, head of the second Philippine Commission, that "yellow journal hypocrites, posing as fanatics," had "created an impression among millions of good people that we have turned Manila into a veritable hell"; letters had inundated the War Department "by the thousands."[53]

Eager to sideline moral objections to the Army Reorganization Bill, Root requested a full accounting from Taft, while the army sent a similar request to MacArthur. It was a sign of ongoing civilian-military clashes that their answers diverged in their degree of disclosure. MacArthur's was a terse, telegraphic denial: "Houses of prostitution are not licensed, protected or encouraged."[54] Taft emphasized regulation's ability to "maintain effectiveness of army" by "subject[ing] known loose women to certificated examination." He argued for situational context: the policy was "better than futile attempts at total suppression in oriental city of 300,000, producing greater evil." He also distanced himself: regulation was an "army police measure outside our jurisdiction; military necessity."[55]

By the early months of 1901 the War Department had decided to openly admit and defend inspection. MacArthur's carefully worded report was issued on February 4 (seven months after Johnson's article) and was printed for mass circulation "in view of the very considerable number of . . . protests."[56] He accused regulation's critics of being "misled as to the facts" and of failing to consider "the disturbed conditions incident to military occupation and the state of war here prevailing." Prostitutes were not "licensed" in the Philippines, and, he boasted, many had been deported. He dedicated only four sentences to the U.S. military's venereal examination of prostitutes, placing it alongside other "sanitary regulations" needed in the tropics. It was a sign of his embattled position that he did not defend regulation by invoking principle but by surrounding the army's dilemma with protective layers of exception. Regulation had been adopted at an exceptional moment: the wartime government had been "necessarily one of emergency." It had been the outgrowth of an exceptional situation: Manila, as the army's chief entry and departure point, had housed sixty-five thousand soldiers "in the prime of life" and "remotely removed from the restraining influences that might be exercised over them by their home surroundings." In its exercise of regulation the United States was—somehow—proving itself to be an exceptional colonial power: Manila's condition was "remarkable in view of the general lack of moral tone pervading the seaports of the East." "No city in America and Europe," he declared, "certainly none in Asia, can today vie with Manila in the good order and morality which have resulted from the practical measures adopted." Ultimately MacArthur threw down the gauntlet, inviting the army's critics to investigate Manila's "social conditions" but insisting they do so in comparison with other "Asiatic" cities or American ones of comparable size.

The antiregulation movement hit a standstill by mid-1901. Social purity, suffrage, and anticolonialist petitioning had achieved a public admission from the army, but progress had halted there. Early in 1902, however, the Washington-based suffragist and social purity reformer Margaret Dye Ellis embraced a dramatic new tactic. At two suffrage meetings she circulated what she claimed was the "official registration book issued by the U.S. authorities" to a "child prostitute" with the name "Maria de La Cruz" (which reformers were careful to translate). According to the suffrage press, the book contained inspection records and a photograph, "the portrait of a girl seemingly about twelve years old, with a childlike face and big, pathetic dark eyes." In February 1902 Ellis apparently left copies of "this dreadful little book" with every member of the Committee on the Philippines; suffrage editors claimed that "circulars left at the homes of the Congressmen fell into the hands

of their wives and stirred them to womanly indignation."[57] Copies of
the booklet were widely distributed within social purity networks and
set loose a renewed flood of letters to the War Department.

Over the next two months Root and President Theodore Roosevelt
appeared to dramatically reverse course, moving from the defensive admission of regulation to its forthright condemnation. In March 1902
critics at last got an American version of the Wolseley order (the British
commander in chief's call for sexual self-restraint), issued by the president himself. Roosevelt's approach to disease prevention was identical
to Wolseley's, and some of his statements were directly cribbed. The only
"efficient" way to control venereal infection was "to diminish the vice
which is the cause of these diseases"; this could be accomplished only
through a sexually restrained and self-disciplined masculinity, which
U.S. officers must inculcate in their soldiers.[58] Roosevelt's order was
hailed by social purity reformers as a "stinging rebuke" to the army's
"European method."[59] Writing in July the APA's president expressed his
hope that it would come to "apply equally well to the soldiers at home,
and equally, also, to people at home who are not soldiers."[60]

Meanwhile local resistance by sex workers, which frustrated inspectors, in combination with activist pressures in the metropolitan United
States, had led to a dramatic alteration in the way venereal inspection
was carried out in the Philippines: U.S. soldiers would now be formally
subject to regular exams. While this had been done earlier in places like
Jolo, it was made general policy on May 21, 1901, with MacArthur's General Order No. 101.[61] Medical officers were directed to make a "thorough
physical inspection" of enlisted men twice a month, with "constitutional and local evidence of venereal infection . . . especially sought for."
The men "must be stripped" for these exams, and those with syphilis,
or "incapacitated" due to other venereal diseases, were to be sent to the
hospital. At the same time, with the "aid of local municipal authorities,"
the inspection of women was to continue in areas where "infectious
disease prevails in the command."

By mid-1901 it appeared that "regulated vice" as reformers had understood it had ceased to exist. In reality Root had discovered through
Ellis the key to ending the dispute: making regulation invisible. Johnson's images of flag-draped brothels had been seized upon by antireg-
ulationists precisely because they had captured colonial regulation in
an arresting form while seeming to resolve ambiguities over the state's
actual role in sexual commerce: the flag as seal of approval. In reply,
military officials had attempted to paper over the system with techni-
cal distinctions; MacArthur had claimed, for example, that prostitution

was not "licensed, protected or encouraged," a statement that, the social purity activist Wilbur Crafts noted bitterly, may have been true "in a Pickwickian sense" since Manila prostitutes were "only certified and superintended."[62]

Ultimately the star-spangled bordello's success as a symbol was registered most by Roosevelt's effort to erase it. In mid-March 1902 he requested information from Manila authorities about the use of flags in brothels with the aim of curtailing it.[63] He received word that Manila's chief of police had already acted, ordering all precinct commanders "to strictly prohibit the flying of flags or the painting of flags on any of the houses of ill-repute."[64] Where reformers made regulation a symbol for what was wrong with colonial empire, hauling down U.S. flags from brothels was a small price to pay for not having to haul them down from the Philippines as a whole.

The other way to render regulation invisible was to do away with the system's other physical artifacts, such as inspection booklets. On February 19 Root cabled Luke Wright, governor-general of the Philippines, advising that "no fees be charged" to inspected prostitutes and "no certificates of examination given." In terms of material traces, if not otherwise, there would be no more Marias de La Cruz. Medical officers could "keep their own records of names, descriptions, residences, and dates of examination," and in this way the program could continue "without the liability of a misunderstanding and the charge of maintaining a system of licensed prostitution."[65] Social purity advocates noted the fact that regulation had continued, even if the double standard had been surmounted. An October 1902 report, titled "More Trouble in Manila," contrasted Roosevelt's "admirable preachment" with the ongoing "tacit toleration" of prostitution in Manila.[66] But antiregulation protest directed at the U.S. military in the Philippines, if it never died out completely, declined precipitously.

Why the end of outrage? It had something to do with the character of social purity lobbying. Ellis, for example, had apparently agreed to end her agitation in exchange for Roosevelt's "preachment." In April, Clarence Edwards, chief of the Bureau of Insular Affairs, confirmed the agreement with Ellis herself, expressing his understanding that WCTU activists "now realized and appreciated that much misinformation from prejudiced sources had gone abroad on this subject" and openly admitting the continued inspection of women, now without fees or certificates.[67] The price that social purity reformers had paid for the image of victory, it turned out, was failure to abolish the regulation of prostitution in the Philippines. But there were other factors too. Roosevelt had declared an "end" to the Philippine-American War preemptively on July 4, 1902; to the extent that critics had tied their attacks to "militarism," and "militarism" to the conduct of war, the declaration (which failed to bring Filipino resistance to a close) undercut them. And regulation became more slippery as it was reassigned from military to civilian authorities. It was no longer a "national" policy carried out by the army—a main source of criticism—but a "municipal" policy undertaken by specific city governments. Regulation in the Philippines was no longer a national-imperial target like the Contagious Diseases Act but a kind of St. Louis in Southeast Asia, far less subject to pressures from the metropolitan United States.

Regulation came to occupy an increasingly important place in U.S. military practice in the years prior to World War I. The Jolo example, which involved the venereal examination of both women and men, appears to have circulated widely in the Philippines, as well as among military-medical educators. As early as 1901 Captain Edward Munson of the Army Medical Department celebrated the experiment of regulation in the Philippines, particularly in Jolo, where venereal diseases were "notably free from the complications so frequently observed in other parts of the Philippines."[68] According to Colonel L. M. Maus of the Medical Corps, the venereal inspection of U.S. troops, first carried out in the Philippines under MacArthur's 1901 orders, had become standard practice at "a large number of Army posts" where soldiers had returned from the Islands.[69] General Order No. 17, issued in May 1912, applied MacArthur's Philippine inspection order to the U.S. Army as a whole, although the specifics of enforcement were printed in a "confidential circular" to avoid "adverse criticism."[70]

Crusaders against regulated vice in the Philippines were not mistaken in their prediction that where U.S. troops circled the globe, commercialized sex, and state efforts to regulate it, would quickly follow. Coiled together during the Philippine-American War, histories of military occupation, sexual labor, disease control, and moral politics would continue to be enmeshed across the "American century." Military-sexual complexes that secured male soldiers' sexual access to women would proliferate from Puerto Rico to Hawai'i and from South Korea to Vietnam, with U.S. military policies or "status of forces" agreements between the United States and "host" states often insulating soldiers engaged in violence or crime against local women from meaningful justice. A critical awareness of the character and costs of these arrangements would dog empire's steps, particularly under the impetus of anticolonial and feminist movements concerned—as late-Victorian activists had been, for the most part, unconcerned—with their impact on the women subjected to them.[71]

Nor were the early twentieth-century reformers wrong about the colonial crossings they had prophesied and feared. At least in the shape of the regular venereal inspection of soldiers—and in other ways they failed to anticipate—the U.S. colonial experience had migrated back to the metropole, even as it was transmuted in the process. Military-medical officials had set out to inspect prostitutes in the Philippines and had ended up examining both them and the U.S. Army as a whole. The intervening scandal had resulted from both the unprecedented character of the regulation experiment in the Philippines and the watchfulness of the American social purity movement, to be sure, but it gained traction—and ultimately resulted in a deluge of angry mail to the War Department—because indignation at U.S. military regulation could be made to mesh with Americans' anxious reflections about what kind of society and polity the United States would be once it was capable of projecting its power halfway around the world. The susceptibility of U.S. soldiers' bodies to disease became particularly charged in such a context. The question of what strategies were permissible in order to protect them—and whether the exclusive coercion and arrest of infected women belonged among them—became closely tied to questions of the United States' own sovereignty and purity in a globalized world. To many, crossings of disease through the protective outer limits of the body became linked imaginatively to the transit of practices and institutions across imperial boundaries.

The reformers' opposition to colonial regulation did not, in the end, abolish regulation in the Philippines, but it did have decisive effects, and not just for U.S. military hygiene. It taught the Islands' new rulers some important lessons about how best an empire might be secured and extended: change the topic, concede to critics, pull down the flags, and, where possible, keep your empire disembodied. The sinister axiom that had informed their efforts to insulate themselves from an empire they could not fully contain—so deeply held that it was advanced without comment—had a long path stretching behind it and ahead of it. Some bodies mattered more than others.

Notes

1. Sweet to Adjutant General, February 6, 1902; Sweet to Commanding Officer (23rd Infantry), March 12, 1902, both in RG 94/417937/B, National Archives and Records Administration, Washington, DC (NARA DC). This essay is a revised and abridged version of the essay "The Military-Sexual Complex: Prostitution, Disease and the Boundaries of Empire during the Philippine-American War," *Asia-Pacific Journal* (July 2011). Due to space constraints, only primary document sources and a few key secondary works are cited here. For full citation, please consult the original essay online at http://japanfocus .org/-Paul_A_-Kramer/3574.

2. On "reflex actions" discourse that anticipated the movement of colonial practices and institutions to the metropole, see Kramer, "Reflex Actions."

3. For a broader exploration of the cultural politics of imperial boundary-making in Philippine-American colonial encounters, see Kramer, *The Blood of Government*. On the status of imperial history as well suited to the task of historicizing actors' definitions of the boundary between "domestic" and "foreign," see Paul A. Kramer, "Power and Connection."

4. See Levine, *Prostitution, Race and Politics*.

5. Tyrrell, *Woman's World/Woman's Empire*.

6. Sawyer, *The Inhabitants of the Philippines*, 114.

7. Terami-Wada, "Karayuki-San of Manila," 289; Ira C. Brown to Acting Adjutant General, May 16, 1900, in George W. Davis, ed., *Report on the Military Government of the City of Manila, P.I., from 1898 to 1901* (Manila: Headquarters Division of the Philippines, 1901), 276.

8. On prostitution in the Philippines in the nineteenth century, see Camagay, *Working Women of Manila in the 19th Century*; Dery, "Prostitution in Colonial Manila."

9. Robert Hughes to Adjutant General, U.S. Army, February 7, 1902, RG 350/2039/8 1/2, Box 246, National Archives and Records Administration, College Park, MD (NARA CP).

10. De Bevoise, *Agents of Apocalypse*, 80–81.

11. Kramer, "Historias Transimperiales."

12. Charles Lynch to President, Board of Health, May 18, 1901, in Davis, *Report on the Military Government of the City of Manila*, 267.

13. Robert Hughes to Adjutant General, U.S. Army, February 7, 1902, RG 350/2039/8 1/2, Box 246, NARA CP; Frank S. Bourns to R. P. Hughes, November 2, 1898, Enclosure 41, in Davis, *Report on the Military Government of the City of Manila*, 261–62.

14. Anderson, *Colonial Pathologies*.

15. Albert Todd to Acting Adjutant General, May 16, 1901, in Davis, *Report on the Military Government of the City of Manila*, 264–66.

16. Charles Lynch to President, Board of Health, May 18, 1901, in Davis, *Report on the Military Government of the City of Manila*, 269.

17. Lynch to President, Board of Health, May 18, 1901, in Davis, *Report on the Military Government of the City of Manila*, 267–68.

18. Lynch to President, Board of Health, May 18, 1901, in Davis, *Report on the Military Government of the City of Manila*, 267–68.

19. Lynch to President, Board of Health, May 18, 1901, in Davis, *Report on the Military Government of the City of Manila*, 268.

20. Major Ira C. Brown to Acting Adjutant General, May 16, 1900, in Davis, *Report on the Military Government of the City of Manila*, 276.

21. Brown to Acting Adjutant General, May 16, 1900, in Davis, *Report on the Military Government of the City of Manila*, 276.

22. Major Charles Lynch to President, Board of Health, May 18, 1901, in Davis, *Report on the Military Government of the City of Manila*, 266–67.

23. J. A. Moore to Adjutant, March 7, 1902, RG 94/417937/B, Enclosure 13, NARA DC.

24. E. B. Pratt to Adjutant, March 11, 1902, RG 94/417937/B, Enclosure 17, NARA DC. See also C. E. Hampton to Adjutant, March 14, 1902 (RG 94/417937/B, Enclosure 19), NARA DC.

25. R. R. Stevens to Adjutant, March 25, 1902, RG 94/417937/B, Enclosure 3, NARA DC.

26. R. C. Croxton to Adjutant, March 10, 1902, RG 94/417937/B, Enclosure 21, NARA DC.

27. W. H. Sage to Adjutant, March 13, 1902, RG 94/417937/B, Enclosure 5, NARA DC.

28. H. C. Bonnycastle to Adjutant, March 8, 1902, RG 94/417937/B, Enclosure 28, NARA DC.

29. D. B. Devore to Adjutant, March 13, 1902, RG 94/417937/B, Enclosure 24, NARA DC; J. H. Sutherland to Adjutant, March 6, 1902, RG 94/417937/B, NARA DC. For reference to an assault charge, see R. C. Croxton to Adjutant, March 10, 1902, RG 94/417937/B, Enclosure 21, NARA DC.

30. C. E. Hampton to Adjutant, March 14, 1902, RG 417937/B, Enclosure 19, NARA DC.

31. Hampton to Adjutant, March 14, 1902.

32. H. G. Cole to Adjutant, March 12, 1902, RG 94/417937/B, Enclosure 22, NARA DC.

33. De Bevoise, *Agents of Apocalypse*, 85.

34. Quoted in De Bevoise, *Agents of Apocalypse*, 89.

35. Quoted in De Bevoise, *Agents of Apocalypse*, 90.

36. Briggs, *The Progressing Philippines*, 122.

37. William B. Johnson, "The Administration's Brothels in the Philippines," *New Voice Leaflets* 1, no. 26 (1900); RG 350/2045/10 (Box 246), NARA CP.

38. "Letter from Dr. O. Edward Janney," *Philanthropist* 14, no. 2 (1899): 6.

39. Mrs. Mariana W. Chapman, "The New Militarism and Purity," *Philanthropist* 14, no. 2 (1899): 2, 3.

40. "Notes and Comments," *Philanthropist* 17, no. 2 (1902).

41. "Notes and Comments," *Philanthropist* 15, no. 4 (1901).

42. Aaron M. Powell, "Appeal for Purity," *Philanthropist* 14, no. 3 (1899): 13.

43. Aaron M. Powell, "Lessons from India," *Philanthropist* 14, no. 3 (1899): 11.

44. September 27, 1900 American Purity Alliance memorial to McKinley, RG 350/2045 (Box 246), NARA CP.

45. "Memorandum Issued by the Commander-In-Chief," April 28, 1898 (London: Harrison and Sons, St. Martin's Lane, 1898), RG 94/343790 (Box 2307), NARA DC.

46. Hoganson, "'As Bad Off as the Filipinos'" and *Fighting for American Manhood*.

47. "A National Disgrace," *Woman's Column*, November 17, 1900.

48. Resolution by the Mississippi Woman Suffrage Association, to William McKinley (ca. February 11, 1901), in RG 94/343790 (Box 2307), NARA DC.

49. On discourses of colonialism as corruption, see Kramer, "Reflex Actions."

50. "Uncle Sam before and after His Wish for Expansion," "Expensive Expansion" (Boston, 1900), in Hoganson, *Fighting for American Manhood*, 182.

51. Edward Atkinson, *The Hell of War and Its Penalties* (Boston: Rockwell and Churchill Press, 1898).

52. Acting Secretary of War to Lillian Stevens, October 8, 1900, RG 94/343790, NARA DC.

53. Elihu Root to William Howard Taft, January 21, 1901, William H. Taft Papers, Microfilm ed. M1584, Series 21, Special Correspondence, vol. 2 (1900–1901), Reel 640. My thanks to Richard Meixsel for identifying this source.

54. MacArthur, quoted in "Moral Conditions in the Philippines," report included with Wilbur Crafts to Theodore Roosevelt, January 22, 1902, 8, RG 94/416181A, NARA DC.

55. Taft, quoted in "Moral Conditions in the Philippines," 9.

56. Major General Arthur MacArthur to Adjutant General of the Army, February 4, 1901, RG 94/343790 (Box 2307) NARA DC.

57. "Against 'Regulated' Vice," *Woman's Column*, May 3, 1902, 1.

58. Roosevelt, quoted in "For Social Purity in the Army," *Outlook*, April 19, 1902, 944–45.

59. "For Social Purity in the Army," *Outlook*, April 19, 1902, 944–45.

60. Editorial, *Philanthropist* 17, no. 2 (1902): 4.

61. General Orders No. 101, May 21, 1901, RG 350/2039/26 (Box 246), NARA CP.

62. "Moral Conditions in the Philippines," 9.

63. George Cortelyou to Elihu Root, March 21, 1902, RG 350/2045/26 (Box 246), NARA CP.

64. Report by George Curry, May 6, 1902, quoted in W. Cary Langer to George Cortelyou, June 11, 1902, RG 350/2045/28 (Box 246), NARA CP.

65. Elihu Root to Luke Wright, February 18, 1902, RG 350/2039 (Box 246), NARA CP.

66. "More Trouble in Manila," *Philanthropist* 17, no. 3 (1902): 4.

67. Clarence Edwards to Mary Dye Ellis, April 3, 1902, RG 350/2039/after-20 (Box 246), NARA CP.

68. Edward Lyman Munson, *The Theory and Practice of Military Hygiene* (New York: William Wood, 1901), 835–37. My thanks to Warwick Anderson for identifying this source.

69. L. M. Maus, "A Brief History of Venereal Diseases in the United States Army and Measures Employed for their Suppression," American Social Hygiene Association, June 14, 1917, 2, 5, Box 131, File 3, ASHA Collection, University of Minnesota.

70. Colonel Joseph F. Siler, *The Prevention and Control of Venereal Diseases in the Army of the United States of America*, Army Medical Bulletin No. 67 (Carlisle Barracks, Pa.: Medical Field Service School, May 1943), 75. My thanks to Richard Meixsel for identifying this source.

71. Höhn and Moon, eds., *Over There.*

two

Moral, Purposeful, and Healthful
The World of Child's Play, Bodybuilding,
and Nation-Building at the American Circus

JANET M. DAVIS

In 1847 the American Sunday-School Union tried to scare children away from the circus with its new novel, *Slim Jack; Or the History of a Circus-Boy*. Bloody, violent, and tragic, the novel chronicled the brief life of an English immigrant trick rider and tightrope walker, John "Slim Jack" Ward.[1] Orphaned at age eight, Jack was sold to a circus and became a star. Yet he paid dearly for his fame. He was beaten, ridiculed for his love of the Bible and prayer, and forced to imbibe daily drams of brandy to anesthetize his exhausted, aching body: "If they who sit in the circus and laugh, and shout, and clap the riders, could only live one month in their company, they would find what fiends they are." At age fifteen Jack fell from the tightrope. Blood pouring from his mouth, he was mortally wounded. Jack spent his final days under the loving care of pious Dr. Frazier, a benevolent physician who brought the wayward circus youth back into Christ's loving fold: "And as his body wasted under the burning fever, beautifully did his soul shine out in its renewed and sanctified nature."[2]

The American Sunday-School Union's cautionary tale of the doomed Jack Ward, his "body wasted," reinforced a common antebellum view of the circus in the United States as dangerous to youthful bodies and minds. In particular, boys with wanderlust were vulnerable to its itinerant excitement. Critics charged that circus troupes were seductive, morally bankrupt spectacles of nearly naked, unruly bodies, such as leg-baring women equestriennes and lithe, body-bending contortionists. The show grounds also crawled with subversive bodies: sneak thieves and pickpockets who preyed upon unsuspecting spectators, and drunken toughs who prowled the crowds looking for fights. During this era several states and individual communities contained this chaotic conglomeration of bodies by banning the circus outright; other communities effectively banished it with excessive taxes and licensing fees.[3] Shortly after the Civil War, moral sentiments remained unchanged. In "A Wise Pastor," published in 1867, a minister told his male Sunday school students that the circus transformed boys into smoking, swearing miscreants. He asked his juvenile flock, "What do you think about it boys? Would you rather go to the circus and have fun, and become vulgar and boisterous, or stay away and be gentlemen?" "'Stay away and be gentlemen,' the boys all shouted," as the preacher looked on approvingly.[4]

Yet by the turn of the twentieth century the cultural place of the American circus was radically changing: purity reformers, religious leaders, educators, and U.S. military officials praised the circus as a site of wholesome bodily improvement and moral instruction, an essential building block of patriotism and citizenship, and a powerful form of international influence. How did the sinful antebellum circus become moral, purposeful, and healthful? In this chapter I examine how interconnected ideologies of the child body, play, physical culture, and state formation at home and overseas remade the place of the circus in American culture. I argue that the rehabilitation of the American circus was inextricably tied to a larger symbiotic process of bodybuilding, nation-building, and empire-building in which the vitality of the child and that of the nation were mutually dependent. In this context the relationship between the child, the body, play, and the newly respectable circus represented a form of Foucauldian biopower, which remade formerly derelict children's bodies into fit, (re)productive civic and national subjects.[5]

Three interconnected bodily sites structure the historical flow of this chapter. The first is the national context of social and cultural thought related to children, strong bodies, citizenship, and play during the Gilded Age and Progressive Era. The second is the circus body itself—as a corporate laboring body and as a constellation of extraordinary performative bodies—and its relationship to children during this period. Showmen became obsessed with bodily regulation and surveillance within the circus as well as without: proprietors established exacting rules of conduct for laborers and performers that disciplined potentially subversive bodies with regimens of punctuality and modesty. The third is the global setting of accelerated bodily mobility during the nineteenth century and early twentieth. European and American wars of colonial conquest and empire-building transformed the content and cultural status of the U.S. circus. Imperialism triggered increased access to colonial bodies—human and animal—that served as instruments of edification, titillation, novelty, and uplift at circus performances. Colonial bodies of color defined the normative white Euro-American body and taxonomies of racial difference through performances of exotic otherness. Accordingly varied circus bodies (spectators, laborers, and performers) were simultaneously imbued with global, national, and local cultural meanings.

Although the historical roots of the circus are global, the late nineteenth- and early twentieth-century circuses that populate this chapter are uniquely American—in name and in structure. British and European showmen staged the first circuses in America in the late eighteenth century, which looked virtually identical to those in Europe: human and animal athletes performed synchronized feats in a ring that was forty-two feet in diameter surrounded by an audience.[6] Yet the circus evolved into a distinctly Americanized cultural form during the nineteenth century owing to the nation's vast size and its scattered population in the rural hinterlands. As new roads, steamboats, canals, and railroads accelerated the movement of people and capital to the western and southern periphery, enterprising showmen quickly recognized new market opportunities; they gladly adopted the canvas tent to show in more places more quickly, and they embraced new transportation technologies to facilitate long-distance travel so that they could reach restive frontier markets clamoring for entertainment.[7]

By the turn of the twentieth century the Americanized circus had evolved into a huge, highly mobile, tented three-ring extravaganza. Barnum and Bailey, Adam Forepaugh, and the Ringling Brothers traveled across the nation by rail and employed over a thousand people and hundreds of animals; the biggest canvas big tops could seat over twelve thousand people. The canvas city itself stretched across nine acres in any given city lot. The expansion and evolution of the American circus—from small, European-style shows to vast three-ring behemoths—was tied directly to national and global expansion. This impressive size and mobility, joined with its newly respectable cultural status as a wholesome site of youthful bodily and moral edification, made the American circus an active structural and ideological participant in nation-building during an era of empire and global migrations.

Progressive-era social reformers and cultural critics were deeply concerned about the fate of the American child's body in an age of global migrations and industrial modernity. Reformers such as the photographer and sociologist Lewis Hine viewed the child's body as an extension of the civic body as well as the national body. In a photographic essay written for the *Survey*, Hine highlighted the plight of impoverished, itinerant children left to languish unsupervised, while their immigrant parents toiled in fields and canneries, ceaselessly moving throughout the summer in search of seasonal labor: "What preparation are they getting for citizenship? . . . There are no playgrounds for these children, no supervision, no schools, no sanitary decencies. The factory owns the tar-paper shacks in which they live." Hine was especially alarmed at the public invisibility of these itinerant children: "These are not the children who tour the country on the stage or with the circus. Such children have the protection of cruelty societies and child labor laws to guard them from the perils of the road." Because these children lived outside the regulatory arms of the state, Hine feared that they were potentially inassimilable and "as foreign as their alien parents."[8]

As future adults holding the rights to full citizenship in an age before women had the constitutional right to vote, boys were of special concern. Social reformers, educators, and politicians spoke frankly about their suspicions of the native-born male body gone soft in the nation's new industrial economy. Although they feared that immigrants were inassimilable, reformers were just as worried that neurasthenic middle-class male brainworkers were at risk of committing "race suicide" because their reproductive rates were being dangerously outpaced by the millions of fecund immigrant "hordes" from southern and eastern Europe.[9] Reformers concluded that the nation's future rested on the fit, fertile, native-born body and the properly assimilated and disciplined immigrant body.

Founded in 1906, the Playground Association of America (PAA) aimed to create fit American citizens out of immigrant children through structured and well-supervised play. Ultimately PAA members saw cooperative play as patriotic play. Such disciplined bodybuilding and citizen building would forcefully combat the unruly, unassimilated youthful bodies that Hine had documented in the impoverished, itinerant labor camps. Henry S. Curtis, creator of the PAA, was a student of the psychologist G. Stanley Hall; he and his colleagues put Hall's theory of recapitulation into programmatic form. Embracing the evolutionary precept that ontogeny recapitulates phylogeny, they posited that children at play reenacted the evolutionary stages of their "primitive" ancestors as they developed. Although this dynamic view of human development recognized now-accepted stages of childhood, such as adolescence, it also validated racialist notions of differential development; that is to say, recapitulation theory put forth a paternalist theory of the white man's burden at the dawning of America's overseas empire. The theory posited that preindustrial "primitive" races were stuck in earlier evolutionary stages of development and needed the guidance and oversight of "advanced" white Anglo-Saxon societies to "grow up" properly.[10]

The PAA grew out of a burgeoning physical culture movement, which was rooted in the gymnastics societies and calisthenics routines that had been popular among German and Scottish immigrants since the 1850s. The advent of state support for children's physical play marked a new chapter in the history of U.S. physical culture during the Gilded Age and Progressive era. The growth of state funding also corresponded to the period in which educators, writers, and reformers began to promote the circus as wholesome child's play. From 1880 to 1920 municipal governments spent in excess of $100 million on the construction and staffing of organized playgrounds, with the majority of this funding coming after the creation of the PAA.[11] The equipment itself helped promote the circus arts: swings, ropes, rings, teeter-totters, twirling push gates, slides, and open spaces for tumbling promoted balancing skills, acrobatics, and upper-body strength.

In fact some playground reformers explicitly argued that the circus was a pleasing alternative to tedious calisthenics and gymnastics, for no child would call such dull, repetitive exercise "play." William H. Allen, secretary of the Bureau of Municipal Research in New York City and the author of Civics and Health, agreed. Allen stressed the link between a clean, healthy body and the health of the national body politic writ large; yet, he observed, children's exercise regimens of supervised gymnastic repetition were utterly boring: "It is too much like taking medicine."[12] Likewise the summer camp founder and physical culture educator Ernest Balch urged children to create their own circus companies as an entertaining and moral form of physical education: "Best of all the stimulus is there, provided by the glamour of the circus and the stage. Given an occasional show—the pupil will practise steadily, without urging, under competent guidance. Can more be said for any game? It is rare indeed that so much can be said for the mechanical exercises. I have never seen it."[13]

Balch provided point-by-point instructions and performance tips for children to create their own successful circus. (He was a seasoned professional, having mentored many youthful circuses at Cloyne House School in Newport, Rhode Island, where the combination of athletics and tenting in the fresh air reportedly created robust children who never got sick.) Yet he cautioned children, advising them to "appear cheerful," to disabuse audiences of any lingering misconceptions that circus children were mistreated. He strongly admonished youthful impresarios to avoid vulgarity, smoking, drinking, and gambling; they had to remain disciplined and virtuous to be good role models and to achieve financial success. An enterprising troupe should charge admission, keep careful accounting records, invest prudently to improve the show, turn a profit, and inculcate thrifty values.[14]

Balch's healthy circus regimen bore a striking resemblance to the boy-centric world of Horatio Alger, whose novels celebrated the circus as a wholesome training ground for productive capitalist values: industry, thrift, and superb physical fitness. Bodily and mental discipline defined the orphaned boy heroes of Alger's circus novels, The Young Circus Rider (1883) and The Young Acrobat of the Great North American Circus (1888).[15] Alger centered each plot on two handsome, deserving boy circus stars who had entered the rollicking nomadic big top as an act of sheer survival. Robert Rudd, a bareback rider, was an orphaned tramp who accepted a showman's offer of training and employment. He quickly became a center ring attraction and the proprietor's favorite. Similarly the orphaned teen Christopher "Kit" Watson joined a circus when his scheming uncle and guardian apprenticed him to a skinflint blacksmith named Aaron Bickford. Kit protested because he wanted to continue his education; he had been a standout student at boarding school, where he learned gymnastics from a former acrobat with Barnum. However, Kit's uncle forced him into the apprenticeship. The circus conveniently was in town; Kit went to the show, saved the crowd from a loose lion (he bravely blinded the beast with a bag of snuff he had just purchased for his uncle's housemaid), and was quickly hired by the grateful proprietor. Like Robert Rudd, Kit quickly became a standout performer.

In sharp contrast to the American Sunday-School Union's degraded portrait of the vice-ridden antebellum circus, Alger's Gilded Age circus was a wholesome institution. Smoking, drinking, and gambling were prohibited; each show comprised friendly, fit, hardworking, temperate performers who welcomed the boys into the nomadic yet capitalist family-like fold. The solidity of these makeshift circus families was especially revealing for Alger's readers in a maturing industrial society where chaotic cycles of economic boom and bust, crop failures, and a 95 percent failure rate for new businesses meant that working-class and lower-middle-class American families teetered perilously on the brink of dissolution; able-bodied men and boys relentlessly searched for work, often many miles from home.[16]

The experiences of Alger's wandering circus boys reflected the ruptures of Gilded Age families and cast a fantastical glow of economic and social mobility. In keeping with Alger's "bootstraps" formula, Robert and Kit succeeded at the circus as a result of pluck and luck. Outstanding physical prowess secured each boy a high position in the show: Robert was a brilliant rider, "tall and slender with a dark complexion and bright eyes" and a keen understanding of the equine mind, "perfectly fearless with horses . . . quick and daring"; Kit could fearlessly leap over three elephants, a skill no one else had ever mastered.[17] Fellow troupers, most notably the father-like sideshow giants, protected the boys from danger: Anak the Giant rescued Robert from a violent farmer named Tarbox who tried to thrash the boy for trespassing on his land, while Achilles the Giant saved Kit from the dirty blacksmith Bickford. Although the boys had a "capital time" with the circus, each wisely knew that the tenting life was temporary, a time of wholesome youthful adventure that would eventually end. Each boy saved his money scrupulously over the season, knowing that he would return to school to improve his station in life. At the conclusion of the novels, Robert and Kit discovered that they had been cheated out of a sizable inheritance by scheming relatives. The novels ended predictably (faithfully adhering to Alger's surefire formula) with the restoration of each boy's rightful riches and honor and the proper social order intact.

Alger's novels were on the forefront of a new mass cultural phenomenon: the literary genre of the children's circus adventure novel. Flourishing at the turn of the twentieth century, these popular novels chronicled the metamorphosis of children who ran away, joined a circus, and blossomed into healthy, productive, and trustworthy citizens.[18] The depiction of upstanding youthful circus life in these novels reflected the ways actual impresarios now successfully marketed their shows to family audiences as sober, vice-free sites of educational pleasure. Months before circus day, bill posters pasted colorful circus posters throughout town—averaging some five thousand posters per stop—that prominently featured neat, orderly children and their parents gazing at exotic people and animals, daring acrobats, and well-toned bareback riders.[19] These images of the circus, the child spectators, and the wider world reminded audiences that the circus was a culturally sanctioned space for children's play, physical fitness, instruction, and coordinated regimens of bodily restraint.

Yet these normative representations of productive, orderly circus bodies belied the ways in which performers simultaneously subverted social and cultural norms. While journalists, novelists, and other cultural observers treated the exquisite muscularity of the superlative circus body as a metonym for ideal manhood, womanhood, and vital nationhood, the circus itself remained a refuge for marginalized bodies—that is to say, transgressive bodies that had "run away" from mainstream society. Male clowns routinely dressed in drag. The "Female Hercules" lifted men and horses. Strength acts placed men in intimate, homoerotic positions as one man slowly balanced his partner's body—often entangled with his own—with a single hand or foot. Annie Jones, the "bearded lady," talked directly to sideshow spectators. She and her fellow sideshow performers supplemented their income by selling postcards of their unusual bodies.[20] William Henry Johnson played "Zip . . . What Is It?," a "missing link from Africa," during his long sideshow career. Although his mute, fur-clad act easily reified racist stereotypes of black "savagery," Johnson socialized and gambled with his sideshow colleagues behind the scenes as part of a racially integrated work culture in Jim Crow America at the turn of the twentieth century. Tiny Kline, a Hungarian-born dancer and aerialist who hung by her teeth at the circus starting in 1919, worked with Johnson, along with hundreds of other performers, including Vander Clyde Broodway, better known as "Barbette," a wire walker and female impersonator.[21] Circus Day saturated its child audiences with a constellation of performative bodies, which offered glimpses of diverse, even possibly liberating alternatives to contemporary norms.[22]

Consequently impresarios worked hard to contain potentially disruptive circus bodies with well-advertised employee conduct rules. Barnum & Bailey's Greatest Show on Earth forbade alcohol, gambling, graft, and blue language on the rails and on the show grounds. As an effective method of surveillance and discipline, Barnum & Bailey and the Ringling Brothers circuses each employed Pinkerton railroad detective agents to monitor circus workers and audiences. At the turn of the century the five Ringling brothers convincingly marketed themselves as "Sunday school" showmen because they ran a "clean," grift-free show.[23] Such regulatory strategies were primarily dependent on disciplining the female circus body. Proprietors openly shared their strict conduct rules for women performers with local newspapers as a form of advertising:

Figure 2.1. The railroad helped transform the American circus into a ubiquitous, trans-continental form of popular entertainment at the turn of the twentieth century. "Ringling Bros. and Barnum & Bailey: 100 Railway Cars," 1923. Poster, printed by the Strobridge Lithographing Company, Cincinnati. Collection of the John and Mable Ringling Museum of Art, Tibbals Digital Collection, ht2001436. Used by permission.

"The rules of the dressing room are very strict, the women being fined $5.00 if they are late one minute; fined if they use bad language; if a glass of wine or beer is found there, or if they step outside the door in their tights only as they go to and from their acts, or are caught flirting outside the dressing room in costume. . . . Women of notably bad reputation will not be hired by the manager of Barnum's circus, and all in his employ are extremely well paid."[24] The kinetic female circus body was potentially disruptive, in part because of its expansive diversity and gender-bending potential: tall, fat, hairy, flexible, muscular, thin, armless, legless, tiny, strong, and often androgynous. Conduct rules rigorously contained the subversive potential of the kinetic female circus body outside the ring, boxing the body and transmogrifying it into a normative female subject.

Children's circus novels and other media paid special attention to the disciplined logistical movement of the show, itself a product of showmen's strict management policies. The tightly organized division of bodily labor in setting up and tearing down the temporary canvas city represented a dazzling spectacle of the national laboring corporate body. Children woke up before dawn to watch the arrival of the first circus trains, which transformed an empty lot into a vast, ephemeral canvas city. Hamlin Garland, Carl Sandburg, Sherwood Anderson, and Willa Cather, among other American writers, remembered Circus Day from their youth, rolling out of bed and streaming to the railroad yard to catch the coming of the circus.[25] Newspapers like the *Waxahachie (Texas) Daily Light* readily noted the flocks of children included in the "living mass of humanity" that witnessed this momentary transmutation. On August 18, 1899, a newspaper in Monroe, Wisconsin, chronicled an insomnia-inducing scene in the wee hours of the morning on what it called "Ringling Day": "The town was thoroughly alive from the time the first section of the circus train arrived from Janesville at 3:20 this morning."[26] Hundreds of circus laborers ("roustabouts" in circus parlance) worked specific jobs: rolling the gilded wagons off the train, marking out the lot, hammering the stakes, raising the tent poles, stringing the guy lines, guiding the animals, and more. The railroad industrialized the labor process at the American circus, transforming the shared duties at the small, animal-powered wagon shows into a speedy, assembly-line labor process at the largest railroad shows, which employed hundreds of laborers and over a thousand performers at the turn of the twentieth century.

Ultimately the division of labor at the biggest railroad circuses became an exhibition of cooperative bodily efficiency that was just as thrilling as the remarkable bodies at the formal big top and side-show performances. Such displays of collective bodily coordination complemented the educational goals of contemporary "child savers." Progressive-era playground reformers and physical culturists viewed group play and team sports as critical tools for adjusting to modern life. In the words of the historian Dominick Cavallo, "Reformers during the Progressive Era tried to orient young Americans toward life in a bureaucratic society."[27] With its myriad tents and delicately calibrated division of labor spread across nine acres of canvas, the railroad circus represented for many of its distant audiences a first intimate encounter with modern bureaucracy.

The vision of the collective laboring circus body had significant national and global resonances. The physical education writer Ernest Balch observed that the circus and the military were large organizations that were founded on synchronized bodily movement, ritual, and pageantry, which could inspire children to become dedicated physical culturists and vigorous, healthy citizens. He cautioned instructors that unless they could "interest the soul," students would care little for exercise: "By the discreet use of the glamour of the circus, tights, shows,

Figure 2.2. In the antebellum United States, showmen marketed their circuses primarily to adult audiences, and social reformers urged children to avoid the circus. However, at the turn of the twentieth century, showmen explicitly promoted the circus to child audiences, and reformers likewise encouraged children to attend. "Barnum & Bailey: Fairyland," 1923. Poster, printed by the Strobridge Lithographing Company, Cincinnati. Collection of the John and Mable Ringling Museum of Art, Tibbals Digital Collection, ht2000042. Used by permission.

etc., the pupil's interest may be maintained at white heat; and there is no need to be athlete or acrobat to do this. . . . Most teachers sooner or later reach this conclusion. These exercises are successful with the majority only in so far as they can interest the soul. In military drill something may be done with the aid of uniforms, flags, guns, mass movements, the stimulation of the attractive side of war, but with the other forms very little is attained."[28]

In the age of the Indian Wars, the Spanish-American War, the Philippine-American War, and World War I, U.S. military leaders took a direct interest in the railroad circus and its ability to move, feed, and encamp human and animal bodies. Army officers periodically rode with railroad circuses to study their organization and punctual transportation techniques; hauling roughly 1,200 people, animals, tents, and supplies across the country, day after day, railroad shows possessed a degree of social order in intimate quarters that was just as impressively disciplined as their scripted canvas performances.[29] In the aftermath of such observational exercises, American showmen eagerly publicized these military endorsements to burnish their patriotic credentials. During Barnum & Bailey's European tour (1897–1902), German army officers also looked to the show's logistical system as a model for its own operations, a fact that the circus press agent Tody Hamilton quickly reported to American newspapers: "What amazed them in Berlin was the way in which we got things in shape. Several staff officers saw us unload 400 horses in seven minutes, and I thought that we would have to get some restoratives for them. After that two or three officers were detailed to go around with us and get ideas from our methods of handling the organization. They were so struck with our folding tables that they have since adopted them in the army."[30] Readily identified from within the United States and from without, the logistical specialization of the American circus body writ large represented a key form of cultural authority for its burgeoning child audience.

With the rise of U.S. expansionism overseas in the late nineteenth century and early twentieth, the railroad circus facilitated intimate bodily contact between American children and the new empire. As a salable source of novelty for an entertainment rooted in its ability to twist the boundaries between normality and alterity, people of color and animals from the nation's overseas territories (such as Emilio Aguinaldo, the Philippine boa constrictor, and midget cattle from Samoa) became stock features. The free parade, sideshows, and the "Ethnological Congress of Strange and Savage Tribes" held in the menagerie tent placed exotic performers within a few feet of audiences.

In this crowded sensory setting, child audiences encountered performances of racial hierarchy that reinforced notions of white native-born superiority. Such ideologies included normative presentations of racialized female beauty. The Ethnological Congress and sideshow juxtaposed "savage" and "grotesque" women of color with animals from their respective country of origin, while "lovely" white European and American "lady dainties" flitted expertly and gracefully under the big top. The Laotian sideshow performer Krao Farini first worked as a "gorilla girl" in her earliest American circus gig in 1885. Thereafter she performed variously as a bearded lady and a "missing link," stationed next to Johanna the Live Gorilla at Barnum & Bailey's circus. Wellworn explorer narratives of capture and rehabilitation were a significant part of Krao's presentation as a "primitive" at the circus. Circus media chronicled how she was seized as a child in a Laotian forest by a Norwegian explorer, Carl Bock, who took her to London, where the showman G. A. Farini hired her. Krao took his name and used it for the rest of her life. As a sideshow performer at American circuses, she became "civilized," according to show programs. She spoke seven languages fluently, possessed "faultless" manners, and volunteered her services as a library tutor in Bridgeport, Connecticut, during Barnum & Bailey's off-season. Nonetheless throughout her career Krao was required to perform as a living artifact of Darwinian evolution and hence represented another form of respectable, educational entertainment for child audiences. Still, Krao's scant, ruffled costume afforded audiences a close, titillating view of her body, thereby demonstrating the ways such child-friendly displays reinforced eroticized Orientalist constructions of female bodies of color at the circus.[31]

Circuses enhanced their authority as a source of educational knowledge about the wider world, and America's place in it, with formal dramas of contemporary or historical events, such as "America's Great Naval Victory at Santiago: The Destruction of the Spanish Fleet," staged at the Barnum & Bailey circus in 1899. The circus showcased the nation's growing diplomatic stature as well. After President Roosevelt mediated the Portsmouth Treaty in 1905, which ended the Russo-Japanese War, Barnum & Bailey staged a reenactment spectacle, "Peace: America's Immortal Triumph," in 1906.[32] The next year Pawnee Bill's Historic Wild West and Great Far East (a virtual amalgam of a circus and Wild West Show, with acrobatic cowboys, marksmanship contests, circus acts, and a sideshow) staged its own "Gorgeous and Realistic Representation of the Russo-Japanese War," complete with contests between "the mighty Slav race and the Yankees of the East, the Japanese." In 1907 Pawnee Bill's program also contained a "Vast Ethnological Congress," described in the show's courier as a constellation of "many strange, queer, quaint and mysterious men," which included "the ever famous Filipinos, whose fierce fighting made it possible for our soldier boys to win unperishable fame and who were with their brave chief Aguinaldo when he was captured." Other performances included a racial hodgepodge of exotic performers: "Indians, Cowboys, Trappers, Boomerang Throwers, South Sea Islanders, Cossacks, Japanese, Arabs, Mexicans, and numerous men of note and remarkable accomplishments from other parts of the world." Pawnee Bill's courier promised that the entire show was "indorsed by the Moral and educated.[33] These circus and Wild West acts offered a close view of exotic bodies of empire, at once alien and reconstituted into familiar domestic tropes of otherness and normativity, featuring the Filipino nationalist Emilio Aguinaldo as a "brave chief" and the Japanese as "the Yankees of the East."

A thriving new industry in circus toys, such as Schoenhut's Humpty Dumpty Circus (1903), gave further form to ideologies of empire-building on display under the American big top. The wooden, jointed animals and human performers could be propped into variable circus-like poses for realistic Circus Day play. These flexible characters were physically inscribed with long-standing aesthetic markers of racial difference and American empire-building. Schoenhut's "Negro Dude" looked effectively identical to an antebellum minstrel show performer, with a big red smiling mouth and surprised, lolling eyes. Schoenhut aficionados have speculated that after the toymaker retired its "Humpty Dumpty in Africa" play set (which transformed the circus into Theodore Roosevelt's African safari of 1909), the company was left with an excess of "African Native" characters. As a money-saving measure, the company reportedly affixed leather ears to the "natives," along with minstrelesque costuming; accordingly a new placeless racial Other was born. Humpty Dumpty's Circus also contained a stock "Chinaman" acrobat character with buckteeth, nearly imperceptible eyes, a long queue, and a rat-like grimace.[34] Eugene W. Metcalf suggests that these popular new circus toys embodied the transformation of the middle-class American child from laborer to consumer in the maturing industrial marketplace: "Removed from the world of adult work, middle-class children became consumers of goods and experience rather than producers of them. . . . No longer only traditional representations of the adult world or small versions of real-world adult tools, playthings became, like the spectacle of the circus, instruments of escape, fantasy, and play."[35] Nonetheless these fantastical playthings had concrete ideological consequences. Circus toys guaranteed that children's encounters with exotic performers and animals would extend far beyond Circus Day, therefore helping to make empire and its racial, gendered, and classed taxonomies of difference a way of life through acts of play and consumption.

In the antebellum United States the American Sunday-School Union condemned the circus as toxic to children. Yet just fifty years later the railroad circus was thoroughly integrated into the cultural and social world of the American child in an age of accelerated immigration, endemic racial and class conflict, and growing anxiety about the effects of child poverty upon the nation's potency. Showmen and "child savers" alike cast the circus's harmonized, disciplined displays of individual and collective bodies as moral expressions of physical fitness, uplift, citizenship, and patriotism at a historical moment when Progressive reformers began to think of the city itself as a body—an organic entity whose relationship with the individual and the nation was ecological. Moreover many reformers, such as the sociologist and civil rights activist W. E. B. Du Bois, used statistics and surveys (see, for example, Du Bois, *The Philadelphia Negro: A Social Study*, published in 1899) to enumerate the overall well-being of the body politic.

In this nation-building milieu the circus became a powerful agent of Americanization overseas as well as at home, thus helping to define what the historian Ian Tyrrell calls America's "moral empire."[36] The Young Men's Christian Association, for one, created a popular Association circus in Shanghai as a pleasurable vehicle for children's physical fitness and uplift. The YMCA branch reported that its Association circus in March 1916 triumphed in its capacity to entertain and educate: "The feature of greatest importance, however, and the one which will certainly make the Circus play a large part in the future life of China is its ideal combination of wholesome fun and helpful suggestion. Men need fun and entertainment, but only such as on a *high plane* is worthy of a real man. One could not look at the drills and feats of strength in the circus without being inspired to attain greater physical fitness for the game of life."[37]

It was precisely this sort of inspiration and edification that General John Pershing had in mind after the Armistice, when he authorized new sport and leisure programs to boost flagging military morale and to prevent vice and Bolshevism among the American Expeditionary Forces.[38] The YMCA and Knights of Columbus helped soldiers stage the American Expeditionary Forces circus, which played across war-beaten Germany and France in the summer of 1919. At Coblenz, Germany, for example, the "Big Show in American Style" on June 6 was the occasion for a festive reunion of some ten thousand U.S. soldiers, who consumed twenty thousand bottles of pop and five thousand bottles of beer and feasted on barbeque. Thousands of German civilians saw the expansive show from surrounding hillsides, "watching something they had never seen before," in terms of the prodigious size and scale of the entertainment. (The circus itself, of course, was a familiar cultural form in Germany; hailing from Hamburg, Carl Hagenbeck was a world-famous circus proprietor, animal dealer, and zoo impresario.)[39] At the massive American Expeditionary circus, each military regiment of the division performed its own signature stunts, and four "elaborate floats" depicted the division's "four major operations" during the war. The YMCA provided a cabaret. A 3rd Division show, "Chop Suey," reportedly "added to the gayety of the occasion," using the name of a

Chinese cuisine (meaning "little pieces") invented in the United States for American consumption, as the basis for a colorful, exotic pageant of domesticated and reconstituted cultural difference.

The press did not describe the contents of this particular "Chop Suey" show, but entertainment reviews of other eponymously named shows suggest that this entertainment primarily took the form of a Ziegfeld Follies–style female or drag chorus line revue consisting of Chinese performers and/or Chinese cultural motifs. At the Pom Pom in Hollywood, one "Chop Suey" musical revue featured a number, "Parade of the Lanterns," imported directly from the Carlton Club in Shanghai: "Each girl will carry a brace of imported Chinese lanterns painted with floral and dragon designs." Another article included "chop suey" in its "Menu of Comedy" (which also included other ethnically identified offerings such as spaghetti, wiener schnitzel, and horse meat). The food scholar Andrew Coe observes that entrepreneurial chop suey restaurateurs added inexpensive entertainment programs to their menus as a way to remain competitive in the expanding urban dining marketplace in the early twentieth century. The name "Chop Suey" stuck as an amusement genre.[40]

By World War I the mutually constitutive relationship between the circus, children, play, the body, and nation-building was in place. During the Gilded Age and Progressive era, child-savers had turned to the circus as a potent form of play that could transform flaccid youthful bodies into muscular models of vigor that were physically fit and fit for the responsibilities of citizenship and nation-building at home and abroad. With its thousands of human and animal performers from America's new empire and beyond, the transcontinental railroad circus offered its far-flung child audiences a "wholesome," jingoistic celebration of U.S. hegemony. Christian organizations that surely would have denounced the circus in the antebellum era now promoted it as a powerful conduit for youthful development and nation-building in war-ravaged Europe and preindustrial China. Working on the transnational front lines, the YMCA and Knights of Columbus worked hand in hand with U.S. military leaders in Europe and American missionaries in China. Promoted by so many people and groups, the big top's youthful gospel of the body helped define America's exceptionalist mission on the world stage for the twentieth century.

Notes

1. The narrative was structured around a conversation between the wise Aunt Fanny and her niece, Sally, who loved the circus. In telling the horrific story of Jack Ward, Aunt Fanny convinced her sweet and now tearful niece that the circus was noxious for children. American Sunday-School Union, *Slim Jack; Or, the History of a Circus-Boy* (Philadelphia: American Sunday-School Union, 1847), 6.

2. American Sunday-School Union, *Slim Jack*, 80, 94.

3. Thayer, "The Anti-Circus Laws in Connecticut," 20; Thayer, "Legislating the Shows," 20.

4. "A Wise Pastor," *Sunday School Teacher: A Monthly Magazine, Devoted to the Interests of Sunday Schools* 2, no. 11 (Chicago, IL: Adams, Blackmer, and Lyon, 1867), 329–30.

5. See Foucault, *The History of Sexuality.*

6. The circus arrived in the new republic in 1792, when a Scottish trick rider named John Bill Ricketts opened a riding school in Philadelphia. In April 1793 Ricketts and a handful of performers opened the new nation's first circus performance with displays of rope dancing, clowning, juggling, and trick riding.

7. See Davis, "The Circus Americanized."

8. National Consumers' League, "Roving Children." National Consumers' League, "Roving Children: Not of the Stage or the Circus; But of the Canning Districts, the Construction Camps, the Stone Quarries and Other Transient or Seasonal Communities. Is Our Civilization Making the Most of Them?," reprinted from *Survey*, New York, January 1, 1910.

9. See for example, Bederman, *Manliness and Civilization*; Jacobson, *Barbarian Virtues.*

10. Cavallo, *Muscles and Morals*, 49–54.

11. In 1905, twenty-four cities had eighty-seven playgrounds; in 1917, 481 cities had 3,940 playgrounds. Cavallo, *Muscles and Morals*, 2, 45.

12. William H. Allen, *Civics and Health* (Boston: Ginn, 1909), 117.

13. Ernest Balch, *Amateur Circus Life: A New Method of Physical Development for Boys and Girls, Based on the Ten Elements of Simple Tumbling and Adapted from the Practice of Professional Acrobats* (New York: Macmillan, 1916), 146.

14. Balch, *Amateur Circus Life*, 132–33.

15. Horatio Alger, *The Young Circus Rider, or the Mystery of Robert Rudd* (Philadelphia: Henry T. Coates, 1883); Horatio Alger, *The Young Acrobat of the Great North American Circus* (1888; Charleston, SC: Nabu Press, 2010).

16. Trachtenberg, *The Incorporation of America*, 80.

17. Alger, *The Young Circus Rider*, 74; Alger, *The Young Acrobat of the Great North American Circus*, 118, 7.

18. See, for example, James Otis, *The Wreck of the Circus* (New York, Thomas Y. Crowell, 1897), and *Toby Tyler, or Ten Weeks with a Circus* (New York: Harper and Bros., 1903); George W. Peck, *Peck's Bad Boy with the Circus* (Chicago, IL: Stan-

ton and Van Vleet, 1905); Peter T. Harkness, *Andy the Acrobat; or, Out with the Greatest Show on Earth* (Cleveland, OH: World Syndicate, 1907); Margaret Mayo, *Polly of the Circus* (New York: Dodd, Mead, 1908); Circus Fiction Collection, Robert L. Parkinson Library and Research Center, Circus World Museum, Baraboo, Wisconsin (hereafter CWM).

19. Davis, *The Circus Age*, 44.

20. See Davis, *The Circus Age*, chapters 4 and 5.

21. Kline, *Circus Queen and Tinker Bell*, 129–31, 304–5, 351n7.

22. Broader perspectives include Putzi, *Identifying Marks*; Martin, *The White African American Body*; Adams, *Sideshow USA*.

23. Davis, *The Circus Age*, 61.

24. "The Ladies of the Circus," unidentified newspaper clipping, 1891, SBK 17, CWM.

25. See Anderson, *Tar*; Garland, *A Son of the Middle Border*; Sandburg, *Always the Young Strangers*. Although Willa Cather did not write directly about her own childhood experiences at the circus, her fictional characters often described the sensory world of circus day. For example, see her frontier trilogy, *O Pioneers!*

26. "The Circus," *Waxahachie (Texas) Daily Light*, November 2, 1898, Newspaper Collection, Dolph Briscoe Center for American History, University of Texas at Austin; "Charms of Circus Draws Big Crowd," unidentified newspaper clipping, Monroe, Wisconsin, August 18, 1899, Newspaper Collection, CWM.

27. Cavallo, *Muscles and Morals*, 10.

28. Balch, *Amateur Circus Life*, 149, 179.

29. Davis, *The Circus Age*, 78–79.

30. "'Tody' Hamilton and His Vocabulary Back," *New York Times*, October 29, 1902.

31. Davis, *The Circus Age*, 128–31; see also Hamlin, "The 'Case of a Bearded Woman.'"

32. Davis, *The Circus Age*, 211.

33. Pawnee Bill's Historic Wild West and Great Far East, show courier, 1907 season, no publishing information given, no page numbers, Circus Program Collection, CWM.

34. Davis, *The Circus Age*, 35–36; "The Schoenhut Humpty Dumpty Circus Identification Guide, accessed January 17, 2012, http://www.oldwoodtoys.com/identification_guide.htm.

35. Metcalf, "Circus Toys in the Gilded Age," 361.

36. Tyrrell, *Reforming the World*.

37. "The Circus a Great Success," *Shanghai Young Men*, March 24, 1916, 27–28; Kautz Family YMCA Archives, Elmer L. Andersen Library, University of Minnesota.

38. See Farwell, *Over There*, 270; Thompson, *The Book of History*, 1258; Robison, "Recreation in World War I and the Practice of Play in *One of Ours*."

39. See Rothfels, *Savages and Beasts.*

40. Edwin L. James, "Coblenz Is Thrilled by Soldiers' Circus," *New York Times*, June 9, 1919; "News of the Cafes," *Los Angeles Times*, August 21, 1929; George Jean Nathan, "The Puppet Shop," *Puck*, July 24, 1915. See Coe, *Chop Suey*, 189–91; Nancy Shute, "In Praise of Chop Suey," *U.S. News and World Report*, August 7, 2005, accessed November 27, 2011, http://www.usnews.com/usnews/culture/articles/050815/15chinese.htm.

three

Making Broken Bodies Whole
in a Shell-Shocked World

ANNESSA C. STAGNER

> In the great crisis of our civilization which we are facing the real
> problem is can we regulate human behavior intelligently? . . . If
> we can, then we have a right to be optimistic about civilization.
> If we can't do it—well! Let us not mention the other alternative.
> —Stewart Patton, 1917

This essay explores discourses of national recovery and national
power that circulated in the interrelated realms of medicine, psychiatry,
and popular representations of soldiers. Acknowledging European historians who have argued that shell shock in Europe became a symbol for
the devastation of the war and Europeans' inability to recover from it,
this essay investigates how the U.S. discourse of shell shock played out
in an international arena. An ocean away from Europe, many medical
and political leaders in the United States articulated a definition of shell
shock that contradicted European notions of permanent injury. Aiming
to prove the validity of their psychiatry and social psychology, American
psychiatrists worked with policy officials to restore the wholeness of
individual bodies and minds. These efforts also became projected as
attempts to restore the health of nations. By the end of the war Americans' optimism regarding their own abilities to restore minds and im-

prove the behavior of individuals and nations fueled a sense of their country's international distinction and even superiority.

When the First World War erupted in Europe in 1914, it brought what many at the time described as a new kind of warfare, characterized by the technological advancements of an industrial age. Machine guns, exploding shells, and deadly gas resulted in massive numbers of casualties. Soldiers suffered physical and psychological wounds difficult even for doctors to describe and define. Particularly problematic were symptoms associated with what the British physician Charles S. Myers first termed "shell shock" in a February 13, 1915, article in the Lancet. Listing five case histories, Myers asserted that impairments to hearing, sight, smell, and taste that many soldiers experienced were the result of "shell-shock"—of the individual having been close to an exploding shell that "burst with considerable noise" and physically shocked the body.[1]

Shell shock became an umbrella diagnosis during the First World War. It covered a variety of bodily ills, ranging from amnesia to limb dysfunction and paralysis. Shell shock formed the basis for international medical discussions related to the neuropsychiatric disorders of soldiers and their treatment. Whether such disorders arose from increased fear, horror or other fatiguing conditions, emotional conflict or excitement, inherited emotional instability, brain damage due to physical impact, or a combination of these remained scientifically unclear. Differences of opinion among medical professionals over the causes of shell shock prompted differing views of diagnostics, treatments, and the possibilities for recovery.[2]

As an unstable category of disability, shell shock and the equally unqualified term war neuroses came to identify the traumatic injuries of thousands of individual soldiers.[3] Simple numbers revealed the immediate importance of these injuries to the war and its outcome. While reporting from France, Thomas Salmon, an American psychiatrist and the director of the National Committee for Mental Hygiene, observed, "No medico-military problems of the war are more striking than those growing out of the extraordinary incidence of mental and functional nervous diseases ('shell shock')." These disorders accounted for one-seventh of all discharges from the British Army.[4] They were toxic to military morale and adversely affected home front attitudes toward war and national strength. In war, a contest among nations in which the central aim is to injure bodies, the ability or inability of nations to recondition those same bodies and minds to an idealized masculine normality became a measure of national victory.[5]

Europe's Wounds

Upon seeing the effects of shell shock on the Western Front firsthand, a University of Georgia neurologist, W. R. Houston, concluded, "This wreckage of men's souls seemed to me to mirror more vividly the horror of war."[6] As early as 1915 individuals in the United States and Europe had begun to see the Great War as an unforgettable nightmare. Nothing captured this sentiment more clearly than the image of the shell-shocked soldier, who seemed to embody the war's most dreadful effects.

European historians have written extensively on the meanings shell shock came to have in Europe. They have described how military officials and sometimes doctors viewed soldiers who were unable to control their mind as emotionally weak. Such soldiers were commonly diagnosed with "hysteria," a neurosis most typically associated with the emotional weakness of women, or were labeled cowards and malingerers.[7] Despite discussions about the condition among psychiatrists throughout Europe, the demands of military expediency during the war often took precedence over treatment programs for such soldiers. Shell shock came to be widely viewed as a permanent disability, and Europeans remained pessimistic about restoring such soldiers.[8]

Each nation developed distinct understandings of shell shock and judged their ability to "cure" soldiers differently. Especially toward the latter part of the war, some reformist European doctors believed they could heal soldiers' minds and tried using what they considered compassionate treatment techniques.[9] Yet for many Europeans both during and after the war, the large numbers of cases of war neuroses suggested an epidemic signifying the mental and spiritual impairment of Europe. Persistent representations of uncured shell-shocked Europeans created a common image of long-lasting mental damage to both European bodies and nations.[10] Eric Leed and other historians have maintained that, at the war's end, Europeans were unable to come to terms with—or forget—the horrors of war and the marked bodies of so many returning soldiers.[11]

The mental fragility of combatants held deep meaning for European and American intellectuals in the early twentieth century who had long been concerned with Western civilization's regression.[12] One historian points out that shell shock was "regarded in much of the literature as a mental state which mirrored a social disease and national degeneration."[13] The Austrian writer and journalist Karl Kraus called it the "harbinger of world decline."[14] For these intellectuals, shell shock seemed to verify the link between advancing industrial technology and Western civilization's ever-weakening bodies. As industrialism spread, so too did cases of what the American neurologist George Miller Beard had called "neurasthenia." Advances in civilization, including capitalism and industrialism, produced "nervelessness—a lack of nerve force," which physically weakened the most intellectually and culturally advanced bodies.[15] War seemed to accelerate this problem. One Englishman, Arthur Davies, stated, "If neurasthenia is due to the strain and stress of a civilization different from those of other periods in the world's history, then we may regard the condition of War neurasthenia . . . as due to the unparalleled conditions of modern War."[16] As with neurasthenia, officers from middle- and upper-class families seemed to suffer from shell shock more than rank-and-file soldiers from the lower class.[17] The apparent weakness of European bodies confirmed, to some, European civilization's decline.[18]

The irrational cruelty with which military superiors treated shell-shocked soldiers only magnified how quickly the supposed advances in European humanity and reason could be reversed.[19] Freud, who associated shell shock with unconscious traumatic neurosis, wrote that physicians who had attempted to heal soldiers with harsh treatment had abandoned scientific judgment in their quest to serve nation-states at war. According to Freud, "Science, herself, had lost her passionless impartiality," and the war "shattered our pride in the achievements of our civilization."[20] Shell shock heralded the breakdown of the highest stratum of modern European civilization and the insubstantiality of modern scientific reason.

For some intellectuals, the inability of soldiers to control their minds also mirrored the irrationality of European nations leading to the outbreak of war.[21] Writers articulating patriotic justifications of the war, for example, were keen to describe their enemy's hysterical mental state. One of America's most popular writers, Owen Wister, blamed Germany's lack of reason for sparking the war.[22] The French social psychologist Gustave Le Bon applied a similar analysis to all European countries. These nations had neglected thought and instead given way to "great collective psychoses," which in turn amplified a regional diplomatic conflict into a world war. Le Bon remained optimistic about the future of civilization, but he acknowledged that the declarations of war in 1914 marked a regression in the mental state of Europe.[23]

Caroline E. Playne, an English pacifist, historian, and writer, drew the conclusion of degeneration most sharply in her 1925 study of France and Germany, *Neuroses of the Nations*. As a member of Britain's National

Peace Council who had supported the creation of the international court at The Hague and attended the International Peace Congress in London in 1908, Playne found no logical explanation for the war and developed a theory of neurosis to explain it. In her study she described society as an organized mental system; beginning in roughly 1889, individual men, inundated by nerve stimulation, had begun losing their ability to reason. Examining primarily France and Germany, Playne argued that the tension found in European civilizations due to industrialization had caused these men to initiate what she labeled an "insane war":

> There was no doubt that the pace of life had affected men's minds in a disastrous way, judging by their temper. This was especially apparent wherever men were collected in clusters, in concourses, in parties, in self-conscious national groups; for these groups, these collectivities were so excited that their emotions were out-of-hand, uncontrolled and uncontrollable. They became possessed of manias and ruled by anxiety-fear. . . . The term "social and national insanity" often used by writers on the war-period is no figure of speech. It is justified by the neurasthenical derangements exhibited by various group-minds. These derangements are exhibited in the literature, in the art of the time, in political action, in the mentality and behavior of leaders and nations, in the teaching of inspirers of groups.[24]

Playne claimed "a saner world" could have avoided the war. Instead Europe had lost its progressive impulse and become "irritable and overstrained" and "too neurasthenical" to think logically about the consequences of war. Germany, she contended, "excited their irritation, their hatred, their abhorrence, their fears; thus a vast complex of anxiety neurosis developed among them."[25] Both individuals and nations had failed to maintain their "nerves" as these societies transformed into modern industrial nations.

Playne followed her study of Germany and France with an analysis of Great Britain, in which she discussed Britain's "psycho-neurotic character."[26] In a following publication, entitled *Society at War*, she described the psychological and nervous mindset of the people in Germany, France, and Great Britain just before the Great War. Using social psychology, she depicted a feverish and neurotic state of public opinion guiding European diplomacy and causing the war.

Playne's studies were not the first to suggest neuroses had led to the outbreak of the Great War, nor were they the last. Her work was reviewed in American and European journals and encountered as much disapproval regarding her research methods as praise for her overall theory.[27] Playne did not include the United States in her studies of national neuroses. Her work emphasized how European nations' role as the protagonists of the Great War set them apart. They engulfed themselves and the rest of the world unnecessarily in war and now seemed powerless, unable to concoct their own cure.

Certainly not all Europeans or Americans believed the Great War marked the weakening of Europe.[28] As historians have rightly pointed out, interpretations of shell shock varied widely from nation to nation, reflecting national differences in perceptions of the war.[29] Still, from the outbreak of the war and through the interwar era, it became common to frame the neuroses of both individuals and nations as an indicator of the decline of Europe's mental strength, scientific and medical abilities, and international diplomatic power.

America's Healing Power

Much like observers on the Western Front, Colonel Pearce Bailey, who served as chief of neuropsychiatry for U.S. Army Medicine, claimed that war neuroses had "their origin in the stress and special horror of modern warfare." Psychiatric advisors to the U.S. Army surgeon general concluded, "A medical service newly confronted like ours with the task of caring for the sick and wounded of a large army cannot ignore such important causes of invalidism."[30] U.S. officials believed the most decisive factor in achieving victory was not physical strength or industrial technology but the soundness of the minds of Americans on the battlefield and at home. Secretary of War Newton Baker declared in 1919, "Wars are battles of the brain."[31] To at least some Americans, "a victory in modern warfare [was] a sign of greater mental efficiency than was necessary among the soldiers a century ago."[32] American psychiatrists, military personnel, and policymakers regarded overcoming neuroses—among U.S. troops and among nations—as an opportunity to demonstrate their country's victorious qualities.

In preparing to deal with shell-shock cases in the war, U.S. Army Surgeon General William Gorgas worked closely with members of the National Committee for Mental Hygiene (NCMH). By 1917, with the funding and support of the Rockefeller Foundation, the NCMH had gained a national and international reputation for its work in changing attitudes about the mentally ill and advancing the prevention and treatment of mental illness. It had risen on the wings of some of the era's most prominent Progressive-era reformers, including William James and Jane Addams, and its membership spanned the nation and included leading neurologists and psychiatrists. Among its members were Thomas Salmon, a psychologist and the director of the National Committee for Mental Hygiene; Stewart Paton, a lecturer in neurobiology at Princeton University; and Pearce Bailey, a New York neurologist. Together they helped to form the conceptual backbone of American neuropsychiatric military policies.

Salmon and other psychiatrists associated with the mental hygiene movement were not unlike many of their European counterparts in treatment and thinking; they had long been part of an Atlantic community that sought to learn more about mental illness. They were also part of the progressive impulse of the early twentieth century that advocated improving society through various kinds of biopolitical social interventions.[33] American psychiatrists contended that soldiers became shell-shocked because of their exposure to modern warfare but that the symptoms soldiers exhibited were little different from those of mentally ill civilians and that their treatment should be similar. The treatment methods they envisioned were eclectic, drawing from many different schools of thought. They attempted to ground their methods in the belief that shell shock was a legitimate wartime injury and framed this approach as compassionate. Still, their efforts at restoration did not simply involve expunging symptoms and returning soldiers to their prewar selves. Many American psychiatrists also suggested that their efforts were aimed at building even better men who would return from war mentally intelligent, emotionally even-tempered, physically strong, instinctively protective, and heterosexual. They strove for this heteronormative ideal believing that such characteristics made men fit not only for warfare but also for citizenship in a healthy nation.

This vision of "curing" individuals had implications beyond the health of the soldier. Many American psychiatrists saw their participation in the First World War as a new opportunity to justify state intervention into the realm of social management. If they could reform the individual soldier, they might afterward be given increased state support to extend their "curative" techniques to other "problem" citizens, including criminals, radicals, and sexual "deviants." They saw their ability to "heal" the mind as directly related to their ability to "heal" societies, particularly in the areas of labor strikes, mob violence, and other disorders they considered symptomatic of national hysteria brought by industrialization.[34] Mental hygiene, with its ramifications for social psychology and biopolitics, was not just about the soundness of the individual mind but about what its advocates saw as furthering the stability of the nation as a whole.

The U.S. Army surgeon general's invitation to create and enact policies concerning shell shock provided a unique opportunity for the NCMH's psychiatrists, one not afforded to many of their European counterparts. The surgeon general remained responsive to each of their policy requests throughout the war.[35] Moreover many of the members of the NCMH accepted important positions of political power. Pierce Bailey became director of a newly created Division of Neurology and Psychiatry in the War Department. Thomas Salmon became the presiding officer in the Division of Psychiatry of the American Expeditionary Forces (AEF). William A. White, director of the army's St. Elizabeths Hospital for the Insane, joined the Medical Advisory Committee of the Council of National Defense. The surgeon general also gave the NCMH authority over recruiting civilian neurologists and psychiatrists for temporary enlistment in the military, which allowed members to nominate like-minded psychiatrists, many of whom were members themselves and supporters of efforts to improve the treatment of the mentally ill. Recruits were also given a rank with some amount of prestige to ensure they had the status necessary to ensure that their ordered treatments were carried out effectively. Although rank was not guaranteed, doctors were often commissioned as majors, or as captains and rapidly advanced to major.[36] At the war's end, the Neuropsychiatry Division of the AEF consisted of 693 commissioned officers, 325 nurses, and forty-five reconstruction aides and social workers, the majority of whom had been recruited through the NCMH and approved by the U.S. Army surgeon general.[37]

American doctors drew from the experiences of Europe in forming their policies. They had volunteered for the war in 1915 and shared their findings in articles in medical journals in the United States. To gain perspective on the best techniques to deal with shell shock some visited military hospitals on the fields of France, in London, in Canada, and on the U.S.-Mexico border, where U.S. troops had been engaged in their "punitive expedition" against Francisco (Pancho) Villa. Such observations influenced American policy.[38] Salmon, for example, admired the talk therapy and reeducation treatments practiced by some English doctors and the French front-line clinics that facilitated soldiers' prompt treatment. Both elements were incorporated into American policies.

American policies diverged significantly from those in Europe, however, primarily because of military support for the NCMH's vision.

Upon the recommendation of the NCMH, policymakers instituted mental health examinations for recruits.[39] This effort allowed doctors to exclude from the military those individuals they perceived as predisposed to psychological illness and thus inherently weak. Men who had been previously hospitalized for mental disturbances, had a family history of instability, or demonstrated what were deemed feminine behaviors or physical characteristics (such as frightening extraordinarily easily or having small genitalia) were classified as men who would not hold up emotionally under the intense environment of trench warfare and were thus excluded from military service. Officials reasoned that subjecting such men to the intense strains of warfare would worsen their condition.

Screening also allowed NCMH members to argue that all those who suffered from shell shock on the battlefield had been mentally fit when admitted to the military. This coincided with the NCMH's vision of shell-shocked soldiers as not conscious malingerers but masculine heroes suffering from legitimate wounds of modern, industrial warfare. Salmon explained this distinction in an extensive article in *Military Surgeon* in 1917 by describing the real suffering of courageous soldiers. Although he acknowledged the existence of malingering, he emphasized the prevalence of war neuroses and the long-term psychological damage done to heroic soldiers who received harsh punishment rather than medical care. Military officials did punish soldiers they perceived to be malingerers. Yet Secretary Baker would boast after the war that unlike European soldiers, U.S. soldiers were not executed for malingering.[40]

Variations in diagnosis in U.S. facilities contributed to the identification of shell shock as a wound that could afflict strong men. Although hysteria was used as a diagnosis, for example, American doctors employed it with less frequency compared to their European counterparts.[41] In fact shortly after the war John H. W. Rhein, professor of diseases of the mind and nervous system at the University of Pennsylvania and a consultant in neuropsychiatry for the AEF, boasted of the lack of use of hysteria as a diagnosis. Like Rhein, many doctors preferred to emphasize psychiatry's medical value and their ability to regenerate mentally strong men.[42]

In order to aid recovery, Bailey and Salmon developed an elaborate system of treatment to validate the soldier's body as wounded and expedite care. Shell-shock patients were treated at the nearest hospital; psychiatrists were assigned to each base hospital and were instructed to administer care as quickly as possible. A special base hospital, number 117, equipped to treat difficult cases, was established in France.[43]

Figure 3.1. Rest and recreation were key elements of American efforts to cure shell shock. During the First World War the U.S. military worked with the American Red Cross and other organizations to provide opportunities for such activities in France. Unlike images of recently diagnosed soldiers, which were carefully guarded, images of recovering "shell-shocked" soldiers participating in recreational activities were made widely available. Courtesy of the National Library of Medicine.

Detailed policy guidelines regulated the placement of soldiers in treatment and provided rules for their transfer between facilities. They also constantly emphasized that the military's aim was to heal soldiers.

American psychiatrists took action to further the perception among troops that the body of the shell-shocked soldier could be restored. Base hospital buildings originally labeled "Isolation-Insane" were renamed "Psychiatric Wards," and open, bright, airy wards replaced small cell-like rooms with heavily barred windows and doors.[44] Each division psychiatrist became responsible for creating "in the minds of troops generally the impression the disorders grouped under the term 'shell shock' are relatively simple and recoverable rather than complex and dangerous."[45] Soldiers were also given extensive propaganda on the ease with which shell shock could be prevented and cured. Officers in training camps received leaflets titled "How the Soldier Keeps His Nerve," courtesy of the Massachusetts Society of the NCMH.[46] Articles published in the Stars and Stripes, the AEF's newspaper published in France in 1918 and 1919, emphasized the U.S. military's ability to enact quick cures.

An article in February 1918 boasted that highly trained army specialists could treat any injury, including shell shock.[47] According to another article, 95 percent of soldiers diagnosed with shell shock improved and were able to return to active duty.[48] Lieutenant Colonel Colin Russell claimed in 1918 that U.S. Army medical officers had mastered shell shock; he asserted that, if properly treated, soldiers could be cured in a matter of minutes.[49]

The military preserved this optimistic image of shell shock partly by keeping hidden images of the bodies of those actually suffering. Film footage of shell-shocked soldiers recently admitted to treatment facilities taken for medical documentation, for example, was closely guarded. YMCA workers were not allowed to watch such films due to their potentially "disturbing" nature. As a medical officer explained, it might "create by suggestion and unconscious imitation of the very conditions we are trying to avoid."[50]

Home front media discussions of shell shock also described it as an injury experienced by healthy, mentally strong soldiers. In their descriptions, American reporters often emphasized the soldiers' heroism, as opposed to cowardice. Stories of those who suffered shell shock often told of their succumbing to illness only after sacrificing themselves and fighting valiantly against the enemy.[51] An article in Scribner's published in August 1918 asserted, "Modern warfare subjects the soldier to a form of emotional strain previously unknown, and these fits of terror occur in men who have shown great bravery."[52] The difficult environment of warfare caused shell shock.

Articles in U.S. newspapers confirmed Americans' abilities to easily cure shell shock through science and medicine. New private camps and redesigned state hospitals were equipped to heal the bodies and minds of returning shell-shocked soldiers after the war's end. Attempting to create calm environments, these facilities provided a "paradise for the soul-weary men from the front." Detailed descriptions of hydrotherapy, previously used in asylums for the insane, were rearticulated to highlight the sophistication of equipment and tools medics had at their disposal to treat soldiers. An article in the Scientific American Supplement aimed at therapists emphasized the importance of breathing exercises using the diaphragm. "In mute cases," the author claimed, "if we can recover [the diaphragm's] use all is likely to go well."[53] Treatments ranged from listening to music to coloring rooms yellow. Some writers described specific individuals who recuperated after enjoying occupational therapy in the form of reading, baking, or various other physical and mental exercises. Farming had a special therapeutic value. Images

Figure 3.2. *After World War I, private organizations continued what had been military efforts to cure shell shock. Mirroring wartime images of treatment, postwar images of this Palm Beach Florida Club House displayed shell-shocked soldiers participating in activities amid nature's serene beauty. Courtesy of* Touchstone *3 (1918): 500.*

of those who mastered such exercises displayed confident and strong men.[54] Such efforts underscored the possibility of recuperation for both veterans and the nation.[55]

American plays, poetry, and films similarly depicted shell shock as a curable wound of courageous soldiers. *Three Live Ghosts*, a comedy by the American author and playwright Frederic Isham appearing on Broadway on September 29, 1920, at Greenwich Village Theatre, tells the story of three veterans returning to England after the war. All three have been German prisoners and reported dead, and the comedy tracks their struggle to reestablish their identities upon their return home. One of the characters, Spoofy, is described as a shell-shocked veteran. He provides comic relief throughout the film as he remains unaware of his own identity and suffers from kleptomania. He eventually steals even his own baby. Despite his comedic role in the film, he is eventually hit over the head and cured, instantly regaining his mind and remembering his identity. He then resumes his role as a nobleman of high prestige and wealth. The production ran 250 performances until May 1921 before being made into a silent film.

Eugene O'Neill's one-act play *Shell Shock*, published in 1918, though not comedic in character, similarly suggested the ease with which one could recover from shell shock. Jack Arnold, an honored veteran of the

World War and a former All-American college football player, is shown to be obsessed with cigarettes, which he hoards. He smokes often and reenacts the motions of smoking by drawing his fingers to his lips when he has no cigarette. During Arnold's encounter with the military psychiatrist Robert Wayne, the audience learns of the horrors he experienced in the Great War. Simultaneously they discover Arnold's heroism in entering No Man's Land during the fierce battle of Chateau-Thierry to rescue a comrade. By the end of the play, Wayne has successfully used talk therapy to reorient Arnold away from his fear. Arnold overcomes his obsession with cigarettes, is cured completely of his shell shock, and reappears as a mentally and physically strengthened heteronormative male.

Characters who at first appear physically and mentally unstable and then regain their prewar selves were prevalent in American stories in the years immediately following the First World War. A poem titled "Shell Shock," for example, describes a valiant soldier who begins to heal after talking with a psychiatrist.[56] The silent film Shootin' for Love (1923) opens with a father who considers his shell-shocked son a coward. As the son begins to heal and regain his senses, the father slowly learns his son is a war hero deserving of respect. In a similar fashion, local townspeople in the film The Trembling Hour (1919) accuse a shell-shocked veteran of committing a murder. Despite his strange habits, he is eventually cleared of the crime and ultimately regains his fellow citizens' trust. In American cultural representations, the shell-shocked character proved to be merely temporarily injured rather than permanently disabled and nearly always regained his status as a respectable, even heroic war veteran.[57]

Images accompanying such stories often displayed the recovered veteran as an idealized embodiment of the era's dominant discourse of masculinity: physically strong, instinctively protective, and heterosexual. The plot of the film The Burning Question (1919), for example, tells of a man who is healed of his shock when he holds his infant child for the first time. In the film's advertising poster, the father is the dominant figure, depicted as composed, calm, and physically strong. His embrace of his infant child suggests his recovery through his resumption of his role as father.

While the dominant discourse of shell shock in America struck a positive tone with regard to healing individual soldiers, it also often advanced a body/nation identification that gave urgency to overcoming the kind of national neuroses that Playne and others described in Europe. Many doctors believed that "war neuroses are the same as peace neuroses," and their contagious nature had the potential to make these diseases of the mind epidemic.[58] Secretary Baker claimed, "Our national problem, the problem in which every man, women—and I was about to say child—can help . . . our national problem is to keep our balance, is not to yield to weary nerves."[59] Keeping one's nerve remained essential to the preservation of the democratic nation.

Efforts on the home front to heal the nation began with healing those individuals who had been rejected from the military due to "mental weakness." The largest number of rejections were men deemed to be mental and nervous cases, and this reinvigorated the efforts of those concerned with mental health and the nation's future. One data analyst concluded, "This rejected material thus turned back into the community has disclosed to a degree never revealed before, the large extent of unsuspected mental disease, instability and defect existing in the world about us."[60] The mentally ill symbolized a sick society, but "a society that is subject to progressive improvement."[61] The common equation drawn between weak men and weak nations would fuel the powerful interwar eugenics movement.

With their knowledge of military hospital treatments of shell shock, the NCMH's members found new reason to pursue civilian mental hygiene programs.[62] They worked with hospitals throughout the United States to improve care and emphasized the need for education about how to withstand the strain and stress of modern life and preserve democracy. The NCMH and other organizations successfully enlisted government agencies, charitable institutions such as the Rockefeller Foundation, and wealthy philanthropists to help finance educational efforts to improve the "mental hygiene" of populations in the United States.

Some psychiatrists and politicians, concerned with keeping the United States separated from the shell-shocked continent of Europe, further advocated the importance of strict immigration screening to prevent Europe's troubled people from entering the country. Lawrence Kolb, who worked at Ellis Island's New York Immigration Station as a specialist in the mental disease of incoming immigrants, argued for careful screening. He wrote, "It is expected that after the war many aliens who have suffered from war neuroses incident to military service or residence in devastated areas will apply for admission to this country." Kolb acknowledged that some immigrants would ultimately make useful citizens; however, he invoked contemporary eugenic doctrines to contend that others, if admitted, would become a financial burden to the state and "transmit neuropathic taint to future generations."[63] Kolb did not overtly distinguish between western and eastern Europeans, nor did he assign shell shock to a particular social class. What he did make clear was that shell shock was a European condition and, in order to serve the best interests of the nation, the borders needed to be sealed against it.

Writing two years earlier, Charles Wagner, president of the American Society of Insanity, had shared Kolb's concerns. The United States had entered the Great War, according to Wagner, on behalf of civilization, national independence, and the rights of humanity. He predicted the number of mentally defective immigrants would rise after the war but took comfort in the restrictions on immigration under federal law. The law stipulated fines for those who knowingly brought insane or mentally defective immigrants into the United States, and it provided a five-year leeway period in which individuals could be deported. Wagner further reassured his readers of the nation's protection against mental degeneration due to recent innovations in American medical science. Because of an increase in knowledge occurring as "the direct result of research in laboratories" on mental symptoms and etiological factors, psychiatrists had gained a better understanding of mental defects and ways to treat them. He believed the ability to treat and cure held the "golden promise" for mental medicine for American citizens and their future.[64]

Just as many American physicians and researchers promised that their approach to medicine could restore the bodies of shell-shocked soldiers and heal citizens and immigrants with mental illness, commentators on international affairs often suggested that American ingenuity could likewise rebuild a shell-shocked and degenerating Europe. Such notions became most clear in discussions of Woodrow Wilson's international effort to establish the League of Nations.

Wilson contended that his effort to implement the League of Nations at the Paris Peace Conference was one step in the "crusade against hate and fear and war."[65] It was a goal for which he would receive the Nobel Peace Prize in 1920, and supportive U.S. journalists frequently associated his efforts with restoring sanity and reason to shell-shocked Europe. One writer described Wilson finding in Europe a people "emaciated, shell-shocked and feverish." Another called Europe "the Shell-Shockt Continent." Wilson, according to the *Los Angeles Times*, was the "sole disinterested moralist" fighting against Europe's "unreasoning panic." His aim was to help European nations make peace quickly to avoid the "serpents of misleading" information who were attempting to "profit by the neuroses of war."[66]

William A. White, director of the army's medical asylum St. Elizabeths, advocated for the League of Nations on the grounds that it would extend America's presumed caregiving role to places outside of Europe as well. Echoing well-worn tropes of imperial paternalism dressed up as Wilsonian internationalism, he argued that just as parents continue to care for children who are mentally deficient, a strong nation should continue to care for those nations with lesser mental capabilities: "A league of nations may include some one that is not culturally in as advanced state of development as the others. Such a nation should be given a chance to develop." Wilson was represented as responsible for ensuring that nations, like the victim of shell shock who faced temporary mental deficiency, would not be punished or abandoned but encouraged and nurtured to health.[67]

Even as late as 1921, despite Wilson's failure to secure U.S. congressional approval of the League, his supporters still held out hope that his League would be the answer to European neuroses. To one opinion writer all of Europe remained in a condition of hysteria. He reasoned that their "sense of weakness and exhaustion" bred fear and was "a case of shattered nerves on both sides." Every nation, including England, seemed to suffer from the same symptoms, and the writer emphasized that "psychological recovery" would take even longer than economic recovery. "It is a case of national shell shock," the writer concluded. The world still required the great stabilizing force of the League of Nations.[68]

Favorable images of Wilson in political cartoons illustrated America's role as the necessary leader for a shell-shocked Europe and a stable world. In one *New York Times* depiction Wilson stands tall, above an inferior female Europe, whose face and tattered clothing suggest the mental and physical trauma her body has endured from years of war. Wilson, by contrast, embodies self-assurance and cultural advancement. His broad arm is extended, showing Europe the way to international agreement and recovery. In another cartoon, entitled "Victory" and published in 1920, the American man stands atop the world. His stance is confident as he plants the American flag, and an eagle beside him spreads its wings across the land. Sunbeams extending from behind the earth suggest the dawning of a new era of American dominance.

Conclusion

Focusing on the meanings inscribed on the individual body of a shell-shocked soldier provides an opportunity to place medical and cultural history in dialogue with international relations. The appearance of the soldier's body, his inability to control his movements and especially his mind, seemed to confirm the existence of an illness born of modern industrial development. It was an illness with tangible consequences for nations. Military casualties hindered battlefield victory and excited concerns about racial weakening and national degeneration. The shell-shocked soldier seemed to embody the nation and its prospects for remaining whole and strong.

The curative discourse so prevalent among U.S. experts during the war promised to overcome weakness in individual male bodies and to build the strength of nations. Although most treatment techniques for shell-shocked soldiers were not new, American psychiatrists, in close relationship with the military, conceptualized shell shock as a legitimate war wound worthy of what they perceived to be humane, scientific medical treatment. The positive language with which they discussed treatment techniques and policies coincided with a public perception about the efficacy of their measures. This view marked the United States as distinct from Europe and, as in descriptions of Wilson's attempt to establish the League of Nations, played into discussions of Europe's recovery from war and of the importance of America's leadership in the world.

In the years after 1920 Americans had to confront the reality that the symptoms associated with shell shock persisted among their veterans. American medical professionals proved as incapable of "curing" mental shocks as they did calming social tensions or securing a lasting peace for Europe. Yet during the war itself—and even after—many Americans advanced the claim that American ingenuity could cure shell shock and that what could be done to restore the character of the individual might be done to restore the stability of the European continent and the world. Thus as Americans looked to their position in world affairs at the war's end, the discourse of curability through science and medicine reinforced faith in their country's exceptionalism and political mission.

Notes

Epigraph: Noted "mental hygienist" Stewart Paton, accepting a medal for Thomas Salmon at the National Institute of Social Sciences, undated (sometime in 1917), Folder: Undated Miscellaneous, Box 4: American Foundation for Mental Hygiene, Thomas Salmon Collection, Oskar Diethelm Library, Institute for the History of Psychiatry, Weill Cornell Medical College, New York City.

1. Charles S. Myers, "A Contribution to the Study of Shell Shock," *Lancet* 185, no. 4772 (1915): 320.

2. Charles S. Myers, "A Final Contribution to the Study of Shell Shock: Being a Consideration of Unsettled Points Needing Investigation," *Lancet* 193, no. 4976 (1919): 51–54.

3. The instability of shell shock as a category of disability is exemplified in contradicting beliefs about recovery. The notion of disability as an unstable category is discussed in Lennard Davis, "Constructing Normalcy," in Davis, *The Disability Studies Reader*, 9–28. For more on disability, see Longmore and Umansky, *The New Disability History*.

4. Thomas W. Salmon, *The Care and Treatment of Mental Diseases and War Neuroses ("Shell Shock") in the British Army* (New York: War Work Committee of the National Committee for Mental Hygiene, 1917), 7.

5. Scarry, *The Body in Pain*; Featherstone et al., *The Body*; Rotundo, *American Manhood*; Kimmel, *Manhood in America*.

6. "War's Amazing Effect on Nerves of Soldiers," *New York Times*, Mar. 25, 1917.

7. The substantial historical literature that examines intersections of shell-shocked bodies, nations, gender, and science within the European context includes "Shell Shock," special issue, *Journal of Contemporary History* 35, no. 1 (2000); Micale and Lerner, *Traumatic Pasts*; Bourke, *Dismembering the Male*; Babington, *Shell-Shock*; Leese, *Shell Shock*; Barham, *Forgotten Lunatics of the Great War*; Lerner, *Hysterical Men*; Thomas, *Treating the Trauma of the Great War*; Mosse, *The Image of Man*; Leed, *No Man's Land*.

8. See, for example, Salmon, *The Care and Treatment of Mental Diseases and War Neuroses*.

9. Among these doctors were the British physician W. H. R. Rivers and doctors at Maudsley hospital in England. John T. MacCurdy, a Canadian who observed British treatments in such hospitals, also maintained a reformist attitude. See Hale, *The Rise and Crisis of Psychoanalysis in the United States*.

10. Fussell, *The Great War and Modern Memory*.

11. See Leed, "Fateful Memories."

12. For more on degeneration see Pick, *Faces of Degeneration*; Kershner, "Degeneration"; Thomas, *Treating the Trauma of the Great War*, 6.

13. Gertz, "Censorship, Propaganda, and the Production of 'Shell Shock' in World War I," 105.

14. Quoted in Hofer, "War Neurosis and Viennese Psychiatry in World War One," 258.

15. Beard, *American Nervousness*, 3; Bederman, *Manliness and Civilization*, 3; Krafft-Ebing, *Psychopathia sexualis*; Gijswijt-Hofstra and Porter, *Cultures of Neurasthenia from Beard to the First World War*.

16. Arthur Templer Davies, presidential address to Assurance Medical Society, 1916, part 3, GC 137.19 in S. H. Foulkes Army Papers 1942–46, PP/SHF/A.5, Wellcome Library, London.

17. Shock, "Healing the Patient, Serving the State," 272.

18. Fussell, *The Great War and Modern Memory*.

19. For discussions of mistreatment, see Brunner, "Psychiatry, Psycho-analysis, and Politics during the First World War"; Eissler, *Freud as an Expert Witness*; Lerner, *Hysterical Men*; Babington, *Shell-Shock*; Thomas, *Treating the Trauma of the Great War*. Also see the *Report of the War Office Committee of Enquiry into "Shell-shock"* (1922; London: Imperial War Museum, 2004).

20. See Freud, "Thoughts for the Times on War and Death" and "On Transience," in *The Standard Edition*, quoted in Brunner, "Psychiatry, Psychoanalysis, and Politics During the First World War," 356.

21. Mosse, "Shell-Shock as a Social Disease," 108.

22. Wister, *The Pentecost of Calamity*, 74; Wister, *A Straight Deal*, 99.

23. Le Bon, *The Psychology of the Great War*.

24. Playne, *Neuroses of the Nations*, 7; Theobald von Bethmann Hollweg, *Reflections on the World War* (London: T. Butterworth, 1920); Kats, *The Will to Civilization* and Trotter, *Instincts of the Herd in Peace and War*.

25. Playne, *Neuroses of the Nations*, 461.

26. Playne, *The Prewar Mind in Britain*, 68–70; Caroline E. Playne, *Society at War, 1914–1918* (Boston: Houghton Mifflin, 1931).

27. See description of Caroline Elizabeth Playne papers, University of London Research Library Services. *Neuroses of the Nations* was reviewed in *Eugenics Review* 18, no. 2 (1926): 150–52; *Economica* 16 (Mar. 1926); and *Advocate of Peace through Justice* 88, no. 11 (1926): 639. *The Prewar Mind in Britain* was reviewed in *Journal of the Royal Institute of International Affairs* 7, no. 4 (1928): 271. *Society at War* was reviewed in *International Affairs* 10, no. 6 (1931); *New York Times Book Review*, Jan. 3, 1932, 17.

28. For an alternative opinion, see MacCurdy, *War Neuroses*, 10.

29. See especially Winter, "Shell Shock and the Cultural History of the Great War."

30. U.S. Army Surgeon General's Office, *The Medical Department of the United States Army in the World War*, vol. 10: *Neuropsychiatry* (Washington, DC: U.S. Government Printing Office, 1929), 1.

31. Newton Baker speech to General Staff College, Folder: Speeches 1919, Box 245: Speeches and Writings 1919–1922, Newton Baker Papers, Library of Congress.

32. Thomas Salmon, "The Conservation of Mental Health: A National Problem," undated (sometime in 1914), Folder: Undated Miscellaneous, Box 4: American Foundation for Mental Hygiene, Thomas Salmon Collection, Courtesy of Oskar Diethelm Library, Institute for the History of Psychiatry, Weill Cornell Medical College, New York City.

33. *Progressive* here refers to the broad movement composed of social theory and movements in early twentieth-century Western nations that sought to take action to better society. For more on Progressivism and psychiatry, see Burnham, "Psychiatry, Psychology and the Progressive Movement"; Rothman, *Conscience and Convenience*. For an overview of the international dimensions of the progressive movement, see Rodgers, *Atlantic Crossings*.

34. Stewart Paton, accepting medal for Thomas Salmon at National Institute of Social Sciences; Frank P. Norbury, "Social Unrest in Times of Stress," *Institution Quarterly* 8, no. 4 (1917): 44; Thomas Salmon, "Preface," Jan. 11, 1922, Folder 1922, Box 4, Thomas Salmon Collection; "Visit with Dr. Meyer," Folder: Biographical Material, Box 6, Thomas Salmon Collection.

35. Pierce Bailey, speech, *American Journal of Insanity* 74, no. 1 (1917): 299.

36. "Neurologists and Psychiatrists for the Medical Department," *Boston Medical and Surgical Journal* 178, no. 15 (1918): 517.

37. United States Surgeon General's Office, *Annual Report of the Surgeon General*, U.S. Army, vols. 1–2 (Washington, DC: Government Printing Office, 1919), 1080.

38. U.S. Army Surgeon General's Office, *The Medical Department of the United States Army in the World War*, 10: 506.

39. E. Stanley Abbot, "The Work of Psychiatrists in Military Camps," *American Journal of Insanity* 75, no. 4 (1919): 459; Edward L. Hanes, *The Minds and Nerves of Soldiers* (Pasadena, Calif.: Logan Press, 1941), 12–19; Pierce Bailey, "Detection and Elimination of Individuals with Nervous or Mental Disease," in U.S. Army Surgeon General's Office, *The Medical Department of the United States Army in the World War*, 10: 57–86.

40. Thomas Salmon, "War Neuroses (Shell Shock)," *Military Surgeon: Journal of the Association of Military Surgeons of the United States* 41 (1917): 675–90; Newton Baker, "Speech to Ohio Federation of Women's Clubs," Oct. 15, 1919, Folder: Speeches 1919, Box 245: Speeches and Writings 1919–22, Newton Baker Papers, Library of Congress; Hale, *The Rise and Crisis of Psychoanalysis in the United States*.

41. U.S. Army Surgeon General's Office, *The Medical Department of the United States Army in the World War*, 10: 451. Caroline Cox confirms the rare use of the term *hysteria* in "Invisible Wounds," in Micale and Lerner, *Traumatic Pasts*, 288.

42. John H. W. Rhein, "Neuropsychiatric Problems at the Front During Combat," *Journal of Abnormal Psychology*, Apr.–July 1919, 9–14.

43. Norman Fenton, *Shell Shock and Its Aftermath* (St. Louis, MO: C. V. Mosby, 1926), 20. For a broad introduction that does not fully distinguish between American and British experiences, see Jones and Wessely, "Psychiatric Battle Casualties."

44. "Shell Shock: Definition and General Consideration," Dec. 12, 1917, Folder Shell Shock, Box 396: 1917–29 General, Record Group 112, National Archives College Park; "Circular No. 35," June 13, 1918, in U.S. Army Surgeon General's Office, *The Medical Department of the United States Army in the World War*, 10: 280–86. For the rules regarding psychiatrists see 313.

45. Letter, "Chief Surgeon to All Division Surgeons," Sept. 8, 1918, in U.S. Army Surgeon General's Office, *The Medical Department of the United States Army in the World War*, 10: 309.

46. Announcement, *Boston Medical and Surgical Journal* 179, no. 25 (1919): 754.

47. "A Hospital of 20,000 Beds," *Stars and Stripes*, Feb. 8, 1918.

48. Comic, "Shelling Is Shocking," *Stars and Stripes*, July 26, 1918; Ad, "Protect Your Hearing," *Stars and Stripes*, Oct. 18, Oct. 25, and Nov. 8, 1918; "Shell Shock Recoveries," *Stars and Stripes*, Dec. 20, 1918.

49. Speech of American Neurological Association, *New York Times*, May 10, 1918.

50. Letter, E. L. Munson to Major Salmon, Winter 1917, Folder Shell Shock, Box 396, Record Group 112, National Archives, College Park.

51. "Chaplain Wallace Succumbs to Gas," *New York Times*, Oct. 7, 1918; "Dogs and Horses Often War Heroes," *New York Times*, Oct. 21, 1917; "General O'Ryan Praises the Spirit and Valor of the New York Soldiers He Led in the War," *New York Times*, Mar. 7, 1919; "Americans Killed at Lens," *New York Times*, Sept. 4, 1917; "New York Officers on the Casualty List," *New York Times*, Sept. 29, 1918.

52. Moses Allen Starr, "Shell Shock," *Scribner's*, Aug. 1918, 185.

53. J. L. Robinson, "Voice Recovery after Shell Shock," *Scientific American Supplement* 83 (May 5, 1917): 288.

54. "Home Letters Reduce 'Shell Shock,'" *Psychological Clinic: A Journal of Orthogenics for the Normal Development of Every Child* 7 (1918–19): 143; "Shell Shock Mastered, Physician Reports," *New York Times*, May 10, 1918; "Men from Trenches in Hospital Here," *New York Times*, Feb. 19, 1918; "Musical Prescriptions for Ailing," *New York Times*, July 13, 1919; "Yellow Paint Cured Shell Shock Victim," *New York Times*, Nov. 13, 1922; "Use Paint to Cure Shell-Shocked Soldier," *Chicago Defender*, Dec. 30, 1922; "Hens Go Home to Roost," *New York Times*, Jan. 26, 1919; "Dumb from War, Now Talks," *New York Times*, Mar. 7, 1918; "Lost Speech in War, Recovers It During Baking Contest," *New York Times*, July 8, 1920; "Wanted: A Book for Every Man 'Over There,'" *Outlook*, Oct. 16, 1918; "Blind Soldier Captures College Prize," *New York Times*, Mar. 4, 1923.

55. See, for example, "Plan Free Clinic for Speech Defects," *New York Times*, Sept. 30, 1917; "Preparing to Care for Shell-shocked Men," *New York Times*, Jan. 16, 1918; "Open Clinic for Men Disabled in War, Equipped by Private Funds," *New York Times*, July 16, 1918; "Working Out Cure for Shell Shock," *New York Times*, Nov. 28, 1918; "Healing the Hurts of Disabled Men," *New York Times*, Jan. 19, 1919; "Camp for War's Maimed," *New York Times*, Aug. 17, 1919; "Snug Harbor for Shell-shocked," *New York Times*, Jan. 2, 1921; "Palm Beach as a Fountain of Youth and Health and Beauty," *Touchstone* 3 (1918): 494–503. Also see Curtis Lakeman, *Home Service and the Disabled Soldier or Sailor* (Washington, DC: American Red Cross, Department of Civilian Relief, 1918).

56. William Ellery Leonard, "Shell Shock," in *Poems of the War and the Peace*, edited by Sterling Andrus Leonard (New York: Harcourt, Brace, 1921), 162.

57. The following films are available for view through UCLA Motion Picture Collection: *Three Live Ghosts* (1922); *The Stolen Ranch* (1926); *The Unknown Soldier* (1926). The following silent films are no longer available, but their plot summaries are available through the American Film Institute's online Silent

Film Database: *Missing* (1918); *Vive La France!* (1918); *The Trembling Hour* (1919); *Shattered Dreams* (1922); *Shell Shocked Sammy* (1923); *Shootin' for Love* (1923); *Wandering Fires* (1925); *Puppets* (1926); *Vanishing Hoofs* (1926); *Closed Gates* (1927); *Absent* (1928); *Burning Bridges* (1928).

58. Hugh T. Patrick, "War Neuroses," *Journal of Indiana State Medical Association* 7 (Feb. 1919), 33.

59. Newton Baker, "Speech to Ohio Federation of Women's Clubs" and "Speech to YMCA: The Unarmed Army," Folder: Speeches 1919, Box 245: Speeches and Writings 1919–22, Newton Baker Papers, Library of Congress.

60. Editorial, "The War's Lessons in Mental Hygiene," *The Sunday Herald*, Boston, Jan. 12, 1919, reprinted in *Mental Hygiene* 3 (National Association for Mental Health: Jan. 1919), 131; Albert Gallantina Love and Charles Benedict Davenport, *Defects Found in Drafted Men: Statistical Information Compiled from the Draft Records* (Washington, DC: Government Printing Office, Senate Committee Print, 1919), 27, 31.

61. Geo. S. Stevenson, "History of the Mental Hygiene Movement in the United States," *Southern Medical Journal* 31 (Aug. 1938): 925.

62. William White, "The Origin, Growth and Significance of the Mental Hygiene Movement," *Science*, n.s. 72, no. 1856 (1930): 79.

63. Lawrence Kolb, "The Bearing of War Neuroses on Immigration," in *Archives of Neurology and Psychiatry*, vol. 1, edited by Hugh Patrick et al. (Chicago: American Medical Association, 1919), 317–29.

64. Charles G. Wagner, "Recent Trends in Psychiatry," *American Journal of Insanity* 74, no. 1 (1917): 8–11.

65. Woodrow Wilson, Nobel Peace Prize acceptance speech, Dec. 10, 1920. Available online at http://www.nobelprize.org.

66. "The Shell-Shockt Continent: As It Looks to an American in Paris," *Independent* (New York), June 21, 1919, 438; "What President Wilson Did at Paris," *New York Times*, Nov. 20, 1919; "Wilson's Darkest Paris Hour, When Withdrawal of America Loomed Near," *Los Angeles Times*, Nov. 5, 1919; "Make Peace and Let the Nations Get to Work," *New York Times*, Mar. 26, 1919.

67. William A. White, *Thoughts of a Psychiatrist on the War and After* (New York: Paul B. Hoeber, 1919), 132–33.

68. "National Hysteria," *Current Opinion*, Jan. 25, 1921, 12–14.

four

Physical Culture's World of Bodies
Transnational Participatory Pastiche
and the Body Politics of America's
Globalized Mass Culture

SHANON FITZPATRICK

In a 1948 issue of the literary journal *Books Abroad*, Gerhard Wiens, professor of modern languages at the University of Oklahoma, reminisced about his childhood in revolutionary Russia. Born to literate, Dutch German Mennonite farmers in southern Ukraine in 1905, Wiens had been lucky. With exceptions made for the occasional famine, he attended school and received a bilingual education in Russian and German. During his free time before and after working his family's land, the boy taught himself how to read and write in English.

One day around 1919, Wiens set out to locate English-language reading material at a time and place when books were dear and paper scarce: "Persistent scouring of the country for miles around uncovered a tattered copy . . . of *Uncle Tom's Cabin*, [and] several issues of *Physical Culture Magazine*," an American health and fitness periodical, which he bought and bound. Decades later Wiens recalled, "I was a healthy, fairly strong youth, but I now realized [upon reading *Physical Culture*] that, if I should ever go to America, I might have to take a lot of pushing around from the Herculean natives."[1]

In the early 1920s Wiens immigrated to the United States. Whether

American physiques measured up to the heightened expectations in-
culcated by *Physical Culture*, I do not know. It is certain, however, that
Wiens encountered more products from Macfadden Publications, Inc.,
the publisher of the magazine that had reached him as a boy. Founded
in 1899 in New York and London by a health reformer and bodybuilder
named Bernarr Macfadden, Macfadden Publications had grown from a
small physical culture press into a national phenomenon. In the wake
of the Great War, the company achieved enormous success churning out
periodicals dedicated to "true stories," pulp fiction, movies, and health
and fitness.[2] A giant sign erected on the roof of the company's New York
headquarters in the 1920s boasted, "The Largest Newsstand Sale in the
World."

To the dismay of elite critics, educators, and the American Medical Association, Macfadden's newsstand sale was particularly strong
among America's multiethnic, heavily immigrant working class. In addition to catering to "foreign" audiences at home, the company's media
also reached readers in other countries, as Wiens's memoir attests. Like
other products of America's burgeoning culture industry, Macfadden's
health and fitness publications flowed beyond the borders of the "first
multicultural modern capitalist society" and out into a wider world
hungry for information and entertainment.[3]

This essay, which draws from my larger study of Macfadden Publications' pulp empire, investigates *Physical Culture*'s transnational
circulations in the first few decades of the twentieth century.[4] These
circulations, I argue, offer a window onto the body politics of America's globalized mass culture during an era of ascendant U.S. power,
widespread population migrations, imperialism, and a flourishing eugenics movement. The fact that the Macfadden Company left behind no
archival material and no clear record of its circulation patterns has until
now rendered its transnational impact almost invisible to historians.[5]
Yet nonelite periodicals such as *Physical Culture* played an important role
in shaping a highly mobile popular culture centered on self-expression,
celebrity, and visual representations of modern bodies that became one
of America's most important—and most difficult to assess—exports to
the world.

By examining the reach, the content, and the reception of *Physical
Culture*, this essay emphasizes the multivocality of *Physical Culture*'s body
politics. In keeping with a widespread and long-running anthropomorphic discourse, the magazine framed "the body politic" in somatic
terms, linking the health and vitality of the state to the physical health
and vitality of its individual members. It also projected, to an increas-

ingly global audience, images of the United States as a strong world power that was fit to regenerate and lead an ailing "Anglo-Saxon" civilization. In many respects the magazine thus promoted ethnonationalist definitions of the U.S. national body and exuded the racial anxieties that powered the era's panoply of regenerative movements.

At the same time, however, *Physical Culture* was formed in dialogue with transnational networks of health reform, a diversifying domestic U.S. market, and an increasingly globalized physique culture industry that positioned the body as the "finest consumer object."[6] The publication's features on performers and athletes, illustrations of fitness routines, articles on natural healing, and ads for food, exercise, and beauty products promoted an ethos of self-fashioning, transformation, and mobility. Moreover *Physical Culture* also developed an interactive formula in which the editor invited readers from around the globe to enter its various competitions and submit their own opinions, narratives, and photos to the magazine. According to Bernarr Macfadden, the loads of intimate letters submitted to *Physical Culture* during its first two decades inspired his creation in 1919 of *True Story*, the pioneering "confession" magazine that would help make Macfadden Publications one of the most successful publishing empires in history.[7]

Examining what I call the "transnational participatory pastiche" that characterized *Physical Culture* in the early twentieth century produces a more concise portrait of flows of America's globalized popular print culture that predated international circulation tracking. It also offers a rare glimpse into various formations of embodied subjectivity formed in dialogue with transnational America's wide-ranging media circulations. *Physical Culture*'s participatory pastiche, I contend, opened the way for messages about bodies and nations that seemed to be every bit as flexible as the physical culture movement's ideal bodies themselves. In this respect the magazine (along with Macfadden Publications' larger pulp empire) calls attention to how America's popular culture, particularly its accessible, nonelite print media, helped foster a proliferation of embodied political imaginaries and adaptable consumerist body politics.

Transnational Circulations, Global Migrations, and "Vigorous Permeation"

Born into poverty in rural Missouri right after the American Civil War as Bernard McFadden, Bernarr Macfadden came of age during an era that one historian has termed "decades of fitness."[8] He was both a product of and a participant in a transnational health reform movement that fueled a boom in fitness-related commodities and entertainments.[9] As a child he attended circuses, trained in gymnastics at a German American *Turnverein*, and participated in the heavily immigrant midwestern wrestling circuit. When the beautiful white body of the Prussian-born strongman Eugen Sandow wowed audiences during the 1893 Columbian Exhibition in Chicago, Macfadden was nearby, demonstrating an exercise apparatus to curious Midway visitors. After the fair Macfadden headed to New York (where he modified his Irish name), then on to England, and back again to New York, chasing his dream of becoming a successful physical culture entrepreneur. In 1899 he started *Physical Culture* magazine.[10]

At first *Physical Culture* was little more than an advertising circular for Macfadden and his ideas and products. Early issues were written, under various pseudonyms, by the editor himself, and they featured image upon image of his own muscular physique—"Macfaddenscapes," one journalist later named them.[11] Initially priced at a nickel, the magazine discussed diet, exercise, morality, natural healing, beauty, travel, and sports, sometimes all at once. It also contained ads for health foods, exercise equipment, collections of "saucy" postcards, and its editor's own ever-growing range of products and publications.

Physical Culture soon doubled in size and price and attracted increasingly diverse contributors, including women.[12] When Macfadden began hosting physique contests, the magazine printed the photographs and measurements of their scantily clad contestants. Before the so-called modern girl became a global phenomenon, the magazine featured a panoply of smiling, athletic women dressed in form-fitting (and sometimes self-fashioned) sportswear. It also contained images of self-possessed, muscular men displaying their sculpted bodies for public inspection. Perhaps not surprisingly, in America during the Progressive era Macfadden's media company provoked the ire of the vice hunter Anthony Comstock as well as urban vice squads dedicated to cracking down on homosexual behavior.[13] However, it also attracted contributions from some of the most well-known and respected writers and reformers on both sides of the Atlantic, including Upton Sinclair, Charlotte Perkins Gilman, Jack London, and George Bernard Shaw. The topics discussed in its pages varied accordingly. A single issue could touch on exercise, child rearing, religion, relations between races and the sexes, comparative ethnographies, and the latest developments in the world of sport, military training, and physical education. Muscular Christians, women's rights activists, eugenicists, politicians, and polemicists of various stripes shared space with savvy advertisers, famous performers, and popular writers who helped Macfadden fill the pages of his magazine.

In the wake of the Great War, Macfadden Publications introduced *True Story* in 1919, and the magazine soon achieved enormous popular success. For his part, Macfadden became a multimillionaire. Yet no matter how many magazines he added to his stable, or dollars he earned, *Physical Culture* and the ideal of the body beautiful remained central to Macfadden's public persona and Macfadden Publications' identity. With an eye on running for political office in the late 1920s, the publisher would work with biographers and the public relations guru Edward L. Bernays to cast his taut body and expansive media empire as symbols of a strong U.S. nation whose global influence grew every day. The resultant stories presented the publisher as a self-made man who had "conquer[ed] New York, and through it America, [and] the world," a narrative that has largely prevailed to this day.[14]

Yet Macfadden's own increasingly patriotic rhetoric and nationalistic narratives should not be permitted to eclipse the importance of transnational currents to the spectacular growth of Macfadden Publications at home and abroad in the first half of the twentieth century. Tracing *Physical Culture's* early circulations reveals how the publisher's transatlantic business ventures, the mobile career of the strongman Eugen Sandow, interconnected imperial geographies, and multidirectional waves of population migration all shaped Macfadden's media and propelled its widespread circulations beyond the borders of the United States.

The London side of Macfadden's business, often neglected by both scholars and journalists, played a central role in fostering the company's ability to reach foreign readers, particularly before the First World War. Macfadden actually published his first magazine, a glorified advertising pamphlet, while demonstrating an exercise apparatus in England in the last years of the nineteenth century. Perhaps not so coincidentally *Macfadden's Magazine* appeared only a few months after Sandow, who was currently residing in London, released a magazine called *Physical Culture* (later retitled *Sandow's Magazine*). Upon returning to New York, Macfadden created his own *Physical Culture* magazine. Within a year he also debuted a London-based edition titled *Physical Development*. The publications shared content but contained locally specific advertising, editorials, and correspondence.

Although Macfadden would never publicly mention Sandow in recounting his start in the publishing industry, Sandow's activities helped lay the groundwork for the international expansion of Macfadden's physical culture media. After completing two very successful circuits of

the United States under the management of Florenz Ziegfeld Jr., the famous strongman set out on an antipodean tour in 1901. A wide-ranging
Far East tour in 1904 took Sandow to South Africa, China, Japan, Dutch
Java, Burma, and India. In all of these places he hawked his magazine
and books and inspired (and drew from) widespread enthusiasm for
strongman performances and for health and fitness media.[15]

Many of the foreign locales from which Macfadden received letters
in the first few years of the century had been part of Sandow's world
tours. For instance, an "admirer in South Africa" became so enamored
with one of Macfadden's pseudonymous female personas that he sent
Macfadden an ivory paper knife and a framed picture of himself, re-
questing a photograph in return.[16] One of *Physical Culture*'s earliest correspondents from New Zealand was F. A. Hornibrook, an Irish immigrant who had trained at Sandow's Institute in London before moving
to Christchurch, where he became "the most popular Sandow instruc-
tor in town."[17] Within five years of their founding, Macfadden's magazines, which included *Physical Culture, Physical Development*, and *Health
and Beauty*, listed, in addition to American and British headquarters,
the names of various "colonial agents." This list included companies
located in Melbourne, Sydney, Adelaide, Brisbane, Cape Town, and, a
few years later, Bombay. Newspaper advertisements from Australia and
New Zealand show that Macfadden's books and magazines were often
sold alongside Sandow's publications.[18]

When *Sandow's Magazine* ceased publication in 1907, Macfadden's
magazines were already well positioned to take its place. This transition from one strongman-publisher to another is suggested by a letter
published in 1908 from H. R. Hyatt, who reported that he was "pleased
to see the increased circulation of *Physical Culture* in New Zealand."[19]
Around the Pacific world at this time, one historian notes, "images of
Sandow's body became less common, only to be replaced with photographs of his American equivalent, Bernarr Macfadden."[20]

By the end of the first decade of the twentieth century, correspondence
from men and women from throughout the Anglophone world became
a constant feature of *Physical Culture*. Writing from Melbourne in 1907,
Dr. C. W. Healy, a physical culture lecturer, noted that he "emphasized
the value of [Macfadden's] interesting magazine to [his] pupils" and requested that Macfadden include more pictures of Australian athletes in
his magazine in order to satisfy his readers abroad. Elsa Schmidt, an
articulate "physical culture girl" from Victoria, told Macfadden that she
had "read several of [his] books, and have lent them and [his] magazines to my friends" and had thus "succeeded in making them interested

in physical culture."[21] When the Australian athlete Reginald "Snowy" Baker debuted his own physical culture magazine in 1912, he cultivated an aesthetic similar to that of Macfadden's publications, complete with didactic editorials, frequent physique competitions, and letters from readers.[22] The covers of the Australian *Withrow's Physical Culture*, a magazine introduced by Walter Withrow in 1920, sometimes appeared almost indistinguishable from those of Macfadden's *Physical Culture*.

Although little is known about Macfadden's circulations in India and South Africa before World War I, letters to the Physical Culture Publishing Company and various biographies provide anecdotal evidence of the presence of Macfadden-brand publications even before the First World War. For example, when Macfadden opened a sanatorium in Brighton around 1912, he hired a South African naturopath named Stanley Lief. Lief had been born in Latvia, where he was diagnosed with a supposedly incurable heart condition as a young boy. In the wake of the social unrest of 1905, his family moved to South Africa. Lief encountered Macfadden's *Physical Culture* magazine during his teens, perhaps in his father's trading store in the eastern Transvaal.[23] Fascinated by Macfadden's methods of natural healing, he traveled to the United States to study at Macfadden's Institute of Physical Culture in Chicago. Eventually Lief would run Macfadden's health home in Brighton and go on to help found the British College of Naturopathy. The politician and diplomat Tommy Boydell, another well-known South African, also remembered being inspired by Macfadden's publications as a young man. Boydell became an "honors diploma graduate" of the Macfadden Institute, which offered mail-order courses. Boydell wrote that he exchanged considerable correspondence with the American publisher while practicing as a "health specialist" in Cape Town during the early twentieth century.[24]

In 1911 a reader in Bombay wrote Macfadden an encouraging letter suggesting that the editor take advantage of "a good economic opportunity" and send students to lecture or open businesses in cities in India, where physical culture had grown in popularity.[25] Historians of India have discussed the importation of Western physical culture via the British military in the nineteenth century, as well as the renewed interest in indigenous bodybuilding methods at this time. India's emergence as an international center of health reform, fitness, and natural healing discourse paralleled the global proliferation of health and fitness mass media, as the letter from Bombay attests. Letters sent to Macfadden from India during the second decade of the twentieth century indicate that *Physical Culture* contributed to some Indians' synthesis of indigenous health and fitness traditions with Western bodybuilding practices.[26] In 1921, for example, *Physical Culture* received a photograph and letter signed, "Hindoo Boy with High Aspirations," who told the editor that he had been "going through every magazine of yours and find them a real blessing." This "physical culture boy from far away" was K. Venkatesa Iyer. Iyer would soon become a national icon in India as well as a world-renowned physical culture celebrity famous for his amazing body and physical culture system that blended hatha-style yoga with "Western" bodybuilding techniques and mass-mediated methods of display.[27]

As these examples from Australasia, South Africa, and India attest, the colonial and neo-imperial channels through which Sandow (and his publications) moved bolstered *Physical Culture*'s success throughout the Anglophone world in the early years of the twentieth century. Thanks in large part to the British side of his business, Macfadden's magazines reached foreign readers through the same networks on which Sandow had so shrewdly capitalized.

Widening spheres of American power also helped broaden the reach of Macfadden's mass-market magazines. *Physical Culture*'s early years coincided with the expansion of U.S. military, political, and cultural power and the formation of an American overseas empire. Flourishing missionary movements, the War of 1898 and the Philippine-American War, the planning and building of the Panama Canal, and intense debates over America's growing empire provided contexts for *Physical Culture*'s first issues. These included various ethnographic articles written by Americans abroad examining the hardy bodies of indigenous Hawaiians, Samoans, and Filipinos, and covers such as "Theodore Roosevelt, 'Rough Rider' and Athlete." The company also acquired distribution agents in the Philippines and the Canal Zone.

Not surprisingly some of Macfadden's earliest letters from abroad came from Anglo-American and other English-speaking intermediaries, such as soldiers, missionaries, and merchants, who both presented potential foreign markets for American companies and acted as conduits for the flow of American consumer goods.[28] Around 1907 William Collins, master of the schooner *Evadne*, wrote the following to Macfadden from the Canary Islands: "While I hate to part with [my copies of *Physical Culture*], I have given away the entire year of 1905 and find a great number of people becoming interested in the movement for a cleaner and better life." Writing from the Canal Zone in 1910, Daniel E. Henriquez wrote that he had been a fan of Macfadden since "long before [he] left his home for the Isthmus of Panama" three years earlier.[29]

As a publication devoted to building up strong bodies, advocating healthy living, and scrutinizing foreign and exotic "others," *Physical Culture* appealed to people involved in the spreading of America's military power and "moral empire."[30] In 1905 a U.S. soldier who had been stationed in the Philippines for six years sent Macfadden a descriptive letter about the popularity of physical culture among his fellow soldiers. Another soldier described having been "run down" by his tour in the Philippines and restored to health after following Macfadden's advice. This reader claimed to have bought extra copies of *Physical Culture* in order to share them with friends.[31]

After Macfadden's ongoing conflict with Comstock led to the publisher's arrest for distributing "obscene material" (a story about venereal disease), a former soldier named R. A. Holman penned a spirited defense for *Tomorrow* magazine, a "monthly magazine for progressive people." Holman recalled, "So sick and emaciated was I after a long siege of campaigning in the Phillipines [sic] . . . that no hopes were entertained of my ever again gaining health." According to Holman, it was the "editor patriot" Macfadden whose teachings helped restore him.[32] As Macfadden stood trial in 1909, he defended himself—unsuccessfully—by referencing the "thousands of letters" of support he had received from throughout the world, hundreds of which had come from YMCA secretaries and ministers.[33] As these examples demonstrate, individuals who participated in America's growing formal and informal empire in the early years of the twentieth century could serve as important intermediaries in the expansion of Macfadden Publications' global range. Certainly *Physical Culture's* constant exhortations to readers to help spread the "creed" of healthy living meshed well with the evangelical ethos of the Progressive era.

Copies of magazines that started out in the hands of Americans did not necessarily remain there. *Physical Culture's* increasingly diverse correspondents attest to the fact that Macfadden-brand media appealed to local populations. One 1920 letter from a Filipino reader told Macfadden, "PHYSICAL CULTURE is one of the most popular magazines here and it finds many earnest readers among the younger generation."[34] One of these "earnest readers," a fourteen-year-old Filipino boy named Arturo Tolentino, described how he first encountered Macfadden's work after discovering a classmate reading *Physical Culture*: "As he turned the pages I had a glimpse of a muscular man. That very minute the longing for a body as massive as that was born in me." Tolentino embarked on his own personal quest to emulate the muscular man he had seen in Macfadden's magazine. He tried to spread physical culture ideas among his family and friends and told *Physical Culture* that he was "thinking of being a Filipino Bernarr Macfadden . . . as [he] kn[e]w of no way in which [he] could benefit [his] people more."[35] Tolentino would eventually go on to become Ferdinand Marcos's strong and energetic vice president of the Philippines.

In addition to the American soldiers, merchants, and missionaries that fanned out across the globe, immigrants to the United States also helped expand the number of people who came into direct contact with the country's commercialized print culture in the early twentieth century. Letters suggest that two important routes through which Macfadden Publications reached an international audience were increased global travel and the prominent phenomenon of reverse immigration. For instance, in 1911 Corrine Erdos from Söpron, Hungary, wrote, "[Two] years ago, my brother, Aurel, came back from the United States of America. He brought several copies of your magazine along. My interest in physical culture teachings grew so high that I resolved to study English."[36] It is very possible that as a young man Aurel was among the over 2.1 million immigrants who moved to the United States from Austria and Hungary between 1901 and 1910. If he had traveled to make money and then returned home, this would not have been unusual; a quarter of Hungarian immigrants who arrived in the United States during that decade went back to Hungary.[37]

Historians have estimated that one-third or more of the "second wave" of American immigrants actually returned to their homelands. While scholars have only begun to analyze the importance of two-way migration to the proliferation of "American" culture, Aurel was certainly not alone in his personal exportation of Macfadden's magazines. Other correspondents, such as H. R. Hyatt in New Zealand, Guy de Villepion in Guatemala, and Dr. Theodor Gatti in Italy, also noted that they first came across *Physical Culture* in the United States in the early years of the century. A letter by the Swedish immigrant Hjalmar Hammersen reminds us that for many people seeking a better life during this era, migrations were multiple. Hammersen first read Macfadden's publications in 1910, but by the time he wrote to *Physical Culture* he was living in Santiago, Chile—and it seems that Macfadden's magazines accompanied him on his travels.[38] Perhaps the copies of *Physical Culture* that Wiens discovered in the Ukrainian countryside had made a similar journey.[39]

As his company grew, Macfadden increasingly presented himself and his magazine as influential leaders in a worldwide physical culture movement. This bombastic, universalist rhetoric, which would grow louder in the wake of the First World War, was typical of the editor and his publications. Yet even in the early years of the century, the pages of *Physical Culture* supported the notion that the movement of which Macfadden claimed himself a leader was a global one, and that some readers around the world—male and female—had been inspired by his works. Between 1899 and the First World War the communications that appeared in *Physical Culture* hailed from increasingly widespread locations as well as from a diverse domestic population. By the early interwar era *Physical Culture*'s correspondence sections contained letters from readers all over the globe.

The early transnational circulations of Macfadden's health and fitness media in the first two decades of the century appear to have helped propel Macfadden Publications' increasingly global reach during the interwar era. The company's popular *True Story*, founded in 1919, soon had Canadian, British, Dutch, German, French, and Scandinavian editions, while a lucrative trade in back issues of the company's fitness and entertainment magazines thrived in Australasia. In 1938 *Scribner's* ran a story about Macfadden Publications' "vigorous permeation of foreign countries," which had, even then, "escaped general attention."[40] Because of its widespread reach and dedication to printing reader correspondence, *Physical Culture* provides rare insights into how and where early forms of American-produced mass print media circulated. In particular the magazine draws our attention to the centrality of British and American colonial and neo-imperial networks, as well as multidirectional flows of human migration, to the expansion of a U.S. culture industry that specialized in disseminating representations of beautiful, fit, and mobile modern bodies.

Cosmopolitan Primitivism and Transnational Participatory Pastiche

Through its far-flung circulation *Physical Culture* brokered widely the argument that the health and vitality of individual bodies were intrinsically linked to the health and vitality of larger social bodies. This idea, however, could mean different things in different contexts to different people, particularly as it was easily linked to debates over gender, race, and nationhood. What constituted a healthy body, and who best embodied this ideal? How could fitness be measured or proven? Which qualities marked certain physical culture practices or characteristics as particularly advanced or modern? What did a fit body politic look like, and who would lead the way to a healthier world? These questions, posed against a backdrop of crystallizing competitive nationalisms, dramatic population shifts and political realignments, a widespread eugenics movement, and the rise of mass consumption, were debated in *Physical Culture.*

Macfadden's early twentieth-century media reflected and helped give shape to the "yearning for regeneration" that characterized American culture, which was tied to concerns over the degenerative effects that urbanization, industrialization, and population mixing had wrought on modern societies.[41] In many respects *Physical Culture*'s globalized circulations helped promote a discourse of civilization that linked modernity and fitness to eugenic notions of biological determinism.[42] Writing from England in early 1913, Macfadden told readers of *Physical Development,* "My life has been devoted to building-up the English-speaking race."[43] In this pronouncement the editor aligned himself and his publications with a powerful transnational racial imaginary that included certain bodies from throughout the Anglophone world while leaving out those marked as racially "other" (whether or not they spoke English).[44] Macfadden's ideal of vitalized Anglo-Saxonhood meshed well with visions of a "eugenic nation" in which African Americans, immigrants, and other "nonwhite" people were represented as possible contagions or pollutants to the U.S. body politic.[45]

Simultaneously, in keeping with a popular tendency in politics and the arts to celebrate "the primitive," *Physical Culture* constantly praised what it saw as "premodern" bodies, usually portraying them as hardy, vigorous, strong, and sometimes even beautiful. Features such as "Our Indians in the West," "Samoa, the Isles of Eternal Summer," "Hawaiians of Yesterday and Today," and "Nudity and Morality among East African Tribes" demonstrated what one article called the "Remarkable Powers of Endurance of Primitive People." As the rich corpus of scholarship on representations of "the other" in early twentieth-century anthropological discourse and popular culture has shown, such displays of "primitive" peoples could propagate "grand narratives of evolutionary progress toward civilization" based on notions of racial incompatibility and evolutionary hierarchy.[46] *Physical Culture*'s ubiquitous representations of so-called primitive people helped mediate the notion of what Teddy Roosevelt called "barbarian virtues," situating the United States as the foil to barbarism but also a conduit for its virtues.[47]

The dark-skinned and "premodern" bodies that appeared in Macfadden publications were often represented via "objective" mid-shots that came from stock photography companies. The people in these images tended to appear unaware of the camera, or at least ignorant about how to show off their physical attributes. For example, "The Igorrotes—A

Figure 4.1. Physical Culture, December 1915. Macfadden's magazines promoted the aesthetic of "cosmopolitan primitivism" for women as well as men. Courtesy of the H. J. Luther Stark Center for Physical Culture and Sports, University of Texas, Austin.

Hardy Vigorous People" (1910) was illustrated with photographs taken at the 1904 St. Louis World Fair, where an indigenous Filipino "tribe" had been displayed at the margins of the forty-seven-acre Philippine Reservation. In the opening photograph several scantily clad "warriors" cluster around a fire; an uncovered buttock, rather than a face, points toward the camera. Just a few feet beyond this cluster, a dozen formally attired fair attendees stand behind a fence, staring at the exposed bodies of their colonial wards. The corresponding text portrayed strong Igorot bodies as the natural result of their crude understanding of agriculture. Its conclusion, in which the author endorsed U.S. tutelage in the Philippines, reminded readers why "barbarian virtues" were so important: "physical excellence" was a prerequisite of (and justification for) national and racial power.[48]

The images of white bodies that dominated *Physical Culture* presented a marked contrast to the magazine's depictions of primitive physiques.

Macfadden Publications helped to develop racially differentiated representational formulas that defined a distinctly modern conception of fitness that celebrated white superiority, American leadership, and barbarian virtues all at once. While Macfadden Publications recapitulated well-established anthropological tropes in its depictions of non-white bodies, it simultaneously fashioned a widely compelling aesthetic that might best be described as "spectacularly visible cosmopolitan primitivism."[49] Such primitivism could be possessed by both men and women and by people outside of the United States, yet it was coded as racially white and presented most often as a quality of American (or American-influenced) physiques.

In *Physical Culture* light-skinned figures from throughout the Anglophone world, including increasing numbers of women after around 1905, gaze confidently and knowingly at the camera, exhibiting their bodies and faces to maximum advantage. Such figures are usually pictured alone, but they also appear as members of fitness clubs, romantic couples, physique contests, or sports teams. ("The line between play and athletics is one that the savage never crosses," one article explained.)[50] The attitudes they strike are flattering and dynamic. In the early twentieth century their poses were usually drawn from a transnational repertoire of "Classical" attitudes. By 1910 *Physical Culture*'s images of white men and women usually referenced aesthetic conventions associated with films (particularly the close-up), modern dance, popular sport, and fitness regimen and beauty advertisements.

Significantly, while African American athletes and reformers were avid participants in the early twentieth-century physical culture movement, Macfadden Publications printed few images of black or dark-skinned American bodies.[51] Furthermore even as bodybuilding and sport became increasingly popular pastimes among some U.S. immigrant groups, *Physical Culture* declared certain ethnic bodies harmful to or inassimilable into the eugenic national body politic and the transnational racial imaginary of vitalized modernity it celebrated. In 1907 Macfadden lamented to his American readers, "We represent an amalgamation of all nations, and I am sorry to relate, the human material that we have had to absorb from the various foreign nations for the last generation, has often been of a low order."[52] In articles such as "Penalty of Intermarriage between Caucasian and Negro" and "The Pride of Race," the magazine emphasized the degenerative consequences of actual racial and ethnic mixing. Writings in *Physical Culture* by prominent early twentieth-century eugenicists such as Havelock Ellis, Margaret Sanger,

Carl Easton Williams, and Charlotte Perkins Gilman reinforced this message.

Contributions from far-flung "Anglo-Saxon" correspondents printed in *Physical Culture*, such as the many white beauty contest entrants from Australasia, could serve to reinforce the linkages between Macfadden's media, exclusionary physical culture imaginaries, and contemporary imperialist and modernization projects that involved the domination, destruction, or denigration of the bodies of nonwhite others. The multitude of letters to Macfadden penned by soldiers in the Philippines, for instance, demonstrates that *Physical Culture's* emphasis on building up white male bodies, combined with its perpetuation of racialized evolutionary discourse, meshed with violent imperial campaigns that accompanied the emergence of "self-styled 'white men's countries.'"[53] Similarly at the tail end of an era that some indigenous Australians called the "Killing Time," one reader named Sydney R. Clifford wrote, "I have been a reader of your paper for some time and have gained much useful information from it. I carry it with me on the track in our skirmishes and battles with the native blacks."[54]

In contrast to both the invisible bodies of ethnically "other" physical culturalists and the hypervisible bodies of premodern people from degraded economic and evolutionary circumstances, *Physical Culture's* white acolytes were depicted as masters of shaping and displaying their figures. Within the context of the magazine, their embodiment of a self-consciously modern identity of spectacularly visible cosmopolitan primitivism could serve to bolster eugenic discourse and exclusionary racial and national imaginaries. While *Physical Culture* brokered globally images of vitalized Anglo-Saxonhood and ethnonationalism, however, it also helped produce a cultural form that opened up space for the articulation of alternative conceptions of modern fitness.

As we have seen, *Physical Culture* constantly solicited reader contributions, particularly personal testimonies and photographs. The magazine's interactive dynamic, when combined with its globalized circulation and the growth of the physique culture industry, resulted in what I call "transnational participatory pastiche." *Physical Culture's* transnational participatory pastiche offers insights into how Macfadden Publications, along with other producers of globalized physical culture media and consumer culture, may have operated to destabilize exclusionary projections of the U.S. body politic and racialized notions of fitness and modernity.

While the term *pastiche* has been used pejoratively to criticize the

Figure 4.2. "A Group of Splendidly Developed Natives of the Fiji Islands," frontispiece, Physical Culture, September 1907. Courtesy of the H. J. Luther Stark Center for Physical Culture and Sports, University of Texas, Austin.

"imitative," "blank," and "dead" products of America's mass culture industry, here it is meant to evoke different associations.[55] First, *pastiche* provides an apt description of *Physical Culture*'s visual aesthetic, in which articles, advertisements, editorials, and reader contributions from increasingly diverse locales came together. Second, the term evokes the notion of *montage*, which played an important role in early twentieth-century cultural theory and continues to inform ideas about how individuals actively make meanings out of (rather than passively absorb) visually disjunctive mass media.[56]

An early example of how *Physical Culture*'s transnational participatory pastiche amplified the magazine's multivocality can be seen in the September 1907 issue. The frontispiece featured the photograph "A Group of Splendidly Developed Natives of the Fiji Islands." Inside the magazine the New Zealand physical culture authority F. A. Hornibrook, who had sent in the photograph, provided a context for Macfadden's readers. He remarked that when these "Natives" attended the New Zealand International Exhibition (where the photograph seems to have been taken), they had been especially impressed by "white physical culturalists, particularly their exercising equipment."[57] Hornibrook's article reflected the discourse of barbarian virtues that dominated many of *Physical Culture*'s representations of foreign peoples; the image of "Splendidly

Developed Natives," however, offered viewers alternative interpretations. Within this photograph the Fiji Islanders, whether standing with flexed biceps, sitting with crossed arms, or standing in profile, are very clearly working to show off their muscles to best advantage. Rather than bodies honed by a "natural" lifestyle, these are *physiques* that have been sculpted and displayed by modern techniques. The men's carefully staged poses and focused facial expressions, which explicitly reference the conventions of contemporary bodybuilding media such as Macfadden's, demonstrate their knowledge of and (successful) participation in modern physical culture.

Significantly the representational formulas that Macfadden Publications modeled and disseminated linked eugenic fitness and modernity not only to race or nation but also to active participation in globalized networks of body-centric entertainment and consumer culture. *Physical Culture*'s advocacy of reader participation, its promotion of a commercial physique culture, and its globalized circulation portrayed modern fitness as an ideal that could be attained and performed rather than an essential biological quality. For example, articles such as "Hints on Posing the Physique Beautiful" detailed how readers without access to a professional photographer might achieve the flattering pictures that could "prove" their spectacularly visible cosmopolitan primitivism: "Outdoors is the best place to photograph a muscular pose. . . . Try to look the pose, submerge self and every distracting thought. . . . It is always best to pose on a pedestal. . . . This lends a statuesque appearance. . . . A pedestal can be improvised at little or no expense, and you can usually find inexpensive substitutes for the . . . devises [sic] your models may be portrayed as holding."[58] The magazine offered a panoply of exemplary "Macfaddenscapes" as well as cheap postcards, statues, photography equipment, and bodybuilding manuals through which physical culture modernity, as codified in the United States, could be purchased, learned, and enacted.

When *Physical Culture*'s circulation widened and as the commercialized physique culture it promoted became increasingly globalized, the magazine's transnational participatory pastiche diversified. While the publication's covers continued to celebrate Anglo-Saxon vitality, letters and photographs sent from "ethnic" Americans, readers outside of the United States, and figures whose bodies were clearly not "white" became staples of its correspondence sections. Its publicized fitness and beauty competitions remained dominated by multipage photo spreads of exclusively white contestants from the United States, England, and Australasia, yet these images were often juxtaposed with impressive physical culture portraits of readers from Mexico, the Caribbean, Central and South America, eastern and southern Europe, and Asia, as well as from "ethnic" America. For instance, on the eve of the First World War the correspondents S. R. Jog and K. A. Mahadker, students at the Jummadada Gymnastic Institute in Baroda, and Jamshedj Kanga from Navsari, India, gave Macfadden's anointed physical culture champions a run for their money with their well-developed physiques. Indeed as scholarship on the role played by physical culture in articulations of Hindu nationalism suggests, *Physical Culture*'s muscular and disciplined Indian readers demonstrated that Macfadden-brand media was "capable of serving any master."[59] Even as Macfadden Publications ran eugenic missives that explicitly denounced eastern and southern Europeans, Mexicans, and Asians as "unfit," *Physical Culture* enthusiasts such as Aurel Erdos and his sister Corrine (from Söpron, Hungary), J. D. Prada (from Celaya, Mexico), and Dr. Theodor Gatti (from Spezia, Italy) wrote to Macfadden in order to display the strong and healthy bodies that they had acquired from exercising, weight lifting, and dieting.

In addition to showing off their bodies, Macfadden's global correspondents also drew attention to their local customs and expertise. Jog and Mahadker professed the advantages of traditional Indian health and fitness practices and ideas, while another Jamaican letter-writer, who signed off as "A Colored Reader," offered readers a cure for seasickness, an illness to which Macfadden himself was prone. Masanobu Sugimoto, writing from Japan, bragged that he had invented a revolutionary machine for strengthening the abdomen. The magazine presented a full-page photographic montage of him demonstrating its merits. Corrine Erdos remarked that she had first been introduced to physical culture principles while a schoolgirl in Hungary, and Gatti included copies of his own publications when he wrote to *Physical Culture*.[60] K. V. Iyer's descriptions of Indian gymnasiums and the practice of Prana-Yam presented Indian physical culturalists as masters of bodily discipline and self-control.[61]

As these examples demonstrate, through *Physical Culture*'s transnational participatory pastiche, Macfadden's global correspondents actively resisted being characterized as unfit or backward. In their letters, photographs, and personal narratives, they exhibited their mastery of spectacular visibility and cosmopolitan primitivism and declared themselves part of a modern physical culture world. Similarly when "ethnic" and immigrant American readers narrated stories of self-improvement or submitted impressive bodily measurements and photographs to *Physical Culture* they implicitly challenged eugenic theories of personal and national "fitness" and called into question the very meaning of concepts such as "white," "American," and "the national body." This is perhaps most prolifically illustrated in the case of Angelo Siciliano, an Italian-born immigrant who first posed as a physique model for *Physical Culture* in 1914. In 1921 Siciliano entered and won Macfadden's "World's Most Perfectly Developed Man" contest. The narrative of Siciliano's transformation from a southern European "ninety-seven pound weakling" into a paragon of American manhood known as Charles Atlas played out in (and helped fuel sales of) *Physical Culture*. Furthermore Atlas's success portrayed transformation, mobility, and improvement—rather than race—as the true markers of physical fitness and the modern American body politic.[62]

The example of Charles Atlas draws attention to the central role that modern advertising played in shaping the meanings of *Physical Culture's* globalized circulation.[63] Macfadden's publications contained pages and pages of ads for products that promised to make readers stronger, healthier, smarter, happier, and more attractive. While some ads, such as those for health home vacations, were aimed at affluent readers, the majority presented relatively cheap consumer products—often available by mail—that promised to dramatically enhance or transform the bodies of nonelite readers. With the help of these products, and the right physical culture media, anyone might achieve spectacular visibility or the cosmopolitan primitivist bodily aesthetic that was the mark of modern fitness and healthy body politics.

What one scholar has termed "the lively play of fitness marketing rhetoric" became especially pronounced within the context of *Physical Culture's* transnational participatory pastiche.[64] Macfadden Publications' widespread circulation, cultivation of a multiethnic readership in the United States, and interactive modes of production influenced the development of an advertising aesthetic that destabilized notions of eugenic determinism and portrayed physical fitness and spectacular visibility as universally attainable. This is perhaps best exemplified by the advertisements of the Swedish American strongman and physical culture entrepreneur Earle A. Liederman. Like both Atlas and Macfadden, Liederman utilized the pages of *Physical Culture* to market muscle-building courses to an international audience. His most eye-catching ads, which debuted in *Physical Culture* in the mid-1920s, were multipage photo spreads that in both content and style echoed the transnational participatory pastiche of Macfadden's magazine. In December 1924, for instance, Liederman announced the winners of his yearly "International Physical Improvement Contest" (Macfadden

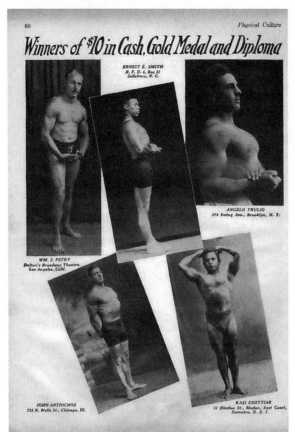

Figure 4.3. Detail from Earle E. Liederman advertisement, Physical Culture, December 1924. Courtesy of the H. J. Luther Stark Center for Physical Culture and Sports, University of Texas, Austin.

was allegedly one of the judges). The pages that followed featured detailed physique portraits of dozens of his (male) pupils from around the globe, along with letters from grateful customers. Liederman's striking ad fit almost seamlessly into Macfadden's magazine, with its collage of physique photographs of men who embodied the ethos of spectacularly visible cosmopolitan primitivism that had become a hallmark of *Physical Culture*. Significantly among the winners Liederman featured were Ernest E. Smith, an African American from North Carolina; Angelo Trulio, an Italian American from Brooklyn; Kasi Chettiar, from Sumatra; Julian Wijeysingha of "Kulala Lumpur [sic]"; Fred Station, from Vancouver; and James T. Sing, of Oahu, Hawaii. On the next page an expansive collection of physique snapshots of men from around the globe created a physical culture collage of striking diversity. "These fellows represent practically every country in the world. It makes no difference where you live, I can do the same for you," Liederman promised, expressing a sentiment that had become the central message of *Physical Culture*'s transnational participatory pastiche.[65]

Conclusion

In July 1949 the director of the U.S. Department of State's Office of International Information (OII) received some exciting news. The president of Macfadden Publications had decided to include State Department propaganda material in the international editions of some of his magazines. Readers of *True Story* and *Photoplay* in Japan, India, Australia, and Italy would encounter featurettes produced by the OII. Apparently State Department officials, though always eager to counter negative stereotypes about American mass culture, saw a unique opportunity to reach the diverse, global range of consumers that had been buying Macfadden Publications' media for years.[66]

Historians have emphasized the important roles played by cultural offensives and transnational economic and cultural brokers, who sometimes worked with and alongside the state, in the expansion of U.S. influence abroad during the Cold War era. Yet as the example of Macfadden Publications attests, this narrative can often be stretched back decades. Retracing *Physical Culture*'s circulation calls attention to the ways early forms of globalized, nonelite, body-centric print culture created and maintained networks of cultural exchange, communications, and commerce that foreshadowed the "American Century."[67] During an era of widespread concern over health and fitness, *Physical Culture* circulated influential messages about American national identity and the nation's place in the world. In particular the magazine's racially differentiated aesthetic conventions and promotion of eugenics bolstered discourses of white racial supremacy, ethnonationalism, and American exceptionalism. Yet analyzing Macfadden Publications' commercialized participatory pastiche emphasizes the multivocality of the company's media and the transnational processes involved in its creation.

Because of its interactive mode of production and global reach, *Physical Culture* provides a case study of what the Modern Girl Around the World Research Group has termed "multi-directional citation," that is, "the mutual, though asymmetrical, influences and circuits of exchange that produce common figurations and practices in multiple locations."[68] As early as the first two decades of the twentieth century, Macfadden Publications circulated globally an accessible vocabulary, range of commodities, and set of aesthetic conventions through which strength, health, attractiveness, and modernity could be defined, acquired, and displayed. Many of the forms of consumption and self-representation that Macfadden Publications helped codify and popularize as modern and healthy encouraged engagement with the products of America's ever-expanding mass culture industry.[69] Paying close attention to the montage of letters submitted by Macfadden's diverse audience suggests, however, how and why media that intertwined bodies, race, and nation within an overarching framework of racial hierarchy were nevertheless able to achieve such a lasting influence on "the global popular."[70] Readers all over the world seem to have viewed *Physical Culture*'s ethos of improvement, self-fashioning, and spectacularly visible cosmopolitan primitivism as a particularly elastic and accessible path to strong, healthy, attractive, and modern personal identities and body politics.

Notes

1. Gerhard Wiens, "Hunger," *Books Abroad* 22 (winter 1948): 5–10.

2. The company that became known as Macfadden Publications was originally the Physical Culture Publishing Company. For consistency, I use the name Macfadden Publications throughout this essay.

3. My reference to the United States as the world's "first multicultural modern capitalist society" is borrowed from Mizruchi, *The Rise of Multicultural America.*

4. See Fitzpatrick, "Pulp Empire."

5. A notable exception that mentions Macfadden's work within a non-U.S. context is Matthews, "Building the Body Beautiful."

6. On the body as "the finest consumer object," see Baudrillard, *The Consumer Society,* 129; Foucault, "Technologies of the Self."

7. Bernarr Macfadden and his third wife, Mary (Williamson) Macfadden, presented conflicting stories about which of them came up with the idea for *True Story.* See Macfadden and Gauvreau, *Dumbbells and Carrot Strips.* On the history of participatory mass media in the Anglophone world, see Griffen-Foley, "From Tit-Bits to Big Brother." Fabian, *The Unvarnished Truth* provides historical domestic U.S. context as well as analysis of Macfadden's true story media.

8. Haley, *The Healthy Body in Victorian Culture,* 3.

9. For more on Anglo and American health and fitness movements of the late nineteenth and early twentieth century, see Green, *Fit for America*; Whorton, *Crusaders for Fitness*; Salazar, *Bodies of Reform*; Putney, *Muscular Christianity*; Engs, *Clean Living Movements*; Budd, *The Sculpture Machine.* On the Swedish and German practices that influenced Anglo and American physical culture, see Hoffman, *Turnen and Sport*; Ottosson, "The First Historical Movements of Kinesiology."

10. The London edition of *Physical Culture* was titled *Physical Development*. I suspect that this was to avoid confusion with Eugen Sandow's *Physical Culture* magazine. This title persisted until Macfadden incorporated the British edition into *Physical Culture* after the Great War.

11. Alva Johnston, "The Great Macfadden," *Saturday Evening Post*, June 21, 1941, 9.

12. On Bernarr Macfadden and physical culture for women, see especially Todd, "Bernarr Macfadden."

13. On Macfadden's battles with Comstock and the AMA, see Ernst, *Weakness Is a Crime*. On *Physical Culture* and U.S. gay subcultures, see Chauncey, *Gay New York*, 116, 204. A more international perspective on gay subcultures and the physique culture industry can be found in Waugh, *Hard to Imagine*.

14. Wood, *Bernarr Macfadden*, 77. Most recently, see Adams, *Mr. America*.

15. For a comprehensive biography of Eugen Sandow, see Chapman, *Sandow the Magnificent*. Sandow's influence in Australasia is discussed in Daley, *Leisure and Pleasure* and "The Strongman of Eugenics." On Sandow's popularity in India, see Singleton, *Yoga Body*; Alter, *Yoga in Modern India*.

16. Bernarr Macfadden, "My Life Story," *Physical Culture*, Jan. 1915, 85.

17. Daley, *Leisure and Pleasure*, 48.

18. For instance, see the ad for H. I. Jones and Sons in *Mercury* (Hobart, Tasmania), July 8, 1902, 4.

19. Letter from H. R. Hyatt, *Physical Culture*, Nov. 1908, 416.

20. Daley, *Leisure and Pleasure*, 60.

21. Letter from C. W. Healy, *Physical Culture*, May 1907; letter from Elsa Schmidt, *Physical Culture*, Aug. 1914.

22. The copies of *Snowy Baker's Magazine* that I consulted are held by the Mitchell Library, State Library of New South Wales, Sydney, Australia.

23. See Kirchfeld and Boyle, *Nature Doctors*.

24. Boydell, *My Beloved Country*, 20–24.

25. Letter from B. P. Madon, *Physical Culture*, June 1911.

26. On "modern" Indian physical culture, see Singleton, *Yoga Body*; Alter, *Yoga in Modern India*; Mills, *Subaltern Sports*.

27. There is little written in English about K. V. Iyer. See Singleton, *Yoga Body*; Aldrich, *Colonialism and Homosexuality*. Some of Iyer's publications and photographs can be found online at Sandow Plus, http://www.sandowplus .co.uk/India/Iyer/iyer-index.htm. Copies of Iyer's physical culture course are held by the Stark Center for Physical Culture, UT Austin.

28. Rosenberg, *Spreading the American Dream*.

29. Letter from William Collins, *Physical Culture*, May 1907, 409; letter from Daniel E. Henriquez, *Physical Culture*, July 1910, 104–5. For corroborating evidence that the enthusiastic William Collins was a "real person," see American Bureau of Shipping, 1905 *Record of American and Foreign Shipping*, 507.

30. See Reeves-Ellington et al., *Competing Kingdoms*; Tyrrell, *Reforming the World*; Zimmerman, *Innocents Abroad*.

31. "Physical Culture in the Philippines," *Physical Culture*, Feb. 1905, 32; letter from Alfred Milor, *Physical Culture*, Oct. 1902, 32.

32. R. A. Holman, "Comstock vs. Macfadden," *Tomorrow*, Feb. 1908, 44.

33. Bernarr Macfadden, "Details of the Prosecution of the Editor," *Physical Culture*, Feb. 1910, 135.

34. Letter from Miguel G. Luna, "P.C. Life in the Philippines," *Physical Culture*, Feb. 1920, 105–6.

35. "From a Filipino Physical Culturalist," *Physical Culture*, Sept. 1927, 85–86.

36. Letter from Corrine Erdos, *Physical Culture*, June 1911, 712.

37. See "Waves of Austro-Hungarian Immigration," in Lehman, *Gale Encyclopedia of Multicultural America*.

38. Letter from H. R. Hyatt, *Physical Culture*, Nov. 1908, 416; "Letter from a Central American Athlete," *Physical Culture*, Mar. 1914, 322; letter from Dr. Theodor Gatti, *Physical Culture*, Dec. 1903, 554; letter from Hjalmar Hammersen, *Physical Culture*, June 1912, 611.

39. See Wyman, *Round-trip to America*.

40. Harland Manchester, "True Story," *Scribner's*, Aug. 1938, 25.

41. Lears, *Rebirth of a Nation*, 1. Also see Kasson, *Houdini, Tarzan, and the Perfect Man*; Putney, *Muscular Christianity*; Green, *Fit for America*; Warren, *Buffalo Bill's America*; Bloom, "Constructing Whiteness."

42. On the racial and gendered dimensions of this multivalent "discourse of civilization," see especially Bederman, *Manliness and Civilization*.

43. Bernarr Macfadden, *Physical Development*, Mar. 1913, 41.

44. My use of the concept of the imaginary is indebted to Anderson, *Imagined Communities*. The powerful phrase "transnational racial imaginary" is borrowed from Lake and Reynolds, *Drawing the Global Color Line*. Also see Ellinghaus et al., *Re-orienting Whiteness*.

45. See Stern, *Eugenic Nation*; Molina, *Fit to Be Citizens?*

46. Kramer, *The Blood of Government*, 269. On representations of "the other" in turn-of-the-century popular culture, including World Fairs, see Rydell, *All the Worlds a Fair*; Pratt, *Imperial Eyes*; Wexler, *Tender Violence*; Hoganson, *Consumers' Imperium*; Hawkins, *American Iconographic*; Goodall, *Performance and Evolution in the Age of Darwin*.

47. See Jacobson, *Barbarian Virtues*, especially 129. There exists a diverse body of scholarship on the popularity of "primitive" and "native" arts, fashions, and iconography among middle- and upper-class consumers in Europe and the United States around the turn of the century. For instance, see Barkan and Bush, *Prehistories of the Future*; Stansell, *American Moderns*; Hershfield, *Imagining La Chica Moderna*; Jacobs, *Engendered Encounters*.

48. Wesley Atkins, "The Igorrotes, a Hardy, Vigorous People," *Physical Culture*, Apr. 1910, 367.

49. As defined in Conor, *The Spectacular Modern Women*, the concept of spectacular visibility refers to a form of "modern subjectivity" generated via

interaction with visual mass media and characterized by fluidity between self-image, public image, and identity. My use of the term *cosmopolitan primitivism* draws from the Modern Girl Around the World Research Group's discussion of cosmopolitanism and multidirectional citation in Weinbaum et al., *The Modern Girl around the World*. Also see Thacker, *Moving through Modernity*.

50. Gordon Reeves, "National Sports and their Significance," *Physical Culture*, July 1914, 64. For an analysis of modernity, nationalism, and sport, see Keys, *Globalizing Sport*.

51. For an excellent analysis of African Americans and the transnational physical culture movement, see Runstedtler, "Visible Men."

52. Macfadden, "My Lecture Tour through England," *Physical Culture*, Mar. 1907, 263.

53. Lake and Reynolds, *Drawing the Global Colour Line*.

54. Letter from R. Clifford to *Physical Culture*, June 1914, 30a.

55. See Jameson, *Postmodernism*.

56. On montage theory, see Eisenstein, "A Dialectical Approach to Film Form"; Kuleshov, *Kuleshov on Film*. For more recent uses of the concept, see Silverberg, *Erotic Grotesque Nonsense*; Conor, *The Spectacular Modern Woman*.

57. F. A. Hornibrook, "The Fijians and Physical Culture," *Physical Culture*, Sept. 1907, 151.

58. L. E. Eubanks, "Hints on Posing the Physique Beautiful," *Physical Culture*, May 1913, 420. Unlike other bodybuilding magazines such as *Sandow's Magazine* or the Australian *Withrow's Physical Culture*, *Physical Culture* encouraged amateur photography and the submission of snapshots.

59. Letters from Indian Physical Culturalists, *Physical Culture*, July 1914, n.p.; Budd, *The Sculpture Machine*, 85. As Budd notes, in India "the cultivation of physical strength thus offered the attractive promise that the British might be beaten at their own game," 85. Also see Valiani, *Militant Publics in India*.

60. Letter from J. D. Prada, *Physical Culture*, June 1911; "Letter from a Colored Reader," *Physical Culture*, Oct. 1910; letter from Masanobu Sugimoto, *Physical Culture*, Dec. 1916; letter from Dr. Theodor Gatti, *Physical Culture*, Dec. 1903.

61. Letter from K. V. Iyer, *Physical Culture*, Apr. 1922.

62. For an excellent treatment of Charles Atlas that pays close attention to issues of both gender and ethnicity, see Reich, "The World's Most Perfectly Developed Man."

63. On American advertising, see especially Marchand, *Advertising the American Dream*; Lears, *Fables of Abundance*.

64. Budd, *The Sculpture Machine*, 30.

65. Liederman advertisement, *Physical Culture*, Dec. 1924, 82–90.

66. See memo from Lloyd A. Free (acting director of OII) to George Allen, July 25, 1949, and memo from Lloyd A. Free to Mr. Bragg, July 21, 1949, both located in Folder: "Macfadden Publications," Box 18, International Information Administration, Private Enterprise Cooperation Staff (IIA/ICO), Subject

File, 1941–53, RG 59, National Archives and Records Administration (NARA) II, College Park, MD.

67. On U.S. cultural influence and power during the Cold War, see Von Eschen, *Satchmo Blows Up the World*; de Grazia, *Irresistible Empire*; Cull, *The Cold War and the United States Information Agency*; Osgood, *Total Cold War and the United States and Public Diplomacy*; Belmonte, *Selling the American Way*; Prevots, *Dance for Export*; Saunders, *The Cultural Cold War*; Falk, *Upstaging the Cold War*.

68. Weinbaum et al., *The Modern Girl around the World*, 4.

69. As Charap, "Teaching the Globalization of American Popular Culture" has put it, "In many places around the world both modernity and its resulting tensions seem to be epitomized by the values enshrined in American popular culture," 225.

70. During, "Popular Culture on a Global Scale."

five

"The Most Beautiful Chinese Girl in the World"

Anna May Wong's Transnational Racial Modernity

SHIRLEY JENNIFER LIM

Chinese American actress Anna May Wong's (1905–61) body maps a complicated discursive terrain that encompasses not only nation-state but transnational racial signifiers. What makes her symbolic body compelling is that the racial and national categories do not neatly align. Instead at times they are contradictory; at other times they are porous and fluid. This essay seeks to explore the development of transnational racial modernity through the lens of Wong's career.

Why does she matter? Anna May Wong broke the codes of yellowface in both American and European cinema to become one of the major global actresses of Asian descent between the world wars. She made close to sixty films that circulated around the world and in 1951 starred in her own television show, *The Gallery of Madame Liu-Tsong*, produced by the now defunct Dumont Network.[1] Examining Wong's career is particularly fruitful because of race's centrality to the motion pictures' construction of the modern American nation-state as well as its significance within the intensifying global circulation of moving images. Gendering the body played a crucial role; as a nonwhite woman, Wong embodied the threat of the Oriental and the primitive, yet her glamour and elegance partially mitigated the threat. Her oeuvre marks differing nodes in the exploration of the body, race, and nation.

This essay discusses representations of Wong's body politic in three different years and locations. The first, marked by the press coverage of her 1929 London stage and screen career, predominantly shows her as an antiquated national Chinese, though hints of modernity do appear. In the second and third portrayals, highlighted by the 1938 cover of *Look* magazine in the United States and her 1939 visit to Australia, hybrid transnational racial modernity dominates. These three sets of materials show that her figure signified the mutability of spatial and temporal racial categories. Her bodily representations were variously intersected by European cosmopolitanism and imperialism, old world Chineseness or Asianness, modern Americana, and transnational, diasporic modernity.

Transnationalism as an analytical category disrupts and denaturalizes nation-state borders. As Laura Briggs, Gladys McCormick, and J. T. Way have postulated, the concept of transnationalism can "provide the conceptual acid that the nation, like sex, is a thing contested, interrupted, and always shot through with contradiction."[2] I use the concept of transnational racial modernity to refer to the ways domestic and imperial racial hierarchies become intermeshed.[3] The deeply racialized history of the United States, for example, began before the nation-state, as a slaveholding colony of Spain, France, and Britain, grafted upon which were the U.S. nation-state's colonial ventures in Asia, the Pacific, and the Caribbean, the continued genocide of indigenous peoples, and the reterritorialization of Mexico. In the twentieth century those global flows of people and cultures rendered the United States the preeminent modern nation-state; it was both imperial and transnational.

Wong's Chinese heritage subjected her to the slipperiness of American racial categories vis-à-vis national citizenship and affiliation. She was born at 351 Flower Street near Los Angeles's Chinatown on January 3, 1905, as the second daughter of two people of Chinese descent. Nation-state citizenship and belonging mapped imperfectly onto her body and rendered her the emblematic transnational. The historian Karen Leong's excellent work on Wong uses the term *accidental transnational* to characterize her career.[4] I instead argue that Wong was necessarily transnational. Asian immigrants are simultaneously bodies to be integrated into the national political sphere and foreign objects always subjected to their alien origins.[5] In material terms, this subjection to alien origins translated into American racial codes, such as Asian immigrants being legally barred from becoming U.S. citizens, alien land laws that forbade noncitizens from owning land, antimiscegenation laws that forbade "Mongolians" from marrying whites, and a whole host of official and unofficial segregation practices that regulated everything from swimming pools and movie theaters to jobs and residential housing. In the United States laws such as the Chinese Exclusion Act (1882), which barred the immigration of Chinese laborers but allowed entry to merchants and students, and the Cable Act (1922), which stipulated that women who married aliens ineligible for citizenship (Chinese male migrants) would lose their own citizenship, prevented Wong from enjoying full citizenship. The United States was not the only country to racially bar the Chinese. Australian settler-colonial and later national identity centered on the exclusion of the Chinese from immigration. Australia's 1901 Immigration Restriction Act created "White Australia" through a dictation test that was intended to exclude the Chinese as well as create provisions for expelling people of Chinese origin. The expulsion to alien origins that rendered people of Chinese descent into an ambiguous nation-state subjectivity, however, also opened up the possibility of extranational affiliation. It was precisely because Wong's American nation-state ties were so tenuous that in her life, body, and career she could come to epitomize transnational racial modernity. I am not arguing that *national* and *transnational* are opposite categories, but that, as shown through Wong's career, they have a vexed and intertwined relationship.

London 1928–1929

Like other racial minority performing artists such as Josephine Baker, Paul Robeson, and Sessue Hayakawa, in 1928 Anna May Wong traveled to London, Berlin, and Paris because limited Hollywood roles discouraged her.[6] Under the ethos of modernity, the racial and primitive "other" was the foil against which Europe proved its civilization.[7] At first glance Wong presented an exotic image to European audiences, one that was ethnically "other" and sexually primitive. She arrived in a Europe primed for her by interests in jazz, chinoiserie, and negritude. As her American national citizenship was frequently subsumed into essentialized racial categories, she functioned as an ambiguous representative of empire. Working in London, Berlin, and Paris during the height of imperialism, Wong represented the desired female colonial body as well as the forbidden dark sexual "other."[8] As she became established in

Figure 5.1. Portrait of Anna May Wong by Carl Van Vechten. Courtesy of Library of Congress, Prints & Photographs Division, Carl Van Vechten Collection, LC-USZ62–54231.

her career in the 1930s, she became legendary for wearing sophisticated designer gowns that contradicted (or perhaps even further adorned) her sexual and "primitive" performances.[9]

Wong's body helped create transnational cinema. The German director Richard Eichberg cast her in films such as *Song/Show Life/Schmutziges Geld* (1928) and *Hai-Tang/Flame of Love/The Road to Dishonour* (1930) that were coproduced in Germany, France, and England and subtitled or shot in multiple languages so that they could screen throughout Europe and, most crucially, the colonial world.[10] Carrying multiple titles, her films played not only in France and Germany but in locations such as Mozambique and South Africa.[11] Thus Wong became a transnational symbol of cosmopolitan femininity, and through her star persona a new pan-European cinema construed more broadly as global cinema could be created. As the film scholar Tim Bergfelder has argued, Wong was an ideal product for European cinema because she could combine exoticism with Americanness, thereby avoiding the limitations of being identified with any particular European nation-state.[12] Wong may have found these starring roles appealing as a way to circumvent the rise in Hollywood's exploitative Orientalist roles as well as the numerous race-based laws that circumscribed her life in California.

While in London, Wong was featured in numerous periodicals, appearing on the cover of the society magazines *Tatler* and *Sketch*, and the industry magazine *Film Weekly*.[13] It is striking that in the British press Wong's Americanness, typically a metaphor for temporal modernity, is largely ignored. Instead her Chineseness comes to the forefront, frequently in inaccurate ways. In *Sketch* on August 22, 1928, the cover reads, "Miss Anna May Wong, in National Dress: By N. Michailow." The caption accompanying the illustration states, "Miss Anna May Wong, the famous Chinese screen star who is visiting England and will shortly make her British screen debut in 'Piccadilly,' usually wears European dress; but when she sat to Professor Nic Michailow, the well-known artist, she chose to be painted in a superb Chinese coat, and with her hair arranged in national style." Hence Wong's American national identity is obfuscated in favor of her high-class Chinese appearance; Chineseness is collapsed into a "national style" associated with China's elite. Note that the piece presents the Chinese dress as Wong's choice and states that she usually wore modern or "European" dress. Another British periodical, the *Tatler*, placed her on the cover on March 20, 1929, also in Chinese dress. These two covers show how Wong's Chineseness in London was an anachronistic, antiquated one, albeit one with high-class standing.

In this London press coverage, Wong's Chinese heritage not only gets collapsed into nation-state historical signifiers, but China and the Chinese become subsumed in temporal noncoevalness.[14] As Johannes Fabian documents in *Time and the Other*, placing the other in noncoeval (noncontemporary) time is central to European domination of the other. The temporal component to modernity is critical. In an age that measured civilization's progress with a linear timeline that posited the modern West as the most evolved stage, the colonized were constructed as primitive (Polynesia, Africa) or decadent (China, Middle East), which meant less evolved and emphatically not modern.

This collapsing of Chinese heritage into Chinese nation-state belonging was not confined to Anna May Wong. Numerous writers confused race and national origins when discussing other actresses of Chinese descent. For example, on March 20, 1929, referring to Wong's performance in *A Circle of Chalk*, the *Sketch* reported, "This celebrated screen star of Chinese birth has been featured in many successful pictures, including the much discussed 'Piccadilly,' but has never before been seen on stage."[15] The article went on to state, "The part of the jealous wife is played by another Chinese actress, Miss Rose Quong." The historian Angela Woollacott has documented that Rose Quong was actually a Chinese Australian from Melbourne who settled in London and capitalized on her Chineseness.[16] In referring to Wong's "Chinese birth" and Quong as "another Chinese actress" both actresses were rendered nationally Chinese.

Perhaps the ultimate testament to the Chinese mode of Wong's appeal came in a theater review of *The Circle of Chalk*, a play in which she garnered top billing over her costar Laurence Olivier. Referring to her role, Hubert Griffith wrote, "I have rarely seen anything more completely beautiful. Rhythm, gesture, the expressiveness of motion—she is mistress of them all. One could sit back and watch the lithe little figure moving across the stage and see how in all the complicated movements of the dance never as much as a finger-tip departed from patterns of the highest grace of felicity."[17] He continued, "The dance was a miracle, a masterpiece. And once again, at the end of the evening, when she at first refused to make a speech at the curtain fall, the actress did so in a gesture that was again arresting in its expressiveness and beauty." Griffith's enchantment with Wong as a physical object was complete.

The critic Griffith, however, preferred Wong silent. He continued in his review, "It is at first a shock to hear that the accent that falls from Celestial lips is a highly Americanised one, and then, when one gets over this as unimportant, to find that it is further an undistinguished one, clipping words leaving many of them almost inaudible. She got no variety into the long speeches, and generally, if I may say so without unpardonable rudeness, was at her most effective when silent. I return in memory to the dance, which I thank her for as a real experience." Wong ruined the illusion of the perfect "Celestial" dance with her voice. In addition to her lack of proper theatrical intonations, Griffith observed that almost the entire cast lacked elocution skills. Although he backed away from his initial position that having an American accent is unimportant, nonetheless he completely elided the history of migration of the Chinese to the United States as a response to British and Western imperialism in China during the middle of the nineteenth century. Such colonial disruptions were effaced through the journalists' categorization of the Chinese as belonging in China, not in the United States or Australia.

Perhaps because of its familiarity with Hollywood, the periodical *Film Weekly* reported that "Anna May Wong . . . though Oriental from her almond-shaped eyes to her long finger nails, was actually born and brought up in Los Angeles, California."[18] In the February 11, 1929, issue, where she appeared on the cover, the text explained, "She became known to the public by playing the role of a Chinese slave girl in 'The

Thief of Bagdad.' Since then, her name has grown famous in such productions as 'Show Life,' 'A Trip to Chinatown,' 'The Chinese Parrot,' and lastly, 'Piccadilly.' . . . Anna May Wong, in English, means Frosted Yellow Willow, a beautiful name for a talented actress." Thus Film Weekly reported on Wong's deeper transnational history.

After theater critics such as Griffith decried her American twang, Wong invested in elocution lessons in order to master an upper-class British accent. For private acting lessons, she sought out theater legends such as Kate Rork and Mabel Terry Lewis.[19] Later, to lend distinction to her work, she invoked traces of that upper-class British accent in her American movie parts. Hiring theater voice coaching was a significant step in Wong's self-fashioning; it enabled her to get starring film and theater roles and allowed her to claim the persona of a cosmopolitan woman of the world—important cultural capital for a person of color in the interwar period.

By insisting on temporal contemporaneity through actions such as elocution lessons, Wong disrupted how European colonialism depended on placing its subjects under noncontemporaneous (noncoeval) time. While in London, Paris, and Berlin, she acquired the credentials that would allow her to become coeval and enter into modernity. In addition to her English-accent training, she learned French and German, utilizing her German in films such as Pavement Butterfly (1929) and the Viennese opera Springtime.[20] Living the life of an upper-class socialite, she met the Prince of Wales, learning to curtsy to royalty in the process, and her elegance and beauty stopped Parliament when she sauntered into the visitors' gallery.[21] As befits a modern movie star, Wong learned how to handle the press and the numerous photo shoots. Thus she gained the social skills and acting polish that, upon her return to the United States, would win her a broader repertoire of starring theater and film roles. All of those acquired upper-class English mannerisms, including voice, ensured that her charms would translate on a global scale.

In the 1920s and 1930s glamorous racial modernity had an uneasy relationship to Orientalism and primitivism, which explains Wong's appeal. As Judith Brown argues, "Glamour derives from a paradoxical indulgence in an aestheticizing distancing of the primitive through formal control and brings into relation orientalist and Africanist primitivism."[22] Hence a prominent film star such as Marlene Dietrich underscored her star persona by embodying the primitive, which highlighted her whiteness and glamour.[23] As Wong's costar, Dietrich played Shanghai Lily, foil to Wong's Hu-Fei, in the Josef von Sternberg film Shanghai Express (1932). Wong and Dietrich acted as sexually threatening women shot through with the exotic. As a nonwhite woman, Wong embodied the threat of the Oriental and the primitive, yet her glamour and elegance partially mitigated the threat. In other words, just as Dietrich needed characters such as Shanghai Lily, Wong needed the elegance and modernity to counteract the threat of her racialized body. It was Wong's ability to play with both the modern and the primitive, in her case the Oriental, that powered her stardom.

Wong's provisionally acknowledged American racial modernity placed her in a complex situation with regard to her Chinese heritage. As a person of Chinese descent, racialized meanings of her body became enmeshed in multiple and overlapping meanings of Chinese, ranging from national Chineseness to antiquated Chineseness, racial Chineseness, and transnational Chineseness. Thus the term *Chinese* as applied to her can change from a racial signifier to a nation-state signifier and to a temporality signifier. One key distinction is between modern transnational Chinese and antiquated national Chinese. Modern transnational Chinese could encompass Wong's Americanness as well as her modernity. Antiquated national Chineseness posited her as noncoeval and as a silent museum curiosity, to be admired but not a threat. Her self-fashioning was her attempt to enter into modernity.

"The World's Most Beautiful Chinese Girl": The United States 1938

Wong's *Look* magazine cover of March 1938, where she was called the "World's Most Beautiful Chinese Girl," offers an opportunity to examine transnational American racial modernity in the United States. Being on the cover of *Look* crowned her status as an American icon. Founded in 1937, *Look* boasted a circulation of two million and a price of ten cents an issue. Now defunct, the chiefly pictorial *Look* featured topics ranging from glamorous University of California Los Angeles sorority women, to raising quintuplets, to exposing fascism.

During the 1930s three historical shifts laid the groundwork for Wong's embodiment of transnational racial modernity by changing the way "Orientals" were portrayed on the screen. First, the *New York Times* on April 14, 1930, castigated Sax Rohmer's novel turned movie, *The Mysterious Dr. Fu Manchu* (1929), for its unreal and overly dramatic "mysterious messages, daggers bathed in blood, opiate druggings, and much gun play."[24] Chinese Americans protested the representation of themselves as Fu Manchus.[25] As a result of such condemnations, liberal pressure drove evil "Orientals" such as Fu Manchu from the screen.[26]

The term *Chinese* signified a different sensitivity to racial hierarchy than the term *Oriental*.[27]

Second, the gains in "positive" portrayals in racialized cinema during the 1930s were paradoxically assisted by the 1934 Hays Code, which not only prohibited interracial sexual relations but also forbade ethnic typecasting.[28] Chinese American actors and actresses noticed the difference that the Hays Code made in their parts; according to oral history interviews, Chinese American actors of the era remembered their roles improving in the mid-1930s. Keye Luke, who played Charlie Chan's number one son, found that his roles changed in the mid-1930s: "It seems I was always cast as a good guy and only 2 or 3 Oriental parts as nasty since 1934."[29] Even though he was not explicitly asked about the Hays Code, in examining his movie career Luke pinpointed 1934 as a turning point.

Third, the Sino-Japanese War, triggered in 1931 by Japan's invasion of Manchuria, resulted in greater sympathy for China and "Chinese Americans," a term that had not been used in the 1920s. The United States sided with China, which signaled a change. Thus in the 1930s, as the United States developed the image of China as a good ally, the term *Orientals* became more ethnically specific. In films Chinese and Chinese Americans gained an identity distinct from that of the Japanese. The changing status of China boosted the value of Wong's portrayals of Chinese patriotism. In the 1932 movie *Shanghai Express*, she plays a patriot loyal to the Chinese nation, whereas in *Daughter of the Dragon* (1931) a year earlier she depicts a woman who does not have national allegiances but swears loyalty to one sinister man, her father.

Look highlighted Wong's glamour, clothing, and, not surprisingly, given the moniker "the world's most beautiful Chinese girl," her physical attributes. The captions and photographs displayed both Wong's Chinese ethnicity and her American citizenship. Underneath a still of Wong from the British movie *Chu Chin Chow* (1934), the pictorial explained that she had only recently visited China and that, despite her appearance, was American born. In case the point was not understood, the next picture clarified Wong's nationality as a sophisticated American citizen. The caption proclaimed, "Anna May Wong, seen here with one of her brothers, Roger Wong, wears clothes unusually well. In 1934 the Mayfair Mannequin society designated her as the world's best-dressed woman. . . . An American citizen, she has given up plans to retire to China." A picture of Wong wearing a modish Western ensemble—long striped tunic belted over a dark skirt with a jacket whose lining and length matched the tunic, accessorized with a dark hat tilted at a rakish

Figure 5.2. Portrait of
Anna May Wong by Carl
Van Vechten. Courtesy of
Library of Congress, Prints
& Photographs Division,
Carl Van Vechten Collec-
tion, LC-USZ62–54231.

angle and black high-heeled pumps—beautifully illustrated the caption. Wong made her only visit to China in 1936, after Metro Goldwyn
Mayer studio refused to cast her in a leading role in the film *The Good
Earth* (1937). Although she had planned to spend more time in China,
her trip dramatized her cultural differences with the Chinese and
demonstrated to her that her true home was in the West.

Look's feature effectively crowned Anna May Wong as the icon of
modern hybrid Chinese American culture. One caption read, "Umpire
Wong. Last summer Anna May Wong showed how completely American
she can be, by umpiring a baseball game, in which Lowell Thomas, with
her here, was a player. In the movies, however, Anna May usually is a
siren type." For the game, Wong dressed in a dark cheongsam with a
pattern of white wavy lines, appearing almost like chain mail. Although
the text called her all-American, given her cheongsam, the photograph
suggested a redefinition of that term. The caption and photograph expanded the concept of Americanness by presenting a visible ambiguity
that evoked wholesomeness. Such a portrait of Chinese American identity worked to alleviate anxiety over race and acculturation. The Chinese
and the Western could coexist and cosignify each other.

In the final photograph, taken with Marlene Dietrich and Leni Riefenstahl, Wong's transnational modernity was highlighted for American audiences. She was clad in a completely Western sleeveless flapper dress in dark material with a chiffon overlay, accented by a knotted long single-strand pearl choker. Like Wong, Dietrich sported a sleeveless flapper dress accessorized by a multistrand beaded necklace. "If Anna May, seen here between Marlene Dietrich and the German actress Leni Riefenstahl, kisses an Englishman in a movie, the scene is cut out by British censors. Despite this, she is very popular in England, where she has made a number of pictures. She first visited China in 1935, was received there like a princess." (Despite the caption's claims, British censors did allow the movie *Java Head* to show a kiss between Wong and a British actor.) Association with Dietrich, dazzling costumes, being received like a princess, and travels to Britain all signified woman-of-the-world glamour and a moneyed lifestyle. This *Look* magazine cover marked the apex of her Hollywood career. Wong had found a way to embody simultaneously a Chinese and an American in a modern way that gained her fame.

Australia 1939

One of the most intriguing twists in Wong's career occurred in Australia, where she functioned as a modern transnational Chinese ambassadorial figure.[30] Wong's ability to portray glamorous racialized modernity was the reason she was brought to Australia in 1939 to perform on the Tivoli Theatre circuit in Sydney and Melbourne. Highlighting Wong was an effective advertising ploy because, for over a decade prior to her visit, audiences throughout Australia had attended her films. As reviews and publicity notices published in newspapers around the country show, almost all of her major films, including more recent hits such as *When Were You Born* (1939) and *King of Chinatown* (1939), played in Australia.

One example of Wong's particular brand of transnational racial modernity appeared in a feature on her in the August 1939 edition of *The Home* that portrayed her as an American of Chinese ancestry. *The Home*, a society-women's monthly magazine published by the *Sydney Morning Herald*, carried a two-page, four-picture spread that starred Wong.[31] The magazine's narrative explained the significance of Wong's body: "Graceful, smartly dressed and possessed of a superb sense of humor, Miss Wong is the Orient and the West in one person—one moment she will be speaking of the mystery of China's lost cities; the next moment the latest Hollywood wise crack will cross her lips. But with it all she has an arresting personality." In this description, Wong herself fashions the alluring hybridity.

Wong's ambassadorial persona was demonstrated in a Fox Movietones Australia newsreel feature that focused on her Australian arrival. In the days before widespread television news, movietones were played before feature films and gave audiences the news of the day. The Fox Movietones newsreel shows Wong as every inch the major international film star akin to royalty. The footage begins with her walking down an outdoor staircase, waving at the crowds that greet her. She wears a long fur coat, a dark dress, and dark high-heeled pumps. Presenting an image of a powerful, modern career woman, Wong says loudly and clearly, "Thank you so much Dr. Pao [consul-general of China] and Madame Pao, you have extended me a most warm welcome and thank you very much. If the rest of my stay in Australia will be as pleasant and happy as today has been then I know that I shall enjoy every moment of it. And to the many Chinese who are listening in may I say [Wong delivers a Chinese greeting]." She smiles broadly and gives a big wave at the end.

Wong's use of the Chinese language, her reference to her Chinese Australian fans, and her mandarin collar all highlight the changing relationship of China to Australia and to Western powers during World War II. In Australia, in contrast to the newly demonized Japanese, the Chinese had become the good Asian ally in the Pacific, aided by the efforts of those who actively worked to inscribe a culturally rich understanding of Chinese culture and society. This changed political dynamic is reflected in the newsreel. Although China was still a source of ambivalence, it was increasingly depicted as a good ally.[32]

On the one hand it is remarkable that Wong was portrayed almost as an ambassador and spokesperson for China, not for the United States. Through her work for China Relief in the United States, she seemed perfectly happy to embrace this Chinese diasporic citizenship.[33] Her racial identity as Chinese constricted her, yet also opened her up to the notion of being Chinese in a broad, transnational sense. Being a nonhyphenated American, which was (and often still is) enmeshed in whiteness and chiefly coded as white, was not an option for her. It must have been highly gratifying to her to be received in such an official manner, for she was not welcomed warmly in China during her 1936 visit.[34]

On the other hand, what becomes apparent in the Fox Movietones newsreel is Wong's commanding World English accent. As the historian Desley Deacon has found, "World English" was an invented accent, considered appropriate to cultured and educated English speakers. Although invented, it resembled some New England speech patterns as well as educated nonregional British English.[35] Wong's British-inflected accent brings her closer to that ideal World English, whose tones ensured her popularity and marketability around the world. Thus the accent coaching and self-fashioning in London a decade earlier proved useful to Wong's transnational Chinese persona. This is particularly significant because language had been a marker of admittance to Australia. The 1901 Immigration Restriction Act, which essentially formalized "White Australia" and restricted Asian migration, was based on "the use of the infamous 'dictation test' (the use of a language test was intended to disguise the fact that the rejection was not on the grounds of colour), [and thus] migration officials were able to exclude Asians and others considered to be undesirable aliens."[36] Though English was the primary language, other European languages were allowed. As is clear from the Fox Movietones Australia episode, Wong spoke with an educated British-inflected accent, which rendered her voice closer to that of an ideal global citizen. Her perfect command of English, down to an accent that would have been the envy of many Australians, therefore represented a threat to the continued application of the White Australia Policy. Through her fashion and voice, Wong's visit to Australia showed how the image of a transnational Chinese was distinctly different from that of an antiquated Chinese national.

Although on one level Wong's status as an ambassadorial figure can be read as the greater acceptance of the Chinese in Australia, at another level it can also be read as an act of erasure of Australia's coolie past.[37] By celebrating her upper-class Chinese markers, not only did Chinese heritage become respectable, but Australia's Chinese past did as well. As Fiona Paisley has argued persuasively in regard to Aboriginals in the 1930s, so much of the project of the modern Australian nation-state involved making settler-colonization respectable.[38] Racial anxieties could be soothed by respectability and class. Positing Wong as a Chinese ambassador assisted in that project, for it placed her as a respectable and nonthreatening public figure securely outside of Australia's nation-state borders.

Conclusion

Anna May Wong's career signified larger transnational changes in cosmopolitanism, race, and gender in the interwar period. A multisite analysis of images of Wong and her travels offers a window into how racial categories of nation-state belonging mutated into the embodiment of transnational modernity.

Unfortunately for Wong, the interwar period represented a moment of possibility that flared up only briefly. After the advent of World War II, her female ambassadorial persona was no longer valued. The visit to Australia was Wong's swan song, one last flickering moment before her transnational fame faded. Wong did not resume her international career in Europe; she never returned to Australia; and she never revisited China. Instead she remained in the United States and sporadically played minor roles such as that of Lana Turner's maid in *Portrait in Black* (1960).

In the interwar period a Chinese American woman could embody glamour, Americanness, and transnational modernity—but this position and the opportunities it offered for personal mobility and redefinition were not without their own stresses and limitations on the very body that made them possible. Wong died of Laennec's cirrhosis, a disease typically stemming from alcoholism, in 1961. Yet, as her legacy shows, for a brief moment, a glamorous Chinese American woman could occupy a position of transnational importance.

Notes

1. I deploy the concept of Asian American as an analytical term, for historically it was not in use during the 1920s and 1930s. At the time Wong would have been called Chinese or Oriental.

2. Briggs et al., "Transnationalism," 627.

3. Walter Benjamin, "Gespräch mit Anne May Wong," *Die Literarische Welt*, July 6, 1928, 1.

4. Leong, *China Mystique*; Lim, *A Feeling of Belonging*. For more works on Wong, see Shimizu, *The Hypersexuality of Race*; Wang, "The Art of Screen Passing"; Metzger, "Patterns of Resistance?"; Hodges, *Anna May Wong*; Leibfried and Lane, *Anna May Wong*; Chan, *Perpetually Cool*.

5. Lowe, *Immigrant Acts*, 4; Wong, *Reading Asian American Literature*; Ngai, *Impossible Subjects*; Chan, *Asian Americans*; Lee, *At America's Gates*; Wu, *Dr. Mom Chung of the Fair-Haired Bastards*.

6. For more on Wong's global career, see Shirley Jennifer Lim, *Performing the Modern*, unpublished manuscript. For a thoughtful overview of Wong's reception in Europe, see Bergfelder, "Negotiating Exoticism."

7. Young, *Colonial Desire*.

8. Nenno et al., *The German Cinema Book*.

9. Since she changed her citizenship to French and remained in Europe,

Baker, unlike Wong, continued her European career into the post–World War II period. For more on Baker's 1950s politics, see Dudziak, "Josephine Baker, Racial Protest, and the Cold War."

10. *Song/Show Life/Schmutziges Geld* (1928), directed by Richard Eichberg, coproduced in France, England, and Germany under Ufa, headquartered in Babelsberg, Germany.

11. Reviews and stories appear in *O Brado Africano* and *South Africa Film and Screen*.

12. Bergfelder, 307.

13. *Tatler*, March 20, 1929; *Sketch*, August 22, 1928.

14. Fabian, *Time and the Other*.

15. *Sketch*, March 20, 1929, 557.

16. Woollacott, "Rose Quong Becomes Chinese."

17. Hubert Griffith, "Anna May Wong on the Stage: Her Dance the One Perfect Moment in a Play," "New Theatre" file, London Theatre Museum.

18. *Film Weekly*, February 11, 1929, cover.

19. Anna May Wong file, Margaret Herrick Library, Academy of Motion Pictures Arts and Sciences (AMPAS), October 26, 1932.

20. Anna May Wong file, AMPAS.

21. Anna May Wong file, AMPAS.

22. Brown, *Glamour in Six Dimensions*, 189n13.

23. See "Dark Continent," in Doane, *Femme Fatales*, 215; Kaplan, *Looking for the Other*, 73.

24. *New York Times*, April 14, 1930.

25. Chun, "'Go West to China,'" 168.

26. Cripps, *Slow Fade to Black*, 306.

27. Yu, *Thinking Orientals*; Lee, *Orientals*.

28. Section 5 cautioned against the use of ethnic slurs: "The Production Code Administration may take cognizance of the fact that the following words and phrases are obviously offensive to patrons of the motion pictures in the United States and more particularly to the patrons of motion pictures in foreign countries: Chink, Dago, Frog, Greaser, Hunkie, Kike, Nigger, Spic, Wop, Yid." Thus the Code encouraged movies more palatable to ethnic Americans and international audiences, such as one featuring a Chinese American female doctor.

29. Keye Luke, Southern California Chinese Historical Association Oral History Interview, 1978–82. Special Collections, University Research Library, University of California, Los Angeles.

30. This research was conducted with the support of an Australian National University Research School for the Humanities Fellowship. I thank David Walker, Agnieszka Sobocinska, and contributors to *Australia's Asia* for feedback on this work. Portions of this research in different form appear in Walker and Sobocinska, *Australia's Asia*.

31. "Anna May Wong," *Home*, August 1939, 50–51.

32. Walker, "Shooting Mabel"; Finnae, "'In the Same Bed Dreaming Differently.'"

33. Leong and Wu, "Filling the Rice Bowls of China."

34. Leong, *China Mystique*, chapter 3.

35. Deacon, "World English?," 76. Watching the newsreel, Deacon confirmed that Wong's accent fit the parameters of World English. An Australian audience member said that it was like hearing the Queen's English.

36. Woollacott, "Rose Quong Becomes Chinese," 16–31; Jayasuirya and Pookong, *The Asianization of Australia?*, 8; Markus, "Chinese Immigration under the 'White Australia Policy'"; Williams, "'Would This Not Help Your Federation.'"

37. Darian-Smith and Hamilton, *Memory and History in Twentieth Century Australia.*

38. Paisley, "'Unnecessary Crimes and Tragedies.'"

six

Roosevelt's Body and National Power

FRANK COSTIGLIOLA

"It is an amazing possibility that the next President of the United States may be a cripple," *Liberty, A Weekly for Everybody*, alerted Americans in its lead article on July 25, 1931. Flashing the title "Is Franklin D. Roosevelt Physically Fit to Be President?," the popular writer Earle Looker emphasized that two of the four most recent U.S. presidents, Woodrow Wilson and Warren G. Harding, had been "broken down by the burden" of their office. "A sound mind in a sound body had more and more come to be a requirement for the Presidency." America's "broken down" economy accentuated the need for robust leadership. Looker referenced the charge, made at a Democratic Party organization meeting and then widely circulated, that the governor of New York, because of the paralysis of his legs, "*is utterly unfit physically*" to be president. Identifying himself as a Republican and "an ardent admirer of the aggressively strenuous tradition of the Roosevelt name," Looker reminisced about playing with Theodore Roosevelt's boisterous brood in the White House. Now he challenged Franklin Roosevelt: "Could [you] stand the strain of the Presidency?"[1]

The origins, discourse, and impact of Looker's article exemplify Roosevelt's body politics from when he contracted polio in 1921 till his death in 1945. As the communications scholars David W. Houck and Amos Kiewe have pointed out, FDR and his aides used a mix of words, silences, and bodily performances to project the image of a leader uniquely gifted for guiding the nation out of the Depression.[2] Roosevelt applied the same strategy in helping persuade Winston Churchill and Joseph Stalin that the United States possessed the grit needed in the struggle against the Axis. As the most successful U.S. politician of the twentieth century, FDR commanded many strategies, including a flirtatious, even androgynous performance of gender. He made a political asset of his struggle against polio. He manipulated public perceptions of his paralysis. He did not attempt to dispel the reigning assumption that a president had to be physically fit. Instead he made it a practice to display himself, particularly his robust upper torso, while obscuring the severity of the paralysis in his legs. He understood, moreover, that his claim of near recovery bolstered his credentials for leading the economically crippled nation back to health. At pivotal, highly public moments, such as the 1924 and 1928 Democratic conventions and the 1941 Atlantic Conference with Churchill, Roosevelt made a show of "walking." The very laboriousness of his effort underscored his refusal to be made immobile—whether by his disease or by the reluctance of the American people to go to war. Roosevelt, who hated flying, also subjected himself to the rigors of journeying to far-off Iran and to Yalta in the Soviet Union to demonstrate to Stalin his determination to secure agreement on wartime and postwar policies. Although FDR was the only Allied leader to die during the war, Churchill and Stalin also bent under the crushing burdens of wartime leadership.

What Looker, with the connivance of Roosevelt and his entourage, presented in *Liberty* as a brusque challenge was really "a spectacular stunt to publicize his fine health," acknowledged FDR's admiring biographer Frank Freidel.[3] According to the article, Roosevelt had invited an autonomous writer to observe him and had agreed to a medical examination by the top doctors of New York State. In actuality, however, in December 1930 Looker had secured from FDR the exclusive right to write about the governor's personality and health. Looker then contacted an agent and a publisher who "enthusiastically" endorsed his project for the magazine article and a follow-up book, entitled *This Man Roosevelt*.[4] The "stunt" played on the faith of early twentieth-century modernity in "facts" arising from what Looker called "cold and dispassionate" observation and what Roosevelt cited as "scientific investigation." The writer spent several days with FDR and interviewed, he claimed, forty-three "disinterested persons in Albany and New York." The latter concurred that Roosevelt "seemed to be more physically able now than he had been four years before." Even after the doctors subjected Roosevelt to a ninety-minute examination, they withheld judgment, Looker related in the article, until "the facts [had] all been checked. And then checked again."[5]

Like many who gazed at Roosevelt, Looker marveled at the man's good looks. He seemed not to notice the withered legs; instead he compared his subject to the boxing champ Jack Dempsey: Roosevelt displayed a "Dempsey-like development of chest, with muscled athlete's wrists and great vigorous hands." The writer drew on racialized notions of physiognomy that associated certain facial features with superior character and ability. Roosevelt's "forehead was broad and high, his eyes widespread and blue, his nose straight, and his lips firm. This face was undeniably fine." Fine did not mean sissy. The tan, weathered skin evidenced exposure "to the glare of the sun and the stinging of salt spray." Looker admired how the governor could recharge his energies by viewing a movie, after which he went back to work on the state's business till 1 a.m. "He seemed able to take more punishment than many men ten years younger. Merely his legs were not much good to him."[6]

Even his handicap worked to the benefit of his constituents, Roosevelt argued. He allowed that he could not take breaks by strolling about his office, but "isn't it better if you have a big job to do, to be held to that job and not be able to waste time indulging in fidgets?" (Years later Roosevelt would claim that his handicap yielded another supposed advantage. Offended by overly solicitous aides, he snapped, "What do you think I am, a sissy? By the way, do you know what a sissy is? A man who gets out of the bathtub to take a piss.")[7] While Eleanor Roosevelt confided to friends her fear that the patriarchal culture of the White House would choke her independence, she recited the party line to Looker, assuring him, "If the paralysis couldn't kill him, the Presidency won't."[8]

In addition to submitting to the supposedly objective gaze of Looker and the doctors, Roosevelt cited "scientific evidence" of his own. He described his long stays at Warm Springs, Georgia, where he had established a rehabilitation facility for himself and other "polios." He claimed, "Recent scientific investigation has proven that exercise while swimming in tepid waters will restore nerve force to paralyzed limbs. Surely I am an example of it." Despite his bravado, Roosevelt had not "restore[d] nerve force" to his legs. Nevertheless he never lost hope—or admitted that he had. What he and his aides did rehabilitate was his image as a person physically "fit" to be president. As part of that campaign, Looker underscored the glowing report of the prestigious medical board. The doctors testified publicly that Roosevelt's "health and powers of endurance are such as to allow him to meet any demand of private and public life."[9] Privately they affirmed that FDR showed "no symptoms of *impotentia coeundi*"; despite the paralysis in his legs, the man remained sexually potent.[10]

Delighted with the *Liberty* article, FDR's campaign manager, James A. Farley, pronounced it a "corker" that "answers fully the questions . . . put to me many times" by worried Democratic Party officials. Longtime aide Louis M. Howe ordered thousands of reprints sent to Democratic Party leaders and journalists around the country.[11] Hoping to secure a permanent place in the rising star's entourage (he would not), Looker wrote Roosevelt, "I think we can be sure that at least seven and a half million readers are sure you are physically fit."[12]

At every Democratic Party convention from 1920 to 1932 Roosevelt advanced closer to national power. At each of those meetings he moved his body in a manner calculated to gain the admiring attention of observers while making the most of the physical capability he could muster at that particular time. Although the kinetics of Roosevelt's tactics differed at each convention, his political strategy remained unaltered. He would impress observing politicians and the wider public with not only his charm but also his enthusiasm, vigor, and mastery of dramatic movement. Regardless of whether it was before or after he contracted polio in 1921, the future president never simply walked to the rostrum. The ways that Roosevelt moved his body at these conventions became a synecdoche for his political style and message. He constantly projected the image of an innovative, resilient, and determined man of action.

Decades after observing FDR at the 1920 Democratic convention at San Francisco, Frances Perkins, the social reformer who became secretary of labor, still marveled at his physical presence. "Nobody who ever saw it will ever forget how handsome Franklin Roosevelt was. . . . He towered quite a bit over the average person . . . [and] he had a big voice. He was always rising. He was always having something to say." At one point, when the chairman refused to recognize his waving hand, Roosevelt, who was sitting well back from the front, "put his hands on the back of the chair in front of him and he vaulted—a regular gymnasium vault—over at least four or five rows of chairs." He scrambled onto the platform. Such athletic self-propulsion helped secure the vice-presidential slot for the ambitious thirty-eight-year-old. Though he and James Cox faced an uphill struggle in a nation weary of Democratic Party rule, FDR campaigned tirelessly. "The miles he covered were enormous," Perkins recalled; "he was young, vigorous, strong, and he didn't falter."[13]

By the time of the 1924 Democratic convention, the chair-vaulter of 1920 had suffered through three years of painful therapy. Despite this effort, he could not stand without braces or walk without crutches. Delegates had heard that Roosevelt "had polio and he was dead, so far they knew."[14] An invitation for Roosevelt to nominate New York governor Al Smith for president offered a chance for resurrection. The challenge lay in negotiating the fine line between displaying courage and evoking pity. Roosevelt devised for the occasion a way to "walk." He had his son James stand to his left so that he could grasp the young man's arm while placing most of his weight on a crutch under his right arm. Roosevelt could jerk forward by pivoting his body alternately right and left with his powerful shoulders. So as not to "scare everybody half to death," father and son bantered as they "walked." James later recalled that while his father's face was "beaming . . . his fingers dug into my arm like pincers—I doubt that he knew how hard he was gripping me. His face was covered with perspiration." The final fifteen feet to the podium Roosevelt shuffled forward alone, using two crutches.[15]

Whether FDR was "fit" for high office remained an issue particularly conducive to individualized interpretation or construction because the evidence was so ambiguous and the emotions so wrenching. As Roosevelt "walked" at the 1924 convention "there was a hush and everybody was holding their breath," Perkins later recounted. "The old-line politicians remembered him as a very vigorous young man at the previous convention. Here was this terribly crippled person. . . . It was a surprise . . . to see that his voice was strong and true and vigorous." Sitting close to the stage, she could see that the hand on the paper of his address "was literally shaking, because of the extreme pain and tenseness with which he held himself up to make that speech." But from a distance, "he looked well. . . . The man in the street just assumed, 'Isn't that wonderful. This fine fellow we thought dead still lives.'"[16]

If potential supporters were to sustain such faith, Roosevelt and his aides had to camouflage his disability. Perkins realized that after his convention speech—and the magic of his voice—wound down, the man with the paralyzed legs would be stuck up on that stage. In front of gawking thousands he would have to make an awkward, painful shift, from leaning on the podium to grasping his crutches and hobbling away on them. As the applause was fading Perkins and another woman rushed up to the stage to stand "in front of him so he didn't show." She later explained, "I realized somebody must do it. I saw all these fat slob politicians—men—around and I knew they wouldn't think of it." At subsequent public events she and other aides perfected "the trick of

Figure 6.1 and Figure 6.2. FDR with 1924 Democratic presidential candidate John W. Davis. In order to regain a footing in the political arena, Roosevelt had to project an image of sound health and radiant cheer. Yet he could not escape the pain and awkwardness imposed by the polio that had paralyzed his legs. Courtesy of the Franklin D. Roosevelt Library.

shielding him. Women could shield him better than men because we had skirts and coats. You could sort of lift your hand to fix your hat and that would make the coat hang like a large screen."[17]

The dual spectacles of the laborious "walk" and the inspiring talk cut two ways. On the one hand Roosevelt beguiled many delegates who, in the deadlocked convention of 1924, eyed him as an attractive dark horse candidate. Yet the assumption persisted that a man burdened by polio could not also take on the responsibilities of the White House. The Los Angeles Times concluded, "He is hopelessly an invalid, his legs paralyzed."[18] That description failed, however, to factor in the force of charisma. Tom Pendergast, the Kansas City political boss who would later launch the career of Harry Truman, remarked, "You know I am seldom carried away . . . but I want to tell you that had Mr. Roosevelt . . . been physically able to withstand the campaign, he would have been named by acclamation. . . . He has the most magnetic personality of any individual I have ever met."[19]

By 1928 that magnetism—assisted by adroit politicking and Governor Al Smith's decision to run for president—enabled Roosevelt to secure the Democratic nomination for governor of New York. At the Democratic convention where FDR nominated Smith, Roosevelt displayed an improved though still laborious method of "walking." Each leg was in a brace. In one hand he grasped a cane while leaning his other arm on the bent arm of his son Elliott. He dragged one foot and then swung his hips to bring the other leg forward. Reaching the podium, his body signaled triumph. Roosevelt beamed, his "head held high this time, braced legs spread wide apart to provide balance, one arm free now to wave and gesture."[20] His voice boomed.

The journalist and writer of popular history Will Durant saw in this body evidence of past torment and future promise. Here was "a figure tall and proud even in suffering; a face of classic profile; pale with years of struggle against paralysis; a frame nervous and yet self-controlled . . . most obviously a gentleman and a scholar. A man softened and cleansed and illumined with pain." An old friend had another reaction to the muscular upper torso: "Frank, you look like a gorilla!" Nevertheless prejudice about sickness, and especially about polio, persisted. Smith, whose personal feelings about Roosevelt would turn poisonous in future years, assured a friend that the younger man would never become a rival; indeed "he won't live a year."[21] FDR not only survived; he would be reelected governor by a huge margin in 1930 and shove Smith aside to secure the Democratic nomination for president in 1932.

In his 1928 campaign for governor, Roosevelt combated doubts about his health with relentless campaigning. He drew attention to his body's ability to endure the rigors of crisscrossing the state. FDR's strategy, Houck and Kiewe have noted, was "not to deny his disability but to modify its appearance, to argue its temporary nature, and to dialectically deflect the most severe accusations with sarcasm and irony—and with his own apparently healthy body."[22] "It seems to me that I am pretty husky," the candidate boasted to a crowd.[23] It was in this context of displaying his infectious charm, good looks, and upper body strength while obscuring the paralysis in his legs that Roosevelt connived with Looker.

By 1932, the fourth year of the Great Depression, the United States itself was suffering economic and political paralysis. Many commentators, whether they advocated or opposed governmental intervention in the economy, used the metaphor of bodily sickness in referring to hard times. In this discursive context, Roosevelt, who at Warm Springs and elsewhere called himself a "doctor," enjoyed an advantage over his opponent Herbert Hoover. Like the economy, FDR had to bear paralysis; he had also made a significant recovery; and he knew, or so he claimed, what it took to regain full health. Roosevelt's supposed triumph over disability also enabled him to snatch the mantle of hero from Hoover, who, having identified himself with the prosperity of the 1920s, was now blamed for the Crash.

After receiving news of his nomination by the Democratic convention in Chicago, Roosevelt stunned the nation by announcing that he would flout the tradition of waiting at home to receive formal notification. Instead he would fly from Albany to Chicago to accept the nomination in person and so jump-start his campaign. Elliott Roosevelt, who was on that flight, later recalled that his father "wanted to demonstrate by this gesture that he was a man of vigorous action, not the semi-invalid depicted without fail by his enemies in both parties."[24] FDR no doubt knew about the dramatic air campaign waged by a future foe, Adolf Hitler, who had recently barnstormed around Germany in seeking the presidency.[25]

Flying so far was risky. Knute Rockne, the famed University of Notre Dame football coach who had popularized the forward pass, had recently died in a plane crash. Roosevelt had never flown before; indeed he would come to hate flying, and he would refuse to travel by airplane again until wartime conferences made it imperative. With his paralyzed legs unable to brace him, his body jerked helplessly as the plane pitched up and down. Flying aggravated his sinus trouble. Though indifferent to most physical dangers, Roosevelt had a phobia about fire. He must have realized that if he did survive a plane crash, he would have to crawl away from the burning wreck. Planes of that era, with their underpowered engines and primitive navigation aids, were dangerous; indeed passengers in 1932 were two hundred times more likely to die in a crash than were those flying in postwar decades. American Airlines offered to put the governor, his family, and staff on a special flight. As a spokesman for the company admitted, "People were afraid to fly. To get a governor on a plane might help spread a little confidence. That's why we were willing to go to so much trouble." Roosevelt, who ordinarily indulged his triskaidekaphobia—refusing, for instance, to start a trip on the thirteenth of the month—allowed that number of family, friends, and staff to board the Ford Tri-Motor plane, the "Tin Goose." The plane was buffeted by winds "like a balloon," the pilot later reported.[26] After the eight-hour ordeal the candidate landed in Chicago.

The New York Times depicted the trip as symbolizing the candidate's manner and message. His "appearance and address" embodied "something of the breeziness that went naturally with his flight through the air. The dash and vigor which he had shown by setting out for Chicago in an airplane also marked his speech."[27] Pretense and aplomb could be effective, as his Republican rival Hoover understood. When an advisor assured Hoover that the assembled delegates "would see Roosevelt's physical helplessness," the president countered that "the audience would not be allowed to see Roosevelt's helplessness but that it would be cleverly concealed by the skillful handling of him."[28] Hoover had observed at a White House conference that aides had shielded FDR whenever photographers seemed about to capture his disability.

A story in the Republican-leaning *Chicago Daily Tribune* titled "The Nominee in Action" suggests that while Roosevelt's disability was apparent, so was his success at surmounting it. The reporter, James O'Donnell Bennett, noted that Roosevelt could walk only "haltingly." He moved "slowly and stiffly, as a very old man might." Nevertheless "he smiles, he nods, he chuckles." Echoing Looker's article, Bennett wrote, "Your first impression is the impression of the commanding stature of the man—his height, his broad shoulders, his big chest. You are not conscious of his lameness, for with the aid of the cane, he holds himself steadily on his feet." "At no time" during his forty-six-minute acceptance speech did Roosevelt "betray weariness." Bennett concluded that while "many may think of [Roosevelt] as a patient invalid, he goes strong." For a nation with an "invalid" economy, a leader who could "go strong" commanded emotional appeal.[29]

Borrowing from what had worked so well in his campaigns for governor, Roosevelt displayed himself. His train would stop wherever there was a gathering. The candidate, leaning on a cane and on the arm of his son James, would "walk" to the rear railing, enabling the crowd to see his robust upper torso. As a reporter observed, "The whole idea of the Governor's managers is to let the people see him during the day and hear him at night over the radios while the vision of his large, handsome features and broad shoulders is still in their minds."[30]

Part of the reason Roosevelt's "splendid deception" succeeded is that so many wanted to believe that the paralysis meant little in terms of how he exercised national power. In Montana "the women are also saying that he appeared in splendid physical condition and that he must be a remarkable man to have overcome his unfortunate physical disabilities in such a complete manner."[31] As president FDR was both praised and pilloried, but he was rarely depicted as paralyzed. The ubiquitous political cartoons of the president often pictured him in motion, walking, running, or jumping. Indeed the 1942 hit film *Yankee Doodle Dandy* featured Jimmy Cagney playing a tap-dancing President Roosevelt.[32] Moreover the president's handlers had the aid of the Secret Service in obscuring the disability. Husky agents prohibited photographs of the president as he was being carried into a building or a car.[33] Journalists, many of whom rooted for Roosevelt despite the Republican bias of their editors and publishers, would assist by "accidentally" knocking to the ground any cameras that violated the rule.

Nevertheless Roosevelt himself remained vulnerable to being knocked to the ground, particularly at those iconic moments when "walking" was crucial to his getting across two key messages: first, that the United States would emerge from the Depression with a more fair and stable economy; second, that despite its reluctance to go to war, the nation would resist Axis aggression. At the 1936 Democratic Party convention thousands in the meeting hall and millions more listening on their radios thrilled as Roosevelt promised, "This generation of Americans has a rendezvous with destiny." He boomed out those words just minutes after a nosedive. As he was laboriously "walking" to the rostrum, stopping frequently to chat with supporters, he was jostled. Suddenly he lost his balance; a leg brace popped open, and Roosevelt collapsed. Diving to the floor, a Secret Service agent managed to get his shoulder under the falling man. The sheets of the speech went flying. Aides clustered round to hide the embarrassment. "Clean me up," Roosevelt snapped. "And keep your feet off those damned sheets." He later admitted, "It was the most frightful five minutes of my life." With the president and his speech put together, he ordered, "Let's go."[34] On reaching the platform he again beamed confidence and control.

Roosevelt's policies, personality, and body politics enabled him to win elections, enact significant reforms, and combat the economic downturn. Despite successes, however, his spending initiatives remained too timid to vanquish the Depression. Only World War II would bring the massive deficit spending needed to restore prosperity. Harbingers of this global conflict appeared only weeks after Looker's article in Liberty. With the Depression choking off its export trade, Japan on September 18, 1931, seized control of Manchuria in order to secure markets and raw materials. Days later Great Britain broke its ties with the dollar-dominated gold standard and took other steps to reserve for itself the resources of its empire. The open global economy of the 1920s was collapsing into the system of closed-door blocs that would strangle world trade and impel military conquest by the Axis. By 1941 Nazi Germany had swallowed much of Europe and seemed likely to gobble up the Middle East. Japan, already controlling much of China, was poised to snatch Southeast Asia or Siberia.

"This is essentially a young man's war," warned Robert Boothby, an advisor to Prime Minister Churchill. To Boothby, Axis aggression figured as a masculine force: a "young, virile, dynamic, and violent" juggernaut "advancing irresistibly to overthrow a decaying old world."[35] In terms of relative youth, in 1941 Hitler would turn fifty-two, Benito Mussolini fifty-eight, Roosevelt fifty-nine, Stalin sixty-three, and Churchill sixty-seven. If Britain, the United States, and the Soviet Union were to halt and eventually destroy that aggression, they had to generate a "virile, dynamic" force of their own.

Churchill, Stalin, and Roosevelt each faced a related personal challenge: persuading the other two leaders that he was fit, trustworthy, capable, and vigorous and that he commanded enough strength, courage, perseverance, and toughness to defeat a frightening, malevolent enemy. Yet each man deviated in some way from the generalized masculine norm that had come to prevail in all three countries despite differences in their national cultures. According to that norm, top leaders should be brave and able-bodied, with a cool demeanor and dependable judgment. Churchill had a history of erratic decision making and a reputation as a heavy drinker who careened from exuberance to depression. A former bank robber and Bolshevik revolutionary, Stalin had killed off most of his military and civilian leadership and had then allied with Hitler. Roosevelt could not walk unaided; he appeared unwilling to challenge public opinion in a nation that still shrank from fighting. Hardly promising material.

Nevertheless the very plasticity of FDR's gender performance proved a winning asset. While quick to acknowledge Roosevelt's essential masculinity, observers also tried to account for why he appealed so intensely to men as well as to women. Lacking a vocabulary for what the feminist and queer theorist Eve Kosofsky Sedgwick has analyzed as "homosocial" feeling, some of FDR's contemporaries labeled as "feminine" an allure that a later generation, more attuned to gender bending, could interpret as flowing from a generic sexuality.[36]

FDR's repertoire of behaviors included some that contemporaries described as feminine. Theodore Roosevelt's daughter, Alice Longworth, called young Franklin a "feather-duster" because "he pranced around and fluttered."[37] The polio he contracted at age thirty-nine further complicated his gender performance.[38] He compensated for the paralysis of his legs by moving with his voice and head. The tendency toward nonstop gesture and talk violated the prevailing stereotype of strong, masculine men. Thomas "Tommy the Cork" Corcoran, an insider who observed Roosevelt at work and play, later described him as "the most androgynous human being I have ever known in my life."[39] That androgyny probably enhanced FDR's glamour and charm. Charm, particularly when distilled into charisma, can prove sexy even if the eroticism remains implicit.

As 1941 dawned, the men who would become the Big Three had few grounds for trusting each other and forging an alliance. They remained largely strangers. Crossing oceans and continents so that they might talk face to face could foster personal attachments, trust, and understandings that might then condition future political decisions. Roosevelt and Churchill believed that at such meetings they could persuade, charm, clarify attitudes, heal rifts, demonstrate respect, and discern trustworthiness. Diplomacy, particularly at the highest levels, entailed homosocial flirtation and seduction. After the November–December 1943 Tehran summit, Stalin would agree. Long-distance journeys, however, remained arduous, especially for Roosevelt, who remained averse to flying. More than Roosevelt or Stalin, Churchill was eager to travel. Moreover he stood out as the petitioner, desperate for U.S. help. Accordingly the first Allied summit took place in Argentia Bay off the coast of Newfoundland in August 1941, where the prime minister risked the submarine-infested Atlantic to meet with the president.

Despite an "extremely cold and violent wind" blowing across the deck of the battleship *Prince of Wales*, Churchill spent hours directing rehearsals for the joint religious service that was planned as the emotional centerpiece of the conference. He expected that FDR, because of his paralysis, would be compelled to stand in place as British officers filed past him.[40] Shortly before the Sunday service, Roosevelt sent word that he would walk, not just stand. He boarded the *Prince of Wales* "leaning on a stick and linking his [other] arm" with his son Elliot. Churchill's aide observed, "It is a very great effort for the President to walk, and it took him a long time to get from the gangway to his chair." On the one hand, FDR was trying to obscure what was obvious: "His legs are evidently rather wasted and he has not much control over them."[41] On the other hand, he was demonstrating—as he had at the Democratic conventions—that he *could* walk. Roosevelt was defying the jibes of the dictators and upending the considerate though patronizing assumptions of Churchill. He wanted his prospective ally to judge him, and the nation he led, as courageous and fit. Resembling, as some onlookers put it, "a sort of marriage service," the procession reflected and reinforced a variety of homosocial emotional reactions.[42]

While conferences in far-off places could prove exhausting, they also packed excitement. Powerful men gathering in "exotic" locations to plan battles and decide the fate of nations were trading the everyday for the enticing and the exotic. At the January 1943 Casablanca Conference in North Africa, Roosevelt and Churchill enjoyed quarters that seemed sensuous to the verge of erotic. FDR delighted in the "most beautiful bedroom he ever had, and the most beautiful bed."[43] He enjoyed sleeping in—and describing—a room that appeared sexy in an androgynous way. His room had belonged to a "very feminine French lady. Plenty of drapes, plenty of frills."[44] He quipped to his body guard, "Mike, what did you do with the madam and the red curtains?"[45] Close by was a library filled with pornography.[46]

With business settled, Churchill invited Roosevelt to his favorite getaway, the ancient city of Marrakech. They stayed at Flower Villa. Even the official log gushed about this "most beautiful" lodging, "furnished in splendor befitting a Sultan."[47] FDR agreed to ascend the tower of the villa to take in the magnificent view of the snow-covered Atlas Mountains. Two aides made a chair with their arms and carried the president up the steps, "his legs dangling like the limbs of a ventriloquist's dummy, limp and flaccid," Churchill's doctor recorded. The setting sun lit the snowy mountains with a pink glow. Churchill murmured, "It's the most lovely spot in the whole world."[48] As the sun set Churchill, in an affectionate gesture, spread a coat over Roosevelt's shoulders.

The homoerotic undertones of the Marrakech interlude were hard to miss. Roosevelt's advisors described their host, the consul Kenneth Pendar, as "a rather effeminate man" playing "hostess" at the dinner.[49] They nicknamed Flower Villa "Pansy Palace."[50] FDR stretched out on the couch, and as Pendar approached, he smiled, saying, "I am the Pasha, you may kiss my hand." At dinner the president displayed his knowledge of the Arabic world, including "the conflict of Koranic law with our type of modern life."[51] At day's end FDR promised Churchill, "I'll be wheeled into your room to kiss you goodbye."[52] The next morning the prime minister—arrayed in black velvet slippers monogrammed "W.C.," a blue air marshal's cap, and a bathrobe patterned with red dragons—accompanied FDR to the airport. As the plane took off, Churchill took Pendar's arm, saying, "If anything should happen to that man, I couldn't stand it. He is the truest friend; he has the farthest vision; he is the greatest man I've ever known."[53] Churchill reclimbed the tower, trying to capture with oil on canvas the view and the intimacy.

In the two years prior to the Tehran summit of November 1943, Roosevelt tried to lure Stalin to a "Marrakech" of their own. He believed that a meeting à deux would enable him to work his charm while offering the suspicious dictator assurance of a lasting entente. FDR envisioned a postwar order run by the "Four Policemen"—the United States, Britain,

Russia, and China—each patrolling its part of the world and cooperating on keeping the peace. Stalin appreciated this implicit recognition of Soviet dominance in Eastern Europe. In May 1943 FDR sent an old friend to Moscow to invite Stalin to a meeting, without Churchill, in either Alaska or Siberia. Stalin assured the emissary, "Your President is a great man. I will be very glad to meet with him." As to whether the conference would take place in Siberia, the Kremlin boss, flashing apparent empathy, said, "No. The President has difficulty in walking, as I understand. It is difficult for me, physically, to come by air, but I will be glad to meet him at Nome or Fairbanks, whichever he prefers. This will make it easier for him."[54] Within days, however, Stalin was probably cursing the very notion of a cozy meeting. He learned that Churchill for the third time since mid-1942 had convinced Roosevelt to postpone the second front desperately needed by the Soviets to relieve the pressure of the German invaders.

Roosevelt's meeting with Stalin did not take place until late November 1943 in Tehran, and then only in the company of Churchill. Nevertheless the president still aimed for accord with the dictator. Dreading another transatlantic flight as he had endured for Casablanca, FDR boarded the battleship USS *Iowa*. An escort vessel accidentally fired a live torpedo at the president's ship. As the captain ordered, "Right full rudder—all engines ahead full" and the ship swerved, Roosevelt flung out his arm to grab hold.[55] His powerful upper body could not have stabilized him in an airplane. In Tehran Roosevelt learned that German agents were plotting his assassination; crossing the city from the U.S. legation could prove deadly. Stalin invited him into the Soviet Embassy while moving to a building nearby. Roosevelt later explained that accepting this hospitality "was a small thing to do to please" them. "If we could woo them"—the phrase was suggestive of FDR's strategy—"in this way, perhaps it was the cheapest thing we could do." He added, "It was a matter of exhibiting my trust in them, my complete confidence in them. And it did please them. No question about it."[56]

One reason it pleased the Soviets was that they had bugged Roosevelt's quarters.[57] Just as FDR had tried to lure the Kremlin chief to Alaska, and Churchill had enticed the president to Marrakech, now Stalin was seeking closer relations Kremlin-style. He assigned agents to transcribe everything FDR said. Attitudes seemed important: Stalin demanded to know "how Roosevelt said something—even what his intonation was."[58] FDR apparently seized the chance to foster trust and intimacy. The transcriber got "the impression that sometimes Roosevelt quite simply said things [into the microphones] he couldn't say to Stalin officially. That he conveyed a whole lot of information to him which it was impossible to convey at a state level."[59]

Valentin Berezhkov, one of Stalin's interpreters, later recalled that his boss "was determined to make a favorable impression on Roosevelt." The dictator seemed anxious that the appearance of his body could have political consequences. He was short and his face was scarred from small pox. "Stalin cased the room, worrying where FDR's wheelchair should be placed and where he himself should sit." He arranged the seating so that his pockmarks would appear in shadow. He put heel-lifts in his shoes.[60]

With the president settled in, the dictator paid him a visit. "With a most engaging grin on his face," Stalin ambled over to Roosevelt, who, sitting in his wheelchair, said, "I am glad to see you. I have tried for a long time to bring this about."[61] Roosevelt suggested their proximity would enable them to confer "more frequently in completely informal and different circumstances."[62] His aide later described such meetings: "Stalin and his interpreter stopped by unannounced for chats. The dictator, who could lavish extraordinary courtesy on favorites—including some he later had executed—would ask Roosevelt, did he need anything? Was he comfortable? . . . all the while smiling and showing great deference for his guest." Each was flirting while showing the other respect. The Georgian "showed genuine liking for Roosevelt," the aide would recall.[63]

Although Tehran outlined a rough schema for postwar cooperation, the meeting and its follow-up were limited by frailties of the body. After the flight into Tehran Stalin appeared "exhausted and for that reason not in the best of humor."[64] Churchill arrived with a head cold. "He is not fit and not in the best of moods," observed his military advisor.[65] The mood of the prime minister worsened; dwelling on "how inadequate" British power seemed, he sank into "black depression," saying, "I want to sleep for billions of years." He begged his doctor, who supplied his barbiturates and other drugs, "Can't you give me something so that I won't feel so exhausted?"[66] Afterward he suffered a bout of severe pneumonia. Though excited about meeting Stalin, FDR had dreaded going "to Tehran, which is full of disease" and lay across mountains requiring, after the *Iowa* docked, a high-altitude flight.[67] Earl Miller, a body guard and family friend, later wrote that the "Boss" "contracted an intestinal bug." He added that "most of the Secret Service was ill most of the time while [in Tehran]—water, food or whatever."[68] After returning to the States, FDR came down with influenza. In March 1944 he would be diagnosed with congestive heart failure.

As the February 1945 Yalta summit approached, Roosevelt was torn between the demands of his duty and his body. His close friend Margaret "Daisy" Suckley recorded, "He doesn't relish this trip at all. . . . Thinks it will be very wearing, & feels that he will have to be so much on the alert, in his conversations with Uncle Joe [Stalin] & W[inston] S. C[hurchill]." Especially with the prime minister present, "the conversations will last interminably & will involve very complicated questions."[69]

Despite the physical strains of getting to the conference and conducting diplomacy there, Roosevelt was not, as some critics later charged, the "sick man of Yalta," too ill to stand up to Stalin. The trip was certainly exhausting. After traveling by ship to the Mediterranean island of Malta, Roosevelt boarded his new plane, the *Sacred Cow*. An aide recalled that no one aboard slept "because a plane took off alongside us every ten minutes until we left" at 3:30 a.m. Even then the vibration and pitching of the aircraft hampered sleep. "The President was already a tired man when we arrived at Saki air field," the aide later recounted. That arrival began what the aide—a robust man who would live for many years—called "one of the most tiring days I have ever experienced."[70] They endured a five-hour, freezing auto trip from Saki to Yalta over curving roads with no retaining walls. FDR slept part of the way. Upon awakening he was stunned at the destruction. "The sight of it now made him want to exact an eye for an eye from the Germans."[71]

Despite the strain, Roosevelt, as usual, bounced back. A British official acknowledged that FDR "looks rather better."[72] Charles E. "Chip" Bohlen, who interpreted for the president, remembered that while his "physical state was certainly not up to normal, his mental and psychological state was certainly not affected." He remained "mentally sharp" and "effective."[73] Berezhkov later testified that "everybody who watched [FDR] said that in spite of his frail appearance, his mental potential was high." He emphasized, "Those who say that Roosevelt did not quite grasp what was going on in Yalta are wrong. Stalin treated Roosevelt with great esteem."[74] Dr. Howard Bruenn, the president's cardiologist, later recalled that at Yalta Roosevelt's "mental clarity was truly remarkable." His "recollection of detail" outshone "associates ten and twenty years younger than himself."[75]

Heart disease did not account for all the bodily problems. Roosevelt's intermittent slack jaw, blank stare, hand tremor, and forgetfulness probably arose from encephalopathy (reduced supply of oxygen to the brain) resulting from heart and obstructive pulmonary disease and the phenobarbital he took.[76] Patients with low-grade encephalopathy often do better when facing challenges.[77] Recurring difficulty in signing his name originated from the polio, which had mildly affected his right hand and sometimes acted up.[78] Despite all these physical problems, Roosevelt remained mentally fit.

By journeying so far to meet with Stalin, Churchill and Roosevelt were, according to diplomatic custom, paying the dictator great respect. Sublimely self-confident, FDR had little compunction about this homage or about his own physical discomfort if he could secure his postwar aims. A close observer later reflected that Stalin seemed to "realize that Roosevelt had shortened his life in order to come meet with him because he cared so much about the future of the world."[79] Other Americans, however, seethed at the perceived humiliation springing from FDR's efforts to overcome his handicap. The Pentagon's liaison to the Red Army, General John R. Deane, later testified, "No single event of the war irritated me more than seeing the President of the United States lifted from wheel chair, to ship, to shore . . . in order to go halfway around the world as the only possible means of meeting J. V. Stalin."[80] The dictator did respond to Roosevelt's show of respect and regard. He arranged for the Americans to live in the conference headquarters, the fifty-room summer home of the czar, Livadia Palace, while he resided six miles away. It was probably no accident that the British were placed ten miles distant. A shop had been set up to produce for the floors marble smooth enough for a wheelchair.

Stalin, abandoning his customary harshness, seemed genuinely to care for Roosevelt. After leaving the president's room, he reportedly stopped, turned to his aides, and asked, "Why did nature have to punish him so? Is he any worse than other people?" The head of the secret police marveled "how full of consideration he is where Roosevelt is concerned, when, as a rule, he is dreadfully rude."[81] A presidential aide later recalled that Stalin "deferred to [Roosevelt] and his whole expression softened when he addressed the President directly."[82] Another observer remembered that Stalin "really admired Roosevelt and had great respect for him."[83] Indeed Churchill complained that on issue after issue, "Stalin made it plain at once that if this was the President's wish, he would accept it."[84] Roosevelt's successor, Harry S. Truman, would never develop the personal and political ties with Stalin that FDR had so carefully cultivated.

Once Roosevelt was back home, Daisy rejoiced "that F[ranklin] looks so much better than anyone can expect—his color is good & his blood pressure is pretty good.[85] Walter Lippmann, who before the 1944 election had called FDR a tired old man, agreed that he had returned "manifestly" in "good health and much refreshed."[86] On March 1 Dr. Bruenn recorded, "Patient has rested well. Cough has disappeared. No cardiac symptoms."[87] But wasn't FDR's death imminent?

Nearly all histories of Roosevelt's last year track an irresistible story line: Great Leader Dies on Eve of Triumph. Pervasive cultural memories—of Moses dying as he approached the Promised Land and of Lincoln being assassinated just after the Confederacy surrendered—add emotional resonance to this grand narrative. Accounts of Roosevelt's demise have clinched the sentimental script. The drama of the fallen war hero seduces us into underplaying the contingency of Roosevelt's death weeks before V-E Day. FDR continued his strategy for cheating death—and for cheating those who calculated on his dying in office. Believing he was a man of destiny, he did not prepare any of his vice presidents. He may well have been deluding himself about his own mortality, but he also had before him the example of people who had performed long after others had given them up for dead: his father, who survived a decade after his heart attack and died at seventy-two, and his mother, who thrived until the age of eighty-six.

After returning from Yalta, FDR focused on issue number one: overall cooperation with Moscow. He resisted pressure from Churchill and others to break with Stalin.[88] He looked forward instead to meeting the Big Three—now institutionalized as the UN Security Council—in a cozy getaway, possibly the Azores. He personally authored the last telegram sent to Churchill before his death: "I would minimize the general Soviet problem as much as possible. . . . We must be firm, however, and our course thus far is correct."[89] Despite failing energy, Roosevelt was working late into the night. By late March he looked "very badly," Bruenn recorded. "Color is poor (grey). Very tired."[90]

Nevertheless within days of arriving at Warm Springs on March 30, FDR showed "decided improvement."[91] His blood pressure levels, however, fluctuated. By April 10 he was eating double helpings, and his face had regained color. He was taking it easy while also working through baskets of papers. He looked like he was recovering, yet again. Then, on Thursday, April 12, he was signing documents when he suddenly bent forward. Roosevelt soon lost consciousness and died at 3:30 p.m.

In projecting the image of a charming, vigorous man on the move, Roosevelt deployed camouflage, a phalanx of aides, emotional control, jaw-clenching exertion, and—not least—a flexible performance of his masculine identity. His body politics underscored that he was a man for his time, a synecdoche of the nation. For a people unsure how to escape the crippling Depression, he embodied confidence that recovery was possible and that he, someone who had restored his own fitness, could lead the way. To a world wondering whether the United States would assume the burdens of helping to defeat the Axis and engaging in the postwar world, Roosevelt demonstrated that America had grit and would venture abroad, however painful the steps. Attuned to emotional reactions, FDR probably understood that the spectacle of his intense effort as well as the appeal of his flirtatious charm—whether at the Democratic conventions, on the deck of the *Prince of Wales,* or in intimate meetings with Stalin and Churchill—could sway and even transform others. An observer recalled how Roosevelt's "slow procession became extremely impressive." People seemed "hypnotized. . . . An audience of strangers had become a group of friends."[92]

Confident in the combined force of his personal charm, the American example, and the U.S. military and economic machine, Roosevelt believed that his face-to-face meetings with top leaders (excepting the extremist Hitler) could ease the thorniest political problems. He risked his precarious health in pursuit of long-term collaboration with Stalin and Churchill. All three leaders came to appreciate the seductive potential of intimate meetings of powerful men. At secluded conclaves they could not only conduct business but also assess each other's mettle and intentions as they joked, argued, drank, ate, and otherwise shared in the daily activities of mind and body. Homosocial emotions inflected their political interactions. While Stalin seized every opportunity to spy on Roosevelt and Churchill, FDR, who also enjoyed secrets, pragmatically used the hidden microphones to amplify his message to the dictator. Mindful of the challenges threatening postwar collaboration, FDR believed that regular summit meetings could help shepherd the difficult transition to a more stable, peaceful world.

Lacking Roosevelt's self-confidence and cosmopolitan outlook, President Truman resolved after the July–August 1945 Potsdam Conference that he would not again attend such meetings, especially not with the Soviets. Churchill and Stalin, by contrast, continued to suggest, even during the worst of the cold war, that a face-to-face get-together might ease tensions. Even as U.S. leaders eschewed intimate meetings with the Soviets in the decade after FDR's death, they underscored the efficacy of such personal contact. Though Truman himself did not relish such contact, his advisors fostered a culture of the Western alliance by instituting regular, lengthy, face-to-face meetings of foreign ministers, defense ministers, economic ministers, and their respective aides. Embodying a political relationship made it more powerful.

Notes

1. Earl Looker, "Is Franklin D. Roosevelt Physically Fit to Be President?," *Liberty Magazine*, July 25, 1931, 6–7; Freidel, *Franklin D. Roosevelt: The Triumph*, 210–11 (emphasis in original).

2. Houck and Kiewe, *FDR's Body Politics*.

3. Freidel, *Roosevelt: The Triumph*, 210.

4. Houck and Kiewe, *FDR's Body Politics*, 66.

5. Looker, "Is Roosevelt Fit," 10.

6. Looker, "Is Roosevelt Fit," 8–10.

7. Roosevelt quoted in memorandum by Drew Pearson, n.d., file F169, Drew Pearson papers, Lyndon B. Johnson Presidential Library, Austin, Texas.

8. Looker, "Is Roosevelt Fit," 8–10.

9. Looker, "Is Roosevelt Fit," 8–10.

10. Smith, FDR, 705n37.

11. Looker, "Is Roosevelt Fit," 10; Freidel, *Roosevelt: The Triumph*, 211.

12. Houck and Kiewe, *FDR's Body Politics*, 67.

13. Reminiscences of Frances Perkins (1955), Columbia University Oral History Research Office Collection (hereafter CUOHRC), 2: 69, 74.

14. Reminiscences of Perkins (1955), CUOHRC, 2: 547.

15. Ward, *A First Class Temperament*, 695–96.

16. Reminiscences of Perkins (1955), CUOHRC, 2: 325, 548.

17. Reminiscences of Perkins (1955), CUOHRC, 2: 325–26, 565.

18. Houck and Kiewe, *FDR's Body Politics*, 31.

19. Freidel, *Franklin D. Roosevelt: The Ordeal*.

20. Smith, FDR, 785.

21. Ward, *A First-Class Temperament*, 785, 789, 788. See also Curell and Cogdell, *Popular Eugenics*.

22. Houck and Kiewe, *FDR's Body Politics*, 50.

23. Houck and Kiewe, *FDR's Body Politics*, 47.

24. Houck and Kiewe, *FDR's Body Politics*, 84.

25. Smith, FDR, 710n117.

26. Smith, FDR, 276.

27. Houck and Kiewe, *FDR's Body Politics*, 92.

28. Houck and Kiewe, *FDR's Body Politics*, 85.

29. James O'Donnell Bennett, "The Nominee in Action," *Chicago Daily Tribune*, July 3, 1932.

30. Houck and Kiewe, *FDR's Body Politics*, 98.

31. Houck and Kiewe, *FDR's Body Politics*, 107.

32. See Off the Record.mp4, http://www.youtube.com/watch?v=bV-U1DJxsAM.

33. For one instance of such enforcement by the Secret Service, see FDR Library, Hyde Park, NY, "FDR in Poughkeepsie," http://www.youtube.com/watch?v=qWYR3eC3hQw.

34. Smith, FDR, 367.

35. Colville, *The Fringes of Power*, 166–67.

36. Sedgwick, *Between Men*.

37. Ward, *First Class Temperament*, 551.

38. On the perceived association between disability and femininity, see Thomson, *Extraordinary Bodies*, 19–29; Kudlick, "Disability History," 108.

39. Reminiscences of Marquis Childs (1959), CUOHRC, 109–10. On androgyny, see Weil, *Androgyny and the Denial of Difference*; Heilbrun, *Toward a Recognition of Androgyny*.

40. Morton, *Atlantic Meeting*, 78.

41. Ian Jacob diary, August 10, 1941, Churchill Archive, University of Cambridge.

42. Borgwardt, *A New Deal for the World*, 1–45, 305.

43. Belle Willard Roosevelt diary, Mar. 1943, box 136, Kermit Roosevelt papers, Library of Congress, Washington.

44. Roosevelt, *As He Saw It*, 66.

45. Reilly, *Reilly of the White House*, 152.

46. Richardson, *From Churchill's Secret Circle to the BBC*, 156.

47. U.S. Department of State, *Foreign Relations of the United States (FRUS): The Conferences at Washington, 1941–1942, and Casablanca, 1943*, 535.

48. Moran, *Churchill at War*, 99 (both quotations).

49. Herbert Feis interview with Harriman, Nov. 16, 1953, box 872, W. Averell Harriman papers, Library of Congress.

50. Kimball, *Forged in War*, 195.

51. Pendar, *Adventure in Diplomacy*, 149–50.

52. Pendar, *Adventure in Diplomacy*, 153.

53. Sherwood, *Roosevelt and Hopkins*, 694; Pendar, *Adventure in Diplomacy*, 154.

54. Joseph E. Davies, "Meetings with Stalin and Molotov," May 20, 1943, box 13, Davies papers, Library of Congress.

55. Captain John L. McCrea, "History of the USS *Iowa*," box 11, John L. McCrea papers, Library of Congress.

56. Reminiscences of Perkins, CUOHRC, 8: 312.

57. U.S. Department of State, FRUS: *The Conferences at Cairo and Tehran*, 461–63; Berezhkov, *History in the Making*, 249–52; Reilly, *Reilly of the White House*, 175–78.

58. CNN interview with Sergo Beria (1996), http://www.kcl.ac.uk/lhcma/cats/coldwar/xc70–28-.shtml.

59. CNN interview with Sergo Beria (1996), http://www.kcl.ac.uk/lhcma/cats/coldwar/xc70–28-.shtml.

60. Schlesinger and Schlesinger, *Journals*, 691.

61. FRUS Tehran, 483; Reilly, *Reilly of the White House*, 179.

62. FRUS Tehran, 483.

63. Rigdon, *White House Sailor*, 81–82.

64. FRUS Tehran, 838.

65. Danchev and Todman, *War Diaries*, 482; Dilks, *The Diaries of Sir Alexander Cadogan*, 578.

66. Moran, *Churchill at War*, 169, 171, 180.

67. Ward, *Closest Companion*, 252, 250.

68. Earl Miller letter to Joseph P. Lash, [1968], box 44, Lash papers, FDR Library.

69. Ward, *Closest Companion*, 390.

70. Wilson Brown, unpublished memoir, 183, FDR Library.

71. Boettiger Yalta diary, Feb. 3, 1945, box 84, Halsted papers, FDR Library; Plokhy, *Yalta*, 37–38.

72. Dilks, *The Diaries of Sir Alexander Cadogan*, 704.

73. Bohlen, *Witness to History*, 172.

74. Valentin Berezhkov to Arthur Schlesinger Jr. [n.d., but probably 1970s], box 2, Miscellaneous Documents, Small Collections, FDR Library.

75. Bruenn to Ross McIntire, Aug. 1, 1946, Bruenn papers, FDR Library.

76. Bruenn, "Clinical Notes," Apr. 23, 1944; Sept. 20, 1944; Mar. 1, 1945, Bruenn papers.

77. Bruenn, "Clinical Notes," Apr. 23, 1944; Sept. 20, 1944; Mar. 1, 1945, Bruenn papers; Lomazow and Fettmann, *FDR's Deadly Secret*, 154.

78. Ward, *Closest Companion*, 396.

79. Kathleen Harriman, interview with Abramson, #4, Dec. 9, 1987, in private possession.

80. Deane, *The Strange Alliance*, 160.

81. Beria, *Beria*, 106.

82. Wilson Brown memoir, 186.

83. Kathleen Harriman, interview with Abramson, #1, May 12, 1983, in private possession.

84. Moran, *Churchill at War*, 279.

85. Ward, *Closest Companion*, 398.

86. Walter Lippmann, *Today and Tomorrow*, Mar. 3, 1945.

87. Bruenn, "Clinical Notes," Mar. 1, 1945, Bruenn papers.

88. Kimball, *Churchill and Roosevelt*, 588.

89. Kimball, *Churchill and Roosevelt*, 630; Glantz, *FDR and the Soviet Union*, 161–62.

90. Bruenn, "Clinical Notes," Mar. 16, 28, 1945, Bruenn papers.

91. Bruenn, "Clinical Notes," Apr. 6, 1945, Bruenn papers.

92. Philip Hamburger, "Talk of the Town," *New Yorker*, Nov. 17, 1962.

seven

Making "Brown Babies"
Race and Gender after World War II

BRENDA GAYLE PLUMMER

"Brown babies," a euphemism the black press popularized, were
the children born of European women and African American soldiers
during the World War II era. Their confused civil status, mixed-race
identity, and urgent material needs engaged the complex intersection
of race, gender, and nation as it unfolded after 1945. They clearly represented the eruption of the biological into the carefully organized—if
wholly self-contradictory—racial hierarchies the United States enforced
in occupied Europe. Brown babies were born as regimes of racial domination toppled in Europe and Asia and as ideological slippage afflicted
Jim Crow in America. U.S. legal segregation survived the Third Reich,
but the seeds of its demise had already germinated by war's end. Exis-
tentially at the margins of the postwar experience, biracial war orphans
exposed the structural racism embedded in the conflicts of the age. This
essay examines these children's place in the broader context of postwar
decision making and demonstrates the intimate relationship between
their plight and American designs for the future, two subjects generally
treated as entirely separate in historical scholarship but joined here to
illuminate a critical intersection in the biopolitics of the age.

By 1945 the U.S. Army had already circumscribed the status of biracial
children yet to be born. In the European Operating Theater commanding officers could veto or approve GI marriages on their own discretion.

Few black soldiers were allowed to marry British and Italian women, for example, even when they had fathered their children.[1] Commanding officers likewise blocked interracial marriages in Germany, where some 1,500 brown babies were born. The brass's interest in racial endogamy took priority over the welfare of children as they sought to preserve proprietary attitudes toward women and the racist and sexist social divisions maintained in peacetime at home. The brown babies' story captures the United States at an important time of transition, before contemporary attitudes naturalized the practice of interracial adoption and when the public perceived mixed-race children as novelties.

In the 1940s and 1950s mixed-race families were relatively uncommon objects of curiosity and disapproval. The initial military response toward the brown babies involved secrecy and suppression. Social workers, including the sympathetic, joined U.S. Army authorities in trying to quiet the issue, claiming that black newspapers in the United States were cheaply sensationalizing it. At a time when African American public opinion endorsed maximum black participation in the armed forces, some civilian leaders and military officials alike feared the brown baby issue could boomerang by achieving domestic notoriety and lending credence to those who advocated black troop reductions in Europe.[2]

Brown babies remained mostly invisible to mainstream audiences, but their popularity with African American readers as human interest stories kept their images in print. Racial transgression was the key to the fascination they generated, as were the interracial exploits of black soldiers in Europe generally. The unusual circumstances of war and occupation provided opportunities for African Americans to thumb their noses at Jim Crow prohibitions, and black readers enjoyed accounts of how this was done.[3] Sympathy among black Americans for mixed-race war orphans was not, however, a foregone conclusion. In the slavery era, white men sired most biracial children in socially mismatched relationships that reflected the inferior status of the black mother in particular and of all black persons in general. After emancipation both whites and blacks continued to associate first-generation mixed-race persons with bastardy. Although the customary U.S. practice of hypodescent—a law in some southern states—made anyone with visible African ancestry black, African Americans did not always believe that all such individuals shared a broadly conceived African American ethnic culture or inhabited its psychological milieu. It is telling that, as late as 1959, authorities found it difficult to place abandoned American-born biracial orphans with either black or white parents.[4]

Military policy placed obstacles in the path of normalizing family life for biracial children born overseas of black fathers and white mothers. Some of these unions were essentially exchange agreements motivated by crisis, where the destitution of one partner encountered the comparative power and opportunism of the other. U.S. policy toward Germany shortly after its defeat in 1944 was initially harsh, though it substantially moderated over the course of the occupation period. Military authorities decided that the German population, as a whole responsible for choosing and sustaining the Nazi regime, should enjoy no priority in the distribution of food and health resources. Only after the needs of the liberated countries were addressed would German living standards be allowed to rise.[5]

Hunger motivated many European women at the end of the war to seek intimate relationships with foreign soldiers. Cynthia Enloe suggests that privation can be understood as a form of coercion. "A military base," Enloe writes, is "a package of presumptions about male soldiers' sexual needs and about the local community's resources for satisfying those needs."[6] The power relationships created from the circumstances of the occupation eroticized German destitution and defeat through submissive and prostituted women. Ute Frevert characterizes the "borderline between rape and prostitution" in the Western zones of occupation as "a fluid one: many American and British soldiers paid for their pleasures in cigarettes, chocolate and bread." A population on the brink of starvation, in early 1947 taking in, on average, 850 calories a day, often condoned the illicit relations between Allied soldiers and local women, both married and single. The Nazi instrumentalist view of women also helped prepare the ground that exigency fertilized.[7]

Army officials did not leave to chance the regulation of sexual relations between soldiers and women in occupied countries in wartime. Monitoring prostitution and other sexual relations was a military necessity that, in Enloe's words, "required explicit American policy-making." How did military authorities regulate, and condone, what they claimed to oppose?[8] While brown babies were born in Britain and Italy as well as Germany,[9] Germany's unique history and former status as an adversary provide a distinctly privileged view of the intersections of race and gender. Military leaders from the United States, where race governed social relations, were confronted by a nation where race had also played a powerful role in constructing the identity of its recently defeated government. How did U.S. officials negotiate these rocky shoals at a historical moment when both nations faced multiple social and political challenges?

In any war personal relationships, whether romantic or commercial, develop between occupiers and nationals. In Germany, although ranking U.S. officers usually viewed interracial relationships negatively, they pursued policies that, given the cultural imperatives they shared with enlisted men, made such relationships inevitable. Men who served in World War II, regardless of rank, tended to assume that all soldiers would seek sexual outlets; thus the solution to the problem of interracial sex was to provide acceptable partners for black soldiers.

The U.S. military was never completely candid about the roles played by female USO workers and by "government girls," the thousands of women civilians recruited to white-collar positions during the war. Ostensibly these were "nice girls" with whom soldiers could socialize, nonprostitutes who provided an alternative to commercial sex.[10] For the black GIs in Germany, however, no African American equivalents existed at first. The military resisted hiring black women civilians to staff the many clerical positions that the occupation government had created. Segregation decreed that black and white government girls could not room together, and residences were available only for the whites. The lack of housing for female African American stenographers and clerks meant that they could not be stationed in Germany, adding another twist to the contradictions surrounding race and gender. Even though many U.S. officers believed that contact with women was an important perquisite for soldiers, black soldiers were thus cut off from both "respectable" and tawdry social outlets.[11]

Government disapproval of both interracial sexual liaisons and the presence of black women illustrate how official thinking about race and sex contradicted itself. Another example is white American reluctance to strip defeated German men of their racial privileges. The army initially tried to avoid assigning black troops to police work that would elevate them to positions of authority over Germans. Though the desire to respect local sensibilities provided the pretext, it should be noted that, in many parts of the United States at the time, black police officers had limited authority over white civilians, which typically prevented them from making arrests across the color line. Marcus H. Ray, an aide to the secretary of war and an advisor on matters related to black soldiers, found army policy in this matter indefensible. "To accept the prejudices of the German people as a reason for nonutilization of the American soldier who happens to be nonwhite," he wrote, "is to negate the very ideals we have made a part of our reeducation program in Germany."[12] Ray might have also argued that it defeated the purpose of the war itself, including the massive propaganda campaign that had been mounted against Nazi racism.

The exaggerated high status of American white women compared to German women in the U.S. zone of occupation also reflects contradictions in U.S. thought and practice. German women did not receive in identical measure the skin and gender privileges that they would have had as white women in America. As members of a nation with which the United States had engaged in bitter and protracted war, they were, in the early years of the occupation, particular targets of hostility from a high command that tacitly encouraged sexual exploitation. This included the creation by a *Stars and Stripes* cartoonist of a buffoonish female character, Veronica Dankeschön ("thank you very much"), referred to as V. D., with acronymic reference to sexually transmitted disease. The plump, hapless Veronica wore the plain braids of the Nazi era and a skirt hemmed with swastikas.[13] Her stereotype enhanced a climate that made possible U.S. military "vice raids" to punish women who clearly were not prostitutes.

In an illustrative incident in Coburg, the Office of the Military Government of the United States (OMGUS) strained its relations with local German leaders after MPs detained "many prominent women of the city, including the Burgermeister's daughter, the wives of prominent businessmen, etc." According to official reports, "they were picked up as they left the opera, stores, etc." Only unaccompanied women were arrested; those with GI escorts were spared. The Coburg raid reneged on an agreement that OMGUS had made to consult German authorities and to refrain from taking women into custody during hours when "respectable" women were on the street. Both occupiers and nationals thus enforced the distinction between "good" and "bad" women.[14]

In this violation of tacitly understood rules, the Coburg raid demonstrates the contours of a bureaucratic control system. U.S. officials, with the acquiescence of local authorities, had first created a double standard. Then, using public health as a rationale, they proceeded to obliterate the standard. The epidemic rate of sexually transmitted diseases among the troops and the creation of an emergency around that statistical fact provided a pretext for the erasure of German women's respectability.

The improbable vice raids were probably intended in part to harass the German population and were especially directed toward humiliating women. Apart from the embarrassment of the arrest itself, arrests were often followed by coerced physical tests for venereal disease. "Patients" complained of rough treatment, doctors who examined them vaginally using cold and dirty specula, and an ethos whereby medical attendants could be bribed to provide written proof of negative results.

In the spring of 1947 authorities conducted a "surprise medical examination" of women working in an OMGUS cafeteria in Bavaria. The German employees and the community at large disbelieved the report that eleven of the workers, including an elderly woman, had gonorrhea and demanded that a German physician reexamine them. Some thought the examination a ploy to fire women who would be replaced by girlfriends of some of the U.S. officers. When the supposedly infected women refused treatment, they were forcibly hospitalized, where a second culture tested negative.[15]

The venereal disease problem in the U.S. military, the ostensible reason for these measures, had a racial angle. Infection rates among black troops in some units were as high as six or seven times that of whites, and the high rate had played a major role in the postwar decision to demobilize large numbers of black troops. MPs disproportionately targeted for arrest those German women who dated black GIs, claiming that they had been shown to have higher rates of infection than those who dated white Americans.[16] During the latter years of the occupation, military authorities toned down the Veronica Dankeschön persona as well as the vice raids, ultimately finding both counterproductive. Dwight P. Griswold, director of OMGUS Internal Affairs and Communications Division, disapproved of these tactics. "Mass examinations of civilian women and so-called 'vice raids' conducted solely to discover cases of venereal disease," he held, "are unsound and hazardous to ideological objectives in Germany." Griswold believed them "wasteful of time and facilities." "Unit commanders . . . conducting venereal disease control activities outside of prescribed channels" hampered German efforts to control the spread of sexually transmitted disease among civilians. The brass came to recognize that this modus operandi did not pay off in reducing the infection rate or identifying more than 20 percent of the local women believed to be carriers.[17]

The militant approach to vice, generally discredited by the late 1940s, nevertheless persisted when interracial sex was involved. In the Rhineland-Palatinate local authorities punished most severely women accused of prostituting themselves to black men. In Kreuznacht a mixed couple was arrested when they could not prove that they were engaged in a serious relationship because they did not have the permit required of engaged couples. When the soldier, in his fiancée's company, later asked his commanding officer for a marriage application, the incredulous C.O. asked the prospective bride why she would wed a black man. Indignant, the GI berated his superior, which only earned him a demotion.[18]

In Birkenfeld a woman was charged with prostitution for allowing black soldiers to buy her a drink. Local authorities resented the fact that blacks subject to segregation laws in their own country had so much freedom in Germany. According to Maria Höhn, when German civilians were no longer starving after 1951, their friendliness toward black soldiers diminished. When Germany regained sovereignty in 1955, criminal prosecutions of interracial friendships increased substantially, while white Americans romantically involved with Germans were left alone. A curtain of white endogamy was drawn over such relationships while "Veronica Dankeschön" was now defined and prosecuted as a woman who slept with blacks. Such associations, more than ever defined as illicit, were driven into lower-class neighborhoods more likely to be targeted by police.[19]

On the American side, racial prejudice could drive hostility toward German women and black men alike. A group of German women boarded the army transport USS *Henry Gibbins* in spring 1949 after the Carrie Chapman Catt Foundation invited them to the United States to study democratic institutions. The army housed them "next to the stokers' quarters" in an unheated stateroom. The women had to walk through the black crews' berths to get to their lavatory and were forced to eat the leftovers of American passengers and use their soiled napkins. Black sailors, who felt sorry for them, slipped them fresh food and water on the sly. The character of the official disrespect shown here is telling; it would have been unthinkable to house middle-class white American women in the bowels of a ship next to low-ranking black troops with whom they would be forced into physical contact on such an intimate level. In the context of U.S. racial conventions and stereotypes of the period, the berth assignment was an open invitation to the black soldiers to rape these unwanted passengers. The black GIs got the message and stood it on its ear, instead extending courtesies to the unlucky passengers.[20] Military propaganda and practice thus helped create an image of the immoral and unworthy German woman that contrasted sharply with that of the good American wife, presumably waiting patiently and virtuously at home. Race played a vital role in this construction.

Germany's former adversarial status influenced all relationships between Americans and Germans during the occupation. Contemporary observers believed that most of the children GIs fathered in Germany were born to married women whose husbands were absent. Early estimates of the numbers of such babies ranged from thirty thousand to fifty-two thousand, of which some three thousand were believed to be of mixed race. Germans joked that, in case of another war, the United

States would not need to send any more soldiers, just new uniforms. Children sired by white Americans could often slip through the cracks of the German nationality law's insistence on "blood," their legitimacy contested only by returning husbands. Black infants could not disappear into German society in this way and presented a prima facie case of bastardy.[21]

The vanquished Third Reich's commitment to racism provided an ironic note. From the standpoint of Nazi eugenics, the brown babies were part of what the war had been fought to prevent. As conditions deteriorated in Germany by mid-April 1945, Himmler tried to barter concentration camp prisoners' lives for Allied pledges that the ss would be treated like ordinary prisoners of war and that black soldiers would not be among the army of occupation.[22] Allied policymaking reflected awareness of such antiblack sentiments in Germany. John R. McCloy, assistant secretary of war, wondered if the Office of War Information and the Bureau of Public Relations should prepare Germans "for the possible use of Negro troops as components of the occupation force." Lieutenant General Thomas T. Hardy, assistant chief of staff, saw black troop deployment as "governed entirely by operational needs" and saw no need to consult the locals. Hardy believed a special campaign to orient Germans to the black presence would "lead to unfortunate publicity in the United States." He advised against any such initiative.[23]

The concern over black troops as occupiers had a history that predated Himmler. After the Allied victory in World War I, France and Belgium sent colonial troops to Germany. The foreign garrisons at that time included Africans, Arabs, and Vietnamese, much to the Germans' chagrin. All the German political parties except the Socialists signed a parliamentary petition calling for the withdrawal of these armies of color on racial purity grounds. A small number of mixed-race children were born as a result of this occupation. Hitler, after coming to power in 1933, moved slowly on the question of mixed-race Germans. For the next four years certain individuals were courted. May Opitz writes, "In consideration of foreign policy interests, caution was exercised not to allow the abuse of Africans and Afro-Germans to go beyond certain bounds. A note of warning from the Foreign Office stated: 'Let us not forget, now that the accusations against Germany over the Jewish question are beginning to abate somewhat, that we must not allow the colored question to provide new substance to the enemy propaganda in the struggle against the new Germany.' In order not to antagonize foreign diplomats traveling to Germany and thereby jeopardize trade relations, a campaign was even begun against xenophobia." At first German offi-

cials perceived certain resident blacks as potentially valuable intermediaries should Germany once again become a colonial power in Africa.
By the late 1930s, however, this view yielded increasingly to those who
favored extermination and sterilization.[24]

Allied policymaking reflected awareness of antiblack sentiments
in Germany. Following the Allied conquest of Italy in 1943, German
propaganda had emphasized to Italians the racial dangers that a black
American military presence presented. A notable propaganda poster
depicted a drunken, leering black GI with one simian arm around the
waist of the chaste, marble Venus de Milo, on which he had placed a
$2 price tag. Planning for the occupation of Germany envisaged the
United States, Soviet Union, and Britain providing most of the garrisons. The Big Three did not want to exclude France for political reasons
but were not enthusiastic about its participation, having learned that
the Free French were readying 175,000 French and 275,000 French African troops in Africa.[25]

African Americans did participate in the Rhineland occupation,
where they encountered hostility from local officialdom and the press.
The police and sectarian welfare agencies firmly associated black soldiers with crime, venereal disease, and vice—both heterosexual and
homosexual. Infractions committed by anonymous American soldiers
were routinely attributed, without proof, to blacks. German newspapers exaggerated the number of black soldiers, as they had done in the
previous war.[26] Racial distinctions and the preservation of white skin
privilege would be a point of friction in postwar race relations.

In Giessen black labor units were made to work alongside POW labor
gangs, both supervised by white Americans. Similar problems occurred
in the United States as well. At Camp Andrews in Maryland, black
women PX workers were fired and replaced by German POWs hired at
sixty cents a day. Stories abound of the favorable treatment of ex-Nazis
in public accommodations and other facilities.[27] What this meant to patriotic black veterans was explained by one of them to journalist Ollie
Harrington: "You fought, if you are a Negro veteran, to tear down the
sign 'No Jews Allowed' in Germany, to find in America the sign 'No
Negroes Allowed.' You fought to wipe out the noose and the whip in
Germany and Japan, to find the noose and the whip in Georgia and Louisiana. One veteran put it to me this way: 'I got through fighting in the
E.T.O.,' he said, 'and now I've got to fight in the S.T.O.' I asked, 'What's
the S.T.O.?' He said, 'Haven't you heard? The Southern Theater of Operations, U.S.A.'"[28]

While the Grand Alliance did not ban black troops as Himmler wished, it made futile efforts to discourage fraternization between black Allied troops and German citizens. Petra Goedde has argued that the initial military policy that prohibited fraternization between German nationals and occupying U.S. troops was widely flouted because most social contacts among Germans and American soldiers involved women. The scarcity of German men in the civilian population and the perception of women as not only relatively harmless but helpless and in need of protection, led to what Goedde calls the "feminization of Germany" in the minds of soldiers and policymakers alike.[29] Once tamed, little separated Germany from an Americanization that some Germans and Americans alike thought desirable. The activities of women in this feminized nation were of political interest to those concerned about Germany's future. "Public discourse in the media and among social critics," Katherine Pence writes, "often made the Americanizing transformation of women's bodies, women's identities, and women's role in German society a site for voicing anxieties about the reconstruction of the German state and civil society within an American alliance."[30] From a race-conscious perspective, Germany, once feminized and Americanized, was now subject to the peculiar racial taboos that inflected sexual relations in U.S. culture.

As of August 9, 1947, the U.S. Army had not approved any applications from black soldiers who wished to marry German women. This did not prevent sexual liaisons from developing, however, and the number of biracial children steadily rose.[31] The reporter William Nunn, on an army-sponsored tour of the ETO, described the improvised communities that resulted: "Now that the sun has brought warm weather to Bavaria . . . Munich . . . Frankfort [sic] . . . Mannheim and other sections thickly populated by Negro soldiers . . . the streets adjoining and approaching Kasernes where Negro troops are stationed, are rendezvous for many attractive Frauleins wheeling carriages bearing their sons and daughters. The girls appear to be happy and jubilant."[32]

The black journalist Cliff MacKay also took a sanguine view. "The tan babies at present are unquestionably the most healthy in Germany, for the simple reason that they are the best fed," he wrote. "It is not an uncommon sight to see these mothers walking up and down in front of colored military posts at mess time, waiting for the fathers of their children to bring out food no other Germans can enjoy." The underground economy worked in their favor. According to MacKay, "A soldier can secure care for a child and mother for a whole week for one package of cigarettes, currently valued on the black market at 80 marks."[33]

Neither reporter focused on what worried less casual observers: What would happen to these army dependents once the GIS left Germany? No one at the time predicted the intensity and longevity of the standoff between the Soviets and the West that wrecked the Grand Alliance. It was reasonable to assume that the military occupation would end after a specified time and that connections forged in the interim would consequently be altered. Close examination had already revealed that German women with biracial children received a different response in their own communities when no Americans were present and that charities did not give them the same consideration as other needy Germans. Nunn heard rumors about "brown babies" being killed, sold, and displayed in carnivals. Such stories revived fears of Germany's all too recent Nazi past. Even if such tales were exaggerations, how would Germany's mixed-race children be socialized? How would they assimilate into German society, and what future would they have? The number of children who were not cared for by their birth mothers further clouded the matter. One group lived in an orphanage in Frankfurt, where many of them were reportedly afraid of black adults.[34]

A strong current of opinion among African Americans favored fathers' assumption of responsibility. The reporter Ollie Stewart criticized black GIS who abandoned their children and girlfriends. The soldiers were quick to respond that they faced the major problem, as in Britain, of surmounting the obstacles to expatriation, including the army's initial ban on all German-American marriages and, subsequently, its continued prohibition of interracial marriages.[35] In spite of these difficulties, many black soldiers bucked the trend. According to statistics of the German Association for Public and Private Assistance, 9 to 10 percent of all U.S. soldiers paid child support. Within that group black soldiers constituted 25 percent of those making payments.[36]

In June 1946 an act of Congress permitted GIS to bring home prospective "war brides" during FY 1946–47 on ninety-day visitors' visas, but the army did not permit its enactment until December of that year. It then created stipulations designed to delay and restrict these unions. Even unit commanders often failed to understand the complicated rules. Only GIS with less than six and more than three months left to serve could apply to marry a German national. Permissions routinely took three months to process, and often the soldier was shipped out before the papers came through. Even the successful applicants had difficulties. Prospective immigrants still had to run a gauntlet of medical examinations, denazification certification, character examination by a cleric, clearance by intelligence officials, and approval by a joint travel security agency. They then faced the expense and scarcity of travel during a period when nonmilitary transport remained restricted.[37]

The degree of scrutiny that newly constituted German-American families faced regarding their moral fitness and political conformity was an extension of pacification policies and eerily echoed the certification policies of the Third Reich. The opposition to paternal adoption reinforced the status boundaries between the conquerors and the vanquished. Needy mothers who could not marry the fathers of their children had no recourse but to apply for charitable assistance. U.S. military archives are filled with "Dear Jane" letters in which officials inform German women that they cannot help them.[38] The stringent rules derived from the extraterritorial rights that the United States bestowed upon itself. The terms of the occupation dictated that German courts, which ruled on adoptions of all children born in Germany of a German mother, did not have jurisdiction over Americans. Neither could "a competent court" simply expatriate German-born orphans for adoption in the United States because the State Department would not issue visas for orphans lacking a determination of paternity. Those courts, however, could not determine that an American had fathered a child by a German woman without the permission of the military government.[39]

In an age when legitimacy held considerable social weight, the army had made every mixed-race child of a black serviceman *necessarily* a bastard. In so doing it ironically replicated slavery-era principles that guaranteed the anonymity of white fathers. Policy made history repeat itself in yet another respect: the shedding of paternal responsibility was a proxy for the shedding of national responsibility. This abdication went all the way to the top. As early as February 1945, when Eleanor Roosevelt approached her husband about brown babies in England, FDR had replied, "I think this is a British problem—not American."[40]

Race posed other obstacles to family constitution. Military judges relied on the laws of the various states to determine whether a proposed union could be approved and compiled the relevant statutes for their own use. Racial record keeping on marriages began in 1947. German courts followed this example. The Allies, having struck down the Nuremberg laws in 1944 and made explicit reference to the abrogation of the 1935 Law for the Protection of German Blood and German Honor, oddly found itself reapplying such legislation in the American zone of occupation, where the German courts followed suit.[41] The Legal Affairs Division's correspondence suggests that it took racial identification seriously in matters of both marriage and adoption. A soldier from a state where interracial marriages were illegal would have his application to marry outside his race rejected. That Americans were not bound to remain in the states where they lived before the war did not seem to dawn on anyone.[42] Additionally, as one military official noted in reply to a German agency's inquiry, "the adoption laws of some of the states of the U.S.A. require that a colored child can only be adopted by a colored adopter and a white child only by a white adopter."[43] Texas and Louisiana forbade the adoption of a child by a prospective parent of different race. South Carolina restricted the adoption of children born out of wedlock and limited the inheritance rights of those who did find adoptive parents. This hypocrisy was not lost on the Germans, and it fed into an indigenous racism that never disappeared.

Legal difficulties and tacit understandings about race and sex, inflected by the bitterness of wartime, helped delay the beginning of positive responses to mixed-race orphans among African Americans. Just as the episode aboard the *Henry Gibbins* underscored the use of race as a marker of subordination, under certain circumstances blacks could "borrow" the identity of the white American conquerors. A *Baltimore Afro-American* feature story described black officers who retained German house servants at $30 a month. The article's accompanying photograph showed a humble German maid serving dinner to a black military man and his wife. In addition to the reversal of German fortunes that the story highlighted, the employment by blacks of white servants also stood customary American race relations on their head and inverted the traditional subservience of black women to white women. From the German domestic's perspective, such jobs commanded vastly higher wages than they could otherwise make, even if some of their compatriots regarded maids who worked for blacks as little better than prostitutes.[44]

The *Pittsburgh Courier* reporter William Nunn, investigating the brown baby question in 1948, found that black servicemen's wives did not sympathize with the mixed-race orphans or their German mothers. The war had enabled the African American army wife to be an honorary white vis-à-vis Germans. She could discuss the "servant problem" in Germany just as glibly as any other American housewife. "A white epidermis here is just nothing at all," the journalist J. A. Rogers observed of European society a few years later. "The masses are poor and color doesn't help. In America it's only the presence of the Negro that gives any value to a white skin."[45] With such unpromising beginnings, what would explain why the black public came to register a concern about the children that black soldiers had left behind in Europe? Here is a case where official policy, evolving cultural attitudes, and large-scale social change collide.

Black Americans shared the ethos of the time. The war had created the terms of citizenship. Society had wanted warriors and defense workers; now the site of production of good citizens had shifted to the family. Blacks were as ready as whites to return to a domesticity once seen as subversive of the war effort and now hailed as the next correct thing to do.[46] Americans renewed their interest in child rearing as the troops came home, a concern reflected in the surging birth rate. Adoption became an increasingly attractive option for infertile couples as the public interest in parenting began to neutralize earlier reservations about the practice. The large numbers of Asian orphans created by World War II and the Korean War also provided an opportunity to link adoption to Cold War concerns. Destitute children could become a destabilizing factor in the power relations between the Eastern and Western blocs. "I have returned from overseas with the realization that the Communists care enough to make very successful capital of democracy's failures," wrote the founder of the Christian Children's Fund. This Richmond, Virginia–based social service agency supported foreign orphanages because of "the strong conviction that we Americans can not close our eyes or stop our ears to the cry of a hungry child anywhere in the world."[47]

There was so much demand for young children that by 1947 a domestic black market in white infants had developed. In the course of the late 1940s many state legislatures changed their adoption laws to require licensing for agencies, establishing conditions under which parental rights could be terminated, guardianship constituted, and the like.[48] The end of racial segregation among adoption agencies also became a practical possibility for the future. In New York City revised Department of Welfare regulations withdrew city financial support to institutions and agencies that discriminated against black children. Some social workers persisted in the view that black children were unadoptable, and non-tax-supported, private organizations continued to set their own standards. Government's expanding role in child welfare, however, foreshadowed integrationist policies in the coming era.[49]

Black communities and organizations shared this natalist enthusiasm. The New York Urban League began the Adopt a Child Project. Photographs of children were featured more frequently in black newspapers, which paid substantial attention, for example, to the Fultz quadruplets of Madison, North Carolina. Multiple births, unassisted then by drugs, were rare, and pictures of the Fultz girls, born in 1946, provided ample human interest during the years of their infancy and toddlerhood.[50] The unprecedented prosperity of the late 1940s for blacks and the sense of optimism attendant on the end of the war also facilitated a *black* baby boom. Like whites, blacks who either could not conceive offspring of their own or wished to enlarge their families through adoption became more aware than previously of the orphan pool.

Ricki Sollinger, in her study of teenage, out-of-wedlock pregnancy in the 1950s, has indicated that white girls were much more likely than black to place their children for adoption. Indeed pregnancy and childbirth for the unwed teenage mother of white middle-class origin was often shrouded in secrecy and shame.[51] While a similar sense of shame affected many black unwed mothers, black families were comparatively more accepting of such offspring and more likely to keep them in the family. The scarcity of black children as subjects for adoption, then, was not only a product of the disinterest of whites in adopting nonwhite children but was also a result of such children's relative acceptance in black communities and consequent unavailability. Adoption of foreign nonwhite children was still rare among whites, although some liberal social workers advocated it. The domestic shortage of orphans consequently made the adoption of brown babies a possibility for black Americans.[52]

It is important to note that some of the racial barriers challenged during the late 1940s involved direct assaults on white social exclusiveness. Unlike the era of *Brown v. Board of Education*, with its comparatively impersonal focus on the desegregation of institutions and facilities, the 1940s faced such intimate issues as marriage, residence, and family formation head-on. In most instances World War II had been the enabler. The legality of interracial marriages, which the Supreme Court would ultimately decide in 1967 in *Loving v. Virginia*, became a heated issue during this period. Military leaders partially ducked it by assigning the few black soldiers with white wives to posts outside the South. Snafus did occur, as in the case of one couple posted to Dixie in error. The unlucky pair went to jail following their attempt to rent off-base housing.[53] Other challenges to housing practices in the wake of the 1948 Supreme Court cases *Shelley v. Kraemer* and *Hurd* resulted from the domestic effects of the war.

The Cold War conflicts that developed between the United States and the USSR after World War II came rapidly to a head in Germany, culminating in the circumstances that led to the Berlin airlift of 1948. The Soviets had been criticized in the Western press for their dogged unwillingness to cooperate on numerous matters. One of these was the refusal to permit Soviet war brides to join their British and American husbands. The Soviet press in turn was more than happy to rake the United States over the coals for its Jim Crow racial practices regarding soldier marriages, which could not be defended as being in the interests of U.S. national security.[54] America's new vulnerability in racial matters abetted subtle transitions across the social spectrum.

By the end of the 1940s, for example, a notable change in attitude about brown babies began occurring among African Americans. The desire by the child welfare establishment to break down black reservations about adopting them played a part. Lester Granger, a social worker and Urban League official, believed that "the state of mind of the Negro community" "would have to [be] built up to accept" it. The black press was a major catalyst in developing such favorable opinion. It had received a warm response to its "human interest" features on the orphans and favored their stateside adoption.[55] Culturally and politically supported desires for family formation and growth among African Americans in the postwar years probably played the determining role. English-born biracial children of black GIs were easier to accept. Britain had been a wartime ally and language barriers did not exist. As early as 1946 a group of African American women in Chicago had sent "care packages" to children in British orphanages whom they wished to bring to the United States. British adoption law foiled the effort, but it demonstrated that attitudes were changing.[56]

African American newspapers were at the height of their influence during the World War II era. Policymakers from the Departments of Justice, State, and War monitored them nervously for fear that black sedition and unrest would compromise the Allied effort. Little escaped the attention of would-be censors and those hoping to deflect black dissatisfaction. Officials regularly clipped articles from such leading periodicals as the *Pittsburgh Courier*, the *Baltimore Afro-American*, and the *Chicago Defender* with an eye to what these papers were saying about war-related subjects. The habit continued during the German occupation. Articles about brown babies circulated among military commanders and social workers alike. The questions the black public asked forced Children's Bureau officials and others to think about the future that these orphans would have.[57]

If the brown babies were not brought to America, they would grow up in Germany. A group of American social welfare professionals discussed this possibility in early 1951. Comprising an ad hoc committee that represented such diverse organizations as the Child Welfare League of America, the NAACP, the Displaced Persons Commission, and the Catholic Committee for Refugees, among others, these officials took up the question at a New York meeting. A representative from the Church World Service had contacted the Venezuelan government, which expressed interest in taking the children. He acknowledged that the option would entail "sending children into a land where they would be entirely strange to the native stock." The Brooklyn Catholic Interracial Council committee member dismissed such expatriation as "tantamount to evasion of the problem." The best solution, the committee ultimately agreed, would be one that would not put the burden of placing the orphans on an economically beleaguered black community alone and that would view the brown babies "as children, as a human problem, and not involving the race and color of the child."[58]

The Children's Bureau, a federal agency with origins in the movement to suppress child labor, had interested itself in the "brown baby" question since the early postwar years. It shared the views of the private agencies and tried to widen the circle of responsibility for war orphans to include the State Department, the High Commissioner for Germany, and the Displaced Persons Commission. Its director, Katherine Lenroot, "felt strongly that the responsibility for some of these international situations rested with a public agency." Children's Bureau officials tacitly communicated disapproval of the War Department's refusal to provide GIs' mailing addresses to women they were believed to have impregnated. The only responsibility the War Department assumed was that of forwarding mail from jilted wives and girlfriends. As a result of pressure from both private and governmental social service organizations, the Departments of State and War concluded a verbal agreement whereby the State Department would assume responsibility for answering the many letters federal agencies were receiving from abandoned, divorced, and exploited foreign women. Public oversight did not permit executive departments charged with making war or overseeing the restoration of peace to completely distance themselves from the messy consequences of troop deployment during the occupations of both Britain and Germany. State Department officials found themselves participating in interagency and joint committees designed to address a problem unprecedented in its scale.[59]

The onset of the Cold War and the military standoff between the superpowers meant the continuous overseas deployment of U.S. troops. Tangled legal and domestic relationships previously associated only with the exigencies of a "hot war" would now be enduring. Yet this permanence did not dissuade federal officials from pursuing policies that made children born out of wedlock a responsibility for the host country and discouraged congressional involvement in creating special legislation for what had become an extraordinary situation. Policymakers chose not to follow Canada's example, whereby after World War I Ottawa made payments to Britain for every child begot there by a Canadian soldier. Brown babies and other children of war would have to rely on the strained social services infrastructure of the countries where they were born.[60]

In 1952 an unusual partnership developed between a black army family and the *Baltimore Afro-American*. Chief Warrant Officer Oscar Grammer and his wife, Mabel, helped to publicize and promote adoptions of German-born biracial children by black parents in the United States. The *Afro-American* celebrated with new parents in lavish photo spreads designed to encourage others to adopt. The Grammers themselves subsequently adopted nine orphans. The law required the visas in such cases to be filed by a recognized agency, but many private U.S. adoption agencies persisted in their refusal to handle black cases, placing the burden of work on the few. Children not admitted under the Displaced Persons Act for purposes of adoption would have to come to America under the German quota. Comparatively few brown babies made the transatlantic crossing. Proponents of transnational adoption faced another hurdle in establishing contact between American prospective parents and German legal guardians: under German law, guardians retained custody until all administrative processes were concluded, and German agencies were not compensated for their work with biracial children. In mid-1954 four thousand children were awaiting transport to the United States under the Refugee Relief Act.[61]

By 1955, when the Federal Republic of Germany became fully autonomous, the oldest of the mixed-race war orphans were already attending school. They faced a hostile German social science establishment that viewed them with condescension, when it was not downright racist and based on Nazi science. Certain people of color had survived the Third Reich because Nazi authorities wanted to use them as an advance phalanx in Africa once Germany's former colonies had been restored. The idea briefly reemerged after the war and abruptly died.[62] Yet the West Germany of the Adenauer years was a different place than the Third Reich. The ultimate repudiation of Nazism involved a revulsion against the American racism that made banner headlines all over the world in the 1950s. In the United States the status of black children became a national issue after the decision of the Supreme Court in *Brown v. Board of Education. Brown* not only concerned education; it was also historic because it at last included black juveniles in the category "children." The sociological jurisprudence the Court exercised indicated its acceptance as a valid argument that racism damaged black children. This acceptance thus acknowledged implicitly—in a manner unprecedented in U.S. law—the humanity of black children. The clash between this recognition and a century of Jim Crow social conventions, including a popular culture that depicted black children as dwarf copies of clownish black adults, embarrassed the United States in its efforts to lead the Western world.

School integration crises in the United States influenced the West German decision to consciously and rationally integrate mixed-race orphans into German society, thus depriving cold war enemies of a race-related issue to which Germany's history made it particularly vulnerable. Dr. Dorothea Struwe of the Nuremberg Youth Office reminded *Ebony* magazine, "The incidents in Little Rock (Ark.) have caused much indignation in Germany. I hope that no one will ever have reason to clean up before our own door. It is essential that our colored children can expand and develop their talents and abilities so that they will be firmly rooted in our community and will not some day constitute a source of unrest." During the era of civil rights insurgency in the United States, the German state made a concerted, conscious, and largely successful effort to integrate the brown babies into the blue-collar workforce. German universities were asked to help plan the assimilation program. The children's social absorption was greatly assisted by the rebounding German economy of the period that muted class and ethnic tensions. Critics subsequently complained, however, that Germans of African descent found barriers in their path when they sought to climb the socioeconomic ladder into the professions by seeking higher education or specialized training.[63]

The brown babies' saga is a tale of war that varies considerably from the official, triumphalist story of the suppression of racism in the U.S. armed forces after 1945. It is also a story of how the United States sorted out the hierarchies of race, nationality, and gender during the occupation's brief "colonial moment." Most military histories of race relations during this time focus on the concentrated efforts of the civil rights establishment, liberal-minded policymakers, and enlightened segments of the public to make the army and other branches abandon their discriminatory treatment of the black GI. Left implicit, rather than made explicit, was how conventional thinking about race and gender could be harnessed to the accomplishment of this task. Equalization of the status of all *men* in the U.S. military required the inclusion of the African American soldier as an equal. Not only did this mean rating black troops above German prisoners of war and treating them accordingly, but it also entailed revising the status and roles of women, and specifically white women, vis-à-vis these newly appraised blacks. Questions related to fraternization and intermarriage plagued an issue that could not be simply reduced to strategic concerns. Ambivalence continued, as did, for example, the prohibition against Japanese-American marriages, still in force in 1949.[64] We are thus presented with an index of the register of changes through which transitions in racial attitudes and behavior were rung.

The black father in the postwar state is at the center of the matter. During the slavery era, black fathers had no legal authority over their offspring. To protect the privileges and status of white men who wished to engage in interracial liaisons, antebellum legal convention held that a slave's father was unknown to the law. It also denied the legitimacy of black paternity, thus undermining black men's ability to assume the same paternal role assumed by their white congeners. This did not make things easy for black women and children, because society assigned them dependent status in any case, and its refusal to recognize black patriarchy left them without conventional protections. Responsible fatherhood, linked to citizenship and property holding, indicated civic entitlement and respectability. It marked the distinction between fathering, as a free man would, and siring, as done by a slave or an animal. During and after World War II, U.S. military authorities had considerable difficulty recognizing the capacity and right of the African American men under their control to father. To see them as men in that sense and not as mere lusting beasts would mean envisioning them as civic persons, a leap of the imagination that the emerging civil rights movement would make possible a decade later.

It is partly for this reason that the military so strongly resisted black GI attempts to establish legitimate paternity and play the male-dominant roles that were conventional in society at large. The reflexive hostility with which many white men viewed interracial relationships was not, as many interpreted it, instinctual. It was instead the product of a tacit, if not entirely conscious chain of thought in which the claims of black challengers to white male supremacy—and endogamy—were denied. In the process the white woman gained a symbolic, if extrinsic, status. That status could be taken away as a penalty for transgression, as the German women's case illustrates. (German men, however, as the POW experience indicates, were not thus punished.) Under the circumstances the existence of the "brown babies" indicated that more than simple indiscretion had occurred: they showed that the barricades had been breached.

Over the past fifteen years scholars have recorded changes in thought and policy about race and gender by looking at a variety of evidence, ranging from popular culture to law. The application of biopolitics to such research provides a deeper look at postwar U.S. society during a period of complex and rapid change. Even before the Berlin airlift institutionalized the cold war rift between the Western powers and the Soviet bloc, race had the power to embarrass the United States, complicate the execution of its laws and policies, confound its most fundamental objectives, and muddle its relations with foreign powers. The war orphans of mixed race are generally treated as footnotes to the main drama of the era, a "human interest" spectacle for the press. But their physicality could not be hidden, nor could their brownness be denied. As exemplars of the relationship between bodies and the nation, and more than the product and subject of policy conflict, they lay near the center of the mission to normalize Europe. In the dilemma they posed for the United States, they joined the discourses of conventional home life, then under reconstruction, and the emerging goal of a more inclusive citizenship. At the same time, the brown babies' story reveals the intricate web connecting national and international practices of race that remained in tension with one another and came to mark our own era.

Notes

An earlier version of this essay appeared in Plummer, *Window On Freedom: Race, Civil Rights, and Foreign Affairs, 1945–1988,* edited by Brenda Gayle Plummer. Copyright ©2003 by the University of North Carolina Press. Used by permission of the publisher.

1. Maj. Gen. Edward F. Witsell to Dr. M. L. Ogan, Apr. 16, 1946; Gianna Del Prede to Director of NAACP, Nov. 11, 1945; Walter White to Robert P. Patterson, Secretary of War, Dec. 20, 1945; NAACP Papers, Part 9: Discrimination in the Armed Forces, Series B, reel 15.Papers of the National Association for the Advancement of Colored People, Library of Congress, microfilm edition (Frederick, Md.: University Publications of America, 1982–1999).

2. The League of Coloured Peoples, *Newsletter* 17, no. 104 (1948): 111, 116; Percival L. Prattis to William Nunn, Mar. 13, 1949, P. L. Prattis Papers, Moorland-Spingarn Research Center, Howard University, Washington, D.C.

3. See, for example, "Italian Woman Weds War Vet," *Baltimore Afro-American,* Aug. 9, 1947; "Affairs with Frauleins Accepted in Germany," *Baltimore Afro-American,* June 5, 1948; "Connecticut Vet Weds Italian Girl," *Amsterdam News,* Nov. 20, 1948; Erich Lissner, "We Adopted a Brown Baby," *Ebony,* May 1953, 36–45.

4. Omi and Winant, *Racial Formation in the United States;* Committee to Con-

sider Possibilities and Resources for the Immigration of a Group of German Orphans of Negro Blood, minutes of Jan. 29, 1951 meeting, p. 4, NAACP Papers, Part 9: Discrimination in the Armed Forces, Series B, reel 8; "The Problem of America's Brown Babies," Ebony, Dec. 1959, 65–72; Dunnigan, A Black Woman's Experience, 371–72. For similar problems affecting Eurasian orphans, see I. Evelyn Smith to Mrs. James A. Michener, Oct. 1, 1952, Children's Bureau Records, RG 102, National Archives and Records Administration (NARA), Washington, D.C. I am grateful to Joanne Meyerowitz for alerting me to the Children's Bureau material and providing many of the citations to that collection.

5. "Germany: Occupation Period: Policy with Respect to Standards of Subsistence for the Civilian Population—Views of the Interdivisional Committee on Germany," July 22, 1944, State Department Documents of the Interdivisional Country and Area Committees, 1943–46, NARA Microfilm Pub. T1221, reel 5 (Washington, 1979).

6. Enloe, The Morning After, 118.

7. Frevert, Women in German History, 258; Stibbe, "Women and the Nazi State." See also Vaizey, Surviving Hitler's War, 70–82; Pine, Education in Nazi Germany, 121–33; Tröger, "Between Rape and Prostitution."

8. Enloe, The Morning After, 118.

9. For Britain, see Smith, When Jim Crow Met John Bull; Rose, "Sex, Citizenship, and the Nation in World War II Britain."

10. See the discussion of this issue in Yellin, Our Mothers' War; Bailey and Farber, The First Strange Place.

11. Francis A. Kornegay to Lt. Col. Marcus Ray, Dec. 14, 1945, Assistant Secretary of War Subject File 1940–47, Records of the Office of the Secretary of War, RG 107, NARA.

12. Dulaney et al., Black Police in America; memorandum, Secretary of War Robert P. Patterson for Deputy Chief of Staff, Jan. 7, 1947; Nalty and MacGregor, Blacks in the Military, 217. Discussions of racism in the U.S. military in occupied Germany can be found in Höhn and Klimke, A Breath of Freedom, 54–60; Höhn, "'We Will Never Go Back to the Old Way Again.'"

13. James P. O'Donnell, "The GI Legacy in Germany," Newsweek, June 16, 1947, 48.

14. Maj. Gen. Frank A. Keating to Lt. Gen. Clarence R Huebner, June 12, 1947, Reports and Programs against Venereal Disease, Prostitution, and Sex Vices, AG 726.1, Records of the Office of the Military Government (OMGUS), Records of U.S. Occupation Headquarters, RG 260, NARA. See also Schroer, Recasting Race after World War II.

15. Edgar G. Conner to OMGUS Bavaria, n.d., Reports and Programs against Venereal Disease, Prostitution, and Sex Vices, AG 726.1, RG 260, NARA.

16. Edgar G. Conner to OMGUS Bavaria, n.d.; Col. Leslie E. Babcock to Chief of Staff, Dec. 2, 1946, Ray's Field Trips, in Office of the Assistant Secretary of War, Civilian Aide to the Secretary, RG 107, NARA.

17. Griswold to Chief of Staff, May 6, 1947, AG 726.1, RG 260, NARA.

18. Höhn, "GIs, Veronikas and Lucky Strikes," 244, 250.

19. Höhn, "GIs, Veronikas and Lucky Strikes," 237, 253–57, 261; Ziemke, The U.S. Army in the Occupation of Germany, 438.

20. Utley, The High Cost of Vengeance, 239–41.

21. O'Donnell, "The GI Legacy in Germany," 48.

22. Lusane, Hitler's Black Victims, 139; Kestling, "Blacks under the Swastika."

23. Lt. Gen. Thomas T. Hardy to John J. McCloy, Sept. 23, 1944, Negro troops—Civilian Aide, ASW 291.2, Formerly Security-Classified Correspondence of John J. McCloy 1941–45, RG 107.

24. Katharine Oguntoye, May Opitz, and Dagmar Schultz, "African and Afro-German Women in the Weimar Republic and under National Socialism," in Oguntoye et al., Showing Our Colors, 50, 52. See also Hügel-Marshall, Invisible Woman; Obermeier, "Afro-German Women." On the World War I–era occupation, see Nelson, "The Black Horror on the Rhine"; Pommerin, "The Fate of the Mixed Blood Children in Germany"; Marks, "Black Watch on the Rhine"; Oguntoye and Opitz, "Showing Our Colours"; May Opitz, "African and Afro-German Women in the Weimar Republic and under National Socialism," in Oguntoye et al., Showing Our Colors, 50, 52.

25. "The Position of France in the Military Occupation of Germany," Country and Area Committee Report No. 133, Mar. 25, 1944, p. 2, State Department Documents of the Interdivisional Country and Area Committees, 1943–46, NARA Microfilm Publication T1221 (Washington, 1979).

26. Höhn, "GIs, Veronikas and Lucky Strikes," 117–21.

27. Including a recollection by the African American historian Nathan Huggins who, on guard duty during World War II, could only stand outside the Jim Crow restaurant where his German POW charges were being served. See Blight, "In Retrospect," 12.

28. Manuscript, No. 22, Aug. 13 1945; Marcus Ray to General Joseph T. McNarney, Nov. 23, 1946, Ray's Field Trips, RG 107 Office of the Assistant Secretary of War, Civilian Aide to the Secretary; Col. Leslie E. Babcock, chief, Inspections Division denied this report in Babcock to Chief of Staff, Dec. 2, 1946; Harrington, Why I Left America and Other Essays, 90–91.

29. Goedde, "From Villains to Victims."

30. Pence, "The 'Fräuleins' Meet the 'Amis.'"

31. Hildegarde Kaiser to Jesse O. Dedmon, Dec. 7, 1946; Howard C. Peterson, Assistant Secretary of War, to Alice Rivkin, May 17, 1947, RG 107, NARA; NAACP Papers, Part 9: Discrimination in the Armed Forces, Series B, reel 15; Douglass Hall, "Don't Disgrace Women, GI's Advised," Baltimore Afro-American, Aug. 9, 1947.

32. George, Berlin Days, 55–56; Ziemke, The U.S. Army in the Occupation of Germany, 321–27; William G. Nunn, "Europe's 'Brown Babies' in Dire Need of Help," Pittsburgh Courier, May 29, 1948.

33. Cliff MacKay, "How Many 'Wild Oats' Babies in Germany," Afro Mag-

azine, May 8, 1948, 11. See also Frevert, *Women in German History*, 261; Höhn, "Frau im Haus und Girl im *Spiegel*," 63–64.

34. Nunn, "Europe's 'Brown Babies' in Dire Need of Help"; Ollie Stewart, "Germany's New Problem," *Afro Magazine*, July 3, 1948, 6; "'Brown Babies' Turned into Side Show Attraction," *Pittsburgh Courier*, July 17, 1948; "Brown Skinned War Babies: An Intimate Story of How These Children Are Cared For inside Hitler's Germany Today," *Chicago Defender*, Nov. 5. 1949, magazine sec., 18, 21.

35. See, for example, "Ohio Claims Three 'Brown Babies,'" *Pittsburgh Courier*, Mar. 2, 1949; Master Sgt. Herman Richardson, letter to the editor, *Sepia*, July 1952, 6.

36. May Opitz, "Afro-Germans after 1945," in Oguntoye et al., *Showing Our Colors*, 90.

37. Robert W. Bruce to T/Sgt. Donald H. Miller, Sept. 21, 1948, Reading File of the Chief and Deputy Chief of the Legal Affairs Division, Records of the U.S. High Commissioner for Germany, RG 466, NARA; OMGUS cable, Aug. 15, 1947, Marriage Policy, AG 291.1; O'Donnell, "The GI Legacy in Germany," 49.

38. Franklin J. Potter to Fred J. Cohn, Sept. 27, 1947; Stanley H. Gaines to S/Sgt. Moe Nehrer, Dec. 27, 1950; Gaines to Lt. Col. Thomas A. Fagan, Jan. 26, 1951; Gaines to Messrs. Gelnhausern and Backer, Apr. 18. 1951; Ernest Anspach, to Genoveva Strohmenger, Mar. 2, 1950; to B. Staedter, Mar. 2, 1950, Reading File, Box 2.

39. Lt. Col. J. V. Sheldon, Asst. Adj.-General, to Commanding Generals, Mar. 5, 1946, OMGUS Records, RG 260, NARA; Robert W. Bruce to Ruth Haas, Dec. 15, 1948, Reading File, Box 2.

40. "Illegitimacy in England Laid to U.S. Ban on Mixed Marriage," *Baltimore Afro-American*, Feb. 1, 1947; "GI's English Kids Labeled 'Apes,'" *Baltimore Afro-American*, April 26, 1947; Emory Ross to Maud Morlock, Mar. 10, 1947, RG 102, NARA; Smith, *When Jim Crow Met John Bull*, 209.

41. Country and Area Committee 37, July 13, 1944, "Germany: Occupation Period: Abrogation of Laws," State Department Documents of the Interdivisional Country and Area Committees, 1943–46, NARA Microfilm Publication T1221, reel 4 (Washington, 1979); Reading File, Box 2. A comprehensive list of states banning intermarriage in 1945 is found in Robert L. Carter to Cpl. Cleophas J. Randall, Nov. 26, 1945. NAACP Papers, Part 9: Discrimination in the Armed Forces, Series B, reel 15.

42. Stanley H. Gaines to Mr. Dunn, May 2, 1951, Reading File; Franklin Potter to OMGUS, Oct. 8, 1947; Potter to Pfc. Horace Bell, Oct. 21, 1947; Potter to Minister of Justice for Hesse, Nov. 4, 1948; Stanley H. Gaines to Capt. A. R. Koval, Dec. 5, 1950; Gaines to Otto Michaelis, July 7, 1950; cable, Dec. 6, 1947, Marriage Policy; Office of the Commanding General, Memorandum, Dec. 13, 1947, Marriages Dec. (1947); Capt. Harry Ross to Commander in Chief, EUROCOM, Dec. 4, 1947, AG 291.1 Marriage Reports, RG 260, NARA.

43. Robert W. Bruce to the Hessischer Landesverein, Jan. 24, 1949, Reading File, Box 2.

44. Höhn, "GIs, Veronikas and Lucky Strikes, 48, 254.

45. Doug Hall, "Christmas Finds These Americans in Germany," *Afro Magazine*, Dec. 27, 1947, M-12; Nunn, "Europe's 'Brown Babies' in Dire Need of Help"; J. A. Rogers column, *Pittsburgh Courier* clipping, 1956, n.d., Tuskegee News Clipping File.

46. Goedde, "From Villains to Victims," 8.

47. Quoted in Klein, "Family Ties and Political Obligation," 47.

48. Manuel Kaufman to Maud Morlock, Aug. 9, 1948, RG 102; "Laws Tightened to End Black Market in Babies," *Baltimore Afro-American*, Mar. 22, 1947; Sollinger, "Race and 'Value,'" 348–50.

49. "New York Bans Agency Jim Crow," *Baltimore Afro-American*, Mar. 22, 1947; Maud Morlock to Esther G. Levitt, May 8, 1950, RG 102, NARA.

50. William S. Jackson to Jean Blackwell, Dec. 31, 1954; and Urban League press release, Jan. 25, 1955 in Schomburg Clipping File, 000,035; New York Public Library; Bettye Cook, "Fultz Quads on Road to Long Life," *Afro Magazine*, Apr. 24, 1947, 1 and photo spread, 3; "Fultz Quadruplets Steal Show at Festival in N.C.," *Baltimore Afro-American*, May 31, 1947.

51. Sollinger, *Wake Up Little Susie.* See also Sollinger, "Race and 'Value.'"

52. Committee to Consider Possibilities, minutes of Jan. 29, 1951, meeting, 5, NAACP Papers, Part 9: Discrimination in the Armed Forces, Series B, reel 8.

53. *Loving v. Virginia*, 388 U.S. 1 (1967); Nichols, *Breakthrough on the Color Front*, 166. For other references to this issue, see Franklin H. Williams to James C. Evans, Apr. 22, 1948, NAACP Papers, Part 9: Discrimination in the Armed Forces, Series B, reel 15.

54. Shukert and Scibetta, *War Brides of World War II.*

55. Committee to Consider Possibilities, minutes of Jan. 29, 1951, meeting, 4–5, NAACP Papers, Part 9: Discrimination in the Armed Forces, Series B, reel 8; "German War Babies: Red Tape Balks Adoption of Orphan by Teacher," *Ebony* 6 (Jan. 1951): 35–38; "German Brown Babies in the United States," *Sepia*, Feb. 1952, 52–54.

56. Beth Muller to Miss Smith, interoffice memorandum, May 26, 1948; Martha Wood's memorandum, June 4, 1948, Social Security Administration, Chicago branch, RG 102.

57. Washburn, *A Question of Sedition*; Louise Noble's report for the Federal Security Agency—Social Security Board, Nov. 1947; Beth Muller, Regional Child Representative, to Louise Noble, Chief of Field Service, Federal Security Agency-Social Security Board, June 4, 1951, RG 102.

58. Committee to Consider Possibilities, minutes of Jan. 29, 1951, meeting, 5–7.

59. Maud Morlock to Miss Nutt, Aug. 1, 1946, Morlock memorandum, Sept. 17, 1946; Willard L. Thorp, Assistant Secretary of State, to Maj. Gen.

Edward F. Witsell, n.d., Children's Bureau copy received Jan. 8, 1947; memorandum of Morlock's telephone conversation with J. Charnow, Jan. 24, 1947; Jane M. Hoey, "Report on Problems Arising from the Presence of United States Troops Overseas," Mar. 21, 1949; I. Evelyn Smith to Dr. Elisabeth Meyer-Spreckels, July 26, 1951, RG 102, NARA.

60. Katherine F. Lenroot to Rep. Joseph R. Farrington, May 31, 1949; Frances K. Kernohan to Irene Murphy, June 8, 1949; I. Evelyn Roberts to Kiyoko Nishi, May 8, 1952, RG 102, NARA.

61. *Baltimore Afro-American*, Aug. 7, 1954; May 17, 1958, 3; *Afro Magazine*, June 20, 1953, 1, 3; Evelyn Roberts to Kiyoko Nishi, May 8, 1952, RG 102; Committee to Consider Possibilities, minutes of Jan. 29, 1951, meeting, 2, NAACP Papers, Part 9: Discrimination in the Armed Forces, Series B, reel 8. See Fehrenbach, *Race after Hitler*, 132–68.

62. Opitz, "African and Afro-German Women in the Weimar Republic and under National Socialism," 52; Opitz, "Afro-Germans after 1945," 79–100; Freda Rippy to Walter White, Mar. 15, 1953; Caroline A. Flexner to Walter White, June 17, 1953, NAACP Papers, Part 9: Discrimination in the Armed Forces, Series B, reel 8.

63. "Brown Babies Go to Work—1,500 Negro Youths Integrated into Germany's Work Force," *Ebony*, Nov. 1960, 98; Opitz, "Afro-Germans after 1945," 97–108.

64. Nichols, *Breakthrough on the Color Front*, 161–68; Cpl. George D. Brown to NAACP Legal Committee, Nov. 20, 1949, NAACP Papers, Part 9: Discrimination in the Armed Forces, Series B, reel 15.

eight

Regulating Borders and Bodies
U.S. Immigration and Public Health Policy

NATALIA MOLINA

Throughout the twentieth century and into the twenty-first, U.S. public health and immigration policies have intersected with and informed one another in the country's response to Mexican immigration. Three historical episodes illustrate how perceived racial differences have influenced disease diagnosis: a 1916 typhus outbreak, the midcentury Bracero Program, and medical deportations that are taking place today. Disease, or just the threat of it, have marked Mexicans as foreign, just as much as phenotype, native language, accent, or clothing. A focus on racialized bodies has rendered other factors and structures, such as poor working conditions or structural inequalities in health care, invisible. This attitude has had long-term effects on immigration policy, as well as on how Mexicans have been received in the United States.

Mexican Immigration and U.S. Public Health Practices in the Twentieth Century

U.S. immigration policy was fairly open until the end of the nineteenth century, because immigrant labor was needed to help build and settle the expanding country. Federal restrictions on immigration did not appear until 1891, when Congress passed the first comprehensive immigration law.[1] The law allowed immigrants to be barred from the United

States for various reasons, ranging from being convicted of a crime to being considered likely to become a public charge, but many involved standards of fitness. Anyone considered "feebleminded," "insane," or likely to spread a "dangerous and loathsome contagious disease" was barred from the United States. An immigrant who was allowed entry but later fell ill and became a public charge (or even was thought likely to become a public charge) faced the possibility of deportation.[2] During the early twentieth century, as public health as a field and profession became more established, it increasingly influenced immigration policy.

At the same time that U.S. immigration and public health policies were becoming more interwoven, Mexican immigration to the United States began to increase. From 1900 to 1930 the Mexican population in the United States more than doubled every ten years. By 1930 an estimated 1.5 million Mexicans and Mexican Americans lived in the United States.[3] Most Mexicans arrived as low-paid laborers who worked mainly in agriculture and railroad building. Nativists denounced Mexican immigrants as unable to assimilate, less intelligent than white Americans, and "for the most part, Indian," and therefore racially inferior.[4] Increasingly these stereotypes took the form of negative medicalized representations, giving rise to significant ramifications for immigration policy and securing the nation's borders. Public health standards based on perceived racial difference influenced both the treatment and perceptions of Mexican immigrants not just at the time they crossed the border but long after they had settled in the United States.

Medicalized Borders in the Nation's Internal Borderlands

Medicalized representations of Mexicans in the United States can be traced back to when what is now the U.S. Southwest was still a part of Mexico. The ideology of Manifest Destiny gained popularity during the Mexican-American War (1846–48) and provided justification for U.S. expansionism. Dedicated believers in Manifest Destiny were compelled to portray white Americans as superior to Mexicans and Native Americans. Expansionists argued that after the U.S. takeover, Mexicans and Native Americans would eventually disappear in the Southwest because they were not as biologically fit as white Americans.[5]

Mexican immigration to the United States increased in the second decade of the twentieth century, driven by the need for laborers, particularly in the Southwest's burgeoning agricultural industry. The demand for laborers was conveniently met by refugees fleeing the ravages of the Mexican Revolution. Mexicans were ideal migrant laborers: sojourner males who traveled to secure work but would eventually return home. Such workers required no capital or social investment; they needed little more than a willing employer and transient housing.

Although immigration laws did not severely restrict Mexican immigration at this time, public health standards helped shape attitudes and regulations directed at this new laboring class. As Amy Fairchild found in a study of the nation's borders, medical inspectors indoctrinated incoming immigrants by demonstrating to them the social and industrial norms needed to succeed as workers in the United States.[6] Thus, far from excluding workers, health inspectors could shape immigrants into an acceptable laboring class. In the borderlands, however, such practices could also stigmatize Mexicans.[7]

Before the enactment of restrictive laws such as the 1917 Immigration Act, which imposed a head tax and literacy test, medical screenings already regulated Mexican immigration. Mexicans underwent intrusive, humiliating, and harmful baths and physical examinations at the hands of the U.S. Public Health Service (USPHS) at the U.S.-Mexico border beginning in 1916. The rationale for this treatment was the belief that Mexicans were bringing disease into the United States.[8] Thus public health policies helped to secure the U.S.-Mexico border and to mark Mexican bodies as outsiders even before the advent of more focused gatekeeping institutions, such as the border patrol, created in 1924.

The connections between public health policies and the development of long-lasting representations of Mexicans as disease carriers are demonstrated by the response to a 1916 typhus outbreak in Los Angeles County. The disease spread from person to person, spurring the creation of local policies derived from the premise that all Mexicans spread disease. The typhus cases in Los Angeles preceded a quarantine on the U.S.-Mexico border in Texas the next year, also spurred by a handful of cases. Nonetheless, as Alexandra Stern, writing about the Texas quarantine, argues, these practices "fostered scientific and popular prejudices about the biological inferiority of Mexicans."[9] These medically driven policies had far-reaching social and political effects.

When a Mexican laborer at a Southern Pacific Railroad camp near Palmdale (twenty miles north of Los Angeles) came down with typhus in June 1916, health officials were alarmed. Typhus is an infectious disease caused by rickettsia (a bacteria-like microorganism) and transmitted to humans through lice and tick bites.[10] In the right conditions (overcrowding, lack of facilities for bathing and washing clothes, poor sanitation), typhus can rapidly become an epidemic.[11] Ultimately twenty-six people contracted the disease (including twenty-two Mexican railroad workers) over a five-month period from June to October 1916. The outbreak killed five people, all of them Mexican.[12]

Public health officials at the county, state, and national levels soon became involved. County measures to contain the outbreak involved hygiene, sanitation, and education campaigns, all aimed exclusively at Mexicans. Dr. Howard D. King of New Orleans warned, "Every individual hailing from Mexico should be regarded as potentially pathogenic."[13] The stigma of the typhus outbreaks marked every area where Mexicans lived as needing inspection. In thirty railroad camps in California, health officials were particularly aggressive; they used cyanide gas to destroy lice, ticks, and other pests.[14]

The California State Board of Health pressured railroad employers to play a role in containing the typhus outbreak. Officials drew up an eight-point list of regulations, printed in both English and Spanish, and labor recruiters distributed the list to the various railroad camps. The regulations applied to every man, woman, and child living in the camps, not just to laborers. All of the regulations focused on improving personal hygiene; not one addressed the inferior living conditions in the camps.

Mexican laborers expressed frustration over the attention paid to their individual actions, with no mention of structural problems in the camps, such as a dearth of toilets and bathing facilities. This frustration is clear in a formal letter of complaint sent to the Mexican consul in Los Angeles by a group of Mexicans who lived in a desert camp about 140 miles east of the city. The men, angry over the crudeness and impracticality of the antityphus procedures and the overt racism of the regulations, submitted their complaint just two weeks after the state board issued the regulations:

Dear Sir:

Due to the difficult circumstances we find ourselves in this foreign country, we look to you asking for help in this case. We are enclosing a copy of the severe law that the railroad line has imposed on us Mexicans who work on the track, which we do not see as a just thing, but only offensive and humiliating. When we crossed the border into this country, the health inspector inspected us. If the railroad line needs or wants to take such precautions it is not necessary that they treat us in this manner. For this, they would need health inspectors who assisted every individual with medical care and give us 2 rooms to live, one to sleep in and one to cook in, and also to pay a fair wage to obtain a change of clothes and a bar of soap. This wage they set is not enough for the nourishment of one person. Health comes from this and these precautions are the basis for achieving sanitation. Health we have. What we need is liberty and the opportunity to achieve it. We need a bathroom in each section of camp and that the toilets that are now next to the sleeping quarters be moved. Many times their bad smell has prevented us from even eating our simple meal. Furthermore, we can disclose many other details which compromise our good health and personal hygiene. With no further ado, we remain yours, graciously and devotedly, your attentive and faithful servants. We thank you in advance for what you may be able to do for us.

Felipe Vaiz, José Martinez, Felipe Martinez, Adolfo Robles, Alejandro Gómez, Alberto Esquivei.[15]

Drawing on an alternative epistemology, the men explained that their living conditions resulted from systemic inequality, not from ingrained cultural habit. Unlike the state and county officials who crafted reports that avoided charging the railroad companies with any responsibility for the presence of disease and dirt in the camps, the workers did not hesitate to assign blame where it belonged. Health officials focused their efforts to stem the typhus outbreaks on remedying Mexicans' "unclean habits," but the letter writers pointed out the obvious: the unsanitary living conditions that so disturbed health officials were created and maintained by the railroad employers, not the laborers.

By failing to treat typhus as a threat to the public at large, officials constructed the disease as uniquely Mexican. This preference for making race the organizing principle for understanding typhus also transformed Mexicans from being the unfortunate victims of a serious disease into being active transmitters of deadly germs, thus adding a medicalized dimension to existing nativism. Armored by their presumed scientific objectivity, health officials gave wide circulation to constructed categories of Mexicans as unclean, ignorant of basic hygiene practices, and unwitting hosts for communicable diseases. These images were embedded in medical and media narratives and in public policy.

Visual depictions of Mexicans effectively linked them with disease. In October 1916, for example, the cover of the California State Board of Health monthly bulletin was emblazoned with a photograph of Mexican men, women, and children who lived in the railroad camps.

The caption, "The type of people who are bringing typhus and other diseases into California from Mexico," ensured that not even the most naïve of readers could miss the point.[16] Used in this way, the word *type* reduced all Mexican immigrants to a static archetype. Race, not symptoms, became shorthand for *disease carrier.*[17]

Although the potential typhus epidemic was contained, it spurred widespread changes in immigration inspection procedures. General inspections at the border increased, even for laborers who crossed daily. The Los Angeles County Health Department received assurances that, in the future, disinfections at the El Paso border would be performed by USPHS staff. Indeed the USPHS planned to establish multiple inspection stations along the Texas border—in El Paso, Eagle Pass, Laredo, and Brownsville—a move county officials applauded.[18] Mandatory inspections continued into the late 1920s, further demonstrating the extent to which Mexican immigrants and disease had become conflated.[19]

The Bracero Program and Health

The idea that Mexicans were likely to spread disease continued to shape immigration policies in the following decades, notably in the Bracero Program. In 1942 the United States and Mexico collaborated in creating this guest worker arrangement, which operated until 1964. The Bracero Program brought four million Mexican men to the United States to work in agriculture and other industries such as railroads to fill World War II labor shortages. The physically rigorous nature of the work for which the U.S. government was recruiting workers necessitated assurances that they would be productive and that they posed no public health threat.

This recruitment took place in the wake of deportation programs carried out just a few years earlier. During the Great Depression everyday citizens and government officials alike scapegoated Mexican immigrants as both drains on the U.S. economy and cultural outsiders. These attitudes led to deportations (voluntary and involuntary) that sent an estimated 1.6 million Mexicans back to their homeland. Although the majority of deportations had ended by 1935, Mexicans who sought medical care at public institutions still risked deportation. The coexistence of the deportations and the guest worker program illustrates the pliability of a racial logic that could view Mexicans as liabilities and resources simultaneously.[20]

Scholars have informed our understanding of the Bracero Program by looking at the complexity of the government policy and administration that drove the program.[21] More recently researchers have shown how the workers themselves exhibited agency as they negotiated this program and how the program affected not just them but also their families, bringing a much-needed gender analysis to this area of study.[22] These recent scholarly works, along with other sources, such as newspaper articles and previously untapped oral interviews, combine to support the conclusion that health policies that were central to the Bracero Program continued to regard Mexicans as health threats rather than critically examining systemic inequalities created and maintained by the program itself. These policies, overseen and sanctioned by the federal government, signaled a new era in medical racial profiling, thus offering a new framework for disciplining labor.

Braceros were recruited in Mexico and underwent health screenings in both Mexico and the United States. In Mexico personnel from the USPHS, along with the War Manpower Commission and the Farm Security Administration, oversaw the contracting of workers, in collaboration with Mexican officials. Mexicans seeking to participate in the program were required to pass a physical examination by both U.S. and Mexican public health doctors in accordance with U.S. immigration policies and railroad company regulations. The practice of sending USPHS personnel to the interior of Mexico for screenings points to the artificiality of the border. In the pursuit of laborers, the border was not a specific geographical location. Instead the Mexican bodies themselves became the sites of border enforcement.

U.S. public health officials used standards developed by the U.S. military for conducting medical screenings. Officials required every prospective bracero to undergo a physical examination, with chest x-rays to check for tuberculosis, serological tests to check for venereal disease, psychological profiling, and a chemical bath. They tested applicants to see whether they were capable of the arduous labor expected of them, checking their hands for callouses and their bodies for scars. Inspectors could interpret fresh scars as evidence of injury or pain, thus potentially disqualifying the applicant.[23]

Mexicans found the examinations tiring and humiliating. In her research the historian Ana Rosas found that men could wait anywhere between six and ten hours to be examined. Physicians directed the men into an examination room that held as many as forty men at a time, where they had to undress and undergo an examination the doctors conducted in English.[24] The scholar Barbara Driscoll notes that recruits complained to Mexican officials that USPHS officials were harassing them.[25] Applicants who passed this examination and were accepted into the program found that their trials were not over: they underwent yet another compulsory physical examination when they arrived in the U.S. bracero camps.[26]

Mexican men did their best to retain their dignity throughout this process. The historian Deborah Cohen interviewed men applying to the Bracero Program and found that they recast parts of the exams in a positive light. They wanted to be seen as strong, healthy, and hardworking, so they willingly extended their calloused hands to inspectors as evidence of these qualities. This image was important to them not just as potential participants in the Bracero Program but as male breadwinners for their family and as part of their own sense of masculinity. Applicants also recalled trying to subvert the x-ray examination by drinking large quantities of milk beforehand. They did this not because they had something to hide but because they feared the physicians might find some small imperfection that could be used to disqualify them from the program.[27]

Despite the perception that Mexicans posed a public health threat, the War Manpower Commission, created during World War II to balance the labor needs of agriculture, industry, and the armed forces, was not always willing to fully fund the USPHS physicians' work. When the USPHS moved from its original location in Mexico City to San Luis Potosí, the employees asked to take the x-ray equipment with them. The War Manpower Commission denied permission on the premise that x-rays were too costly. In 1945, however, a railroad company in eastern Florida complained that a bracero in its employ had an active case of tuberculosis. After this complaint, the USPHS received permission to move the x-ray equipment to its new office, although the head of the War Manpower Commission refused to purchase any more medical equipment.[28]

In the United States contracted workers underwent a second inspection at USPHS processing centers that duplicated the procedures they experienced in Mexico. The USPHS centers in and around El Paso, Texas, the largest port of entry into the United States from Mexico, processed many of the braceros. Often the braceros were transported in cattle cars.[29] Personnel routinely processed 800 to 1,600 braceros at a time and in some cases more than 3,100.[30] Carlos Cordelia, a processing employee, described how braceros were asked to strip and then were sprayed with a white powder on their hair, face, and "lower area," a procedure that embarrassed them. Some tolerated the situation with humor, declaring, "I guess we're gringos now."[31]

Many other problems arose in the U.S. inspections. Dr. Pedro Ortega reported that U.S. doctors sold the x-ray films of men who had passed the physical exam to braceros who worried about passing. He also reported that doctors occasionally gave penicillin to braceros with the goal of keeping them in good health for six months, the length of their contract.[32]

Although health standards were ostensibly important selection criteria, once braceros were hired, the employers did not adhere to the same standards in providing working and living conditions. According to a report from California's State Senate Fact Finding Committee on Labor and Welfare, inadequate health and accident insurance and employee housing ranked among the laborers' most frequent complaints.[33]

In one case in Santa Barbara, California, in 1963, the U.S. Department of Labor was called into a work camp to conduct a special investigation after receiving reports that "wretched conditions existed in the camps." The laborers charged that they had been threatened with return to Mexico if they filed any complaints. Braceros with health problems claimed that they received "unsympathetic treatment from camp doctors." They also complained that they were not given enough to eat and were often served spoiled meat and that their wages were not paid in full.[34] It is striking that concerns about access to health care and the standard of living persisted throughout the Bracero Program's twenty-two-year existence. It is also striking that these concerns involved a government program, carried out by the very same government that was enacting laws and policies dedicated to eradicating the diseases that were spawned by the conditions in which the workers were forced to live.

In its final years the Bracero Program faced a congressional opponent in Representative Edward Roybal. Roybal began his career as a public educator with the California Tuberculosis Association and is remembered for his many years of fighting for the rights of his constituents in East Los Angeles, first as a council member and then as a member of Congress for more than three decades. He publicly denounced the substandard living conditions in the bracero camps and the poor health of the workers and argued against renewing the program.[35]

Thus, although the Bracero Program ostensibly upheld strict health standards, in practice it stigmatized Mexicans as bearers of disease while ignoring the systemic conditions that gave rise to disease. Even when investigations repeatedly brought to light problems in the camps, government officials did not rush to ameliorate the problems. Conditions found in the bracero camps were reminiscent of those found in railroad camps fifty years earlier, but change would have required dealing with widespread systemic problems and would have threatened the very existence of the Bracero Program.

Medical Deportations

The consistent representation of Mexicans as disease carriers unworthy of social membership in U.S. society led to the conclusion that they were unworthy recipients of publicly funded health care. This philosophy is exemplified by the frightening modern-day practice of patient deportation by hospitals. Some hospitals, without prompting from the federal government, are taking it upon themselves to return patients to their home country if they are undocumented, without insurance, and in need of long-term care. This occurs because, by law, hospitals that accept Medicare are required to secure continuing care before discharging Medicare patients. Except in California and New York, Medicare does not pay for long-term care for undocumented patients, so hospitals undertake a large financial burden when they accept such patients.

Hospital administrators who deport patients do not necessarily secure health care in the patients' home country. One attorney, whose practice specializes in these cases, objected, "If somebody has a serious illness and needs continuing care, a hospital can't simply discharge them onto the street, much less put them onto a plane."[36] These hospital-initiated deportations shine a light on how deportations are being performed today outside the purview of Homeland Security.

In today's climate, in which many view Latino immigrants as an economic, cultural, and social threat, it is not surprising that Latino immigrants are often the targets of medical deportations. Although the deportation of immigrants by hospitals is not a practice originated to regulate immigration from Latin America, but rather is a response to the perceived burden of patients from other countries who are unable to pay for their care, these deportations are nonetheless undergirded by the same racial logic that led to public health screenings during the 1916 typhus outbreak and the Bracero Program, in which immigrant Mexicans were consistently characterized as a problem for or threat to U.S. society.

In addition, these deportations are connected to other contemporary medical practices and acts that stigmatize Mexicans, such as the passage of California Proposition 187 in 1994, which sought to withhold public services from undocumented immigrants.[37] The anthropologist Leo Chavez provides a fascinating look at the contemporary categorization of Latinos as threats in medical discourse in his examination of immigrants as organ transplant recipients.[38] Similarly the anthropologist Jonathan Inda examines how immigrants are constructed as incapable of governing themselves; his research focused on changes in immigration and welfare policy, such as the Personal Responsibility and Work Opportunity Reconciliation Act of 1996.[39] The sociologist Lisa Sun-Hee Park demonstrates how immigration and welfare reform in 1996 particularly stigmatized low-income Latina immigrants of childbearing age, documented and undocumented alike, as unworthy public health and service seekers.[40]

Hospital deportations suggest that little has changed in the workplace for immigrants since the early twentieth century. Low-wage, low-skilled immigrants routinely perform the most dangerous jobs yet are not provided health care as part of their employment and earn too little to purchase their own health insurance. According to a recent special issue of the *American Journal of Industrial Medicine* on occupational health disparities, "Immigrant Latino workers have fatal traumatic injury rates that are one-third higher than U.S. workers overall. Hispanic workers also experience high rates of non-fatal, lost-work injured and prolonged recovery times. Studies show that such workers commonly work in the more dangerous jobs, receive little training, and are exploited by employers."[41]

Focusing on the cost of providing long-term care to injured immigrants reinforces the image of Latinos as a threat and potential burden, obviating the need to examine the systemic inequalities that place Latinos in this position. The journalist Deborah Sontag has documented cases of deportations resulting from what she terms a "collision of two deeply flawed American systems, immigration and health care." She writes about Luis Alberto Jimenez, an undocumented Guatemalan immigrant, who was working as a gardener in Florida when he became the victim of a drunk driver in an auto accident. Uninsured, Jimenez owed hospital and rehabilitation bills of $1.5 million. The hospital, Martin Memorial, obtained a court order and "forcibly returned him to his home country," according to a hospital administrator, although an appeal was pending. The hospital did not notify Jimenez's family of the deportation.[42] In Phoenix, Arizona, as a Mexican patient lay in a coma, hospital personnel, without the family's permission, took her fingerprints to begin deportation proceedings.[43] Not all deported immigrants are undocumented. Some hospitals routinely return both documented and undocumented immigrants simply because they are uninsured. A Tucson, Arizona, hospital attempted to send a sick baby, born in the United States to an undocumented Mexican couple, to the parents' home country. The process was stopped only after legal intervention.[44]

Because these deportations are not part of an official government program, no official statistics exist on how many immigrants have been affected, but the increasing prevalence of examples suggests a trend. St. Joseph's Hospital in Phoenix, which has a large Mexican immigrant population, has reported deporting ninety-six immigrants. Since 2007 ten immigrants have been returned to Honduras from Chicago hospitals. In San Diego, California, the Mexican consulate reported eighty-seven medical cases, most of which ended in deportation. The Guatemalan foreign ministry listed fifty-three deportations by U.S. hospitals from 2003 to 2008.[45]

In addition, medicalized repatriation programs have been privatized as companies have developed to provide the services usually undertaken by federal immigration authorities. One such company is MexCare, located in San Diego, which bills itself as "an alternative choice for the care of the unfunded Latin American national." MexCare works with "any hospital seeking to defray un-reimbursed medical expenses" to transport patients to their home country. MexCare emphasizes that it only transports patients when they have received the authorization of the patient or family.[46] By contrast, Dr. Steven Larsoa, an expert on migrant health and an emergency room physician, considers repatriation a "death sentence" in some cases: "I've seen patients bundled onto the plane and out of the country, and once that person is out of sight, he's out of mind."[47]

 MexCare is also vague about the hospitals it has collaborated with, thereby raising some doubt about the transparency of its practices. Although its website includes a testimonial section, it does not attribute the sources of the testimonials. One such anonymous quote reads, "Our hospital has used MexCare several times. They help us provide care to our unfunded Latin American patients. They do it all, from start to finish. We are very pleased with their service." Because MexCare is a private company performing a function usually reserved for the federal government it is difficult to independently verify the legality or ethics of its practices.

Although transnational patient dumping is a recent phenomenon, it nonetheless follows patterns established throughout the twentieth century, in which medical discourse is used to distinguish desirable from undesirable members of society. The emergence of private companies, such as MexCare, is symptomatic of a neoliberal era in which private companies take over activities once performed by public entities. The seeming ease with which a private company can transport a patient in critical condition from Chicago to Honduras is also a feature of the era of globalization. In these cases we see how the same racial logic that gave rise to harmful policies and practices in the typhus epidemic and Bracero Program continues to affect Mexicans and other Latin American immigrants.

Conclusion

How a problem is defined shapes its solution. Negative representations of Mexican bodies as disease carriers and health burdens shaped the programs, policies, and practices of immigration and health agencies. Many documented cases illustrate the medicalization of the Mexican immigrant historically. The reaction to typhus outbreaks in the early twentieth century and the development of health policy standards in the Bracero Program revolved around representations of Mexicans as a threat to public health. Race served as an interpretive framework for explaining the typhus outbreaks and for developing a double-screening policy for braceros entering the United States and thus precluded any need to ameliorate the living conditions of workers once they had settled in the United States. Such reasoning, firmly established, obviated the need for a deeper investigation into the systemic inequality that fostered the inferior health and living conditions of Mexican laborers. Because medical discourse has the power to naturalize racial categories, it has also in some cases naturalized societal inequalities.

The fact that medical discourse has had a demonstrable influence on perceptions and consequently on the treatment of Mexican immigrants does not mean that all programs failed to implement changes that improved the public's overall health and welfare. To the contrary, public health agencies and practitioners have carried out many genuinely successful efforts, from reducing infant mortality rates to maintaining pure water supplies. Nonetheless the power of public health discourse to affect perceptions of race and to contribute to inequalities continues in the twenty-first century.

Latino immigrants who face deportation by U.S. hospitals today, like their counterparts before them, are perceived as unworthy of U.S. aid. Hospital deportations continue to obscure the global structure of inequality: people immigrate to developed nations in search of work; the destination countries benefit from the cheap labor without providing the necessities of a sustainable community; and then the immigrants become scapegoats for the problems that inevitably arise. The situation today did not arise spontaneously but rather flows from the long history of negative representations of Mexicans as foreign bodies who are unfit to be citizens.

Notes

This article, slightly revised, is reproduced with permission of the *American Journal of Public Health* 101, no. 6 (June, 2011): 1024–31, American Public Health Association, http://www.apha.org/.

1. The federal government had regulated immigration before, most notably with the 1882 Chinese Exclusion Act, but this was an act that discriminated based on race and class and not a comprehensive act. See Lee, *At America's Gates.*

2. Kraut, *Germs, Genes, and the "Immigrant Menace."*

3. Reisler, *By the Sweat of Their Brow*, 56.

4. U.S. Congress, House Committee on Immigration and Naturalization, *Hearings before the Committee on Immigration and Naturalization*, House of Representatives, 70th Congress, First Session, Feb. 21–Apr. 5, 1928 (Washington, DC: Government Printing Office, 1928).

5. For more on Manifest Destiny, see Horsman, *Race and Manifest Destiny.*

6. Fairchild, *Science at the Borders.*

7. On the West Coast, the Chinese also came under the purview of public health officials. See Shah, *Contagious Divides.*

8. Stern, *Eugenic Nation*, 57.

9. Stern, *Eugenic Nation*, 59.

10. Typhus symptoms can include high fever, headaches, chills, and severe muscular pain, followed by the appearance of a rash. The disease is serious and can be fatal for the very young, the elderly, and those already in poor health. See World Health Organization, "Epidemic Louse-Borne Typhus," May 1997, accessed March 2, 2011, http://www.who.int/mediacentre/factsheets/fs162/en/index.html.

11. The World Health Organization notes, "Louse-borne Typhus is the only rickettsial disease which can cause explosive epidemics in humans" ("Epidemic Louse-Borne Typhus").

12. In addition to the twenty-two Mexican railroad workers, one person in the city of Los Angeles contracted typhus, two people in the county (but not from the railroad camps) were affected, and no details are available regarding the one remaining case. There were also outbreaks in areas outside the county: seven cases in Banning (Riverside County), one in Livermore (Alameda County), one in Bakersfield (Kern County), and three in Tulare (Tulare County). California State Board of Health monthly bulletin (Sacramento: State Board of Health), June–December 1916.

13. Howard D. King, "Frequency of Tuberculosis among Negro Laundresses," *Journal of Outdoor Life* 11 (1914): 275. King also wrote about the prob-

lems of miscegenation; see "Miscegenation: An Old Social Problem," *New Orleans Medical and Surgical Journal* 66 (1914).

14. Los Angeles County Health Department, "Quarterly Health Report, 7/1–9/30/16," Records, Los Angeles County Department of Health Services Library, Main Office, Los Angeles (DHS). De-lousing procedures at this time typically involved routine baths, laundering clothes, and cleaning living quarters. Use of cyanide gas was not common because of the effects chemical gases could have on the central nervous system. In Prussia, however, the military used hydrocyanic acid to fumigate gypsy dwellings and railway carriages. The key ingredient was sodium cyanide, and the substance also contained sulphuric acid and water. See Weindling, *Epidemics and Genocide in Eastern Europe*, especially chapter 4, "The First World War and Combating Lice."

15. F. Vaiz et al. to Mexican consul, Oct. 17, 1916, Foreign Consulate Records for Los Angeles, Archives Secretaria de Relaciones Exteriores [Secretary of Foreign Relations], Mexico City.

16. California State Board of Health monthly bulletin, Oct. 1916, cover.

17. Rafael, "White Love." Rafael argues that these types of photographs flatten out identity, causing individuals to be seen merely as racial types.

18. Los Angeles County Health Department, "Quarterly Health Report, 7/1–9/30/16," 5.

19. Markel and Stern, "Which Face? Whose Nation?"; McKiernan-Gonzalez, "Fevered Measures"; Stern, "Buildings, Boundaries, and Blood."

20. Molina, *Fit to Be Citizens?*, 141.

21. Calavita, *Inside the State*.

22. Rosas, "Flexible Families"; Cohen, "Masculine Sweat, Stoop-Labor Modernity."

23. Driscoll, *The Tracks North*, 55, 73, 91; Cohen, "Masculine Sweat, Stoop-Labor Modernity," 267.

24. Rosas, "Flexible Families," 67.

25. Driscoll, *Tracks North*, 93.

26. Rosas, "Flexible Families," 197.

27. Cohen, "Masculine Sweat, Stoop-Labor Modernity," 267–68, 71–74, 87–89.

28. Driscoll, *Tracks North*, 93–94.

29. J. Lowenberg, oral interview, Bracero History Archive, accessed December 8, 2009, http://braceroarchive.org/about.

30. S. Sánchez, oral interview, Bracero History Archive.

31. C. Corella, oral interview, Bracero History Archive.

32. P. Ortega, oral interview. Bracero History Archive.

33. R. Salazar, "Braceros Cast in Complex Role," *Los Angeles Times*, Nov. 26, 1962.

34. R. Salazar, "U.S. Probe of Bracero Complaints Scheduled: Charges of 'Special Nature' on 'Wretched Conditions' Cited; Full Report Promised," *Los Angeles Times*, Nov. 14, 1963.

35. "Bracero Plan to Be Opposed by Rep. Roybal," *Los Angeles Times*, Jan. 10, 1963.

36. Deborah Sontag, "Deported by U.S. Hospitals," *New York Times*, Aug. 3, 2008.

37. California Proposition 187 was approved via referendum by California voters in 1994 to prevent undocumented immigrants from receiving public benefits or services, including health care and education. Legal challenges prevented it from being implemented. Ostensibly Proposition 187 was directed at all undocumented immigrants, but within California's political and cultural climate, it was understood that the proposition's primary target was Mexicans. Hondagneu-Sotelo, "Women and Children First."

38. Chavez, *The Latino Threat*.

39. Inda, *Targeting Immigrants*.

40. Park, "Perpetuation of Poverty through Public Charge."

41. Solis, "Foreword to Disparities Special Issue," 81.

42. Sontag, "Deported by U.S. Hospitals." See also Deborah Sontag, "Jury Rules for Hospital That Deported Patient," *New York Times*, July 28, 2009; Deborah Sontag, "Deported in Coma, Saved Back in U.S.," *New York Times*, Nov. 9, 2008.

43. "Mexicano Es Deportada En Estado Vegetativo" [Mexican is deported in vegetative state], *La Opinion*, Mar. 12, 2008, accessed Mar. 2, 2011, http://www.proquest.com.

44. Sontag, "Deported by U.S. Hospitals."

45. Sontag, "Deported by U.S. Hospitals."

46. MexCare, accessed Sept. 18, 2008, http://mexcare.com.

47. Sontag, "Deported by U.S. Hospitals."

nine

The American Look
The Nation in the Shape of a Woman

EMILY S. ROSENBERG

The American Look, introduced briefly in the 1930s but relaunched at the end of World War II, became a part of the lexicon of American nationalism in the early Cold War and illuminates the early days of what the *Time-Life* publisher Henry Luce predicted would be an "American Century." Arising from the campaigns of Dorothy Shaver and Claire McCardell in the world of women's fashion, it styled "American women"—exemplifying the nation itself—as wholesome, fun-loving, friendly, resourceful, and self-confident. Picked up by home design professionals and the automotive and other industries, the American Look then broadened its meaning and became an emblem of a desirable modernity—a descriptor for a future that everyone in the world should wish to embrace. As U.S. State Department officials stepped up their global propaganda efforts in the Cold War rivalry of the 1950s, they invoked the American Look in designing exhibitions abroad. This essay examines the meanings involved in inscribing the nation onto particular women's bodies styled as the American Look.

Historians of international relations have noted the implications of the common practice of gender-coding national states and of the ways that such coding constructs the categories both of nation and of masculine and feminine genders. In the early Cold War—a time preoccupied with the superior attributes of masculinity—it might seem that the world's new superpower would be represented primarily by a male body. Indeed Eisenhower's New Look policy, with its emphasis on nuclear weaponry and brinksmanship, contained an implicit male coding, one that *Dr. Strangelove* so acerbically satirized. The often extravagant displays of masculinity in discourses of Cold War rivalry, however, makes the American Look, which projects the nation in the shape of a young, modern, white woman, all the more interesting.[1]

This essay focuses on a *Life* magazine photo spread called "What Is the American Look?," from May 21, 1945.[2] Thirteen photos of "American women" are presented, most titled to exemplify a particular attribute: good grooming, naturalness, simplicity, well-brushed, well-shod, glamour, cleanliness, confidence, agelessness, domesticity, long legs. Under each photo and caption is a block of text briefly describing and explaining the attribute. This photo feature provides a starting point for examining how representations of women's bodies in the American Look came to refract larger postwar issues and, ultimately, became powerful signifiers in America's Cold War contests.

This issue of *Life* is particularly interesting. It announces the Allied victory in Europe; Winston Churchill is on the cover with a story about his "lives," and other top stories are titled "The Germans Sign the Surrender," "Victory Wreath Placed on Franklin Roosevelt's Grave," "Last Days of Berlin," and "London Goes Wild on V-E Day." It also foreshadows future Cold War tensions: an article on the recent French election announces "Free Europe's First Elections Show Definite Shift to the Left." Significantly this article leads by tying the leftist gains in France to the fact that this was the first French election in which women had the vote: "Communists polled 25% of the total vote; many those of disgruntled women." Most of the accompanying pictures show women rallying at socialist and communist gatherings. In this article and its images, the threat from the Left is identified with—and embodied by—women. At first glance the American Look photos seem to stand very much apart from such articles on the geopolitics of victory and danger. The closer one examines this feature, however, the clearer it becomes that its placement in this issue of *Life* fittingly heralds the end of the war and the new era that *Life*'s publisher had called the American Century.

In its overall layout, the six-page spread on the American Look resembles *Life*'s extensive advertising copy rather than its news stories. Like typical ads from this period, it presents large photos with small accompanying text. Also like many ads, the photos attract attention by displaying compelling female images. That *Life* drew upon advertising styles for such photo features (for which it was, of course, famous) raises an intriguing question: What was being "sold" here? Why, in this important issue celebrating the end of the war in Europe, would *Life* project America in the shape of a woman, and why would it offer these particular women's images and attributes as representational of America? I read this photo feature as a not so veiled form of advertising copy, asking what the American Look was intended to sell and to whom. Any successful imagescape—whether an advertisement, a film, or a photo spread—contains multiple appeals at once. Exploring four of the several appeals of the American Look frames this analysis.

Selling American Women as Mates

The first, and most obvious, audience for *Life*'s pictorial on the American Look is returning soldiers. The short lead paragraph opens with a direct appeal to returning American servicemen, who are presumed to have had encounters with foreign women during the war: "In this most immense of wars Americans have involuntarily absorbed such a knowledge of people and races as would never have come their way in peacetime years. Naturally the GIs' interest in racial strains involves girls. They have seen and evaluated the relative endowments of English girls, French girls, Australian girls, and Polynesian girls. They have found some to be beautiful, some pretty, some exotic. But none of them look like the American girls and the GI has come to appreciate and miss, with a deep and genuine poignance, the look that sets American girls apart from those of all other lands." Framed within the rhetoric of a male gaze, and more specifically a GI gaze, the article exhibits apprehension about the possible attractions of foreign women but then repudiates such unease by advancing American women as the best possible choices for American men. "It appears to roving GIs that quantitatively there are more attractive women on their own shores than anywhere else on earth."

The military's wartime campaigns against venereal disease would have been a familiar subtext to the soldier-readers addressed in this feature.[3] These anti-VD campaigns often marked foreign women as carriers of disease and exhorted men to keep themselves healthy—not only for the sake of the war effort and themselves but also for their present and future wives back home. In line with this wartime message, the healthy women pictured here, especially with captions such as "cleanliness" and "domesticity," are free of the corruptions of war and available to returning servicemen who seek to build a wholesome nation.[4]

In addition, the photo spread implicitly addresses the military's

A CLEAN, READY SMILE, WITH TEETH WHICH SHOW THE RESULT OF PLENTY OF MILK AND ORANGE JUICE AND OF BRACES WHEN YOUNG, IS THE BADGE OF THE AMERICAN GIRL

WHAT IS
THE AMERICAN LOOK?

THE GIRLS OF THE U. S. HAVE AN AIR ALL THEIR OWN

In this most immense of wars Americans have involuntarily absorbed such a knowledge of people and races as would never have come their way in peacetime years. Naturally the GIs' interest in racial strains involves girls. They have seen and evaluated the relative endowments of English girls, French girls, Australian girls, Polynesian girls. They have found some to be beautiful, some pretty, some exotic. But none of them look like American girls and the GI has come to appreciate and miss, with a deep

and genuine poignance, the look that sets American girls apart from those of all other lands.

Although the U. S. has not, perhaps, evolved girls of more surpassing beauty, it appears to roving GIs that quantitatively there are more attractive women on their home shores than anywhere else on earth. For all the racial streams of America, its girls have somehow acquired an unmistakable American look that has become as much a part of the national scene as the corner drugstore or the Mississippi River.

What precisely is the "American Look?" In a current campaign to promote American fashions Dorothy Shaver, first vice president of Lord & Taylor, New York department store, has tried to answer this question. The American Look involves many things — a natural manner, freshness and enthusiasm, a friendly smile, an easy, confident stride with head held high, an unaffected elegance in make-up and dress. On the pages that follow LIFE Photographer Nina Leen translates these qualities into pictures.

CONTINUED ON NEXT PAGE 87

Figure 9.1 "What Is the American Look?," Life, May 21, 1945. Copyright 1945. The Picture Collection Inc. Reprinted with permission. All rights reserved. Printed with permission of Getty Images: Nina Leen/Time Life Pictures/Getty Images.

larger dilemmas about "fraternization" and about what to do about GIs who applied to marry foreign women. The burgeoning scholarly litera-ture on the gender politics of "foreign affairs" between servicemen and overseas women provides an important context within which this fea-ture should be read. In every theater of the war, the American military sought to discourage fraternization but also felt pressure to accommo-date soldiers who had married foreign women and wanted to return home with them. Reminding soldiers about the benefits of marrying American women dovetails with the military's concerns about the pos-sibly growing number of war brides.[5]

In this context it is worthwhile to pause to consider how *American* is defined by the writers of the *Life* photo essay. The opening text carefully reinforces the common "melting pot" discourse of ethnic pluralism so common to wartime culture: "For all the racial streams of America, its girls have somehow acquired an unmistakable American Look that has become as much a part of the national scene as the corner drug store or Mississippi River."

"Racial streams"? Actually the images presented in the photos be-lie the phrase. It is, of course, hardly surprising that a *Life* magazine from 1945 does not suggest that America's "racial streams" included African Americans, Mexican Americans, Asian Americans, or Native Americans, but not even the immigrant streams of the earlier twenti-eth century can be easily detected in these photos. Only three of the seven women shown have dark hair, and none displays the features that were, at that time, largely associated with the Jewish or Italian im-migrants that composed the most numerous immigrant groups of the early twentieth-century wave. The pictures and the text, then, are some-what at odds, but their mixed messages can be read as an expression of the cultural ambivalence of the war years: the selection of photos and models overwhelmingly represents "American" women as Northern European, but the text nonetheless embraces the common wartime dis-course of melting pot, antiracism, and tolerance for the multiple "racial streams" that made up America.

The important point here is the text's embrace of what approaches a postethnic definition of America. The caption on the lead picture de-clares, "A clean ready smile, with teeth that show the results of plenty of milk and orange juice, and of braces when young, is *the badge* of the American girl" (my emphasis). Note how the distinguishing badge of Americanism is something that can be obtained through better food and dental braces. "American" women are the products of a land of abundance and of a broad middle class. That they are collectively constructed by environment and performance rather than marked by heredity pushes toward the repudiation of racial and ethnic barriers, even if the photos work to visually reinscribe those barriers.

While servicemen are being reminded of the healthy women waiting at home, then, there is a larger message that suggests that Americanism is not biologically rooted but is a potentially universalizable trait. To be sure, these photos show only a projection of "white" and presumably heterosexual women, but whiteness and heteronormativity here serve partly to signal a previously constituted, performative code for respectability and health—a code that these photos invoke and then, of course, help perpetuate.[6] Portraying such white women remained, in this period, a successful technique in global advertising—even in countries whose population was predominantly not white. The text opens the possibility that foreigners themselves may one day restore healthy food supplies, offer cosmetic dentistry, and develop women who also display the most important—and acquirable—attributes of these "Americans." (I'll return to this universalizing message later.)

The American Look photos provide a window onto what became a larger postwar project of inviting servicemen back to seek consorts in a land of abundance and health. America is a place where women reflect the exceptionalism of the nation, not because of their ethnic roots but because of the vibrant system that provides the nutrition and health care that melds and molds a new type of people. Servicemen are cast as the primary audience of this feature, although it also clearly informs potential women readers about the need to wholesomely appeal to returning soldiers. The message is clear: American women can and must beat the foreign competition.

Selling American Fashions

A second obvious appeal made in Life's photo essay relates to the marketing of American-made fashions. This sales campaign emerged during the early 1930s when Dorothy Shaver of the Lord and Taylor department store promoted "American fashions for American women" as a way to challenge the dominance of French couture. Shaver advocated building a domestic market to support American fashion designers and manufacturers, and Lord and Taylor became the first major store to present a show featuring all American-made fashions.[7]

This made-in-America campaign of the 1930s was a potentially brilliant marketing ploy for the U.S. fashion industry. It took the very qualities often used by foreigners to denigrate American goods—that they were inexpensive and mass-produced—and promoted them as assets. Shaver proclaimed that American fashion designers could offer affordable but stylish ready-to-wear fashions to women of all classes. The *New York Evening Post* reported, "[Shaver] believes that this year of low economic ebb is the ideal time, psychologically, to win a hearing for the Americana designers." Casual dress could proudly, rather than defensively, express a distinctive national style. American women, in Shaver's view, did not have to yearn for one-of-a-kind high fashions from France; they could have the freedom to choose from a variety of casual clothes that fit the many different lifestyles available to them. American "separates" and "sportswear" became features in Hollywood movies, which displayed thin, young, sporty women and associated active lifestyles with leisure.[8]

The appeal to frugality in fashion and to nationalism seemed a perfect fit for a retailing strategy launched in the Depression decade, but World War II brought even greater opportunities. Despite rationing and scarcity, the war created favorable conditions for American fashions. First, it helped popularize sturdy, attractive work clothes for women, and new job opportunities, especially in clerical work, created a reliable segment of buyers for ready-to-wear fashions. High wartime salaries meant that more and more women had the means to purchase clothing. Second, the war dealt a blow to the French fashion industry, whose designers and exports had been cut off from American department stores. Third, the continued popularity of Hollywood, linked with the burgeoning sportswear industry inspired by California's leisurely lifestyles, imparted glamour to casual, sporty clothes. American designers consolidated their new opportunities in promotional campaigns. In 1940 *Vogue* magazine, which had generally ignored American designers, devoted its two September issues to a new "American collection"; *Vogue* also adapted the British "Beauty Is Your Duty" campaign to exhort American women to keep up wartime morale by attiring themselves attractively; and the *New York Times* gave star billing to American designers in its newly expanded fashion section.[9]

As the postwar world dawned, American designers and manufacturers planned new ways to expand their reputations and markets. Shaver issued a press release in January 1945 announcing a major ad campaign in New York newspapers. She proclaimed, "I believe that the American look will be copied all over the world. . . . This contribution is as distinctly American as the jeep, nylon hose, the movies, and a clear complexion."[10] That year Shaver became president of Lord and Taylor, the first woman to head a major department store.

Life magazine, in effect, became one vehicle for this relaunch of the American Look. Shaver was the inspiration for the *Life* spread, and one of the photos shows her and the photographer interviewing women models to select just the attributes they wanted. This careful selection suggests that the American Look was assuming a more expansive significance. In the 1930s the American Look had been a nationalistic, buy-American *fashion statement*. In 1945, however, *Life* quotes Shaver as describing the American Look in this way: "The American Look involves many things—a natural manner, freshness, and enthusiasm, a friendly smile, and easy confident stride with head held high, and unaffected elegance in make-up and dress." *Women's Wear Daily* applauded Shaver and Lord and Taylor for promoting the American Look campaign, which, it wrote, was typically American in its emphasis on "youth, gaiety, freedom, and animation" and was now being lauded all over the world.[11] Note how the American Look was being described not only as a clothing style but as a *description of bodies* that signified health, affluence, self-confidence, freedom, and youth.

In 1955 *Time* reported the success of American Look fashions: "Whatever they buy, most American women this summer will have one thing in common: a style that has come to be known the world over as the American Look." Dorothy Shaver was now one of the highest profile women business executives of the era. In the late 1940s the French designer Christian Dior had introduced his widely acclaimed "New Look," which signaled a return to luxurious feminine clothes that announced the end of wartime scarcity. But the American Look, associated with mass-produced casuals, also flourished. *Time* explained that American fashion exemplified a "leisure of action—barbecue parties in the backyard, motor trips along country roads and across the country, weekend golf and water skiing. From America's lively leisure has evolved a new, home-grown fashion, as different from Paris fashion as apple pie from crepes suzette."[12]

Claire McCardell, a major American Look designer in this era, inspired a host of new American designers, especially after publication of her practical guide to "democratic" fashion, *What Shall I Wear*, came out in 1956.[13] McCardell, through her company Townley Frocks, Inc., was best known for her bias-cut dresses and skirts, which had adjustable waistlines and side pockets, and for her versatile "popover" dress. She eliminated the girdle, a restrictive undergarment, and used simple fabrics like denim and wool jersey, a soft, stretchy woven fabric. Together with her new spring line of clothing, she was featured on the cover of *Time* in the issue of May 2, 1955. The feature story, "The American Look," boasted that the U.S. fashion industry was busy turning out garments "that are as at home in the front seat of a station wagon as in the back seat of a Rolls. . . . Sports clothes must swing as easily on the laundry line as on the golf course." The huge popularity of sports clothes coincided with the rise of the tourist industry, national highways, and the growing cultural influence of the sunbelt, especially Florida and California, with its relaxed lifestyles.[14] Nearly anyone could afford the American Look, and nearly anyone could wear it. American Look clothes were simple and practical. Often featured by the fashion photographer Louise Dahl-Wolfe, whose work from the 1930s on had appeared in *Harper's Bazaar* and elsewhere, the American Look became associated with nature, outdoor locations, active lifestyles, and simple functional lines.[15]

The demand for casual separates—in daring colors such as orange, chartreuse, and hot pink—boosted a new industry, which became a signature of American manufacturing during the early Cold War (before it migrated to low-cost labor environments off-shore beginning in the 1960s). By 1955 there were 14,500 women's-apparel manufacturers employing 450,000 people and creating $6 billion worth of goods a year. St. Louis, Chicago, Philadelphia, Dallas, and Miami and California all developed garment-making industries, although Manhattan remained the center of the trade. A new generation of American designers, working in McCardell's shadow, gave the concept of "American design" (which once had seemed an oxymoron) a new respect worldwide.[16]

Viewed from this framework, the American Look photo feature becomes a window onto economic—and export—promotion. The American Look represented a tasteful consumerism that combined wholesome bodies with a burgeoning U.S. fashion industry. Unlike other sectors of the economy, this new postwar industry succeeded very substantially through the leadership of women, both designers and business leaders. American Look fashion, however, had broader implications than the promotion of an important new manufacturing and retailing sector.

Selling America

The American Look's emphasis on bodies as well as fashions suggests a third message of this photo spread, one aligned with publisher Henry Luce's vision of an American Century. Its portrayals are clearly designed to advertise not just one industry but America itself. In this context it might be asked how the American Look uses the bodies of American women as vehicles to proclaim the virtues of the political and economic system of the world's now most powerful nation.

The central feature of the American Look in *Life* is the "friendly, luminous smile," with its straight, white, healthy teeth. American children, the text reads, have good teeth because of balanced diets and good dental care. As a symbol, the smile represents more than wholesomeness, however. It signals friendship and openness. The America represented in the American Look is not a figure to be feared but a figure to be dated and loved. She is full of energy and fun. She is not old, not authoritarian, and certainly incapable of brutality. She nurtures rather than coerces. She is the perfect partner.

As mentioned earlier, the American Look portrayed in *Life* is less biologically inherited than acquired. The comments that adorn the captions of the photo spread confirm this view as they describe the physical and social characteristics of Americans: The "American" figure, the reader is told, is long-legged, slim-waisted, broad-shouldered, and high-bosomed, but people who don't have these qualities can achieve them by carriage, manner, and choice of clothes. The American woman is a product of the richness of the country because America "mass produces good looking clothes" and has inexpensive cosmetics and lots of bathtubs. Its schools have competitive sports and free medical clinics. And because America is a country of moviegoers, Hollywood sets the standard for the desirability of smooth skin, bright lips, and lustrous hair. American women have long legs because nutrition and good health care has made women in America taller, and most of this new height comes from longer legs. The reader is also informed that American women's feet are larger than those in the rest of the world, but that this is a beauty advantage because it makes the ankles appear more slender. In World War II culture, a veritable cult—spurred by pin-up art and the Betty Grable rage—had developed around women's legs.[17] This fascination with long legs persisted into the 1950s as a symbol of the American Look. The final full-page photo, taken from the back in a manner reminiscent of Grable's most famous image, shows the shapely legs of a young woman dressed in short shorts and wheeling a bicycle.

Such physical attributes are presented as signs of character traits that caption writers depict as typically American: poise, freshness, friendliness, animation, all borne of democracy in the school and home. "Most American girls live happy, unregimented lives during their school years." They form friendships and make dates in a self-confident

THEIR LEGS ARE LONG The American girl is growing taller and most of the additional length seems to go to her legs. She is about twice as long from waist to toes as from waist to the top of her head. Even the daughters of the small "average" 5-ft. 4-in. woman are getting to look more like the ideal Powers or Conover models,

Average 1945 height of Powers' 12 leading models is 5 ft. 7 in., of Conover's models, 5 ft. 4 in. This is two inches taller than ten years ago. Their feet are getting longer (size 7 shoe vs. 6½ ten years ago), but as compensation that has the effect of making their ankles appear proportionately slimmer.

91

Figure 9.2 "What Is the American Look?," *Life*, May 21, 1945. Copyright 1945. The Picture Collection Inc. Reprinted with permission. All rights reserved. Printed with permission of Getty Images: Nina Leen/Time Life Pictures/Getty Images.

manner. Thus the American Look is an "authentic" outgrowth of the democratic American way of life. It is *made, not born.*

The cold warriors who mounted propaganda campaigns to sell the American Way of Life during the early Cold War realized the popularity and potential of the American Look—that is, the nation in the shape of a healthy young woman. From Shaver, McCardell, and *Life* the American Look migrated to the fashion shows of the Cold War exhibitions in Brussels in 1958 and Moscow in 1959 (there called the Young American Look). Exposition planners well understood the importance of appealing to women in the Cold War competition (remember the alleged problem of women voters in France?) and teamed up with *Vogue* magazine and with various cosmetics companies to create appealing displays.

At the Brussels exposition, while the Soviet pavilion featured heavy machinery and imposing statuary, the American pavilion advanced the theme of "human aspiration and fulfillment, and the freedom of the individual and his institutions."[18] A central element of this "freedom" was the exhibit "Islands for Living," which concentrated on home life and placed at its center a fashion show on runways and platforms. The U.S. pavilion also displayed a street scene with fifteen shopping windows and a soda fountain. Loop films showed American shopping centers, houses, gas stations, and other snippets of life, while Walt Disney's *Circarama*, a 360-degree motion picture compilation shown by twelve projectors, culminated with clips from *High Noon*. Consumer culture, in short, held center stage.[19]

The fashion show proved the most popular exhibit in the American pavilion (with the possible exception of *Circarama*). Here the Young American Look, under *Vogue*'s general supervision, showed an array of sportswear, work clothes, and evening attire—all emphasizing affordability, style, and the "freedom" to change clothes in accordance with women's many different roles and kinds of activities. Nine models showed five dresses per hour for eight hours a day, six days a week, and attendance was huge. The press release from U.S. officials echoed the themes already popularized as the American Look: "[Showing] the inexpensive, ready-to-wear clothes . . . is a colorful demonstration of why so many American women are among the well-dressed of the world." Expensive evening gowns dazzled while sportswear projected casual living. Moreover viewers were told that, even as they were seeing these clothes at the pavilion, women everywhere in America were able to buy duplicates because 175 shops around the country were stocking selections from the collection modeled in Brussels. Clothes shown in a Sears Roebuck catalogue—another popular exhibit—also underscored generally how widely and easily available were American ready-to-wear offerings. And in another form of modeling, all U.S. women guides at the pavilion wore simple, clean-cut uniforms "designed for easy care": pleated skirts, solid gray jackets, white nylon blouses, bronze berets, and gray shoes and hose.[20] One program session highlighted "American women who work," featuring Assistant Secretary of Labor Alice Leopold. Some American critics savaged the Brussels's displays for presenting America as a frivolous consumer culture, but planners well understood the importance of making a strong appeal to women abroad.

At the U.S. exhibition in Moscow the next year, fashion shows and consumer displays expanded. Taking mass produced consumer displays into the heart of the communist empire, American designers featured a ranch-style home that became the most talked-about exhibit. Here took place the famed kitchen debate in which the leaders of the two superpowers contested what their systems meant, especially for the lives of women. While Premier Nikita Khrushchev derided capitalism's trivialities and "gadgets," Vice President Richard Nixon proclaimed that household consumer appliances accomplished the manly goal of liberating women from drudgery. Model kitchens featured American-produced convenience food; *Vogue* magazine showcased American fashions; and Coty and Helena Rubenstein offered beauty treatments and free cosmetic products—at least until Soviet authorities banned the practice. The American Look in Moscow exuded tasteful affluence, promoted as being within the reach of Americans, especially women, of all classes.

As in the *Life* photo essay, the Cold War fashion shows in Brussels and Moscow seemed on the surface to be about an American fashion trend, but the women on stage conveyed far more: they identified American life with youth, freedom, affluence, choice, leisure, and fun. One U.S. press release quoted a French model in the fashion show reportedly commenting that the fashions provided "a relaxing and refreshing change of pace. Just wearing these clothes makes me more anxious than ever to visit America."[21] The land of the American Look became the expression of an ascendant postwar nation whose allure came from "her" confidence and ready smile. Who wouldn't want the embodiment of the American Look as a friend or ally?

In Cold War propaganda efforts, of course, America was not always represented as a woman. Yet historians should recognize the America-as-woman trope as perhaps America's most attractive face during the early Cold War years. As postwar capitalism colonized the representational body of American women, it boosted its allure. The youthfulness and consumer attractions embodied in the American Look challenged communist claims about women's oppression under capitalism.[22] American Look images were not simply foisted on women at home or internationally; they were aspirational images easily embraced by many women after more than a decade of depression and war.[23]

America in the shape of a woman offered decided advantages in the realm of informational diplomacy. It did not threaten; it did not bore; it seemed nurturing and reserved; it employed simplicity. It enlisted rather than demanded support. And any good teacher or propagandist recognizes these as the most important ingredients in getting a lesson across.

Selling a Universalized American Modernity

The American Look had an even more expansive career, however, than advertising American women, American fashions, and America itself. In the early Cold War, it also became a broader description of a modernist style that transcended national borders by exemplifying a future shaped by stylish, functional design principles. The American Look presented itself as a universalized modernity, available to anyone who wished to embrace it. *Life's* photo feature, as suggested earlier, describes the Look as authentically American yet also acquirable. It highlights the ways American exceptionalism has always been a nationalism cloaked in universalism. It also invites a closer look at the longer semiotic association among women, fashion, and codes of modernity.

Jean Baudrillard has emphasized the relationship between fashion and modernity: "Modernity is a code and fashion its emblem."[24] In this sense the American Look, as a fashion emblem, signaled the ever-moving and always unfinished bodies of modernity. Fashion, like the bodies it adorns, is never stable; it projects an ever-changing system of signs that may be acquired, assembled, and reassembled. In the American Look the "modern" body, as we have seen, came not from inherited status but from the semiotic array of teeth, clothes, stance, activities, and consumer objects that surrounded and altered it.

The use of women to project codes of modernity had a genealogy in American advertising that predated the Cold War. Women had long figured prominently in appeals to sell American products partly because advertisers consistently, throughout the twentieth century, reported that women made approximately 80 percent of all purchasing decisions. As American advertising traveled abroad, products for and featuring women often symbolized a "modern" style of consumerism, born of independence and leisure, and a future in which America's democratic capitalism could help "free" other peoples. For example, America's most important manufactured global export at the turn of the century, the Singer sewing machine, was marketed mainly to women. It built its appeal as a practical and sturdy product that, bought on time, could boost women's economic independence and status. America's simple sewing machines symbolized potential gains in both economic and fashion independence for women. From the interwar era the automobile offers another example. America's inexpensive and reliable cars exploded onto world markets after World War I, and in the late 1920s and 1930s auto companies developed extensive advertising campaigns to market to women both at home and abroad. Often drawn in art deco style, featuring tall, slim, stylish, and sporty women-on-the-move, the ads appealed to women by emphasizing the cars' beauty and ease of handling. Their images and text stressed themes that equated automobiles with independence and mobility.[25]

Such American products and appeals, however, pushed against constant challenges in foreign markets. Anti-American critics around the world decried rather than welcomed American modernity in the shape of a consuming woman. For many, America represented the home of standardization, Taylorization, materialism, crass mass culture, women running wild, and emasculated men who often seemed little better than wage slaves beholden to women's consumerist addictions. Americans often touted their democratizing impulses and large middle class, but critics could easily render these very qualities as devolution and stultifying mid-cult. Anti-American critics for decades had complained that American life was feminized, anti-intellectual, and artless. They portrayed American women especially as trivial and highly sexualized beings who overpowered men with the voraciousness of their desires.

The American Look, especially as it began to broaden its scope beyond the world of women's fashions, directly confronted this long tradition of anti-American complaints. In the early 1950s Shaver had begun to push the American Look into the realm of household design. In a 1953 article for *House Beautiful* she wrote that although the American woman is now "entirely a free citizen in her dress, using fashion to please herself and express herself and suit herself, in home decoration she has just begun to declare her independence." She predicted that just as the American Look in fashion was virtually unknown twenty years earlier and now "is known around the world," so an American Look was now taking hold in home decor, "the expression of a free people, a

happy people, a prosperous people, a young people." Echoing her earlier fashion campaign and with themes that the State Department's
anticommunist informational offensive also embraced, she wrote that
American dress and home decor showed one did not need to be rich
to live with exciting and delightful design: "In our land human values
come before all others, proof that from the diversity of cultures from
which America grew, a spirit of both equality and independence has
arisen which is uniquely ours and new in the world." Like fashion separates, she wrote, today's modern home accommodates the many different roles of the woman who runs it—professional, civic leader, wife,
mother—and can be individualized to suit each family.[26]

This American Look in design provided the basis for the "Islands of
Living" display at the Brussels exhibition. Planners decided that there
was no such thing as a "typical" American home, so they showcased
the things with which Americans surrounded themselves. Push-but-
ton stoves, washers, dryers, electric blankets, radios, cars, heat and air
conditioning controls emphasized convenience. Office machines, toys,
household and garden furniture, sports equipment, and all kinds of
recreational gear highlighted modern working conditions and leisure
activities. The fashion show models walked through these "islands
for living," connecting the design trends in women's fashions to those
in daily living to create a gracefully integrated vision of the American
Look.[27]

General Motors also adapted the label of the American Look in its
celebrated 1958 promotional film by that name, a film that directly
confronted the widespread anti-American discourses that associated
the country with crass commercial culture, the soulless materialism
of standardized mass production, and the tastelessness of insatia-
ble women. The company broadened the American Look far beyond
a term connoting women's fashions and deployed it to describe an
American-led modernist design movement. The ostensible purpose of
the GM film, now a classic of midcentury modernism, was to provide
a "tribute to men and women who design." It celebrated "free spirits,"
"grace," and "glamour." It lauded democratization and prominently
featured women, while it associated democracy, home decor, and
mass-produced goods with social achievement and, above all, impec-
cable taste. The American Look equaled a modernity characterized by
ease, simplicity, and refinement—a look that is now popularly called
(and admired) as midcentury modern design. Although promoted as
an American Look, the supposedly universal appeal of the modernist
styles presented in the film subtlety found affirmation in the way they

drew from the kinds of transnational influences associated with design traditions variously called Bauhaus, international style, functionalism, and Danish modern.

Made to appeal to global audiences, GM's film The American Look celebrated America as a land of the future in which "the things we have are ever-changing because of designers." The first third of the film, which has very little voiceover and a striking musical score, features an amazing array of truly dazzling household products. By foregrounding the home and what were considered to be women's products, GM's American Look retains a gendered characteristic. Telephones, dishes, furniture, vacuums, and every other conceivable type of household item dance in and out in vibrant colors and variety. Open-plan homes, and especially kitchens, provide arresting settings for these artful products of daily living. The voice announces, "Homes have new patterns for living because of new kinds of living spaces and color." Together the products and the homes express Americans' "love of beauty" and "Americans' love of freedom, which is the freedom of individual choice." The film then shifts to places of work and leisure. Office furniture, implements, machines (typewriters), and trucks bespeak a stylish efficiency. Outdoor equipment—mowers, boats, water skis, pools, baseball fields, golf, camping, bowling—all emphasize how "modern fashion has the active look, the casual look." Modern, urban architecture is shown as design's crowning achievement: walls of glass in offices and in homes merge inside spaces with outdoor vistas, and this use of glass heralds a new urban artistry. The third part of GM's film provides the closer: the automobile as the ultimate representation of freedom, individuality, a desirable future—and of the artistic design processes represented in the American Look.[28]

The American Look images are set against an orchestral score that carries out its themes. It is, by turns, stentorian and playful; at times it sounds like American symphonic music (serious stuff) and at other times like popular movie scores. The opening and ending sequences showing sunrise and sunset add a celestial chorus that highlights the film's sense of grandeur. By singing in "la, la" rather than language, the chorus carries out the themes of universality and globalism.

Within this motion picture, graceful motion itself is really the protagonist: the products are proclaimed to be "ever changing" as they drift and move across the screen; the varied musical background provides a sense of motion; the highlighting of sports activity keeps the focus on people in motion. Of course, the centrality of automobiles to the "look" of the future also emphasizes a society in which to be free means to be constantly on the move. Bodies in motion; goods in motion; identities in motion.

General Motors' American Look, like the informational displays at the Cold War exhibitions, staged a close identification between modern technology, modern women, freedom, movement, and the future. America was positioned at the vanguard of transnational modern design—the new capital of ever-changing artistry and technology; the capital in which women and women's products brought grace and good taste; the new capital of the world of tomorrow.

Conclusion

The early Cold War is generally remembered as a time of muscularity and masculinity. The "containment" of women, the "lavender scare" that targeted homosexuality, the masculine display evident among so many public intellectuals, policymakers, and even rebels provide the usual symbolic markers for scholars of this era. The American Look that projected the nation in the shape of a respectable, white, modern woman does not undermine such a view. In fact it rests alongside it (and thus helps give it definition). The American Look may perhaps be seen as the consort of Eisenhower's nuclear-teethed New Look—the female companion that smiled and seduced as the fearsome thrust of weaponry grew ever more powerful. She was the healthy and wholesome woman to whom American servicemen tempted by foreign allures should come home. She was the face of a new postwar world of casual and inexpensive fashion that had slipped out of the shadow of Paris, projected its own enviable "look," and became an export powerhouse. She was the embodiment of capitalism's success, advertising a broad middle class that could afford good nutrition, long legs, and good teeth. She was the Cold War weapon that seduced by advancing a compelling modernity. This American modernity—sleek, elegant, and broadly affordable—challenged the mass-culture critics who proclaimed to see in America nothing but crass standardization, materialism, and bad taste. By the 1950s the American Look was as important to the Cold War cultural rivalry as Eisenhower's New Look was to the military rivalry. Each enhanced the presence of the other, and both embodied the expansive energy of postwar America, a nation that both compelled and seduced its rivals.

Notes

1. Works that emphasize the connection between masculinity and Cold War policies include May, *Homeward Bound*; Rosenberg, "'Foreign Affairs' after World War II"; Dean, *Imperial Brotherhood*; Cuordileone, *Manhood and American Political Culture in the Cold War*.

2. "What Is the American Look?," *Life*, Mar. 12, 1945, http://books.google .com/ books?id=5okEAAAAMBAJ&printsec=frontcover&source=gbs_ge_ summary_r&cad=0#v=onepage&q&f=false. The photographer Nina Leen was one of *Life*'s first women photographers. The website Quite Continental, accessed June 15, 2011, http://quitecontinental.net/2011/03/06/life-archives-the-american-look/ contains the photos and some not published.

3. Parascandola, "Quarantining Women."

4. Brown, *Foul Bodies*, provides historical perspective on the links between women's roles and cleanliness.

5. Zeiger, *Entangling Alliances*, 71–202 provides an overview and other citations to the literature. On the issue of postwar sexual liaisons and the difficulties of marriage, see also the essay by Plummer in this volume.

6. Here, Butler's *Bodies That Matter* and her other work, which emphasizes identities as performative, provide an important context for my reading of race and gender in these photos.

7. The media attention to this campaign is reflected in articles from the *Christian Science Monitor*, July 28, 1931; *New York Evening Post*, May 3, 1932, and Apr. 10, 1933; *Women's Wear Daily*, Apr. 13, 1932, and others in Folder 6, Box 4, Dorothy Shaver Papers, Collection 631, National Museum of American History, Washington, DC. On Shaver, see Webber-Hanchett, "Dorothy Shaver." See also Schweitzer, "American Fashions for American Women."

8. *New York Evening Post*, May 3, 1932 (quote); Warner, "The Americanization of Fashion."

9. Arnold, *The American Look*; Robinson, "American Sportswear"; Buckland, "Promoting American Designers"; McEuen, *Making War*, 136–38.

10. Press Release, Jan. 12, 1945, and appreciative responses from retailers around the country, Folder 9, Box 4, Dorothy Shaver Papers; "'American Look' Ads Planned by Lord and Taylor," *Women's Wear Daily*, Jan. 12, 1945, Folder 8, Box 4, Dorothy Shaver Papers. Quote from "Says U.S. Will Alter Postwar Fashiondom, *Toledo (Ohio) Times*, Jan. 16, 1945, Folder 6, Box 4, Dorothy Shaver Papers.

11. Winefred J. Ovitte, "Applause for Leadership," *Women's Wear Daily*, Jan. 12, 1945.

12. "Fashion: The American Look," *Time*, May 2, 1955, accessed Oct. 2, 2008, at http://www.time.com/time/magazine/article/0,9171,866314–1,00.html.

13. On the designers inspired by and associated with McCardell, see Farrell-Beck and Parsons, *20th Century Dress in the United States*, 120–23. On McCardell, see Yohannan and Nolf, *Claire McCardell*.

14. See Campbell, *When the Girls Came Out to Play* for background. It is also important to note that the American Look, stressing youthfulness, consumption, and freedom for women, built upon already circulating global memes about "modern girls." See Weinbaum et al., *Modern Girl around the World*.

15. Arnold, "Looking American."

16. "Fashion: The American Look," *Time*, May 2, 1955.

17. McEuen, *Making War*, 91–98.

18. Memo, "U.S. Participation at the Brussels Exhibition, 1958," Folder "General Themes," Box 4, Records Relating to U.S. Participation in the Brussels Universal and International Exhibition of 1958, Record Group 43, Records of International Conferences, Commissions, and Expositions, National Archives, Washington (hereafter RG 43, Brussels Exhibition).

19. Folder "Reports," Box 6, Folder "Films," Box 12, RG 43, Brussels Exhibition.

20. Various press releases in Folder "Press Releases," Boxes 12 and 14, RG 43, Brussels Exhibition. On women as both vehicles and targets of U.S. postwar cultural diplomacy, see, among others, Haddow, *Pavilions of Plenty*, 135–68; Belmonte, *Selling the American Way*; Laville, "'Our Country Endangered by Underwear'"; Osgood, *Total Cold War*; Smulyan, *Popular Ideologies*, 41–81. Yarrow, "Selling a New Vision of America to the World" analyzes ways in which early cold war propaganda emphasized the symbolic connections between America and affluence.

21. Folder "Press Releases," Box 12, RG 43, Brussels Exhibition.

22. For more elaboration, see Rosenberg, "Consumer Capitalism and the End of the Cold War"; Hixson, *Parting the Curtain*.

23. This makes an argument neither for writing women out of their own subject creation nor for making them the masters of it. It assumes that women "choose" their attractions and identities but always within an environment already discursively structured.

24. Baudrillard, *Symbolic Exchange and Death*, 90.

25. See, for example, the collection of ads from the 1930s in Ford Motor Company, Series 3, Box 220, 222, N. W. Ayer Collection #59, National Museum of American History, Washington, DC.

26. Dorothy Shaver, "The American Look in Living," *House Beautiful*, June 1953, in Folder 6, Box 4, Dorothy Shaver Papers.

27. "Press Release" No. 20, Folder "Press Releases," Box 13 and Folder "Islands for Living," Box 20, RG 43, Brussels Exhibition. See also Castillo, *Cold War on the Home Front*.

28. *The American Look*, parts 1, 2, and 3 may be viewed at the Prelinger Archives, http://www.archive.org/details/prelinger.

ten

Sammy Lee
Narratives of Asian American Masculinity
and Race in Decolonizing Asia

MARY TING YI LUI

In the fall of 1954 the U.S. State Department dispatched the Korean
American diver Sammy Lee to several Asian countries to provide a series
of diving demonstrations as part of its public diplomacy efforts to shore
up U.S. prestige abroad. This was not Lee's first time as a goodwill ambassador for the United States. A double gold medalist on the platform
and springboard events in the 1948 London Olympics who successfully
defended his platform title in the 1952 Helsinki Olympics, Lee had been
accustomed to representing his country on the international stage. A
practicing ear, nose, and throat specialist and major in the U.S. Army
stationed in Korea since 1953, Lee on occasion gave impromptu diving
demonstrations to local Korean audiences that proved to be enormous
crowd pleasers. As a clutch performer who could easily adapt to local
conditions in war-torn Asia, Lee embodied exactly the perfect goodwill
ambassador to navigate the unknown political and physical terrain of
decolonizing Asia.

In the early years of the Cold War, the State Department, with cooperation from American sports institutions such as the Amateur Athletic Association (AAU), made great efforts to bring U.S. athletic stars
into its public diplomacy work around the globe. Particularly beginning
in 1954, President Eisenhower lobbied Congress to establish a $5 mil-

lion Emergency Fund for International Affairs to counter the surge in
Soviet propaganda and appointed Theodore Streibert, director of the
United States Information Agency (USIA), as the executive agent of the
fund.[1] Eisenhower established the fund to promote U.S. participation
in international trade fairs and increase the presentation of American
cultural artists and groups abroad to demonstrate that "America too
can lay claim to high cultural and artistic accomplishments."[2] Streibert
would also employ the fund to support goodwill tours featuring athletes such as Sammy Lee and the African American gold medal runner
Mal Whitfield.[3]

Sports, with its recent history of some progress toward racial integration, as seen in Jackie Robinson's much celebrated entry into Major
League Baseball in 1947, provided evidence of improvement in domestic
U.S. race relations.[4] Even though the bureaucratic machinery changing
U.S. policies and law was slow to enact and ensure racial integration
in all aspects of American life, at least in the sports arena strides were
being made to include nonwhites in the nation's favorite pastimes.
Successful minority athletes such as Lee and Whitfield embodied this
new postwar vision of an integrated body politic. At the same time,
their athletic bodies exemplified the American nation's postwar health
and vigor, as demonstrated by their physical prowess and competitive
successes.

Still, even as U.S. newspapers and State Department officials rushed
to proclaim the value of American athletes in courting nonaligned
states such as India, the goodwill tours of American athletes held open
a number of possible interpretations for local audiences. As suggested
by the quote of a young boy in Bombay after seeing pole-vaulter Bob
Richards perform, "Mr. Richards good American, teaching Indians
how to win Olympics," the individual athlete may not necessarily stand
in for the entire U.S. nation-state and its foreign policies.[5] While Richards was a "good American," other Americans presumably remained
suspect. Moreover the boy's idea that Richards's mission was to teach
Indians how to outperform and defeat the world's elite athletes expressed popular notions of Indian sovereignty and nationalism. The
rising tide of popular nationalism in the Third World was exactly what
U.S. leaders feared could undermine U.S. hegemony in the region if it
were not channeled in pro-American and pro-capitalist directions.

The place of sports in U.S. cultural diplomacy in Cold War Asia, as
I explore in this essay, becomes even less clear with the presence of
Asian American athletes such as Sammy Lee, whose Asian American
male body left open a range of possible interpretations by local Asian

audiences. I focus on Lee's fall 1954 tour throughout Asia, paying particular attention to his stay in Vietnam, in order to relate the familiar
discussions of Asian American citizenship and post–World War II racial
formation stateside to Cold War geopolitics in Asia. I argue that Asian
American goodwill ambassadors to Asia in this period—particularly
because of their racialized bodies—found themselves a part of the remaking of understandings of race and citizenship both at home and
abroad. In the case of Lee's visit to Vietnam, his acceptance and popularity during his whirlwind tour resulted from his ability to embody
simultaneously postwar racial liberalist discourses as well as competing decolonization narratives of race and nation-building in Southeast Asia—narratives that offered multiple and at times contradictory
versions of the Vietnamese struggle against Western imperialism and
could either support or undermine U.S. influence in the region.

International Sports, Politics, and the Nation

The popularity and success of American athletes on these goodwill
tours in Asia reflect a long history of Western sports in this part of the
globe as a result of nineteenth-century labor migrations, Christian missionary work, and Western colonialism.[6] Historians, moreover, have
long looked to professional and amateur sports and physical culture
more broadly as important sites for the formation of national identity
and citizenship as well as international politics. C. L. R. James, in his
seminal work on West Indian cricket, for example, used this sport as
a text for understanding indigenous colonial resistance, while other
scholars questioned to what extent the sport served as a form of imperial discipline and control over its colonial masses.[7] Asian American
studies similarly looked to the sport of boxing in creating notions of national identity, masculinity, and modernity through the mass consumption and celebration of the Filipino fighter's agile and powerful body.[8]
Other scholars in the field examined the role of American team sports
such as baseball and basketball in the molding of loyalty, belonging,
and citizenship for Japanese American and Chinese American youth.
Organized youth sports disciplined Asian American physiques while
providing a public arena to display their physical skills. Asian American
youth in turn used sports to lay claim to an American cultural identity
and employed their particular physicality to introduce new skills and
strategies that could transform the mode of play.[9] Yet other scholars
have looked to sports as a dynamic site of national formation, a place
where national identity and the meanings of nationhood may be ex-

pressed, contested, and affirmed.[10] International sporting events, such as the Olympics, bring together the nation's top athletes and place these corporeal representatives of the nation-state into direct physical competitions that mirror as well as shape international cultural and political relations.[11]

In the twentieth century the establishment of the Far Eastern Championship Games in 1913 brought international Western sporting contests to the region. Forty years later the creation of the Asian Games in 1951 brought Olympics-style competitions to that continent. Although only eight nations competed in the 1951 Asian Games in New Delhi, by the time of the second Asian Games four years later in Manila, the number of participating countries expanded to eighteen, including new nations such as Vietnam.[12] The Asian Games, organized under the patronage of the International Olympic Committee, noticeably omitted the newly emergent communist nations of Asia—the People's Republic of China, established in 1949, and the Democratic People's Republic of Korea, founded in 1948—in favor of pro-U.S. or nonaligned governments such as the Philippines and India or European colonial possessions such as Singapore, which remained under British control until 1957.

The absence of communist Asian nations served State Department aims to further the ideational integration of decolonizing Asian nations into the U.S.-led "free world." As seen in the comments of Philippines vice president Carlos P. Garcia at the beginning of the second Asian Games in Manila, the Games could serve a larger goal of promoting the U.S. liberal democratic agenda in Asia: "All that is important is that democracy will triumph in all its splendor and magnificence and this coming Asian games will afford to the Asians the rare opportunity of proving to the world that they can act as one man and perform their role in the realization of a common objective the perpetuation of democracy as an institution so necessary to man in his pursuit of real happiness."[13] As Garcia's statement also makes clear, the international stage of the Asian Games, comprising eighteen countries, far surpassed games played in the Philippines or elsewhere in Asia. Though conceived as an event to bring "Asian Countries together on the field of Sports," the Asian Games served a larger purpose of proving each participating nation's readiness for self-governance and support of a U.S.-led Asia alliance.[14] Each country's athletes bore the responsibility to properly demonstrate their country's fitness to join the international community.

Asian solidarity remained politically suspect, however, as the specter of a united Asia against the nations of the West remained a concern even as Cold War geopolitics emerged to replace older imperial geographies of Asia. The Asian Games—even when occurring in Manila—left room for declarations of Asian self-determination against U.S. intrusion, as seen in a political cartoon titled "On the Warpath" appearing on the front page of the Filipino newspaper *Daily Mirror.* The cartoon featured a sports stadium with a number of Asian national flags representing the competing countries. Excluded from the international competition, a group of American Indians portrayed in "war dress" and holding weapons march around the stadium wall while carrying a banner proclaiming them "The Scalpers." The cartoon inverts the familiar mid-twentieth-century racial and national hierarchies. Americans appear as the premodern primitives existing outside of civilizing discourse, exemplified by the stadium's walls, while Asians have organized themselves into modern territorial nations bound together by peaceful competition and exchange.[15] Furthermore headlines such as "Red China Urges 'Asia for Asians' at Geneva," also appearing on the front page of the same issue, reminded readers of the possibility of a pro-communist Asian solidarity that excluded the West.[16]

Within the U.S. domestic context of desegregation and social unrest and the international context of decolonization and ensuing questions around Asian self-determination and solidarity, the State Department's selection of Sammy Lee for an Asian goodwill tour could not have been more appropriate. Lee was born in Fresno, California, to Korean immigrants who arrived in the United States at the turn of the century. The Lees relocated to Los Angeles and ran a small grocery store in Highland Park, where his mother cooked "chop suey" to sell to their customers. He excelled in both diving and academics, earning a BA from Occidental College and a medical degree from the University of Southern California before entering the U.S. Army Medical Corps during World War II. Lee earned national and international fame following his remarkable double victory in both the platform and springboard competitions in the 1948 London Olympics. In that same competition the Filipina American Victoria Manalo Draves echoed Lee's performance by earning gold medals in both the springboard and platform events. Writing in the *New York Times,* Benjamin Welles captured the dramatic celebration of these Asian American divers for American readers back home: "After twisting cleanly into the water following her final voluntary dive from the highboard, Mrs. Draves was seen wiping both pool water and tears from her eyes as America's Sammy Lee—winner of the men's high-board championship yesterday—hurried to the pool's edge to tell her she had won. 'I am so happy,' she said, 'I just can't believe it.'"[17] Photographers snapped pictures of the Asian American divers with their hands clasped in celebration of Draves's history-making victory. If the Asian bodies of the two athletes momentarily confused American readers, Lee's immediately recognizable U.S. Army uniform and Draves's U.S. Swim Team swimsuit, with its familiar striped crest, indisputably made clear that these Asian bodies belonged to the U.S. nation. Photo captions likewise marked these athletes as local, home-grown champions, as the *Los Angeles Times* wrote, "HEROES—Mrs. Vicki Draves of Pasadena, maker of Olympic history in women's diving events, clasps hands with a fellow-Pasadenan, Dr. Sammy Lee, Army medic, who captured the high platform diving championship in the Wembley Pool."[18]

The 1948 London Games should also be understood as the first international games to be held since the controversial 1936 Berlin Olympics, where Adolf Hitler and the Third Reich's racial ideologies of Aryan supremacy became part of the international sporting spectacle. For U.S. audiences, the 1936 Games would be best remembered as a series of dazzling triumphs by African American athletes such as Cornelius Johnson, Ralph Metcalfe, and Jesse Owens in defiance of Nazi racial ideologies.[19] Whereas the 1936 Berlin Olympics remained associated with the Nazi regime and its repugnant racial ideologies, the 1948 Olympics represented a postwar victory celebration of Western allied nations and a reaffirmation of their support for liberal democracy.

The 1948 victories of Lee, the child of Korean immigrants, and Draves, the daughter of a Filipino father and English mother, could not have been better timed to coincide with postwar U.S. domestic and foreign policy needs. As U.S. leaders charted a new postwar global order built around an anticommunist political consensus in defense of free economic markets and liberal democracy, popular images of Asian American success, especially in the international arena of the Olympiad, helped to project the United States as a modern, robust nation whose greatness derived from the full participation of racially and ethnically diverse men and women. These widely circulated celebratory images of the Asian American gold medal divers, along with prominent African American athletes such as Alice Coachman, the first African American woman to win a gold medal in track and field, and the gold medal sprinter Harrison Dillard, would help to convey the message of U.S. racial liberalism to audiences around the globe and in the United States. Meanwhile seventeen-year-old Bob Mathias's stunning victory as the youngest athlete to win the grueling decathlon projected an image of American vitality and strength against the backdrop of a still recovering postwar Europe. The postwar American nation, embodied by these incredible athletes, presented to the world an image of racial diversity, tolerance, and youthful vigor.

Four years later the U.S. sporting world expected the 1952 Olympics in Helsinki to be just as successful in showcasing the nation's athletic talent as well as its ongoing commitments to racial progress at home and liberal democracy around the world. On the eve of the Olympics, Avery Brundage, the president of the U.S. Olympic Association, summed up the hope for a diverse contingent of U.S. athletes to serve as the nation's best representatives: "At Helsinki we look for tremendous things from Bob Mathias, a country doctor's son from Tulare, Calif., and a past Olympic winner in the decathlon at 17; a fabulous vaulting preacher, Rev. Bob Richards; a Korean-born diver named Capt. Sammy Lee; a fine Negro broad jumper, George Brown; a young Navy airman named Dick Attlesey in the hurdles, and many others. As always, our athletic ambassadors will come from every state in the Union and every walk of life."[20] But for Brundage, the athletes were more than "ambassadors" who brought the nation's goodwill and sportsmanship to the international sporting arena. Indeed he saw these athletes ready to engage in battle as the 1952 Olympics hosted the first postwar appearance of the Soviet Union in the games, "the first display of Russian sport strength in the Games since 1912."

Sammy Lee's Fall 1954 Tour to Vietnam

At the 1952 Olympics Lee successfully defended his gold medal in the ten-meter platform diving competition. Although Victoria Draves had retired from Olympic competition, the Asian Americans Yoshinobu Oyakawa and Ford Konno of Hawai'i won gold medals in swimming events and Evelyn Kawamoto, also from Hawai'i, won bronze in the 400-meter freestyle.[21] The following year the AAU awarded Lee the James E. Sullivan Award. Lee became not only the first Asian American but also the first diver and oldest recipient of the prestigious award to be given to an American athlete who did the most to "advance the cause of good sportsmanship during the year."[22] In the postwar years domestic civil rights and international Cold War political pressures intruded into the world of American professional sports, making Lee an appropriate winner for that year. In Sammy Lee, America had a wonderful example of socioeconomic progress for the nation's small Korean American population, a minority within a minority.

In the realm of public diplomacy rather than in the competitive sporting arena, Lee embodied the aims of the Sullivan Award. The

Figure 10.1. Syngman Rhee, president of South Korea, greets Sammy Lee at a diving demonstration in Seoul, September 20, 1953. Courtesy of University of Southern California, on behalf of the USC Korean Heritage Library.

accompanying citation highlighted his congeniality and popularity, particularly in the international field of competitors: "The trail of international friends made by Dr. Lee is as lengthy and encircling as the equator."[23] Moreover Lee had a long career in the American military that stretched back to World War II, when he entered the army through a special medical training program. The army funded his medical school education in return for his military service after graduation. Lee juggled his medical school training, military duties stateside, and diving training and competitions throughout the 1940s and early 1950s, until he retired from diving competition.[24] In early 1953 he received orders to transfer to South Korea but arrived after the war concluded. The citation further noted Lee's personal sacrifices to the nation: "While his Army duties have kept him from competing regularly in the American championships in recent years, Maj. Lee has given unstintingly of his free time to entertain our troops stationed abroad with exhibitions of his matchless form off the high platform."[25]

The AAU's selection of a Korean American athlete—coming just a few months after the disappointing stalemate of the Korean War—announced the American sports world's intent to take up an activist role in the nation's social and political affairs. The AAU saw the role of sports as facilitating the end of racial discrimination and segregation while simultaneously aiding in the U.S. mission to integrate Asia's de-colonizing nations into an American postwar liberal consensus in the global Cold War. The following year, 1954, months after the landmark *Brown v. Board of Education* Supreme Court decision, the AAU gave the award to its first African American recipient, the track and field star and former Tuskegee Airman Mal Whitfield. The AAU voting membership's decision to give the nation's prestigious all-around amateur sports award to an Asian American and an African American athlete in consecutive years sent a strong message to both domestic and international sports audiences.[26]

By the time of Lee's visit to Southeast Asia in the fall of 1954, United States Information Service (USIS) outposts throughout the region had been working on diffusing anti-U.S. propaganda that emphasized the problems of racial discrimination stateside. In 1951 USIS officers in the region turned their attention to the issue through hiring and propaganda initiatives such as placing more African American information workers in the field. (The USIS was a predecessor of the USIA.) Attempts to hire an African American in the Malaya office failed, however, because the Selection Board rejected the candidate. Instead USIS officers planned to arrange for Myrtle Thorne, a Howard graduate and USIS public affairs officer already stationed in Mendan in North Sumatra, to tour and speak to local audiences in the region.[27]

In addition, USIS solicited the cooperation and assistance of British information officers in the battle to shape narratives of progress in U.S. race relations circulating in the region. British information officers in the field regularly reported that "South-east Asians, like other non-Europeans, when talking privately to British people, do tend to raise the question of racial discrimination in the States."[28] Increasingly alarmed at the negative effects of such questioning on the local populace, the Foreign Office in London directed the British Embassy in Washington to ask the U.S. State Department to provide "suitable material on recent improvements in racial legislation and practice in the United States" that could be circulated to various embassy outposts and colonial offices in the region. As one British information officer put it, "This is a case where I think we might be able to give the Americans some real help since facts quoted by an Englishman may carry more weight than facts quoted by an American."[29] A few months later Adam Watson, a British information liaison officer, forwarded a list of books on the topic of "Negroes in America" as well as a retyped recent *Ebony* article that em-

ployed 1950 census statistics to illustrate the postwar "advancement of
the Negro."[30] By early 1952, USIS officers had created the "Background
and Action Kit No. 5 United States Minorities—A Progress Report" to
distribute to USIS outposts in the region as well as to the British regional information officer in the Office of the Commissioner General
in Singapore for potential redistribution to U.K. officers in Djakarta,
Rangoon, Bangkok, Saigon, and Tokyo. The kits instructed British and
U.S. officers in these regions on how best to address "accusations about
the treatment of minorities, especially negroes in the United States."[31]
In 1953 the USIA was created, and usually referred to the centralized
office in Washington, but the USIS remained the name for the outposts
outside of the country. The USIA continued to send out such press
kits advertising the improvement of U.S. race relations throughout the
1950s. For example, a kit that circulated around the time of Lee's fall
trip involved the story of Clifford Alexander becoming the first African
American student to be elected president of the Student Council of Harvard University.[32] Aside from a USIA press release detailing Alexander's
biography and many achievements, three black-and-white photographs
showcased his life at Harvard as the president of the Student Council
and as a star athlete on the university's baseball team. Beginning in the
late 1940s USIS–Hong Kong began production of a series of popular
magazines, such as World Today (Jin Ri Shi Jieh) and Four Seas (Si Hai), that
often ran feature stories of Chinese Americans that emphasized the social freedoms and economic mobility they enjoyed.[33]

   With Lee touring on behalf of the U.S. State Department, USIS officers in the field had a more effective propaganda weapon than any
media kit or magazine consisting of press releases and static black-
and-white photographs portraying the lives of nonwhites in the United
States. In Lee USIS officers had the real-life embodiment of postwar
U.S. racial progress. USIS officers unanimously pronounced Lee's visit
to their respective jurisdictions a grand success. John K. Emmerson,
the chargé d'affaires at the U.S. Embassy in Karachi reported the unusually "large number of enquiries that the Embassy received regarding
the schedule and performance of the visitor."[34] In Bombay police held
back "crowds seeking autographs and interviews."[35] Officers with USIS-
Rangoon claimed that the Burmese press's coverage of Lee's visit was
"second only to Vice-President Nixon among visiting American celebri-
ties."[36] In all his visits, USIS officers commented on the importance of
Lee's race in his acceptance by local audiences, following a racial logic
that grouped Lee with the diverse peoples of Southeast Asia. The report from USIS-Rangoon, for example, claimed that Lee, as a person of

Asian descent, "possesses a perhaps instinctive understanding of the Asian mind which enables him to communicate immediately and fully with audiences and individuals of this area."[37]

State Department correspondence regarding Lee's visit to Vietnam from September 28 to October 8, however, provides important evidence that complicates U.S. officials' emphatic pronouncements of Lee's success as a symbol of American racial progress. Similar to the other country visits on his tour, Vietnamese audiences heartily embraced Lee and his impressive aerial acrobatics. The political instability following the signing of the Geneva Accords in July 1954 and the partition of Vietnam at the seventeenth parallel made Lee's work as a U.S. cultural ambassador in this country of critical necessity. In Vietnam and the Southeast Asia region, the popularity and standing of the United States as a force for liberal democracy had slipped by the 1950s, perhaps partly as a result of its financial support of France's unsuccessful war to retain colonial possession of Indochina.[38] One British information officer, reporting on a recent meeting with Theodore Streibert, noted, "With the experience of Indo-China fresh in its mind, the U.S. would in future studiously avoid identification with colonial interests and, in this way, hope to gain the confidence of free Asia, Latin America, etc."[39]

With the July 1954 division of Vietnam into two zones, the United States worked to strengthen the government of Ngo Dinh Diem in the South and to improve the image of the United States in all of Vietnam and the region. At the same time, however, U.S. leaders understood that Diem did not command the popular support that North Vietnam's communist-nationalist leader Ho Chi Minh and the Viet Minh did among the Vietnamese people. They read the postwar surge of Vietnamese nationalism as both a potential source of support and a possible challenge to the popular legitimacy of Diem's rule and a pro-U.S., anticommunist, South Vietnamese state. U.S. officials greatly hoped that Lee's visit, at this crucial point in the new nation's founding, would help mobilize popular support for U.S. involvement in the region. Indeed U.S. officials' decision to have Lee tour South Vietnam for ten days suggests the degree to which they deemed his visit important to the new government led by Diem.[40]

The partition and political changes of 1954 caused great confusion for Lee's USIA-Saigon handlers, who had to navigate a new working relationship with the Vietnamese National Army (VNA) and curtail earlier planned activities to visit Hanoi and other sites in the North. Furthermore USIA-Saigon's lack of experience with the sport of diving led to other complications, such as the search for swimming pools large enough to accommodate his diving demonstration; embarrassingly, USIA-Saigon had committed to the lengthy ten-day visit before locating proper facilities. Fortunately the VNA solicited the cooperation of French officials who retained private possession of some of the only adequate facilities in the entire country. On the eve of Lee's arrival in Saigon, USIA officials found themselves scrambling to build a new itinerary that could make full use of Lee's stay in Vietnam.[41]

In the end, Lee's lengthy visit included only three diving demonstrations; two took place at the French Sports Club in Saigon (Cercle Sportif Saigonnais), where one event reached an audience of nearly one thousand. The third demonstration took place in Dalat, the site of the French colonial hill station that boasted a geography and architecture reminiscent of the French Beaux Arts movement. With its wide boulevards and opulent resorts designed for the French colonial ruling class and Vietnamese elites, the complex included facilities for the promotion of such Western sports as rowing, tennis, and horseback riding. French colonial officials had promoted such sports as critical to the social reproduction of the French ruling class as well as the disciplining and training of a French colonial and military elite. More important, Dalat also boasted a top-flight military academy, where the French had begun training Vietnamese officers for the VNA during the French-Indochinese War back in 1951. Here, in the heart of French imperial martial culture, an adequate diving pool could be found.[42]

If USIA officials hoped to use the Lee visit to showcase American national and physical strength to local audiences and cement new relationships between the United States and the new South Vietnamese regime, the physical backdrop for these demonstrations reminded spectators of the lingering and pervasive French colonial presence in official and everyday Vietnamese life. Moreover, with Lee's itinerary managed by the Forces Morales Division of the French-trained VNA, USIS-Saigon had little control over his public appearances. In the case of the two diving demonstrations at the Cercle Sportif Saigonnais, the occasion became an opportunity to showcase French swimming talents and young Vietnamese hopefuls while exemplifying the ongoing collaboration between the South Vietnamese regime and its French former colonial rulers. A headline for the French-language Vietnamese newspaper Union Française, for example, announced in large bold letters the upcoming "swim gala" while tacking onto the end in small letters, "with Olympic champion Sammy Lee."[43]

Not only did Lee's itinerary become a challenge for his USIS handlers not used to hunting for swimming pools with diving facilities as part of their usual diplomatic duties, but how exactly to channel Lee's Asian American body and physical talents into an unabashedly pro-American message to diverse audiences throughout Vietnam also posed some difficulties. In Lee the USIA found a most willing and cooperative cultural ambassador, as he eagerly presented himself as an example for racial progress in the United States. He recalled in a 1999 interview, "I g[a]ve diving exhibitions and then I'd have a little session to talk about Americanism, prejudice, bigotry, and I always, in order to top them, say that the majority of the American people didn't practice what they preach. I could not be here as a two-time Olympian, doctor of medicine, major in the U.S. Army and winner of the James E. Sullivan award otherwise. That was my punch line. Nobody could top that."[44]

Indeed Lee's statements supported U.S. claims of postwar domestic racial progress in terms similar to those found in the USIA press kits and news articles that highlighted the socioeconomic advancement of African Americans and Chinese Americans. Moreover Lee's affability and general acceptance by the local Vietnamese populace also pointed to the possibilities for improving U.S.-Vietnamese relations that might bode well for integrating postcolonial Asian nations into an American liberal consensus. Yet there was another possibility: particularly in the spectacular diving displays of this Korean American athlete and military officer, Lee's body could also represent the discourses of Vietnamese nation-building that worked to construct a virile and martial Vietnamese nationalism. Such an image could, on the one hand, support a U.S.-aligned South Vietnamese nation-state or, on the other hand, give rise to a popular nationalism that would challenge the U.S. alliance. Arriving on the heels of the French withdrawal from Indochina and the emergence of two Vietnamese states, each rivaling to lead a newly independent Vietnam, this model specimen of Asian American masculinity and athleticism could resonate with popular Vietnamese narratives of their underdog efforts to end French colonial rule. Lee's small physical stature—at slightly over five feet tall—and unassuming, modest manner, as well as his Korean ethnicity, played well to David-versus-Goliath narratives of anticolonial resistance.

The collective excitement of USIA officials in the region over Lee's visit temporarily pushed away their concerns with anti-U.S. sentiment. While he could easily represent Vietnamese nationalist discourses of nationhood and postcoloniality that would support Vietnamese sovereignty and self-determination, however, there were no guarantees that such expressions of nationalism could be contained and channeled back to support the emerging state of South Vietnam, the leadership of

Diem, and the presence of the United States in the region. Indeed Lee's small stature and consistently stunning victories over larger Western opponents could easily remind Vietnamese audiences of their claims to sovereignty and ability to withstand Western intervention in their national affairs.

While we cannot ascertain the full extent of audience reactions to Lee's tour, newspaper articles provide a glimpse into the ways the story was communicated to different audiences in Vietnam. Articles did not just present Lee as an American athlete or a U.S. military officer, but also commented on his family background, specifically emphasizing his Korean parentage. In the French-, Chinese-, and Vietnamese-language press announcements of Lee's visit, reporters took care to go beyond using a geographic or quasi-racial "Asian" label to emphasize his Korean ancestry; some newspapers described his family's origins in Seoul and circulated the photograph of Lee's diving performance in Seoul that summer.[45] Lee's Koreanness, rather than a generic Asianness, heightened his appeal to his Vietnamese audiences. The former colonial subjugation of Korea, his ancestral homeland, by Japan made Lee's story familiar to the Vietnamese people, who had similarly been colonized by Japan during World War II, before the eight-year-long fight for independence from the French. Moreover Korea had just experienced what Vietnam had begun to undergo, the partition of the country into separate north and south governments, along with civil strife that was deeply imbricated in global Cold War geopolitics. The emphasis on Lee's roots in South Korea easily resonated with the attempts of the Diem-led South Vietnamese government to legitimize its rule vis-à-vis the Ho Chi Minh–led Viet Minh government in the North.[46] The South Korean association, however, could also work to remind readers of the perils that faced divided countries.

Lee's phenomenal diving success competing among the best athletes of the Western world resonated within the national Vietnamese renaissance of indigenous folk cultures that had emerged during and after World War II and contributed to a reappraisal of pre–French colonial Vietnamese history and culture that paid particular attention to war heroes who struggled against alien invaders. Vietnamese literati and historians infused music, literary, and athletic practices with martial themes promoting nationalist sentiment.[47] In the immediate postcolonial years, northern intellectuals continued to look to indigenous folk traditions to recuperate an innovative precolonial Vietnamese culture and society that countered French colonial narratives of Vietnamese primitivity.[48] Prime Minister Ngo Dinh Diem in the South launched a series of moral self-strengthening programs using Catholic and Confucian models that honored discipline and sacrifice to build a strong, healthy nation.[49] Even as Vietnam underwent partition, then, narratives of renovation and self-discipline in the construction of a strong nation continued to gain purchase among Vietnamese at opposite ends of the political spectrum. As a result Lee's skilled performance, despite his own anticommunist views, might easily appeal even to groups who were critical of Diem's government and the place of U.S. intervention in the region.

Vietnamese newspapers' numerous photographs of Lee's nearly naked body—wearing just skin-tight swim trunks—captured in midair somersaults showcased his compact muscular build, agility, and masculine virility. In a group photograph of divers at a 1953 exhibition in Seoul published in the Saigon newspaper Phong Su (Reportage), audiences could see Lee's diminutive size compared to his Western opponents. The only Asian among the group, Lee stands a full head shorter than the white divers pictured. [50] But if Lee was small by Western physical standards, his Korean body fit easily within the groups of Vietnamese with whom he was photographed throughout his trip. Shots of Lee in a U.S. Army uniform visiting VNA hospitals in Saigon, for example, show him comfortably moving within the infirmary and visually blending in with the VNA officers. A photograph of Lee at the military academy in Dalat shows him observing a judo demonstration performed by VNA cadets for his benefit—as one martial artist to another.[51]

The USIA included these photographs in their official reports as evidence of Lee's success in building goodwill between American and VNA soldiers, but, perhaps concerned about the image of the United States as a military aggressor in the Pacific, in their publicity to Vietnamese audiences USIA officials rarely showcased these images of Lee the U.S. military man. Instead the visual narrative throughout the tour presented him not as a member of the U.S. armed forces but as an athlete and Olympic champion. Most significantly, USIA publicity photographs sent to newspapers in advance of his tour usually portrayed Lee in mid-dive. Images of his near-naked body—taut with rippling muscles flexed in pike formation or fully extended in a graceful swan dive—demonstrated his physical prowess as a diver and athlete and recalled his Olympic glory and good sportsmanship. In his military uniform Lee was inextricably linked to the powerful American nation-state and its growing military presence in the region that could arouse fear and suspicion among Asia's decolonizing populace; without his military uniform Lee's national identity could be more readily effaced even as his racialized body marked him as Asian.

Diving, a sport developed in the West, shared much in common with several indigenous forms of physical culture in Asia, including martial arts, in terms of its demands on strict physical and mental discipline to control the body's movements.⁵² Unlike the more recognizably Western team sports such as soccer or basketball that resembled the territorial wars of modern nation-states, with agreed-upon rules and boundaries and the strict regulation of time, diving remained at its core a competition that pitted individuals against one another. The movements themselves, graceful and powerful gravity-defying twists and tumbles, resembled familiar indigenous forms of acrobatics found throughout Asia in popular folk performances. Not surprisingly Vietnamese-language newspapers used the word for *tumbling* instead of *diving* when describing Lee's sport.⁵³ Well-known martial arts schools such as the Jingwu Tiyu Hui (Pure Martial Athletic Association) that promoted a national formulation of indigenous Chinese martial arts began establishing branches throughout Southeast Asia, including Vietnam, to cater to overseas Chinese populations. The essence of this physical culture emphasized the sharpening and disciplining of the mind and body to create a strong modern nation. Lee's successes as a diver in international competition confirmed the familiar principles of the martial arts movement in demonstrating that the well-disciplined Asian male body could vanquish any challenge to his person or nation.⁵⁴ While Lee's presence helped to support the making of a strong South Vietnamese state, it also bolstered Vietnamese nationalism generally. An independent South Vietnam—even if anticommunist—might depart from and obstruct U.S. policies in the region.

The question that dominated U.S. relations with South Vietnam in the fall of 1954 as Lee conducted his tour was to what extent Diem would be successful in harnessing and channeling the groundswell of Vietnamese popular nationalism in support of his heavily U.S.-subsidized leadership. The multiple competing discourses of nationhood in Vietnam in the period following the official French withdrawal from Indochina demands that historians look more critically at the State Department's glowing reports of the power of U.S. cultural diplomacy to sway postcolonial nations to accept U.S. political leadership in the region. No doubt, as an athlete with enormous physical skill and talent, Lee could easily put on a spellbinding spectacle to entertain and win over Vietnamese audiences. While USIA officers in the region firmly believed his Asian Americanness and professional achievements provided the definitive proof of U.S. liberal democracy, his Asian American body left room for multiple interpretations. In effect the brilliant success of Lee's visit lay not so much in his unequivocal celebration of American ideals, as his USIA handlers claimed in their reports, but in his racialized body's ability to appeal simultaneously to competing discourses of postwar U.S. empire-making and to various styles of Vietnamese nation-building.

Notes

1. Acting Secretary of State to the Director of the United States Information Agency (Streibert), Sept. 10, 1954, U.S. Department of State, *Foreign Relations of the United States* (FRUS), 1952–1954, 1791.

2. President to President of the Senate, July 27, 1954, FRUS, 1776. For two studies that examine parallel examples of cultural diplomacy, see Von Eschen, *Satchmo Blows Up the World*; Prevots, *Dance for Export*.

3. Bass, *Not the Triumph but the Struggle*, 6–10.

4. Von Eschen, *Race against Empire*, 177. See also Thomas, "Playing the 'Race Card'" and "'The Good Negroes'"; Kelly, "Exclusionary America."

5. "Pole Vaulting Diplomat Wins Friends for U.S.," *Chronicle Telegram*, Elyria, Ohio, Nov. 17, 1954. Aside from being an accomplished pole-vaulter, in 1958 Bob Richards was the first Olympic champion to grace a Wheaties cereal box, a commercial practice that has since become a routine part of the commercialization of the Olympic Games. "Health, Wealth, and Wheaties," *Time*, June 16, 1967.

6. Morris, "Native Songs and Dances."

7. James, *Beyond a Boundary*; Nandy, *The Tao of Cricket*; Beckles and Stoddart, *Liberation Cricket*, 9–32. To see how the discussion of professional sports and empire has emerged in other sports, see Dubois, *Soccer Empire*; LaFeber, *Michael Jordan and the New Global Capitalism*.

8. España-Maram, *Creating Masculinity in Los Angeles's Little Manila*.

9. Nomura, "Beyond a Level Playing Field"; Yep, *Outside the Paint*. In many ways these studies are connected to works on sports and physical culture coming out of immigration and ethnic studies that have largely looked at the role of sports and youth organizations in shaping the next generation of American citizens. See, for example, Eisen and Wiggins, *Ethnicity and Sport in North American History and Culture*; Mormino, "The Playing Fields of St. Louis"; Aronowitz, *Choosing Sides*.

10. Brownell, *Training the Body for China*; Morris, *Marrow of the Nation*; Morris, *Colonial Project, National Game*; Perez, "Between Baseball and Bullfighting"; Creak, "Cold War Rhetoric and the Body," 103–10.

11. Keys, *Globalizing Sport*; Guthrie-Shimizu, *Transpacific Field of Dreams*; Wagg and Andrews, *East Plays West*.

12. "History of Other Asian Games Organisations," *Bulletin du Comite International Olympique*, no. 25 (Jan. 1951): 24–25; "The First Asian Games Championships Will Be Held in March 1951 at New Delhi," *Bulletin du Comite International Olympique*, no. 25 (Jan. 1951): 22–24; "Report of the First Asian Games

in New Delhi," *Bulletin du Comite International Olympique*, no. 27 (June 27, 1951): 43.

13. "Mag'say Opens Asian Games Today at Stadium," *Daily Mirror* (Manila), May 1, 1954.

14. "The First Asian Games Championships Will Be Held in March 1951 at New Delhi," 24.

15. "On the Warpath," *Daily Mirror* (Manila), Apr. 29, 1954.

16. "Red China Urges 'Asia for Asians' at Geneva," *Daily Mirror* (Manila), Apr. 29, 1954.

17. Benjamin Welles, "Ann Curtis Excels in 400-Meter Swim," *New York Times*, Aug. 7, 1948.

18. "Vicki Draves, Wins Second Diving Title," *Los Angeles Times*, Aug. 7, 1948.

19. Arthur J. Daley, "110,000 See Owens Set World Record at Olympic Games," *New York Times*, Aug. 3, 1936; Arthur J. Daley, "Owens Captures Olympic Title, Equals World 100-Meter-Record," *New York Times*, Aug. 4, 1936. See also Keys, *Globalizing Sport*, 134–57.

20. Avery Brundage, "My Biggest Olympic Battles," *Baltimore Sun*, June 29, 1952. This was a syndicated essay published in newspapers throughout the country.

21. Allison Danzig, "Lee and Oyakawa Triumph as U.S. Gains 34 Points in Olympics Swim," *New York Times*, Aug. 2, 1952.

22. "Sammy Lee Sullivan Victor," *Oakland Tribune*, Dec. 31, 1953; "Maj. Sammy Lee Wins Sullivan Memorial Award for Diving before Korean GIs," *Daily Register*, Harrisburg, Illinois, Dec. 31, 1953.

23. "Maj. Sammy Lee Wins Sullivan Memorial Award for Diving before Korean GIs."

24. "An Olympian's Oral History: Sammy Lee," interview by Dr. Margaret Costa, Amateur Athletic Foundation of Los Angeles, Dec. 1999 (hereafter "Sammy Lee Oral History").

25. "Sammy Lee Oral History."

26. The State Department also recruited Whitfield to conduct goodwill athletic tours throughout the decolonizing world. In fact Whitfield received news of his Sullivan Award while touring in the Middle East on behalf of the State Department and the AAU. He eventually established a career for himself working for the State Department serving as an athletic consultant in Africa. Joseph M. Sheehan, "Whitfield Is First Negro to Gain the Sullivan Trophy in Amateur Athletics," *New York Times*, Dec. 31, 1954; "Diplomat in Short Pants," *Sports Illustrated*, Feb. 7, 1955, 12–15; Loosbrock, "Mal Whitfield," 402.

27. "Minutes of the Eighth Meeting of the United States and British Information Officers in Malaya," Aug. 31, 1951, Folder FO 953/1200, FO 953 Series, National Archives, U.K.; "Howard University Grad Fights Communist Claims in Sumatra," *Afro American*, July 17, 1954, 6.

28. A. C. E. Malcolm to J. H. A. Watson, Aug. 22, 1951, Folder FO 953/1200, FO 953 Series, National Archives, U.K. For more on Anglo-American cooper-

ation in the field of anticommunist propaganda, see Defty, *Britain, America, and Anti-Communist Propaganda*, 144–62.

29. A. C. E. Malcolm to J. H. A. Watson, Aug. 22, 1951, Folder FO 953/1200, FO 953 Series, National Archives, U.K.

30. Adam Watson to A. C. E. Malcolm, Nov. 9, 1951, Folder FO 953/1200, FO 953 Series, National Archives, U.K.

31. Information Policy Department to Regional Information Officer, Mar. 12, 1952, Folder FO 953/1200, FO 953 Series, National Archives, U.K.

32. "Negro Student Heads Harvard's Student Council," Folder FO 953/1529, FO 953 Series, National Archives, U.K.

33. For example, see "Emma Ping Lum," *World Today*, Hong Kong. Apr. 1, 1952; "Overseas Chinese Newspapers in America," *World Today*, Hong Kong. May 5, 1952. *Four Seas* also ran lengthy stories on Chinese Americans as well as a recurring "Overseas Chinese" feature located at the end of the magazine that included stories and photographs of Chinese migrant communities around the globe, including in the United States. See for example, *Four Seas*, no. 6 (Feb. 25, 1952).

34. Foreign service dispatch from John K. Emmerson, Chargé d'Affaires a. i., Karachi, Pakistan, to Department of State, Washington, Sept. 14, 1954, Folder 511.903—Sammy Lee, RG 59, National Archives and Records Administration, College Park, Maryland (NARA CP).

35. Rube Samuelson, "Sammy Lee Wins Friends for America as a . . . 'Diving Diplomat,'" *Oakland Tribune*, Apr. 10, 1955.

36. Foreign service dispatch from Lionel Landry, Public Affairs Officer, Rangoon, Burma, to Department of State, Washington, Oct. 27, 1954, Folder 511.903—Sammy Lee, RG 59, NARA CP.

37. Foreign service dispatch from Lionel Landry to Department of State, Oct. 27, 1954.

38. On anti-American sentiment in the region during the early 1950s, see Cohen and Tucker, "America in Asian Eyes"; Finkelstein, "U.S. at Impasse in Southeast Asia."

39. Confidential Memorandum, n.d., FO 953/1528, FO 953 Series, National Archives, U.K. See also in this same series, J. W. Nicholls to J. H. A. Watson, May 20, 1954, regarding U.S. concerns about working publicly with the British in the Middle East.

40. By contrast, Lee spent six days in Burma and seven days in Pakistan. For more on Diem and his relationship to U.S. leaders, see Jacobs, *America's Miracle Man in Vietnam*.

41. Foreign service dispatch from Donald R. Heath to Department of State, Oct. 20, 1954. Folder 511.903—Sammy Lee, RG 59, NARA CP. The political chaos of that visit clearly stuck with Lee, who in a 1999 oral history interview recounted that he "went to Saigon and . . . was there when Dien Bien Phu had fallen about a month before." In fact the battle of Dien Bien Phu had ended more than three months earlier. Sammy Lee Oral History, 23.

42. Jennings, "From Indochine to Indochic"; Lam, *The Twenty-five Year Century*, 25–31.

43. "Deux Grands Galas de Natation Cet Après-midi et Demain Matin à la Piscine du c.s.s. avec le Champion Olympique Sammy Lee," *Union Française*, Saigon, Oct. 4, 1954, 2. See also "Deux Grandes Manifestations au Cours du Prochain 'Weekend,'" *Le Journal D'Extreme Orient*, Saigon, Sept. 30, 1954; "Sports Local: Natation," *Nouvelles du Dimanche*, Saigon, Oct. 1954, 15.

44. "Sammy Lee Oral History," 23.

45. See, for example, "Samuel Lee: Double Champion Olymique de Haut Vol," *Union Française*, Saigon, Sept. 30, 1954; "Major Sammy Lee, Olympic Diving Champion Arrives in Saigon," *Viet Nam Thoi Bao*, Saigon, Sept. 30, 1954; *Dan Thanh*, Saigon, Oct. 2, 1954. *Viet Nam Thoi Bao* was published in Chinese; *Dan Thanh* was published in Vietnamese.

46. As discussed by historians of Vietnam during World War II and the early postcolonial period, the South Vietnamese regime faced a legitimacy problem. The government under the leadership of Bao Dai, who was named emperor of Annam in 1926, had retained his position throughout the French colonial period as well as during the wartime joint administration between the French Vichy government and Japanese occupiers. He abdicated his throne in August 1945 in preparation for the creation of a new Vietnamese state at war's end but was reinstalled by the French as part of the March 1949 Elycée Agreement to grant more independence to Vietnam by establishing an indigenous regime as an alternative to a Ho Chi Minh–led Viet Minh administration installed in Hanoi. See Marr, *Vietnam 1945*; Statler, *Replacing France*; Bradley, *Imagining Vietnam and America*, 173–87; Young, *The Vietnam Wars*, 29–30, 42–43.

47. Marr, *Vietnam 1945*, 92–96.

48. Pelley, "'Barbarians' and 'Younger Brothers.'" For more on how Vietnamese postcolonial scholars in the North established a new national history, see also Pelley, *Postcolonial Vietnam*.

49. Donnell, "National Renovation Campaigns in Vietnam."

50. *Phong Su*, Saigon, Oct. 2, 1954.

51. See, for example, photographs USIA-STEM No. 25635 and USIA-STEM No. 25633, RG 59, Folder 511.903—Sammy Lee, NARA CP, where Lee is pictured inspecting military hospitals in Saigon. In USIA-STEM No. 25518, Lee is viewing the judo demonstration. The Japanese military promoted judo in Vietnam during World War II as part of a larger Japanese imperialist project of transmitting Japanese culture throughout the occupied territories in Asia (Marr, *Vietnam 1945*, 81).

52. Competitive diving was first introduced at the St. Louis Games in 1904 and featured only competitors from the United States and Germany (Matthews, *America's First Olympics*, 165–66).

53. "Sponsored by the Army General Staff of the Republic of Vietnam. Major Sammy Lee Performs Tumbling," *Tin Mai*, Saigon, Oct. 2, 1954. See also

Tieng Chuong, Oct. 1, 1954. Interestingly Chinese Vietnamese newspapers did employ the term *diver* (*tiaoshui*, literally translated as "jump water"), so such a term could have been used by Vietnamese journalists. French newspapers also likened his performance to acrobatics. See "A Diving Acrobat: Major Samuel Lee," *La Press D'Extreme Orient*, Saigon, Oct. 9, 1954; "World Diving Champion Arrives in Saigon to Perform," *Luan Dan*, Sept. 30, 1954. Note that all headlines are translated into English from their original language.

54. Morris, "Native Songs and Dances," 52–57.

eleven

Counting the Bodies in Vietnam

MARILYN B. YOUNG

When all else is forgotten about statistical reporting in the Vietnamese war, the body count will be remembered.
—Brigadier General (ret.) Douglas Kinnard, *The War Managers*

Well, we don't do body counts on other people.
—Secretary of Defense Donald Rumsfeld on *Fox News*, November 2, 2003

The body counts are back. For the first time since Vietnam, the U.S. military has begun regularly reporting the number of enemy killed in the war zone—in contradiction, apparently, to prior statements by its own top brass.
—Mark Benjamin, "Return of the Body Count," *Salon*, June 11, 2005

Not everything that counts can be counted. Not everything that can be counted counts.
—Albert Einstein, quoted in Lawrence Kaplan, "Vietnamization," *New Republic*, March 24, 2011

The first reference to the phrase *body count* on Google is to the American heavy metal band of the same name. The lyrics of their most famous song, "Body Count," describe the war on the streets of Los Angeles in 1991: "I hear it every night / another gunfight / the tension mounts / on with the Body Count."

Ice-T, who served four years in the U.S. Army (1979 to 1983), no doubt first heard the phrase in reference to the Vietnam War, where daily body counts were how the military tracked success for the public and for itself. As a way of measuring progress, the body count had the virtue of simplicity and apparently scientific certainty; before long it also became the focus of criticism of American military tactics at home and abroad. As in so much else that once marked the Vietnam War as exceptional, from civilian massacres to massive bombing, the body count was common practice in the Korean War, starting in 1951, when the war stabilized at or near the 38th parallel. "We want maximum casualties on the enemy," General James Van Fleet instructed the commanding officers of the 8th Army in the spring of 1951. "Terrain in itself doesn't mean much." Decades later General Bruce Palmer observed that in both Korea and Vietnam the absence of any territorial objective meant that "it was not possible to demonstrate or assess progress in terms of territory gained and held." Counting the enemy dead was one of the only ways of indicating "how the war was going. . . . At one point in the Korean War, the explicit, if crudely stated, military objective was to kill as many Chinese ('Chinks') as possible."[1]

The war of attrition in Korea seems not to have been a matter of public concern in the United States. Some congressmen did wonder what U.S. objectives were and were told they were "to kill as many Chinese Communists as possible without enlarging the war at the present in Korea." Ultimately, the reasoning went, such punishment would "bring them to the negotiating table."[2] The number of bombing sorties was reported daily, but unlike in Vietnam, there was no daily toll of the enemy dead. Nor, given that at this point in the Korean War the enemy consisted of regular troops rather than guerrillas, was there as great a possibility of counting civilian as military dead, except when death was the result of aerial bombing. In these cases the things that were counted were "structures."

In Vietnam, by contrast, counting bodies began early in the U.S. war effort. In 1963 George Tanham, a researcher for the RAND Corporation, went to Vietnam to assess progress. RAND (Research and Development) was itself the perfect instrument for Secretary of Defense, Robert S. McNamara, committed to advanced management techniques. Founded in 1945 by the Douglas Aircraft Company, Project RAND reported directly to General Curtis LeMay. In 1948 it separated from Douglas and, with the help of Ford Foundation funding, became an independent, nonprofit research organization whose mission was to "further and promote scientific, educational, and charitable purposes, all for the public welfare and security of the United States of America." *Pravda*, with some justice, called it the "academy of science and death."[3] Tanham checked in with General Rollen "Buck" Anthis, commander of the 2nd Air Force Division, whose approach to the issues was numerical: the combination of U.S. and Vietnamese air operations was responsible for two-thirds of all enemy casualties that year. Mai Elliott, in her study of RAND, has observed, "Measuring progress by tracking statistics was the general tendency of the U.S. military in Vietnam. In a war without a front line, in which the enemy's objective was not to capture and hold territory and in which the U.S. goal was to grind down the enemy, the key measure of progress was the number of enemy killed in action—known as the *kill ratio*, or, later, as the *body count*." Tanham was not persuaded that "achievement by numbers" was an adequate measurement and worried about the practice, already in use, of establishing an "'enemy zone'" in which anything that moved was a legitimate target. But concerns about civilian deaths were dismissed by Anthis as isolated incidents and in any case the responsibility of the South Vietnamese officials who told him whom and what to bomb.[4]

By 1964 the military had established a system for counting bodies. The Operations Division of the Military Assistance Command in Vietnam counted weapons captured, sorties flown, and enemy bodies, and of these, according to Brigadier General Douglas Kinnard, the body count was "regarded as one of the most important indicators of progress." As more and more U.S. troops arrived in Vietnam and General William Westmoreland's war of attrition expanded, statistics from various sectors of the country were incorporated into monthly Measurement of Progress reports, which showed both the absolute numbers killed and the kill ratio comparing American deaths to National Liberation Front (NLF) and North Vietnamese deaths. Kinnard recalls his surprise when he attended a briefing in the spring of 1969: "The first seven charts concerned body count and kill ratio: this unit compared with that unit; this year compared with last year; night compared with day, and so on."[5]

The goal was to reach a "crossover point" at which more enemy soldiers were being killed than could be replaced. Only body counts would indicate when that point had arrived. Moreover body counts satisfied Secretary McNamara's passion for measurements, for statistics, for production. When he expressed his displeasure with the low body count of one unit during a visit to Vietnam in 1966, the message was clear: the way to advance one's career was to produce more bodies. The Battle of the Ia Drang Valley in 1965 was the sort of engagement Westmoreland and McNamara had in mind. There, in only a few days, Lieutenant Colonel Harold Moore's troops had killed 1,894 men; early in the next year Moore's score was even more impressive: a kill ratio of 40:1.[6]

One problem was finding the enemy so as to be able to use U.S. firepower and then count the results. The overwhelming majority of combat engagements were initiated by the enemy, leaving the U.S. military to send out patrols—bait, really—to search for and then destroy whomever they found. Soldiers remembered the exhilaration, "like that experienced when one's football team scored a touchdown," of a countable kill. There were contests among platoons, a point system with a sliding scale of value, an "efficiency index" based on the kill ratio (enemy to U.S. dead or wounded).[7] To count the dead, you've got to, in the words of the helicopter tail gunner in the film Full Metal Jacket, "get some." It was sometimes difficult to record precise numbers. After one engagement in the Central Highlands, the military historian S. L. A. Marshall observed that it was difficult even to estimate how many had been killed because the bodies "had been brayed [sic] apart by the blast and arms, legs, and heads had been scattered over a wide space."[8]

Often bodies could be collected without any combat at all. David Bressem, a helicopter pilot, told an ad hoc congressional committee that his unit had equipped their helicopters with sirens. "Anyone taking evasive action could be fired on," he said, by which he understood "someone running or trying to evade a helicopter or any fire." His unit flew over a group of farmers who failed to scatter: "We then hovered a few feet off the ground among them with two helicopters, turned on the police sirens and when they heard the police sirens, they started to disperse and we opened up on them and just shot them all down."[9] The massacre of over four hundred civilians at My Lai in the spring of 1968 was initially reported as a successful operation yielding 128 enemy dead. My Lai was not an aberration but rather, as Ron Ridenhour, the solider who worked hard to expose it, wrote, "an operation."[10] The shift from Westmoreland's "war of attrition" to General Creighton Abrams's "accelerated pacification" did not mean an end to the body count. General Julian Ewell, known within the military by his nickname, the "Butcher of the Mekong," was congratulated by Abrams on the success of Operation Speedy Express, which lasted from early December 1968 to the end of May 1969.[11] Ewell's pressure on his commanding officers to increase the kill ratio spurred them to exceed even Moore's record, achieving a ratio of 40.8:1. Units with low body counts were told they would have to remain in the field until they improved, and officers were given 3 x 5 index cards on which to record their monthly totals. One American military observer witnessed the strafing of a group of boys and the water buffalo they tended, which had turned the paddy field in which they stood "into a bloody ooze littered with bits of mangled flesh. The dead boys and the water buffalo were added to the official body count of the Viet Cong."[12] A reporter for *Newsweek* observed that despite a body count of almost eleven thousand, only 748 weapons had been collected in the Speedy Express operation. The use of firepower, Kevin Buckley concluded, was "indiscriminate" but "quite discriminating . . . as a matter of policy, in populated areas." One after-action report offered a dubious explanation: "Many individuals in VC guerrilla units are not armed with weapons."[13]

The Phoenix Program, the showcase counterinsurgency effort that occupied the waning years of the American effort in Vietnam, did not change the statistical focus on piling up bodies. Robert "Blowtorch Bob" Komer led the effort, which was intended to directly contest NLF control of villages and hamlets throughout the country by imitating the tactics of the guerrillas as Komer understood them. In addition to welfare projects, teams of Vietnamese with their American advisors would gather information so as to target and eliminate the "Viet Cong infrastructure (VCI)," the network of people, soldiers, and political cadres that RAND and other American analysts credited with sustaining the NLF in the face of American firepower. Komer set a quota of three thousand VCI to be "neutralized" each month. From 1968 to mid-1971, twenty-eight thousand VCI were captured, twenty thousand assassinated, and seventeen thousand persuaded to defect. How many of these people were actually affiliated with the NLF is anyone's guess, for the program was an extortionist's paradise, with payoffs available for denunciation on the one hand or protection on the other. K. Barton Osborne, a military intelligence officer, recalled, "Bringing these people in and interrogating them, the process of even considering legal recourses, was just too overpowering, considering the mania for the body count and the quotas assigned for v.c.i. and neutralization. Quite often it was just a matter of expediency just to eliminate a person in the field rather than deal with the paperwork."[14]

Morley Safer, who had been a CBS news reporter in Vietnam, described the effort to locate and "neutralize" local NLF cadres as "a monster child with its computer brain and assassin's instinct [that] would make the Vietcong wither from within": "So out into the countryside went teams of accountants and case officers, Vietnamese assassins and their American counterparts, with bags and bags of money, the whole effort tethered to a computer in the United States Embassy in Saigon. And from the embassy came reports again and again that the program was working. Body count became our most important product. The bodies turned out to be just about anyone who got in the way, sometimes even genuine, certifiable 'infrastructures.'"[15] The disparity between the piles of bodies, the lack of weapons collected, and the lack of notable progress in winning the war gradually brought the practice of counting bodies into disrepute. Some criticism was simply skepticism about the numbers: Were all of the dead really armed enemy soldiers? But skepticism moved readily into an appalled realization: If they weren't enemy soldiers, who were they? With the withdrawal of all American troops in 1973, counting dead Vietnamese was left to those who lived there.

All along, in Korea as in Vietnam, the bookkeeping had been double entry: the fewer American bodies the better; the more enemy bodies the better. American bodies had names, and every effort was made to recover the dead and ship them home along with their personal effects.[16] After the war the American bodies left in Vietnam became a major political issue, and in the effort to restore relations with the United States the Vietnamese government, in the words of Senator John Kerry, launched "the most significant remains retrieval and identification effort in the history of warfare."[17] As Michael Allen has pointed out, by the standard of other wars, the numbers were modest, about 5 percent of those who had died in Vietnam. By contrast, 20 percent "of all Americans killed in World War II—over 78,000 were never found and 8,500 more were never identified. More than 8,000 Americans are still missing from the Korean War, nearly a quarter of American losses." In each of these wars, some effort was made to recover the dead, but "nothing so extensive as the post-Vietnam accounting effort had ever been attempted." Talk of these "lost warriors," Allen explains, "became a way to talk about a lost war, and the effort to account for them was as much a means to establish accountability for their loss as it was a search for their remains."[18] The government had betrayed its citizens, not by sending its young men to fight in Vietnam but by leaving their bodies behind. Americans, not Vietnamese, were the true victims of the war. By 1993 the U.S. government was spending $100 million on recovery efforts, which, given the paucity of results, came to approximately $1.7 million per recovery. Neil Sheehan observed that there was something "bizarre, perhaps even morally obscene—and an insult to the bravery of the dead, to spend so much money searching for bones in a country where children die for want of anti-biotics and thousands of amputees from the war, many of them former Saigon-government soldiers . . . hobble on crutches or go armless, because they cannot afford prosthetic devices."[19]

Vietnamese bodies had no names and were left where they lay, gathered in great nets and helicoptered to mass graves, dragged behind a departing tank, mutilated, their ears trophies for their killers, or left marked with a playing card thought to terrify Vietnamese peasants, the ace of spades.[20] After the war the 300,000 Vietnamese missing in action were not considered an American problem. For many Vietnamese, these unburied dead are doomed to wander the earth, grieving, angry, a constant reproach to the living.[21]

For some American veterans, however, the Vietnamese dead *were* an American problem, or in any case, their problem. George Evans, a poet who had served as a combat medic in Vietnam in 1969, returned thirty years later ready to bear what he thought would be the deserved hostility of the village he was visiting. According to his companion on the trip, Wayne Karlin, Evans was perhaps "remembering the children he told me he had seen early in his tour, when he went into the emergency room and saw two dead Vietnamese children—run over by an American truck engaged in a game the drivers called 'gook hockey,' betting on whether or not they could run down the kids on the roads—lying on gurneys, 'like little dolls.' Their mother came in screaming, running back and forth between them, beating at George's chest, her spittle wetting his face, hysterical, lost, her face burned into his mind. They were not the last dead children he saw." Walking through the village, Evans felt he was "running a grief gauntlet—faces twisted in pain, moans and keening sounds." Grief, and also "pure anger." Later he remembered thinking, "Now they have me, finally and now I pay." He braced to face it, telling himself "Take it, be strong, they deserve to give it and you deserve to get it, it's your responsibility, their pain belongs to you." Karlin, walking beside him, felt no hostility and wondered whether they had each seen what they needed to see.[22]

Karlin's book, *Wandering Souls*, is an account of the effort of one veteran, Homer Steedly Jr., who had fought in Kontum province in 1969, to return the belongings of the young Vietnamese soldier he had killed to the soldier's family.[23] Steedly never explains why he went through the pockets of the man he had just shot, removed the documents he found there, and sent them home to his own mother for safekeeping. Years later, in the course of putting together a website on his war experience, Steedly examined them for the first time. Hoang Ngoc Dam had been trained as a medic, and his notebooks were full of carefully drawn anatomical studies. "I realized that I wanted to try and get those back to whoever they belonged to, just simply because it belonged to them."[24] With Karlin's help Steedly returned to Dam's village and, in an elaborate ceremony, carried a tray of fruit for the family altar. "I'm Homer Steedly," he told the assembled villagers. "I'm a farmer's son that got sent halfway around the world and wound up killing people that I didn't mean to." Later he traveled with the family to retrieve Dam's bones for reburial. In a mystical moment, stopping casually on the trip back north with what were presumed to be Dam's bones, Steedly found himself at the very spot on the trail where Dam had died. He does not feel forgiven. Only Dam himself can offer that, Steedly believes, and perhaps will, should they indeed meet after death.[25]

In the main, however, neither American soldiers nor the American public knew the names of the Vietnamese killed by American arms. Yet every now and then a photograph would inscribe a particular face on public consciousness; later the face might be named. Kim Phuoc, the young girl, her clothes burned off by napalm, her face frozen in shock, was one. Over time, rather like the "Hiroshima maidens" brought to the United States for plastic surgery in 1955, Kim Phuoc came to symbolize all the unnamed Vietnamese dead. Kim Phuoc was treated for her injuries in Saigon; after the war, having studied in Cuba and emigrated to Canada, she established a foundation to assist child victims of war. In a ceremony at the Vietnam Veterans Memorial in Washington in 1996, she accepted an apology from a U.S. serviceman who claimed he may have helped target the bombing raid that burned her. Other faces and other names from those years of war, however, have remained in the shadows of a past the American public wants to forget.

The war continues to mark Vietnamese bodies. The United States had so liberally seeded Vietnam with land mines that they have killed and maimed some 105,000 people between 1975 and 2000. And then there is Agent Orange, as liberally sprayed over South Vietnamese forests and fields. From 1962 to 1971 19 million gallons of herbicide were sprayed over 6 million acres in South Vietnam. Eleven million of those gallons, stored in drums with an orange stripe at the top, contained a highly toxic byproduct, 2,4,5-T, Agent Orange. Put another way, some 12 percent of the population of what was then South Vietnam was exposed to this toxic spraying. According to a recent estimate by Fred Wilcox, three million Vietnamese continue to suffer the effects of the chemical warfare the United States conducted during the war, and a "third and even fourth generation of Agent Orange babies have been born." The deformities, recorded in a book of photographs by Philip Jones Griffith, are extreme: not only blind, but eyeless; not only paralyzed, but limbless; not only a misshapen head, but two heads.[26]

It was hardly surprising that the military decided to give up on counting bodies, though not on war itself. Initially General Tommy Franks and Secretary of State Donald Rumsfeld were both firm: there would be no body counts in Iraq after the 2003 invasion. Until a successful Freedom of Information request in 2007, the official number of Iraqis killed by American forces was classified information. According to Lawrence Kaplan, some units in Afghanistan did publicize their kill ratios, but "the practice remained controversial."[27] As the war in Afghanistan began its tenth year, however, the body count returned, with regular reports of the numbers killed, divided into "leaders" and "rank and file."

The new American way of war, which shifts the burden of combat to contract soldiers, Special Forces, and drones, has reintroduced a problem familiar from the Vietnam War: Exactly whose bodies are they? The precision with which drones and Special Forces hunter-killer teams operate depends on the quality of the targeting intelligence available. With some regularity, the targets turn out to be wedding parties, Pakistani military units, Afghani military and police, even, on one occasion, American Marines. Moreover the quota system returned with a capitalist twist. The contractors who operated some of the targeting programs had quotas. As Joshua Foust has reported, this means that "their continued employment depends on their ability to satisfy the stated performance metrics. So they have a financial incentive to make life-or-death decisions about possible kill targets just to stay employed."[28]

Kaplan wrote that counting bodies meant that the United States was losing the war. The trouble with body counts, he concluded, was the "lack of strategic underpinnings, its tenuous moral legitimacy."[29] That's one way of looking at it. The other is to observe what it reliably reveals: whose bodies count.

Notes

1. Quoted in Gartner and Myers, "Body Counts and 'Success' in the Vietnam and Korean Wars," 386, 388–89. So far as I know Gartner and Myers were the first to point out the use of body counts as a marker of success in the Korean War.

2. Gartner and Myers, "Body Counts and 'Success' in the Vietnam and Korean Wars," 386, 393.

3. See Abella, Soldiers of Reason, 92.

4. The mission statement appears in the official "About" section of the online history of RAND, accessed July 20, 2012, www.rand.org. Elliott, RAND in Southeast Asia, 36, 37.

5. Kinnard, The War Managers, 73.

6. Daddis, No Sure Victory, 99–108. As Daddis explains, Westmoreland was

convinced that the NLF were the proper concern of the South Vietnamese Army; Americans should be engaging main force North Vietnamese units, while behind the security lines thus established, the South Vietnamese would take care of "pacification" (91–92). For Ia Drang, see 79–85. Daddis also summarizes Hanoi's very different assessment of the battle and its meaning.

7. Daddis, *No Sure Victory*, 96.

8. Quoted in Daddis, *No Sure Victory*, 102–3.

9. Testimony before the Dellums Committee, quoted in Young et al., *The Vietnam War*, 113.

10. Seymour Hersh, "Lieutenant Accused of Murdering 109 Civilians," *St. Louis Post-Dispatch*, Nov. 13, 1969, reprinted on Candide's Notebooks, accessed Dec. 16, 2011, http://pierretristam.com/Bobst/library/wf-200.htm. This site contains all of Hersh's original dispatches. For Ridenhour, see Turse, *Kill Anything That Moves*.

11. See Austin Long, "Doctrine of Eternal Recurrence: The U.S. Military and Counterinsurgency Doctrine, 1960–1970 and 2003–2006," RAND Counterinsurgency Study, Paper 6, prepared for the Office of the Secretary of Defense (Santa Monica, CA: RAND, 2008), 18.

12. Nick Turse, "A My Lai a Month," *Nation*, Nov. 13, 2008, accessed Dec. 17, 2011, http:www.thenation.com/article/my-lai-month. The title refers to the estimate made by a soldier who took part in Operation Speedy Express. Turse also discusses his use of the cache of official U.S. documents, declassified in the 1990s and subsequently reclassified, that have revealed how body count drove a blindness to civilian casualties and undercut any claim that the killings at My Lai were a one-time aberration. See also Nick Turse and Deborah Nelson, "A Tortured Past," *Los Angeles Times*, Aug. 20, 2006, and the second in their series, "Civilian Killings Went Unpunished," Aug. 25, 2006.

13. Daddis, *No Sure Victory*, 164–66; Young et al., *The Vietnam War*, 223. See also Turse, *Kill Anything That Moves*.

14. See Young et al., *The Vietnam War*, 213. This account of Phoenix is drawn from 212–13, 240–41.

15. Morley Safer, "Body Count Was Their Most Important Product," review of Douglas Valentine's book *The Phoenix Program*, *New York Times*, Oct. 21, 1990, accessed Dec. 16, 2011, http://www.nytimes.com/1990/10/21/books/body-count-was-their-most-important-product.html.

16. When this is violated, as occurred recently with respect to what the air force has been doing with the bodies of the unidentifiable American dead in Iraq and Afghanistan, there was a serious public outcry. Bodies that proved difficult to identify had been cremated and then dumped in landfills. A report by Brad Knickerbocker quoted from a CNN account: "Backtracking on initial information about how it handled the remains of American service members killed in Iraq and Afghanistan, the Air Force now says the cremated body parts of hundreds of the fallen were burned and dumped in the landfill. . . . The Air Force also said that 1,762 body parts

were never identified and also were disposed of, first by cremation, then by further incineration and then buried in a landfill." The practice is said to have ended in 2008. Brad Knickerbocker, "Remains of Hundreds of Fallen American Soldiers Sent to Landfill," *Christian Science Monitor*, Dec. 8, 2011, accessed Dec. 12, 2011, http://www.csmonitor.com/USA/Military/2011/1208/Remains-of-hundreds-of-fallen-American-soldiers-sent-to-landfill.

17. Quoted in Allen, *Until the Last Man Comes Home*, 286. See also Neil Sheehan, "Prisoners of the Past," *New Yorker*, May 24, 1993, 46–51.

18. Allen, *Until the Last Man Comes Home*, 2, 4.

19. Sheehan, "Prisoners of the Past," 46. Total U.S. aid for prosthetic devices came to $1 million.

20. One can buy "Ace of Spades Death Card Patches" on eBay for a song.

21. Memorialization of the dead in Vietnam is complicated by state politics and local religious practice. See Kwon, *The Ghosts of War in Vietnam*.

22. Karlin, *Wandering Souls*, 218, 219.

23. Karlin, *Wandering Souls*, 218.

24. Karlin, *Wandering Souls*, 176.

25. Karlin, *Wandering Souls*, 256, 286, 305.

26. See Wilcox, "'Dead Forests, Dying People.'" In 2007 a congressional earmark introduced by Senator Patrick Leahy (Democrat, Vermont) to a huge Bush administration appropriation for the War on Terror promised $3 million to clean up dioxin storage sites in Vietnam and support public health programs in the surrounding countryside. It should be noted that this was less than half the amount appropriated by the Ford Foundation for dioxin-related projects in Vietnam.

27. Lawrence Kaplan, "Vietnamization," *New Republic*, Mar. 24, 2011, 9. The FOIA suit was brought by the American Civil Liberties Union.

28. Joshua Foust, "Unaccountable Killing Machines: The True Cost of U.S. Drones," *Atlantic*, Dec. 30, 2011, accessed Jan. 15, 2012, www.theatlantic.com/international/archive/2011/12/.

29. Kaplan, "Vietnamization," 9. Kill ratios are less frequently cited, perhaps because on the whole the disparity between Afghan and U.S. dead is so great. An article in the Toronto *Globe and Mail* quoted former chief of the defense staff of Canadian forces Rick Hillier, who succinctly stated the military's objective, "to kill 'scumbags,'" but noted that the enemy's "kill ratios are uncomfortably high and growing." Michael Bell, "Afghanistan, Iraq and the Limits of Foreign Intervention," *Globe and Mail*, July 23, 2010, accessed Dec. 17, 2011. Of course, with drones doing much of the killing, the ratio is pure sci-fi: man against machine.

twelve

"Nobody Wants These People"
Reagan's Immigration Crisis and the Containment of Foreign Bodies

KRISTINA SHULL

Between April 21 and September 29, 1980, 125,266 Cuban refugees arrived in Key West, Florida, transported on American vessels from Mariel Harbor, Cuba, in what is now known as the Mariel Boatlift. This exodus, sparked by many factors, including economic and political strife in Cuba and U.S.-Cuban negotiations for family reunification, began under assumptions that the United States would accept 3,500 refugees. But shortly after Fidel Castro announced the opening of Mariel Harbor to American vessels wishing to pick up family members, the operation spiraled out of control, and five months of mass migration ensued. Shortly after the first arrivals in the United States, reports of Castro purposefully infiltrating the boatlift with criminals and other social "undesirables" began to circulate in the media. Overwhelmed, President Jimmy Carter's administration declared a state of emergency in South Florida. While roughly half of the arrivals were reunited with family members or resettled in the Miami area in a relatively timely manner, the other half were sent to one of four military bases across the country that served as temporary camps for processing.[1]

On the night of May 26, 1980, two hundred of the eighteen thousand Cuban refugees housed at Fort Chaffee, Arkansas, walked out of an unlocked gate in protest against their detainment by the Immigration and

Naturalization Service (INS) and the slow resettlement process. As they entered the adjacent rural community of Jenny Lind, armed residents on rooftops fired hundreds of rounds into the night sky. No one was harmed, and U.S. Army officers in charge of camp security rounded up and returned the Cubans with little incident. Later that night, hooded Ku Klux Klan members appeared outside the fort carrying torches and signs reading, "Kill the Communist Criminals," while a vigilante security patrol of armed Jenny Lind residents circled the camp in pickup trucks.[2]

Six nights later, on June 1, tensions flared again. An estimated one thousand Mariel Cubans set fire to five army buildings and stormed the front gates, chanting "Libertad!" as they marched down Route 22 toward the small community of Barling. Arkansas state troopers fired over their heads and held them back with rifle butts and billy clubs just outside the town limits, while the Cubans threw rocks, bottles, and pieces of concrete. Federal troops, unable to intervene due to the law of *posse comitatus*, stood in the middle yelling, "Don't hit them! Don't hit them!" to the troopers and onlooking armed civilians. After a couple of hours the state troopers, using clubs and tear gas, finally contained the unruly Cubans within the camp. The "Fort Chaffee incident" left one Cuban dead, forty injured, and eighty-four jailed. One civilian and fifteen state troopers were also injured.[3]

Livid that federal troops were unable to use restraining force, Governor Bill Clinton immediately called in the National Guard and summoned President Carter's aide Gene Eidenberg to demand tighter security at the refugee camp. The night after the disturbance, Clinton took Eidenberg on a tour of Barling and Jenny Lind in his car; he recalled, "It was well after midnight, but down every street we drove, at every house, armed residents were on alert, sitting on their lawns, on their porches, and, in one case, on the roof. I'll never forget one lady, who looked to be in her seventies, sitting stoically in her lawn chair with her shotgun across her lap. Eidenberg was shocked by what he saw. After we finished the tour he looked at me and said, 'I had no idea.'"[4] Clinton also recalled that there had been a run on handguns and rifles in every gun store within fifty miles of Chaffee, while Gun City in Barling sold T-shirts after the incident depicting crowds of Cubans through a gun sight with the caption, "I survived the Cuban Rock Festival."[5]

The panic displayed by local residents at Fort Chaffee mirrored widespread panic expressed in local and national media reports. On May 26, coincidentally the same day as the initial disturbance at Fort Chaffee, *People* magazine quoted an INS officer claiming that "85 percent of the refugees are convicts, robbers, murderers, homosexuals, and prostitutes." This figure was a gross overestimate, but it fueled fear. [6] On June 7 White House press secretary Jody Powell further stoked Cold War anxieties and xenophobia by announcing that among the agitators were a "few hardened criminals" positively linked with Cuban Intelligence efforts.[7]

Eidenberg reflected on the media's role in the incident: "I was in Chicago in 1968. What happened at Ft. Chaffee was a disturbance but it became a riot in the public mind. The national media defined the character of 127,000 Cubans. . . . People wandered off the base on a hot summer night to stretch their legs, they were scared, nervous, bored, but not about to take on the U.S. Army."[8] Lieutenant Francisco Bazán, stationed at Fort Chaffee during the disturbances, later recalled, "The majority who wandered off that night were not considered undesirables when the investigation was completed." He cited frustration with bureaucratic delays as the cause of the protests. He also added, "The locals were not very hospitable, and some had reason not to be. They did not feel adequately protected by their police, and they were being told daily by television, newspapers, and radio that these Cuban refugees right at their doorstep were potentially dangerous people." One Cuban detainee, Estanislao Menendez, did not condone the actions of the agitators who escaped that night but identified with their grievances, saying, "I was taught as a child to respect the law and the military. . . . I would never do what the others were doing. . . . But I can see there was a reason for what they were doing—throwing stones, running away—and the reason was that we were not free, and we did not know what was going to happen to us."[9]

The Fort Chaffee incident did not occur in isolation; disturbances ranging from peaceful protests to hunger strikes and outright violence frequently punctuated the indefinite detention of Mariel Cubans that, for some, lasted for years. This specific incident, however, introduces the various actors that were involved in what would be called a growing national immigration "crisis": displaced migrants, the mass media, local communities, camp administrators, and various levels of government officials. It also reveals some of the many administrative questions that arose: Where do migrants seeking asylum belong? Who should house them? Who should adjudicate their cases? Who has the right to exert physical control over their bodies? Fort Chaffee provides a fitting beginning for an exploration of the "mass immigration emergency" that the administration of Ronald Reagan, which entered office in 1981, felt it inherited. The fear associated with the Mariel migrants powered the Reagan administration's establishment of a new kind of biopolitics: a system of immigration detention characterized by extensive privatized facilities along with a virulent rhetoric of xenophobic American nationalism.

The U.S. immigration detention center is both a transnational space and a foreign policy microcosm. Its detainees reside physically within the nation yet legally outside, while its walls, fences, and doors clearly demarcate those bodies that do not belong to the nation from those that do. The detention center is not merely a domestic place where foreign policy is executed. It is a place both locally and globally defined, where social interactions and cultural narratives transcend concrete walls and nation-state boundaries. Bodies are controlled, marked, and contested in this liminal space. This essay explores the detention and processing of Mariel Cubans at Fort Chaffee as exercises of biopolitical management in the era of Reagan's revitalized nationalism. Through a process of inclusion and exclusion, a previously welcomed "anticommunist" exile group suddenly became cast by the media and politicians as "undesirable." While some Cuban refugees were rendered acceptable additions to the national body through "American" cultural training, sponsorship, and resettlement, nonnational "excludables" were simultaneously rendered invisible through the act of detention.

From Open Arms to State of Emergency

Large-scale migration to the United States from Cuba during Castro's reign was not an unprecedented phenomenon. Since its diplomatic break with Cuba in January 1961, the United States had adhered to a policy of granting entering Cubans immediate parole and hailing them as "freedom fighters" who had bravely escaped Castro's communist regime.[10] In September 1965 Castro announced the opening of Camarioca port in Cuba to Cuban Americans wishing to pick up relatives for emigration to the United States. Through mutual negotiations between Cuba and the United States, this began an eight-year "Freedom Flight" during which 268,000 Cubans entered the United States as legal refugees.

Despite this precedent of Cuban migration, the Mariel boatlift of 1980 posed new problems for the United States. The boatlift brought in approximately half of the number of refugees that came in 1965 in only six months' time and with far less notice, greatly straining government resources.[11] The demographic composition of the Mariel Cubans also differed from those who had emigrated previously. Whereas the earlier wave consisted mainly of older, white, and upper- or middle-class

Cubans seeking family reunification, the Mariel Cubans comprised a predominantly younger, male, and single population, representing "a mix of races more typical of the island's multiracial population."[12] Even though the Mariel Cubans were on average more educated than their predecessors, the racial composition of this group aided in their ultimate labeling by the government as "undesirables."

A confluence of political factors further distinguished the Mariel Cubans from previous refugees, leading them to become one of the most stigmatized groups in recent history.[13] While the Carter administration's initial response to the boatlift aligned with the customarily receptive stance of the United States toward refugees from communist countries, this stance was quickly revised upon rumors that Castro's real aim was to relieve Cuba of its prisoners and social undesirables. Less than three weeks after the boatlift began, President Carter announced at a press conference on May 5, 1980, "We'll continue to provide an open heart and open arms to refugees seeking freedom from Communist domination, brought about primarily by Fidel Castro and his government."[14] At the same time, however, stirrings of negative publicity began surrounding the Mariel exodus, and the very next day Carter declared a state of emergency in southern Florida. A week after Carter's initial endorsement, a U.S. State Department bulletin accused Castro's government of "taking hardened criminals out of prison and mental patients out of hospitals and forcing boat captains to take them to the United States." The bulletin concluded, "We will not permit our country to be used as a dumping ground for criminals who present a danger to society."[15]

Indeed Castro wanted to perpetuate the belief that Cuba was purposefully infiltrating the boatlift with a hard-core element in order to combat the embarrassment caused by the unexpected and overwhelming numbers of Cubans trying to emigrate. Eyewitness accounts confirm that Cuban officials were releasing people whom they deemed "lumpen," so-called loafers, parasites, criminals, and addicts, from prisons and forcing them onto boats bound for the United States, as Castro announced in a May Day rally speech. However, the actual extent of the infiltration of hardened criminals in the boatlift was grossly magnified both by the Cuban government's commitment to remaining ambiguous on the subject and by U.S. media and bureaucratic responses to the Mariel Cubans.[16]

The Carter administration faced a dilemma, wanting to offer open arms to refugees from communist countries while also appearing tough on illegal immigration. The United States had traditionally defined refugees as persons fleeing from countries ideologically opposed to the United States, but the 1980 U.S. Refugee Act, which went into effect in March, a month before the boatlift arrivals began, expanded this category to any persons fleeing fear of persecution. Despite this, the Carter administration sidestepped its dilemma by determining that the Mariel Cubans did not qualify as refugee bodies under the new Act. Even though they are often referred to as "refugees" in media and government sources, they were granted the temporary status of "entrant"—not yet an accepted part of the nation. Ironically a month after the Refugee Act's passage, the Mariel Cubans were the first immigrant group from a communist country since the start of the Cold War to whom the U.S. government denied refugee status.[17]

The political climate in 1980 played a large role in this decision to exclude the Mariel Cubans. During the previous decade the United States had accepted thousands of refugees in the wake of war and persecution, most notably from Vietnam and Southeast Asia, the Middle East, the Soviet Union, Central and South America, and the Caribbean. Americans' rising hostility toward the Mariel Cubans and immigrants in general, labeled in the media as "compassion fatigue," was compounded by an economic recession marked by oil embargoes and high interest and unemployment rates. Many believed immigration burdened social services and increased job competition. Reports that the U.S. government had spent $400 million on processing and resettling Cuban and Haitian entrants by August 1980 only aggravated these sentiments. In the economic downturn U.S. citizens were reluctant to sponsor refugees, while Cuban entrants also had to compete with refugees from other countries, including the fourteen thousand a month who were arriving from Southeast Asia.

Cuban émigré communities in Miami and throughout the United States were initially sympathetic to the Mariel Cubans. In the early days of the boatlift, government agencies provided security and kept order at makeshift camps, and the local Cuban American community and charitable organizations raised funds to provide for the welfare needs of the migrants. As reporting of Castro's plan and Mariel criminality increased, however, anxiety flared and émigrés took care to distinguish themselves from the new immigrants by calling them *Marielitos*, a term that quickly took on pejorative connotations. Nicasio Lopez-Puerta, a first-wave émigré and Cuban American political leader, explained this process: "[Castro] tried to get the American people to turn against us by sending . . . his worst social beings to pollute the image we had so carefully cultivated. . . . I have relatives who came in from Mariel. I am aware of the suffering and the sacrifice. That's not new. What is new is that our relationships with other communities in Miami deteriorated, and xenophobia reared its ugly head."[18]

The "compassion fatigue" displayed by Americans during this time is indicative of a larger shift rightward in U.S. political culture after the end of the Vietnam War. Historian Natasha Zaretsky identifies a resurgent Cold War nationalism that she labels a "conservative counteroffensive" in reaction to both the failure of the Vietnam War and the visibility of the New Left movements of the 1960s and early 1970s. Zaretsky links this nationalism to a constructed perception of national decline that was "experienced as a crisis of reproduction: reproduction of national authority, reproduction of collective sentiments of patriotism, reproduction of postwar affluence, and reproduction of U.S. world dominance . . . also cast as a crisis of generational reproduction."[19] Zaretsky's familial description of nationalism as a reproductive crisis helps facilitate an understanding of growing anti-immigrant sentiment as migrants seemingly posed a threat to the national body. Together these larger national trends set the stage for the real and imagined immigration "crisis" in which bodies that were increasingly represented as dark, criminal, and deviant took on symbolic overtones that resonated with larger narratives of national decline.

Shortly after the Fort Chaffee incident and at Governor Clinton's urging, the Pentagon granted federal troops the emergency power to use restraining force to contain Cubans within the camps across the country where they were being processed, and the White House promised that no more Cubans would be sent to Fort Chaffee. However, as the boatlift drew to a close, Fort Chaffee became the consolidation site for 9,500 unsettled Mariel Cuban detainees in the fall of 1980. A total of 19,060 Cubans were processed through Fort Chaffee, until the fort's closure in February 1982 sent the remaining 392 who were labeled "antisocial" to several prisons across the country. There they joined 1,200 Cubans who were already imprisoned based on suspected felony charges. An additional 600 labeled "serious mental cases" were housed at St. Elizabeths Hospital in Washington, D.C.[20] Many of these detainees, still with indefinite legal status and unable to repatriate due to cold relations between the United States and Cuba, remained in INS or Bureau of Prisons custody for years, and some for well over a decade.

Fort Chaffee, the largest resettlement camp in the United States and in operation the longest, serves as a site of inquiry into the narratives concerning the need to contain foreign bodies that reverberated throughout the media, among governmental officials, and in expressions of xenophobia in the adjacent town of Fort Smith, Arkansas.

"Fort Chaffee's Unwanted Cubans": Resettlement and Detention as Exercises of Inclusion and Exclusion

After the Fort Chaffee incident, Siro del Castillo, a Cuban émigré and the associate director of human resources for Carter's Cuban-Haitian Task Force stationed at the camp, addressed the Cuban community there. Reminding them of their conditional freedom, he stated, "Let's compare this waiting period with that of those Cubans who stayed in Cuba. . . . Let's have, as we said before, a little more humility and maybe a little gratitude. . . . Let's keep in mind that the behavior of each and every one of you who leaves the camp and the behavior of every one of you inside the camp, this is what will determine if the doors of Fort Chaffee are opened or closed to each and every one of you."[21] Castillo seemed to warn detainees that the doors to joining the outside society were open to them only if they acted not only more civilly but more *American* as well.

A close look at the local community interactions and life inside Fort Chaffee will help explain the dynamics behind Castillo's words. Efforts to obtain sponsorship and resettlement for Cubans involved cultural training and an affirmation of "American" values; by contrast, those who remained excludable to the nation were rendered invisible by continued detention. Moreover the stigma attached to the Mariel Cubans extended beyond the walls of the camp and ultimately colored the entire migrant population inside and outside of the detention center.

The largely xenophobic reception of the Mariel Cubans in the adjacent town of Fort Smith highlights familiar anti-immigrant themes seen at various times throughout U.S. history: namely, the foreign threats to national security of criminality, financial burden, disease, and sexuality. The national media's role in circulating these themes helped shape local concerns even before the Cubans arrived at Fort Chaffee. The first 128 Mariel Cubans to arrive in Arkansas on May 9, 1980, received a mostly warm welcome. However, the *New York Times* reported that "some residents of the Fort Smith area were concerned about reports that there were diseased people and criminals among the refugees." And right before the refugees' plane landed, a man dressed in Ku Klux Klan robes ran through the Air National Guard Station, yelling, "Don't let them Cubans in! Hoodlums! They're gonna come in here and get a free ride for everything!"[22] On February 12, 1982, after the last Cubans were moved out of Fort Chaffee, a *Times* article noted, "What is left behind, in the case of Fort Smith, is 71,000 people with a touch of xenophobia," and quoted Fort Smith mayor Jack Freeze as he recounted the experience: "People here decided they didn't want the Cubans before they saw them. The press had already said they were bad. I knew they couldn't be productive. There might be a Desi Arnaz or two out there, but mostly they were going to be killing one another."²³ Both of these articles make reference to how the preexistence of negative press surrounding the Mariel Cubans helped shape local perceptions.

In addition to widespread media coverage of Cuban criminality, concerns over the economic impact of the Mariel Cuban population also greatly influenced the views of Fort Smith residents. A May 10, 1980, *New York Times* article describing a picket at Fort Chaffee cited fears of economic recession as paramount. One young and unemployed mother carried a sign reading, "What are they going to do now—relocate us Americans?" Another young man remembered that Fort Chaffee served as a processing site for fifty thousand Vietnamese refugees back in 1975, relating, "Everywhere you go there's a Vietnamese working now— at least one."²⁴ A June 30 article quoted a man standing in an unemployment line in Illinois, saying, "I bet that if we were Cubans we wouldn't have to wait this long." However, the same article also mentioned the softening of attitudes toward Cubans in Fort Chaffee due to the two thousand jobs that detention had created for local residents.²⁵ This economic concern continued, however, as evidenced by a letter from a citizen addressed to President Reagan on March 28, 1981. The letter asks why "good, law abiding, concerned, underpriviledged [sic] Americans" were paying the expenses of "bad, unlawful, non-caring, CUBAN PRISONERS." The letter concludes with the plea, "Please do something about this predicment [sic] that Carter got us into!"²⁶ Here the recurring themes of financial burden, Cuban criminality, and Carter's failure became intertwined. Economics would continue to play a key role in the Reagan administration's handling of Fort Chaffee and the immigration crisis.

The threat of disease and sexual deviance was also a concern, as reporting highlighted the spread of tuberculosis and sexually transmitted diseases like gonorrhea and syphilis inside the camp. Male homosexual detainees also received much media attention and were segregated in separate barracks.²⁷ A memorandum from Fort Smith chief of police Henry J. Oliver in February 1981 details the death of a young Cuban male in a Fort Smith bar. Oliver describes the need to perform an autopsy: "We were all concerned that even though foul play might not be involved, some contagious disease might be involved." The memo also addresses the dilemma of Cubans being able to acquire guns: "Fort Smith has many, many outlets for firearms. . . . There is no gun registration law in Arkansas and as a result there is no legal way to know whether a Cuban has or does not have a gun. . . . It is felt these people will continue to be a problem as long as they are in this area."[28] After a disturbance in April 1981 in which one Cuban was shot, the local newspaper, *Arkansas Democrat*, ran an article with the opening "Fort Chaffee—The insane who huddle under blankets are sedated lest they cut their wrists to get attention. Homosexuals swish along dusty streets in drag. Single young women bear children conceived in the American resettlement camp. These are the unwanted Cubans at Fort Chaffee." The Republican governor of Arkansas Frank White sent this article to the White House with a note relaying the "desperate need to resolve this situation."[29]

With a lack of government funding, refugee resettlement required the help and sponsorship of private volunteer organizations such as Church World Service and Lutheran Immigration and Refugee Service. Despite xenophobic responses to the resettlement camp expressed by the local community, Mariel Cubans did receive some community support, especially in the boatlift's earlier days, preceding consolidation. Before the Fort Chaffee incident, KKK members demonstrated outside the camp's fences, but so did those in support of Cubans receiving refugee status. Many community members from churches, volunteer agencies, and local schools and colleges volunteered their time, money, and energies at the camp, providing English lessons, trade classes, sports and recreational activities, and training in job interviewing and life skills. Contestations over their status show how Cubans became symbols of very different views of how to protect and promote the American national body.

While at capacity of around nineteen thousand Cuban detainees in addition to army officers and camp administrators, Fort Chaffee became the third largest "city" in Arkansas. It was a truly transnational space—at once American, Cuban, both, and neither. Some detainees had experienced the outside world and returned after their sponsorships broke down for a variety of reasons. Fort Chaffee ran two newspapers, *La Vida Nueva*, initially in Spanish and later in Spanish and English, for the Cubans, and *Crossroads*, for camp and army personnel. At first detainees were fairly free to re-create Cuban social structures and cultural activities. They were encouraged to play traditional sports and games such as boxing, baseball, and dominoes, and they followed Catholic religious practices. Single men, single women, homosexuals, and families were housed separately, but personal relations and the development of a black market based on cigarettes, blue jeans, and other commodities, including sex, was not regulated.[30] Sylvia Gonzalez of the

*Figure 12.1. "Jane Ramos Teaching English to Cuban Refugees at Fort Chaffee, 1980."
Picture Collection, number 4801. Special Collections, University of Arkansas Libraries,
Fayetteville. Used by permission.*

Cuban-Haitian Task Force noted that homosexual life in the camp was
freer than in Cuba or the United States: "We have to impress upon them
that homosexuality is not an accepted thing by Americans at large. . . .
So once they've been assigned a sponsor, you'll see that the eyebrows
tend to grow out and the make-up fades as they prepare for reality."[31]
This freedom inside the camp proved a liability for obtaining freedom
outside the camp, however, as an abundance of media reporting on the
phenomenon of male detainees dressing in drag highlighted public
anxieties surrounding sexual deviance.

Instrumental to sponsorship and resettlement was Cubans' demonstration of willingness and ability to "fit in" with American society. As
Paula Dominique of the Church World Service told the *New York Times*,
"There are people who call up and request a white, college-educated Cuban who speaks English. . . . We remind them that we're not a Sears catalogue."[32] Most sponsors preferred women, children, or entire families,
but the majority of detainees at Fort Chaffee were young, single men.
Over half were Afro- or dark-skinned Cubans, many were unskilled or
uneducated, and 16 percent were reported to have spent time in jail in
Cuba or the United States.[33] Efforts in the camp to increase Cubans'
prospects for sponsorship included a variety of educational techniques

and programs focused on the teaching of English, American cultural practices, and democratic values. Local high school students visited the camp for boxing matches, baseball games, and on one occasion to give Cubans a presentation on the success of capitalism in the United States. The fact that male detainees were encouraged to engage in masculine activities such as sports and discouraged from overtly expressing non-normative gender identities in order to obtain sponsorship exemplifies camp efforts to prepare detainees to become model American citizens.[34]

The La Vida Nueva newsletter, edited by the Cuban-Haitian Task Force in charge of camp administration with the help of detainees, served as an educational tool as well as a form of transnational media that tried to mediate the detainees' liminal status. The newsletter, which ran three times a week, provided updates on camp happenings, world news, health tips, lessons on U.S. history and politics, and messages from the camp director Barbara Lawson. The newsletter also took opportunities such as holidays to educate detainees about American customs and values. On Thanksgiving in 1980, for example, the camp held a "Turkey Trot" race, served a Thanksgiving dinner, and published Lawson's message in La Vida Nueva: "On this first Thanksgiving, it is especially important to remember those first refugees, the pilgrims. . . . They had been able to overcome obstacles and . . . reach their proposed goal: freedom, just like millions of immigrants after them who triumphed over the barriers of language and culture. My prayer on this day of giving thanks is that we will soon have sponsors for each of you, so you can begin your new life in the U.S. as thousands of refugees have done before you." Cuban detainees contributed to this effort to weave themselves into this Thanksgiving narrative of American immigration history. Ramón Valdes Hevia's piece in the Thanksgiving newsletter read, "We Cuban exiles, who have found freedom in this land of open arms, which opens the great gates of life, we join the Christian sense of this town commemorating the 27th of November. . . . I thank God for being in this land of freedom."[35] A group of older Cubans in the camp known as "the Abuelas" held a small demonstration to show what Thanksgiving meant to them, with signs that read, "The Communism Is Cancer," "Muera el Comunisma," and "Thanks to the American People!"[36]

Despite Cuban efforts such as these to combat negative stereotypes in the media and claim belonging in American society, and despite the fact that all but several thousand Mariel Cubans were resettled within two years of arrival, the act of detention itself perpetuated the stigma of criminalization placed on the Mariel Cubans. As time went on, especially after the disturbances and consolidation at Fort Chaffee, the "camp" environment became increasingly more punitive as the concentration of hard-to-sponsor Cubans increased. As conditions deteriorated, so did Cubans' hopes, as they faced a lack of employment, boredom, and frustration. The longer they remained at Fort Chaffee, the lower their chances of being sponsored. A December 1980 *New York Times* article titled "Fort Chaffee's Unwanted Cubans" detailed the hardships detainees faced in obtaining sponsors, a situation exacerbated by negative media reporting and lack of coordination between government bureaucracies and volunteer agencies.

The experience of detention often hardened detainees and kept them from the doors to freedom. Dave Lewis of the Catholic Conference, in explaining a system of green, yellow, and red lights for profiling Cubans for sponsorship, noted, "There's no telling how many have crossed from green to yellow because of their experiences in here . . . but you know there have been casualties."[37] Immigration guards carrying Mace and clubs had by this time taken control over a "segregation" area at the fort called "Level II," where fence jumpers and troublemakers were kept. The "stockade" was a place of solitary confinement for those who committed more serious crimes, and those who were considered most threatening were sent to prisons in Texas and throughout the South to be detained indefinitely. Criminals were not the only detainees that were further isolated at Fort Chaffee; mental patients who were considered "red" lights were kept in a psychiatric ward that barred journalists from entering. In one example, accusations of negligence surrounded the October 1980 death of a twenty-three-year-old female patient with a history of seizures left alone in a seclusion area.[38] The more "excludable" that Cubans were deemed to be, the more hidden in the vast network of detention centers, mental facilities, and prisons they became.

"Nobody Wants These People": From Panic to Policy

Mariel Cuban detention at Fort Chaffee was so contentious in Arkansas that it became the central issue during the gubernatorial election of 1980. Republican candidate Frank White used Fort Chaffee against incumbent Bill Clinton, saying that Clinton had not "stood up" to the White House and that he had passively accepted the refugees. White promised to empty Fort Chaffee within a year and aired commercials showing rioting Cubans to assist his successful election in November.[39] A White House memorandum in June 1981 concluded, "It is the opinion of the Governor, his political advisors, and those of us who have analyzed the 1980 election that Governor White was elected solely on the basis of this issue."⁴⁰ The *New York Times*, detailing the upcoming rematch of White and Clinton in 1982, also confirmed that Fort Chaffee was a central issue in the previous election by recalling that Clinton was "perceived as having allowed the state to be used as a dumping ground for Cuban refugees."⁴¹

On a national level, Reagan's election linked a rhetoric of national renewal with denunciation of an immigration "crisis" inherited from the Carter administration. On the campaign trail, Reagan promised to "renew" America and to "get tough with Cuba" by threatening a naval blockade.⁴² Once in office, he sought ways to further restrict contact with Castro, a move that prolonged the detention and indefinite status of the Mariel Cubans, as Cuba continued to refuse repatriation. Extensive media focus on the Mariel boatlift, and on Fort Chaffee in particular, made immigration an issue the incoming administration could not ignore.

When Reagan took office 5,200 unsettled Cubans still remained at Fort Chaffee, and on March 6 Reagan formed the President's Task Force on Immigration and Refugee Policy headed by Attorney General William French Smith.⁴³ Reagan highlighted the prominence of the Fort Chaffee dilemma in his diary: "Bill Smith came in with a task force report on immigration. Our 1st problem is what to do with 1000's of Cubans—criminals & the insane that Castro loaded on refugee boats & sent here."⁴⁴ Reagan had quickly adopted the dominant yet simplified view of the Mariel Cuban migration. White House files reveal that the dilemma of how to handle the Cubans at Fort Chaffee remained a pressing issue for the administration in its first year, and both the political fallout from the Mariel migration and the specter of future potential mass migrations played a central role in immigration policy formation in the coming years.

Closing Fort Chaffee was a priority for the Reagan administration, but the political problem remained of where to send the remaining Cubans. Chief of Staff James Baker and Vice President George H. W. Bush both expressed to Governor White their commitment to solving the problem. Baker wrote to White on May 4, 1981, "Your problem at Fort Chaffee is receiving priority attention at the cabinet level. Nobody wants these people. As you pointed out, the Reagan Administration did not admit them." On June 3 Bush wrote, "I have your letter on the undesirables at Fort Chaffee and have been pressing the system for an answer. Your concern is widely shared but by no one as strongly as me. . . . This is a high priority matter in the Administration. As soon as I can report progress on the undesirables, I will be in touch with you."⁴⁵ Both letters express solidarity with White and agree upon the excludable status of the Cubans.

Shortly thereafter Baker wrote to Presidential Counselor Edwin Meese recommending the closure of Fort Chaffee based on political concerns: "White was elected solely on the basis of this issue. His re-election in 1982 is contingent upon a favorable resolution of the situation. . . . The Governor indicates he was under extreme political pressure in Arkansas to close Ft. Chaffee immediately.[46] A White House fact sheet confirms the administration's dilemma, stating that, regarding Fort Chaffee, "political obstacles prevent a solution" and "political commitments prevent its use."[47] On January 4, 1982, the *New York Times* opined that the unsettled Cubans remaining at Fort Chaffee "have become more important as political symbols than as individuals," citing a letter from White to Secretary of Health and Human Services Richard S. Schweiker, stating, "I don't need to tell you how important it is to the Republican Party and to my own political future that these people be moved."[48]

Finding an alternative home for the unsettled Cubans, however, became increasingly difficult. An idea to return them through the U.S. military base at Guantánamo Bay circulated in government and in the media. An internal White House memo noted that using Guantánamo Bay "would avoid the domestic political costs of continuing to hold them within the United States; getting undesirable Cubans out of the U.S. would be viewed as an Administration victory."[49] However, this solution was untenable given relations with Cuba. The White House and the State Department later denied reports that the administration was considering Guantánamo as a means of solving the problem.[50]

As efforts to relocate the detained Cubans within the United States proved equally difficult, the White House expressed an increased sense of emergency in the search for long-term detention solutions. Most states were unwilling to accept or detain the Cuban population. Texas state representative Buck Florence said that he did not want Cubans moving to Texas because "they urinate in public and are prone to masturbation."[51] Governor Harry Hughes of Maryland declared his "most vigorous opposition" to a proposal to build a detention facility in Bainbridge, and the mayor of Port Deposit stated, "There is apprehension here and a few people have become so alarmed as to say, 'Oh, I have to buy a gun.'"[52] Attorney General William French Smith noted that Cuban and Haitian "release into Florida adversely affects the local community; Governor Graham and the Congressional delegation urge dispersal of the illegals to other areas of the country." He also called for the expansion of other facilities to "meet a possible immigration emergency."[53]

Doris Meissner, commissioner of the INS, said the remaining detainees at Fort Chaffee were "mostly single men, with limited education, limited skills, almost no English ability. . . . We believe that most of these people will have to be held for some considerable period."[54] On August 9, 1981, the *New York Times* reported that there were "720 refugees left at Fort Chaffee, Ark., most of them classified as 'antisocial,' and, according to Federal officials, no one wants them."[55] As negative publicity continued, viable options for the transfer of Mariel Cubans grew slimmer for the administration.

The need to pass off the political hot potato of Cuban detention ultimately led the administration to arrive at the most expedient solution available. As a White House proposal outlined, "Termination of Ft. Chaffee operations is the major priority at this time. . . . If greater speed is required . . . [an] alternative would be faster and millions of dollars less expensive. . . . Our proposal will permit Ft. Chaffee to be closed sooner and can be implemented at less cost."[56] The proposal recommended that Cubans from Fort Chaffee be transferred to various Bureau of Prisons facilities instead of a permanent facility to be built in Glasgow, Montana. This recommendation became a reality. As Fort Chaffee closed and the last Cuban detainees disappeared into the prison system in February 1982, Justice Department officials legitimized the decision, claiming, "It's cheaper to keep them there" and that it was an "interim solution."[57] It was also the least visible, and therefore least politically costly, solution.

The unrelenting need for an expedient solution for the placement of Mariel Cubans and anticipated future migrant flows continued to influence decisions on the administration's handling of immigrants and refugees. In April 1981 Kenneth Starr, counselor to the attorney general, declared the new administration's commitment to preventing another Mariel crisis: "It is absolutely clear that this administration would not tolerate a massive influx of the type we witnessed in 1980."[58] This sentiment was reflected in two proposals by the Task Force on Immigration on detention policy that summer. Under the heading "Contingency Planning," the Task Force recommended the following: "Identify suitable facilities to hold 10,000 to 20,000 people; plan for activation of the facilities on short notice, but maintain the facilities on an inactive basis prior to an emergency." And under the heading "Enforcement Options," it suggested, "Detain undocumented aliens upon arrival pending exclusion or granting of asylum. This requires facilities with a capacity of 5,000–10,000 assuming more rapid exclusion hearings and high apprehensions."[59] These policy recommendations mark important new strategies utilized by the Reagan administration to assure the exclusion of unwanted immigrants: the use of the specter of another "Mariel" to legitimize more permanent detention facilities, the use of detention as a deterrent to illegal immigration, and the detention of asylum seekers upon arrival. In July Attorney General Smith addressed the House, claiming, "The problem has been out of control for years. . . . Detention of aliens seeking asylum was necessary to discourage people like the Haitians from setting sail in the first place."[60]

In an interview on December 3, 1981, Reagan was asked about the current refugee problem. He replied, "In 1980—the administration then was caught by the great exodus from Cuba. . . . No planning had been made for that. We're also looking at available sites and facilities for a detention center for those who are apprehended and are illegal aliens, who will probably be returned." Here Reagan alluded to plans for larger illegal immigration enforcement structures for detention and deportation. He also admitted problems with "finding [a site] that the inhabitants of the State would be willing—you'd be surprised how difficult it is to find some State that wants it."[61] These statements reveal an important transformation that occurred within the administration; the refugee "resettlement camp" had now become inseparable from the "detention center" for the "illegal alien." They also highlight the continued need to render such unwanted bodies invisible within the nation.

The Reagan administration's handling of Fort Chaffee left its legacy: the continued criminalization of Mariel Cubans and the buildup of a more permanent immigration detention system that included the unprecedented use of private contract facilities beginning in 1983. In March 1982 the Office of the Attorney General described the foreseen need for detention: "A very real possibility exists for other major movements of illegal entrants from Central America and the Caribbean into the United States during the next several years. A new permanent detention facility would allow the Department to enforce its illegal alien detention policy more equitably nation-wide."[62] Not only more equitably, but more palatably, as prison building served the dual function of bringing jobs to low-income communities and keeping unwanted immigrants out of sight. The journalist Mark Dow credits the Reagan administration for the establishment of what began as a "contingency plan," based on the "detention of hundreds of thousands of undocumented aliens in the case of an unspecified national emergency," but is now common practice. In 2011 the U.S. government held around thirty-four thousand undocumented persons at any given time in a network of nearly four hundred local, federal, and private facilities. Immigration and Customs Enforcement's target for 2012 was to detain and expel 400,000 people.[63] The perceived threat of immigrant bodies remained pervasive and continued to buttress a highly racialized and lucrative private prison and detention industry.

Conclusion

> Are we gonna keep people forever? That's the issue. Do you warehouse people, or do you provide some kinds of services so that we can release them into our country?
> —Barbara Lawson, director of Fort Chaffee, "RE Montana Transfer," interview with reporter, August 1981, cassette tape, Fort Chaffee Collection, Cuban Heritage Collection, University of Miami

Paul Heath Hoeffel presciently commented in the *New York Times* in December 1980 that "the plight of the Cubans at Fort Chaffee may be the beginning rather than the end of a problem of national and international proportions."[64] Shortly after all of the Mariel Cubans had been moved from Fort Chaffee in February 1982 and while the problem of their detention still remained, Reagan wrote in his diary, "What to do with 3000 jailed Cubans. Castro infiltrated with the Mariel refugees. These have criminal records and history of mental problems. They are truly violent and were evidently released from prison and hospitals in Cuba just to be dumped on us. A judge threatens to release them from our jails and turn them loose on society. The problem—as yet unsolved is how to return them."[65]

The status of Mariel Cubans was finally resolved in 2005, when the U.S. Supreme Court ruled unconstitutional the indefinite detention of Cubans who arrived in the boatlift. For twenty-five years the United States had reserved the right to keep Mariel Cubans imprisoned, even after they had served their sentences for crimes. This ruling freed around 750 Cubans still being detained, and as Mark Dow concludes, "Detainees who came here during the 1980 Mariel boatlift are probably the most lasting victims of U.S. immigration detention."[66]

Cubans were not the only immigrant group to be detained en masse during this time, nor was the practice of immigration detention a new phenomenon.[67] However, the size and scope of the U.S. immigration detention system grew exponentially after the "crisis" of the early 1980s. As this essay shows, Mariel Cubans became a key symbol of the specter of future immigration emergencies for the United States, and narratives surrounding the urgent need to contain and eradicate the threat of foreign bodies became the necessary counterpart of a reinforced vision of who was to be included in the nation. The policies outlined by the Reagan administration marked a new departure in U.S. immigration policy that remains firmly in place today.

While the U.S. government created private detention centers and controlled the flow of who went in and out, wider-reaching currents of anti-immigrant sentiment, fostered by the resurgent nationalism of what Sean Wilentz calls the "Age of Reagan," preceded the migrants before they entered and followed them after they left. Since Mariel, the detention system has grown rapidly and now partners with a multibillion-dollar private prison industry. The "detention center," though a center of private profit, transcends the categories of nation and place, as circulating narratives of the threat posed by foreigners and the need for physical containment of bodies reinforce the legitimacy of detention policies within a feedback loop that simultaneously buttresses the bio-politics of who belongs in and out of the nation.

Notes

1. The four military bases were Eglin Air Force Base in Florida, Fort Chaffee in Arkansas, Fort Indiantown Gap in Pennsylvania, and Fort McCoy in Wisconsin. See Larzelere, *The 1980 Cuban Boatlift* for boatlift statistics.

2. Hamm, *The Abandoned Ones*, 55; Llanes, *Cuban Americans*, 178.

3. "Cubans Refugees Riot at Fort Chaffee," *Washington Post*, June 2, 1980; "The Refugees: Rebels with a Cause," *Newsweek*, June 16, 1980, 28–29.

4. Clinton, *My Life*, 275–77.

5. Karen De Witt, "New Cuban Influx at Fort Chaffee Arouses Hostility," *New York Times*, Aug. 11, 1980.

6. "Freedom Flotilla: A Brave Skipper, a Grateful Family and Angry Florida Critics," *People*, May 26, 1980, 29. The sociologists Brian Hufker and Gray Cavender, in a study on negative portrayals of the Mariel Cubans in national newspapers, concluded that actual criminals, homosexuals, and mental patients "constituted less than 5% of the immigrants." However, "the attention focused on that small group eventually stigmatized the entire population" ("From Freedom Flotilla to America's Burden," 322).

7. Rivera, *Decision and Structure*, 10.

8. "Gene Eidenberg unrehearsed conversation Sept 3 81," Folder 1, "Barbara Lawson: Cuban-Haitian Task Force Documents, 1980–1981," Box 1, Fort Chaffee Collection, Cuban Heritage Collection, University of Miami, Miami, FL.

9. Llanes, *Cuban Americans*, 179–81.

10. Engstrom, *Presidential Decision Making Adrift*, 28.

11. Engstrom, *Presidential Decision Making Adrift*, 63.

12. Gonzalez-Pando, *The Cuban Americans*, 66 (quote); García, *Havana USA*, 68. While the term *undesirables* quickly increased in usage throughout media and government sources, it appeared earliest in a White House policy memorandum dated May 13, 1980. See Engstrom, *Presidential Decision Making Adrift*, 105–6.

13. García, *Havana USA*, 69–74.

14. Steven R. Weisman, "President Says U.S. Offers 'Open Arms' to Cuban Refugees," *New York Times*, May 6, 1980.

15. U.S. Department of State, *Cuban Refugees*, 71.

16. Cuba did not cooperate with U.S. efforts to obtain immigrant prison records, which caused further screening burdens and delays for the U.S. government. The situation was further complicated by the fact that many were jailed in Cuba for crimes that the United States would not have considered worthy of incarceration, such as participation in the black market, homosexuality, and dissenting from the communist government. For more on Castro's purported purposeful infiltration of the boatlift and the Cuban government's and media's role in mobilizing a narrative of Mariel deviance, see Fernández, *The Mariel Exodus*, 23–41.

17. To complicate matters, the Carter administration established a Cuban-Haitian Task Force to deal with the unprecedented number of both Cuban and Haitian arrivals by sea in the summer of 1980, which remained in place into Reagan's first term. Policy discussions regarding this "immigration emergency" in the Reagan administration often lumped Cubans and Haitians together, despite their different classifications in the U.S. legal system and the varying stances on Cuba's communist and Haiti's oppressive governments. However, their shared experience of detention and their being considered together in policy discussions may have further contributed to the stigmatization of Mariel Cubans.

18. García, *Havana USA*, 69–73; Llanes, *Cuban Americans*, 164–65.

19. Zaretsky, *No Direction Home*, 144–45.

20. Larzelere, *The 1980 Cuban Boatlift*, 379, 434.

21. Siro del Castillo, "One Day More or One Day Less," Folder 1, "Barbara Lawson: Cuban-Haitian Task Force Documents, 1980–1981," Box 1, Fort Chaffee Collection, Cuban Heritage Collection, University of Miami, Miami, FL.

22. William K. Stevens, "Arkansas Fort Receives First of Thousands of Cubans," *New York Times*, May 10, 1980.

23. Gregory Jaynes, "Fort Smith Has a Bad Morning After," *New York Times*, Feb. 12, 1982; Hufker and Cavender, "From Freedom Flotilla to America's Burden," 332.

24. William K. Stevens, "Pickets Add to Problems for Refugees in Arkansas," *New York Times*, May 11, 1980.

25. Nathaniel Sheppard Jr., "Economic Standings Reflect Attitudes on Cuban Refugees," *New York Times*, June 30, 1980. That immigrants pose a threat

of job competition with citizens has been a long-standing argument against immigration in the United States; however, this prospect of job creation that immigration detention provides foreshadows the dynamics underlying the creation of the highly racialized privatized prison industrial complex. See Alexander, *The New Jim Crow.*

26. Letter, unsigned, to Ronald Reagan, Mar. 28, 1981, folder "General Correspondence," box 9, Francis S. M. (Frank) Hodsoll Files, Ronald Reagan Library, Simi Valley, California.

27. Homosexuality was a potential ground for exclusion from the United States during this time, justified under the 1965 amendment to the 1952 Immigration and Nationality Act, which added the phrase *sexual deviation* as a medical ground for exclusion. The Immigration Act of 1990 withdrew this phrase.

28. Memo, Henry J. Oliver to Mr. Steve Lease, Feb. 16, 1981, folder "Detention Center and Chaffee Working Files (2)," box 8, Francis S. M. (Frank) Hodsoll Files, Ronald Reagan Library.

29. Letter, Frank White to Rich Williamson, Apr. 20, 1981; Peter Arnett, "Cubans Caught in 'Beauty, Tragedy' of System," *Arkansas Democrat,* Apr. 19, 1981, folder "General Correspondence," box 9, Francis S. M. (Frank) Hodsoll Files, Ronald Reagan Library.

30. Fernández, *The Mariel Exodus,* 42–43.

31. Paul Heath Hoeffel, "Fort Chaffee's Unwanted Cubans," *New York Times,* Dec. 21, 1980.

32. Hoeffel, "Fort Chaffee's Unwanted Cubans."

33. García, *Havana USA,* 71.

34. *La Vida Nueva* (Fort Chaffee), no. 152 (Dec. 13, 1980), CHC Exile Journals, Cuban Heritage Collection, University of Miami. Translated from Spanish by author. (Hereafter CHC Exile Journals).

35. *La Vida Nueva,* no. 142 (Nov. 27, 1980), CHC Exile Journals.

36. *La Vida Nueva,* no. 143 (Nov. 29, 1980), CHC Exile Journals.

37. Hoefel, "Fort Chaffee's Unwanted Cubans."

38. Hoefel, "Fort Chaffee's Unwanted Cubans."

39. "Politics Key to the Fate of Camp's Last Cubans," *New York Times,* Jan. 4, 1982.

40. Memo, Lyn Nofziger and Richard Williamson to James Baker and Edwin Meese, June 11, 1981, folder "Detention Center and Chaffee Working Files (2)," box 8, Francis S. M. (Frank) Hodsoll Files, Ronald Reagan Library.

41. Wendell Rawls Jr., "Arkansas Gubernatorial Candidates in Close Race," *New York Times,* Oct. 28, 1982.

42. Torres, *In the Land of Mirrors,* 105, 117; Reagan, "First Inaugural Address," 335.

43. Robert Pear, "Plan Aims to Free Refugees in Jails for Crimes in Cuba; Most Have Confessed Crimes Refugees Await Sponsors," *New York Times,* Jan. 30, 1981.

44. Reagan, "May 18, 1981," *The Reagan Diaries*, 20.

45. Letter, George Bush to Frank White, June 3, 1981, folder "Detention Center and Chaffee Working Files (2)," box 8, Francis S. M. (Frank) Hodsoll Files, Ronald Reagan Library.

46. Memo, Lyn Nofziger and Richard Williamson to James Baker and Edwin Meese, June 11, 1981, folder "Detention Center and Chaffee Working Files (2)," box 8, Francis S. M. (Frank) Hodsoll Files, Ronald Reagan Library.

47. "INS Detention Policy," undated, folder "Detention Center and Chaffee Working Files (6)," box 8, Francis S. M. (Frank) Hodsoll Files, Ronald Reagan Library.

48. "Politics Key to the Fate of Camp's Last Cubans," *New York Times*, Jan. 4, 1982.

49. "Using Guantanamo to Hold the Undesirables who Arrived in the Mariel Boatlift," undated, folder "Detention Center and Chaffee Working Files (5)," box 8, Francis S. M. (Frank) Hodsoll Files, Ronald Reagan Library.

50. "U.S. Officials Call Cuba Deal Story 'Absolutely False,'" *Washington Post*, July 5, 1981.

51. Charles R. Babcock, "Resettling of Cuban Refugees Is Proceeding at a Slow Pace: Criminal Records, Homosexuality, Mental Illness Are Factors," *Washington Post*, Feb. 10, 1981.

52. Jura Koncius, "Bainbridge Is Leading Refugee Site Choice," *Washington Post*, July 13, 1981.

53. "Cabinet Administration Staffing Memorandum," from William French Smith, July 6, 1981, folder "Detention Center and Chaffee Working Files (2)," box 8, Francis S. M. (Frank) Hodsoll Files, Ronald Reagan Library.

54. Dale Russakoff, "Bainbridge Is Unlikely Refugee Site," *Washington Post*, July 14, 1981.

55. Robert Lindsey, "U.S. Is Finding That No One Wants to Accept Last Cuban Refugees," *New York Times*, Aug. 9, 1981.

56. "Termination of Ft. Chaffee Operations," undated, folder "Immigration Policy: Cubans and Haitians," box 10, James Cicconi Files, Ronald Reagan Library.

57. "Cubans in Arkansas Will Be Transferred to 2 Federal Prisons," *New York Times*, Jan. 23, 1982.

58. Edward Walsh, "Next Cuban Exodus May Not Get as Warm a Welcome as '80 Boatlift," *Washington Post*, Apr. 28, 1981.

59. Memo, William French Smith to Ronald Reagan, June 26, 1981, folder "Report of the President's Task Force on Immigration and Refugee Policy," box 15, Francis S. M. (Frank) Hodsoll Files, Ronald Reagan Library.

60. Charles R. Babcock, "Immigration Plan Includes Amnesty, Tighter Controls," *Washington Post*, July 31, 1981; Dunn, *The Militarization of the U.S.-Mexico Border*, 46.

61. "Remarks in an Interview with Managing Editors on Domestic Issues December 3, 1981," *The Public Papers of President Ronald W. Reagan*, Ronald Rea-

gan Presidential Library, accessed Nov. 4, 2013, http://www.reagan.utexas .edu/archives/speeches/1981/120381e.htm.

62. "Federal Prison and Alien Detention Policy" from Edward C. Schmults to James A. Baker III, Edwin L. Harper, Annelise Anderson, and James W. Cicconi, Mar. 10, 1982, folder "Immigration Policy: Cubans and Haitians," box 10, James Cicconi Files, Ronald Reagan Library.

63. Dow, *American Gulag*, 8–9. In effect, ICE removed 409,849 people in FY2012. Immigration and Customs Enforcement, "Removal Statistics," http:// www.ice.gov/removal-statistics/.

64. Hoeffel, "Fort Chaffee's Unwanted Cubans."

65. Reagan, "February 26, 1982," *The Reagan Diaries*, 71.

66. Dow, *American Gulag*, 16, 297; Mirta Ojito, "The Long Voyage from Mariel Ends," *New York Times*, Jan. 16, 2005.

67. Haitian boat people, for example, were being systematically detained since the early 1970s. See Rivera, *Decision and Structure*, 13–16; Miller, *The Plight of Haitian Refugees*.

epilogue

When the Body Disappears

EMILY S. ROSENBERG AND SHANON FITZPATRICK

A few weeks after American pilots dropped atomic bombs on Hiroshima and Nagasaki in August 1945, a member of Hollywood's First Motion Picture Unit arrived in Japan. Dispatched with the army's U.S. Strategic Bombing Survey to study the effects of the air war, he assembled an eleven-person film crew employing Technicolor and Kodachrome film and began to document the aftermath of the bombing. He also discovered that Japanese camera crews, deployed immediately after the bombs fell, had already filmed twenty-six thousand feet of color footage, a cache that U.S. authorities confiscated and over which he assumed control. After returning to the United States with ninety thousand feet of both sets of color film, he used the footage to make several short documentaries intended for military purposes and began discussing a possible project with Warner Brothers. Top military officials, however, raised alarms about the negative impact that the scenes might have on America's atomic bomb building and testing programs. Images of dead and burned bodies and of men, women, and children in shock and in pain—that is, the chilling evidence of the true horror of atomic weaponry—disappeared into a classified container in the United States. Photos of burned-out trolleys surrounded by rows of skulls and bones, of children with burned and distorted faces, of people clustered around water wells clogged with radioactive sand remained unseen. As radiation illness took its toll on human bodies in Japan over the ensuing months and years of U.S. occupation, American authorities continued to confiscate photos of human damage. Even *Chicago Daily News* war correspondent George Weller's powerful verbal descriptions of atomic horror, especially of radiation illness, were hidden away, to be published only in 2005.

Instead the images that American (and world) viewers initially saw of the two bombings showed awesome black-and-white mushroom clouds and the destruction of cities but not their residents. Meanwhile U.S. leaders built up stockpiles of atomic weapons and war-gamed how to make them into useful levers of power. The invisibility in photos of bodies of atomic victims, concludes one researcher, was "part of a broad effort to suppress a wide range of material related to the atomic bombings, including photographs, newspaper reports on radiation effects, information about the decision to drop the bomb." President Harry Truman's increasingly hard-line advisors feared that gruesome pictures might tilt public debate over atomic power in favor of its critics. The images were too troublesome.[1]

This epilogue closes the *Body and Nation* volume by asking about bodies that, deemed dispensable, become obscured from view. Carrying out the major themes explored throughout this volume and focusing on the post–World War II era, we consider the "disappearance" of othered, foreign bodies whose fates, if fully seen and acknowledged, might challenge not only prevailing national security policy but also cherished notions about America's "benevolent supremacy."[2] Being absent from view—being erased—is the most profound kind of bodily marking. Bodies rendered invisible by the security state and within mass media cannot easily command attention. This process of erasure "silences the past" and distorts history and public memory.[3]

The Trouble with History

In law the absence of a body can occlude a full inquiry into a death. So it is with history: burying real and metaphorical bodies out of sight can shield them from public investigation.

Alfred Hitchcock's 1955 film *The Trouble with Harry* likely offered no intentional reference to victims of international violence, but we may still imagine the film as a postwar parable. Harry's shot-dead body is repeatedly dug up and reburied, sometimes dressed up to camouflage its fate, sometimes secreted away. A widening circle of people encounter the body, but they care little about it except as something that must be hidden lest the circumstances of the shooting point to them and interrupt the normality of their lives. The trouble with Harry is less that he was shot than that his dead body is troublesome to good and ordinary people and must be repeatedly concealed.

In an analogous drama we might call "The Trouble with History," bodies also do not always stay buried. Despite classifications and locks, for example, images of those dead and wounded from the atomic blasts returned to media visibility. In 1967 the United States finally agreed to repatriate the footage shot by Japanese film crews, and it was shown in Japan.[4] The journalist Erik Barnouw edited it into a sixteen-minute mini-documentary called *Hiroshima-Nagasaki 1945*, but no U.S. TV network would show it. The Strategic Bombing Survey's footage was declassified in the mid-1970s, and a 1982 documentary, *Dark Circle*, used it to warn about nuclear hazards, including nuclear power and testing at home. The film reached some festivals but received little media coverage. In short, by the time the horrific images that included humans became theoretically visible, they attracted little attention in the United States. The storylines of the bomb's necessity and even its benevolence had by then become firmly entrenched as a historical narrative of patriotism, and such images might have troubled this now normalized storyline.

One very visible image of atomic injury even enhanced the discourse of American benevolence. In 1955 the antinuclear activist Norman Cousins sponsored a trip to the United States by twenty-five young Japanese women students whose faces had been severely disfigured when they looked up at the incoming bomb. The story of how these "Hiroshima Maidens" received restorative surgeries in New York became a media sensation. Cousins had hoped the women would help dramatize atomic afflictions, but the mainstream press instead highlighted their grateful embrace of American life, fashion, and culture. *Time* magazine, which had attained an enormous international circulation, carried "before" and "after" photos labeled "From horror to triumph." Self-congratulatory stories of heroic medical science and deep compassion effaced accounts of bodily disfiguration.[5]

Concealing disturbing bodies seemed perpetually in order. In the mid-1980s the Smithsonian Air and Space Museum designed an exhibit around the *Enola Gay*, the plane that dropped the bomb on Hiroshima. Curators planned to display graphic photos showing the bomb's effects on human bodies. A furor developed over the proposed exhibit as critics charged, among other things to which they objected, that such photos made the Japanese seem like victims in a war they had started. Advising historians responded that an exhibit on the first use of atomic power, the onset of the atomic age, should convey at least some sense of its lethal enormity. Under heavy pressure from veterans' organizations and conservative lobbying groups, however, Congress settled the controversy. Threatening the museum's funding, Congress forced cancelation of the exhibit. (Later the *Enola Gay* went on view in a new museum without interpretive panels.) Years after the atomic bomb, a willful looking away obscured visibility perhaps even more effectively than official secrecy had done. Unearthing the silences of history, after all, might be troublesome.[6]

The lack of visibility of atomic victims—enforced first by classification and then maintained through cultural denial—coincided with the expansion of the U.S. nuclear program. The fallout from the extensive bomb testing in the Pacific and the American West poisoned land and waters, dislocated peoples, and sickened those downwind. The massive production of new atomic and hydrogen bombs left canisters of atomic waste secreted in government facilities and brought cancers and birth defects to thousands of unsuspecting workers and residents. These atomic bomb testing and production processes fed the intricate and voracious systems of missile targeting directed by secretive underground offices of the Strategic Air Command in Omaha. Yet the escalation of nuclear capacities remained an abstraction for most Americans. The real and potential price of such a "defense" strategy had no human face. Even in the "hottest" zones, such as Rocky Flats, Colorado, and Hanford, Washington, there was a culture of secrecy in which few would speak of plutonium's dangers. To be a critic of the nuclear industry or to warn against its potential health effects was to become a cultural outcast, some kind of radical crank. Kristen Iversen, who has written a moving memoir of radiation poisoning, *Full Body Burden*, writes, "We weren't supposed to know about Rocky Flats during the production years, and now we're supposed to forget it ever existed." She expresses what many living near the residue of nuclear sites know: "We don't talk about plutonium. It's bad for business. It reminds us of what we don't want to acknowledge about ourselves."[7]

After the end of the Cold War, the Clinton administration declassified medical records and moved toward greater acknowledgment of the atomic industry's costs to health and environment at home and abroad. But by then many of the afflicted had died, and Cold War triumphalism worked against a full public reckoning. The government turned Rocky Flats into a wildlife refuge because the costs of clean-up to allow for human habitation would have been astronomical. Staring down the human casualties of the nuclear age might trouble the history of Cold War righteousness and technological progress.

The invisibility of atomic bodies became part of a pattern replicated in many other contexts over the course of the Cold War. After World War II, the United States denounced, indeed held war trials for those who abused "human rights." U.S. leaders proclaimed a commitment to being the global champions of individual freedom, using a rhetoric shaped during World War II and refined in the many propaganda campaigns that framed the Cold War as a battle between "freedom" and "slavery." Yet the fight for freedoms preserved through democratic forms of governance paradoxically justified the hiding of those bodies that might bear witness to a more complicated narrative. The victims of America's often blind and capriciously zealous anticommunism raised more trouble with history.

Cold War Bodies

After World War II, anticommunism became increasingly centered on the treatment of bodies. Discourses of human rights accompanied the development of new transnational organizations, new governmental offices, and even new ratings systems to help protect people from brutal regimes. Americans played leadership roles in this new activism promoting human rights. Meanwhile bodies also became the ground zero for a new front in Cold War national security policy: behavioral scientists engaged in clandestine "mind control" experimentation. Scares over communist "brainwashing," fed by an array of popular images during the Korean War, justified secret spending to devise techniques for stressing bodies in ways that might provide access to information and even reprogram minds.[8] Alfred W. McCoy sums up the seen and unseen foreign policies related to human bodies: "Publicly, Washington opposed torture and led the world in drafting the United Nation's Universal Declaration of Human Rights in 1948 and the Geneva Conventions in 1949. Simultaneously and secretly, however, the Central Intelligence Agency began developing ingenious new torture techniques in contravention of these same international conventions."[9]

Like the atomic program, psychological experimentation with new methods of bodily stress developed in an environment of government-enforced secrecy compounded by a willful looking away. McCoy and others have traced how Central Intelligence Agency researchers, especially in the secret MKUltra program, tested drugs as part of mind control programs. They point out, however, that experimentation with other behavioral methods seemed more promising and left no marks or residue. These methods combined techniques of sensory disorientation and self-inflicted pain to assault personal identity while making victims feel responsible for their own pain—and thus more quickly capitulate to stop it. The program of inflicting systematic physical and psychological trauma on bodies involved tortures that sounded like rather simple disciplines: long periods of sensory isolation; maintenance of stress poses that could induce stages of bodily collapse; manipulation of heat and cold, light and dark, noise and silence. Their very banality obscured the horrifying mental and bodily effects. In the hands of improvising torturers ("interrogators"), use of such techniques easily devolved into sadism and became compounded with more traditional brutalities inflicted on body parts, especially sexual organs.[10]

The silences about how such bodily experimentation became the terrain of national security policies have increasingly distorted Americans' popular understandings of their country's international policies. If America's use of torture techniques became public, and even controversial, during the George W. Bush administration's "war on terror" after 9/11, it was not because the practices were especially new, or even especially hidden. For years psychophysiological techniques of manipulation and stress had been a standard part of the formula of covert action, a practice that played an important, if only intermittently visible, role in Cold War battles. From Latin America to the Philippines, Vietnam, and secret prisons throughout the world, sensory deprivation, stress positions, and an escalating array of other techniques for inflicting fear had made "enemy" bodies the terrain of national security policy.

These Cold War covert actions—particularly in Latin America, Asia, and Africa and often directed most brutally against nonwhite populations—often aligned with and empowered regimes that maintained themselves through brutality and torture rather than through processes of democratic consent. Why? First, from the Truman administration on, the United States elevated anticommunism above all other goals and gradually came to support conservative elites who were reliably anticommunist. Even if communist parties in many countries were small, these elites often exaggerated the threat and then expanded the definition of communist to include labor leaders, agrarian reformers, or anyone else who might threaten their political and economic dominance. Second, in the name of fighting communism, U.S. programs of foreign military assistance increased in size during and after the Korean War. As military sectors in weak countries grew more powerful, they often became effective tools of reactionary regimes that sought to suppress democratic challenges to their control. Third, powerful economic interests sometimes lobbied the U.S. government to maintain

"stability," a code word for docile labor and favorable trade and investment environments. Fourth, U.S. politicians embraced anticommunist
rhetoric and policies because hard-line credentials helped them win in
bureaucratic power struggles and in elections at home. Especially after
the Chinese communist revolution of 1949, anyone who could be labeled
"soft" on communism became politically vulnerable; being "tough" on
communism often implied a willingness to look beyond the niceties
of democracy and human rights rhetoric. Moreover demonstrations of
covert action in the early 1950s seemed to prove to policymakers that
operating in shadowy, secret realms, while publicly proclaiming fealty
to democracy and human rights, could be cheap and effective. In a vola-
tile world, operating covertly and through ferociously anticommunist
clients seemed a security asset.

The case of America's decades-long involvement in Guatemala provides a chilling example of "the trouble with history." The fate of perhaps 200,000 Guatemalan victims of state-orchestrated violence who
were buried over several decades of U.S.-supported terror remained
classified for a while and then gradually became visible, but few in the
United States have cared to see.

This story began with the "successful" covert action of 1954 code-
named PBSUCCESS. The Truman administration's new Central Intelligence Agency (created in 1947) had begun to plot against the reformist
democratic government in Guatemala, and the Eisenhower administration finally gave the official go-ahead for a secret action. The Guatemalan government of Jacobo Arbenz had enacted new labor laws, new
rights for union organizers, and an agrarian reform bill—all measures
that antagonized both the landed elite of the country and the dominant
U.S. investor, United Fruit Company. In the hypercharged anticommunist atmosphere of Washington, policymakers determined that any
move to the left in Guatemala had to be stopped. Executing a carefully
planned secret campaign, CIA operatives orchestrated false and over-
blown charges about communist influence in the government and plotted with local military leaders to secure the government's overthrow.
When the military takeover occurred, President Eisenhower proclaimed
publicly that Guatemalans had beaten back communism and preserved
democracy, but the American public remained ignorant that their government had just overthrown democracy in favor of a military dictatorship. In the aftermath of the coup, as the CIA basked in its success and
planned covert actions elsewhere, U.S.-allied elites consolidated power
and rained terror on reformers and especially on the indigenous, mostly
Mayan communities that made up half of Guatemala. They repealed la-

bor and land laws and attacked unions as communistic. Agricultural workers slipped into a state of near slavery. Resistance justified ever greater repression.

For well over three decades after 1954, a small privileged class continued to run Guatemala in the name of anticommunism by relying on repressive techniques that were known to, financed by, and often taught in conjunction with U.S. officials.[11] A 1963 U.S. manual used to train anticommunist squads in Guatemala and elsewhere in counterinsurgency tactics, declassified in 1997, provides a window onto how the psychological techniques developed in CIA-funded experiments intersected with the newly successful strategies of covert action. The authors of this manual write, "American psychologists have . . . conducted scientific inquiries into many subjects that are closely related to interrogation: the effects of debility and isolation, the polygraph, reactions to pain and fear, hypnosis and heightened suggestibility, narcosis, etc. . . . For this reason a major purpose of this study is to focus relevant scientific findings upon CIA interrogation."

The manual then presents interrogation techniques "in an order of increasing intensity as the focus on source resistance grows sharper," and it ends with a "check-list" of do's and don'ts. In many ways, compared to the practices allowed by the George W. Bush administration forty years later, the manual cautions restraint; it explains why, for example, psychological studies suggested that the use of pain, fear, and threats of death might often be counterproductive, especially if prolonged. It did, however, provide extensive guidance drawn from other techniques that had been the focus of postwar behaviorist experimentation: isolation, hypnosis, drugs, and use of electric shocks appeared as useful tools of interrogation.[12]

Thus while covert action included economic destabilization, propaganda campaigns with invented claims, and money spread to reliably anticommunist militaries, the accompanying "science" of interrogation involved psychological and corporeal stress techniques that had been under development since the Korean War. Although known to America's diplomats there, some of whom detailed the outrages in confidential memos from Tegucigalpa and vainly tried to convince the State Department that such extreme abuses were counterproductive as well as immoral, the American public had little awareness of the escalation of bodily terrors committed in the name of "freedom" and their national security.[13] By the 1980s, as the Reagan administration renewed support for conservative elites in Guatemala and the rest of Central America, these techniques—as well as many old-fashioned kinds of physical brutality—escalated into an even broader array of tortures and mass killings visited upon opponents. Following the general pattern we have observed, however, even when the documentation of appalling abuse became widely public during the 1990s, most Americans turned away. The dirty history of U.S. involvement in Guatemala, although revealed in a growing number of easily available documents and scholarly books, has hardly entered the Cold War narrative held by most of the American public—a narrative that has continued to frame a story of America's four-decade-long Cold War fight for democracy and human dignity.[14]

Guatemala's thirty-five-year-long experience with harsh interrogations, terrorist tactics, and death squads was not an aberration in the bipolar Cold War world. From the early 1950s into the 1980s dictatorships in the Third World spread as proxies for one side or the other. Odd Arne Westad has detailed the ways in which Cold War rivalries ravaged the states emerging from formal or informal colonization by refracting their domestic rivalries into global geopolitics that ultimately offered new forms of dependency. As rival domestic groups appealed for support from superpowers, the superpowers reciprocated, strengthening and arming their localized supporters around the world.[15] This dynamic stoked civil wars and brutal dictatorships aligned with each side, and covert action became a weapon of choice. In his short few years as president, John F. Kennedy expanded greatly on Eisenhower's "success" in Guatemala and authorized 163 major actions.[16]

In Asia, Vietnam became a manifestation of this dynamic. There, in fighting a potential communist dictatorship, the United States sponsored a dictatorship of its own, developed kill ratios that justified massive human casualties, poisoned the land and people with Agent Orange, and developed forms of psychological terrors (in the Phoenix Program). The U.S. counterinsurgency manuals adapted for use in Vietnam and in various other places during the 1960s called for plunging prisoners into a strange and traumatic world in which all that was familiar, including self-image, disappeared. Such techniques targeted less the life in the body than the body's very humanity and singularity. U.S. involvement in Southeast Asia also took a severe, ongoing toll on the bodies of the Americans conscripted to fight there. Although images of some of the war's violence, especially the killings at My Lai, entered American living rooms through television and photojournalism, it took decades for the scope of Vietnam-era atrocities to become part of the public record, and even then, such knowledge hardly penetrated public memory.[17]

To prevent "other Vietnams," policymakers of the 1960s and early 1970s supported increasingly brutal anticommunist dictatorships such as those in the Philippines, South Korea, Indonesia, and Iran. In these countries, as well as throughout Latin America, U.S. military training programs taught an expanding array of bodily inflictions and supported regimes that developed death squads, which eliminated opponents by the application of torture and, sometimes, by simply "disappearing" bodies. In the late Vietnam War era (the early 1970s) nearly every country in Latin America, even the large ones with democratic traditions such as Brazil, Argentina, Uruguay, and Chile, were headed by U.S.-allied anticommunist dictatorships propped up by murderous, often sadistic death squads. Hundreds of opponents were disappeared—often dropped alive into the ocean. Women's bodies became special targets of anticommunist generals for whom counterinsurgency justified rape, electric shock and mutilation of sexual organs, and stealing of babies from disappeared women.[18]

Throughout these years the United States trumpeted concern for the human rights of those living under communist regimes but turned a blind eye to its own covert actions, counterinsurgency practices, and anticommunist allies. Although the Carter administration mounted a brief attempt to steer U.S. policy behind its rhetoric on human rights, the renewal of Cold War tactics under Reagan again cemented support for some anticommunist death squads. In the 1980s, while the major South American countries began to shed their military regimes and return to democratic practices in the 1980s, the Sandinista victory in Nicaragua spurred another round of anticommunism among U.S. policymakers. Throughout Central America the Reagan administration doubled down on support for anticommunist elites, and new levels of violence flared, along with new inflictions of bodily pain. During the 1980s, as before, architects of U.S. policy frequently assured themselves that some Latin American, Asian, and African countries neither preferred nor were mature enough to be governed by democratic elections. And besides, they convinced themselves, U.S. national security demanded a stalwart and unblinking embrace of whatever groups stood against "radicals." In the Middle East during the 1980s the U.S. policy to build the capacity of Islamic militants who opposed the Soviet Union in Afghanistan and elsewhere would, within a few years, prove tragic once these same groups turned their terrorism on Americans. Harsh tactics and questionable allies became elements in the renewed anticommunism that characterized the Reagan presidency.[19]

The bodies from all of these decades of Cold War brutalities did not stay out of sight. In the aftermath of communism's fall, people in some countries demanded a reckoning. New regimes reburied those who had been dumped in mass graves and tried to document identities of the disappeared. Torture victims came forward with their stories, and some played new roles in their country's political life. A few countries launched truth commissions. Guatemala's 1999 Commission for Historical Clarification, for example, put out a multivolume study that graphically described the special cruelties that had been visited on bodies in the name of national security:

> Acts such as the killing of defenceless children, often by beating them against walls or throwing them alive into pits where the corpses of adults were later thrown; the amputation of limbs; the impaling of victims; the killing of persons by covering them in petrol and burning them alive; the extraction, in the presence of others, of the viscera of victims who were still alive; the confinement of people who had been mortally tortured, in agony for days; the opening of the wombs of pregnant women, and other similarly atrocious acts, were not only actions of extreme cruelty against the victims, but also morally degraded the perpetrators and those who inspired, ordered or tolerated these actions.[20]

Reports and recollections confirm that the death of enemies seldom seemed enough. In the anticommunist "dirty wars" of this era, physical and psychological degradation through torture became a biopolitical tactic to discipline populations. Indeed it helped create a new aesthetic of war.

The accounts from the many countries that suffered under America's dictator-allies confirm how anticommunism justified what Eileen Scarry called "the body in pain." In her seminal book by that title, Scarry writes that torture, like war, blends the "real and the fictional." "The incontestable reality of the body—the body in pain, the body maimed, the body dead and hard to dispose of—is separated from its source and conferred on an ideology or issue or instance of political authority." Enemy bodies become not persons but representations of the nonnation.[21]

Scarry also interrogates the silences that surround bodies in pain. She writes that torture proves so incommensurate with the moral intuitions of most people's daily lives that it either recedes into silence because of its incomprehensibility or the voice of pain silences all else by making interpretation seem inappropriate. Her book helps explain why U.S. complicity in the Cold War regimes of "bodies in pain," although increasingly a matter of public record, scarcely penetrated the American media or the public's consciousness. Much evidence gradually became available for all to see; journalists and historians in the United

States and in the affected countries piled up documentation from country after country both at the time and, even more, in the years after the Cold War ended.[22] Bill Clinton traveled to Guatemala and stated that U.S. "support for military forces or intelligence units which engage in violent and widespread repression of the kind described in the [Truth Commission] report was wrong, and the United States must not repeat that mistake."[23] But the documentation of U.S. complicity in abuses and even the quasi-apology from a sitting American president got little news coverage in the United States. Silences engulfed the unspeakable acts against human bodies.[24]

For most Americans, the visibility of their Cold War killing fields, unlike those sponsored by fascist and communist regimes, remained limited even after the Cold War's end. Researchers report that people remember things that fit their preexisting frames, and the frame of America as the sponsor of democratic freedom had become so strong that many Americans apparently looked away from bodies of evidence and evidence of bodies. Public airing, after all, would trouble the history of U.S. benevolence during the Cold War; it might disturb good and ordinary people.

Torture, Rendition, Drones, and Asymmetric Visibility after 9/11

Scarry's book about the silences of "the body in pain" proved perceptive in the mid-1980s, when it was written. She could at that time write that "torture is such an extreme event . . . that there is a reluctance to place it in conversation by the side of other subjects."[25] But times were changing. Images of violence inflicted on bodies increasingly worked their way into most media genres: TV, movies, video games. And after the dramatic attacks of 9/11, an insistent public defense of the need for engaging in extreme bodily abuse of enemies emerged in politics as well. Mark Danner, a *New York Times* reporter who had written a stunning exposé of a massacre in Guatemala, has contrasted the harsh techniques of the Cold War period with those of the post-9/11 environment. The United States had embraced brutal regimes during the Cold War, he notes, but policymakers at least tried to hide or excuse that action. Atrocities mostly hid within the silences that Scarry had theorized. As Danner writes, however, "what is indisputably distinct about what has happened . . . [after 9/11] is that there is available a full official record produced by the very government in which decisions were made, policies were disputed, legal opinions were rendered. What is different, in other words, is that much of that official record of the very government that made torture the official policy of the United States of America is publicly available to us almost in, as it were, real time."[26]

Torturous, body-centric national security policies developed within the post-9/11 environment in two ways: through "rendition," the practice of spiriting away suspected persons to unknown black sites in foreign countries, and through "harsh interrogations" conducted in U.S.-run prisons abroad. The first often outsourced torture, putting suspects in the hands of allies in Egypt, Syria, Jordan, Morocco, Libya, Uzbekistan, and Eastern Europe. Carefully camouflaged U.S. advisors were also often reported present at the "interrogation" sessions.[27] The second accepted what once had been called torture as an acceptable method of dealing with anyone who might fall under suspicion of being complicit in "terrorism."

The record of how, after 9/11, the United States moved away from accepting and championing the standards of humane treatment under the Geneva Convention (which bans "torture" and "cruel, inhuman, and degrading treatment") is well documented. Invoking what became called the "torture memos" written by Deputy Assistant Attorney General John Yoo and White House Counsel Alberto Gonzales, the Bush administration, in effect, rendered the Geneva Convention "principles" that could be waived. Yoo and Gonzales argued that the Geneva Convention applied to states but that Al Qaeda was not a state and that members of the Taliban in Afghanistan were bodies from a "failed state."[28] Although other officials in the Justice Department dissented from this reasoning, an order signed by President Bush on February 7, 2002, outlining treatment of Al Qaeda and Taliban detainees, proclaimed U.S. humane values and adherence to Geneva Convention "principles" while nevertheless opening a huge (and potentially self-fulfilling) exception that allowed their violation: "Of course, our values as a nation, values that we share with many nations in the world, call for us to treat detainees humanely, including those who are not legally entitled to such treatment. Our nation has been and will continue to be a strong supporter of Geneva and its principles. As a matter of policy, the United States Armed Forces shall continue to treat detainees humanely and, *to the extent appropriate and consistent with military necessity,* in a manner consistent with the principles of Geneva" (emphasis added).[29]

In 2004 photos of U.S. military personnel administering extreme psychological and bodily abuse of prisoners at Abu Ghraib in Iraq caused a furor when they appeared in newspapers and on TV. After the International Committee of the Red Cross managed to interview detainees to assess compliance with Geneva principles in 2006, its report unequivocally concluded that U.S. treatment of detainees "constituted torture" and "constituted cruel, inhuman or degrading treatment."[30] Although President Bush continued to maintain that "we are a nation of laws" and many of his supporters attacked the Red Cross as a meddlesome organization, the documentary record of specious legal decisions, of euphemisms, and of cover-ups has continued to unfold. More and more evidence has revealed the broad network of secret prisons around the world and graphically described what went on in them— and at the legally liminal U.S. base in Guantánamo Bay, Cuba. Even as the Abu Ghraib photos were provoking outrage at U.S. techniques, it appears that officials sent a veteran of the counterinsurgency (death squad) campaigns in Central America in the 1980s to organize similar squads in Iraq.[31]

But visible practices are not always seen. Again the compulsion to look away can seem an even more powerful obscurant than secrecy. No high-level officials were brought to justice for disregarding international law on the treatment of prisoners. After President Obama's election in 2008, Senator Patrick Leahy, chair of the Judiciary Committee, called for some kind of truth commission to investigate how U.S. detention practices had come to violate America's rule of law, and Obama issued an executive order to stop the use of techniques that fell under the accepted international definitions of torture. But Obama also asked Americans, including those in his party and administration, to move on, to look forward and not backward. In other words, the president asked citizens to turn their gaze away from America's very public record of condoning and facilitating "the body in pain" in the years after 9/11.[32]

In post-9/11 America torturing bodies appeared acceptable not only in the administration of President Bush but in media as well. Immediately after the 9/11 attack the Bush administration sent emissaries to Hollywood to rally support for its policies. Media moguls, already profiting from violence-infused thrillers, needed little convincing, and many eagerly enhanced storylines about imminent danger and plots based on the need for extreme measures. Within less than two months emerged the quintessential post-9/11 TV show: 24. This widely watched and internationally syndicated show built each episode around the premise that torture would be required to stop attacks on the nation and its leaders. With the structure of the plot, the ticking-time-bomb sounds, and the split-screen techniques, the show appealed on a visceral and emotional level for viewers to accept, even cheer torture techniques that, within the "reality" of the show, were positioned as effective and even heroic.

Although its brutal images sparked some controversy, the show became a sensation and lasted for 192 episodes and eight seasons. In the post-9/11 environment, stimulated by the heightened sense of vulnerability, images of bodies in pain apparently brought solace rather than the silence upon which Scarry had commented. Graphic brutality recruited a large audience of people who apparently enjoyed watching Jack Bauer (Kiefer Sutherland) torture those deemed to be threats. The ability to inflict pain on foreign bodies seemed to ease fear in an age of anxiety; the world of Jack Bauer and Dick Cheney seemed to soothe some viewers by offering illusions of empowerment and control.[33]

The show 24 was only the most obvious example of a media culture (and business model) that elevated ever-higher levels of violence and bodily harm to the status of the commonplace. Image-laden media provides viewers with what François Debrix and Alexander Barder have called "biopolitical frames of respectability," in which the body is placed as the visual center of operations of power, but some body images are framed as life-giving (for example, wounded U.S. soldiers), while others either remain off-frame or are framed as enemies whose very humanity is questionable and disposable.[34] Torturing bodies became a thing so implied or visible in mass culture that the reality of afflicted persons disappeared almost completely into abstracted representations of threat. As in the political realm after 9/11, so in entertainment: "harsh interrogation" techniques, which the U.S. government had earlier defined as torture and some of which had even (as seen in the Guatemalan training manual) been declared operationally unwise, became widely portrayed as an acceptable and ordinary method of conducting national security policy. The acclaimed film Zero Dark Thirty (2012) showed graphic scenes, which erroneously implied, critics charged, that torture had provided significant information that led to the U.S. raid against Osama bin Laden, the architect of the 9/11 attacks.[35]

When torture comes to seem like normal and productive behavior, it hides in plain sight. It provokes little news, little controversy, little notice. Even after President Obama's Justice Department repudiated use of the "harsh interrogation" techniques that fell under the definition of torture, no prosecutions of torturers were pursued; no major officials were held responsible; no reckoning with the past ensued. Troublesome history was kept aloof from the lives of good and ordinary people, many of whom enjoyed and perhaps absorbed lessons from the "realities" of television, video games, and film.

If post-9/11 torture practices hid within representational formulas that accepted and normalized them, new security technologies could make images of troublesome bodies less visible than ever. The rapidly expanding technology of drones, which is one aspect of a more general revolution that robotics is bringing to warfare, exemplifies a newly important dynamic related to visibility and bodies.

Drones have become big business since 9/11. In 2000 the Department of Defense had ninety drones and planned to double that number in a decade. The wars in Iraq and Afghanistan, however, became testing grounds for unmanned systems, and the global "war on terrorism" brought surveillance and targeting to every continent even as it swelled the U.S. military budgets needed to develop new technologies. By 2012 the United States had deployed more than 9,500 remotely piloted aircraft, and improvements in drone technologies were driving development of ever greater numbers and designs.[36]

Although drones may be most useful for surveillance, their role in transforming combat may be more significant. In 2012 the Pentagon projected that by 2015 the air force would need more than two thousand pilots to guide unmanned air combat missions, which would run twenty-four hours a day worldwide. Many drones operate from remote-control centers often not far from their operators' suburban homes in the United States but perhaps seven thousand miles away from their targets. Those targeted to be killed by this remote method are not necessarily anonymous to the person who pulls the trigger. Often they have been watched for hours, days, and weeks as they played with their children and went about their ordinary lives.[37]

Many security strategists present drones as an enormously humane advance in warfare. Enemies can be identified and eliminated with a greatly reduced ratio of collateral damage to civilians than is usually found in conventional aerial (or even ground) warfare. Vietnam's "free fire zones" and emphasis on body count, for example, look callously killing-intensive beside the close and careful scrutiny promised by today's drone controllers. Moreover drones dramatically lessen the risk to American pilots, lowering the human and material costs of aerial activity. Drones are a flexible technology and can be inexpensively adapted to hundreds of purposes that may serve both war-making and peace-building.

But might whatever gains seem possible be diminished because of other consequences of the new technology? Might drones become a "quick fix" implement to be used any time that U.S. leaders would like to eliminate someone? If drones become not an alternative to bombing in war but a substitute for policing and capture in nonwar situations, they may expand rather than narrow areas of conflict and increase killing that might have been unnecessary. In a drone-saturated world, what is the line between war and peace? Do the traditional laws of war apply? Are drones a first or a last resort to achieving international objectives? The temptations are great. Drone kills, for example, could help eliminate the thorny issues of "enemy combatants," rendition, and confinement in liminal sites like Guantánamo. Dead bodies are less visible than those in custody or on trial, as are the identities of the people indirectly responsible for their demise. Killing by drone, in short, may expand simply because it is cheap and easy and avoids the difficult legal and practical problems presented by visible and present bodies captured especially in nonwar situations.[38]

The growing use of drones ratchets up the disparity between visibility and invisibility. It creates an increasingly asymmetrical visual field in which citizens who supposedly sponsor the killing may not know the action is happening, may not even have heard of the enemy being targeted. Drones and robotic battlefields, as Peter W. Singer has explored, enhance both the physical and the emotional distance of combat for their users.[39] Yet the associates of those who are attacked or killed certainly see the afflicted bodies up close and know who sponsored the perpetrators' actions. After the 9/11 attacks and in light of the menace posed by truck bombings in Iraq and Afghanistan, U.S. strategists worried over what they called "asymmetric warfare." But drones bring asymmetric warfare of another kind, where the sponsoring side may not even know a war is on (or with whom) while the other side suffers, sees death and maiming raining down from the air, and pledges revenge.

If Americans do not know the actions against which revenge is plotted, then their opponents can seem nothing but irrational—striking out for no apparent reason against a well-meaning nation that seemed to be doing them no harm. Drones are the perfect weapon for preserving the illusion of innocence but also for stimulating blowback in the form of counterattacks. When bodies that are nearly invisible to some are very visible to others, that asymmetry can feed an accelerating cycle of misunderstanding and ever more vicious violence.

Many of the essays in this book have stressed the importance of historicizing the media environment that provides context for discourses of body and nation. The disappeared body provides another powerful example of the importance of media—and of how its changing nature may alter the body and nation formulations. To come back to the earlier examples, U.S. media censorship in the decades after World War II obscured the bodies of atomic victims to most audiences in the world—even initially in Japan—because American media dominated global circulations. Major changes in the global media landscape of the late twentieth and early twenty-first century, however, reshaped the transnational flows and influence of America's mass media.[40] The most significant of these changes have been the rise of competing national and regional media industries and the growth of the Internet and social media technologies that have expanded access to news consumption and production. The simultaneous multipolarity and permeability of the contemporary global mediascape have had significant effects on media culture in the United States and on America's role as a transnational "semiotic center."[41] As media has become more and more globally owned and diversified, and as new forms of social media have expanded, the idea that any one nation or group could control visibility becomes increasingly problematic. The changing media environment of the twenty-first century thus augments the asymmetric visibility of counterinsurgency actions, rendition programs, and drones by accentuating the fact that bodies hardly visible in dominant American media are often highly visible to others.

Body and Nation in an Age of Biosecurity

As the use of drones spreads for policing at home as well as for shadow wars abroad, the geographical definitions of space and place may fade in importance. Both a nation's sovereignty and a body's vulnerability may become unbounded and at large. Whenever fear prevails, drones permit attackers to smash geopolitical logics, and the nation/nonnation divide, along with other forms of alterity, may become ever less distinct. As the relationship between the nation and the bodies that occupy any specific geography becomes increasingly flexible, disturbing questions emerge: Might a new generation of biosecurity technologies, applied in transnational ways, gradually colonize the bodies of individuals on a personal level? Are new security technologies ushering in an age in which both nations and bodies become so indistinct that the Foucauldian biopolitics of population management shifts its grounds?

National security in the post-9/11 period brought government resources pouring into new intelligence and research projects. The Cold War emphasis given to research in physics (atomic power) and to psychological theories and behavioral effects (so-called mind control and "interrogation" techniques) has morphed into an emphasis on new high-tech research in neuroscience and bioscience. Bodies, more than ever and in new ways, have become the principal terrain of national security research.

Fresh pipelines of funds cascaded into university research centers to develop innovative scientific approaches to manipulating what was now, with greater sophistication, understood to be the mind-body connection. Building on a Marine Corps effort in the mid-1990s to develop nonlethal weapons, for example, national security research grants sought to promote methods that could be used in war or non-war situations, such as crowd control or the capture of criminals and terrorists. Experiments with pharmaceutical compounds such as muscle relaxants and anti-anxiety drugs sought to produce effective calmative agents. A variety of sensory weapons also went into development: acoustic devices such as painful "sonic bullets" and hypersonic sound that could beam messages to specific individuals while leaving others in silence; malodorants; microwaves that could create severe burning sensations with no burns; genetically engineered biological weapons that could target the brain or nervous system to debilitate. Compared to highly visible physical wounds of war, the consequences of such neuroscientific approaches appear almost benign—like a gentler way to wage combat. Their overall effect, however, has been to foster a new science of "neurosecurity" that invites security agencies and militaries to intrude upon individual bodies both domestically and abroad in unprecedented, often barely visible ways. Migrating or "outsider" bodies, which our essays show have historically been subject to special scrutiny, may fall under even greater surveillance, and people once designated "insider" citizens may themselves become objects that are easily monitored.[42]

National security research after 9/11 not only boosted the emerging discipline of neuroscience but also emphasized other branches of bioscience, especially genetic engineering, immunology, biometrics, and "synthetic biology," a discipline that approaches biology from an engineering standpoint to design and construct new biological parts, devices, and systems. This new research uses genetics (including genomics) to engineer bodily systems and draws upon informatics to analyze biological data in ways hitherto unimaginable. Could soldiers, for example, become less vulnerable, require less sleep, regenerate body parts? In what innovative ways might the military use biometric scanning to identify and control suspect populations, a technique that began to be used in the wars in Iraq and Afghanistan? Diverse applications of biotechnology may find new ways of protecting, reengineering, and destroying people. Still in their infancy, such applications promise the capacity to dramatically alter bodily systems.

The post-9/11 flow of dollars into neuroscience and bioscience accompanied a political and media atmosphere preoccupied by threat. The 24/7 media culture thrives on a constant escalation of alarm: warnings over militarized attacks merge with terrorist bombings, with bioterrorist threats, with mass gun-murders, with anxiety over pandemics, with the erratic weather systems provoked by climate change, and with pervasive and graphic visual presentations of mass death as an aesthetic form. Threat has become "as ubiquitous as the wind, and its source as imperceptible."[43] National security regimes (and their expenditures) flourish in a state of what might be called "fear to the second power"—that is, not fear of a particular threat so much as fear of fear itself.

When fear to the second power becomes omnipresent and magnified through a media-drenched culture, then national security truly may know no bounds, no inside/outside, and no geography. Security measures may move toward, first, an intermittent and then a permanent "state of exception" in which technologies and boundlessness erase any distinction between "home" and "abroad," military and civilian, nation and body.[44] In this atmosphere new technologies and regimes of biosecurity raise issues about biopolitics. Will such innovations efface individual bodies even as they obliterate once sovereign borders? Will efforts at fear reduction, enforced at the most individual and personal level, work to disappear individual bodies into a new form of security state that has become nonnational (or supranational)? Such questions show how bodies and body politics in the twenty-first century continue to shape the themes highlighted in this volume: issues related to migration and belonging, the ever-changing roles of mass media and popular culture, and the shifting discourse of national security.

The near invisibility of atomic victims, the silences surrounding America's covert wars since the 1950s, and the visual asymmetries related to torture, rendition, drone strikes, and biosecurity over the past decade provide examples that raise questions about the meanings of disappeared bodies. Such not-seen bodies may often be hidden behind narratives of life-preserving benevolence and exceptionalism. But the trouble with history is that their ghosts may also surface and appear to good and ordinary people—who may, or may not, see them.

Notes

1. The story of this footage, now declassified but still hardly seen by the public, is told in Mitchell, *Atomic Cover-up;* Lifton and Mitchell, *Hiroshima in America.* The quote is from "The Great Hiroshima Film Cover-up," *Nation,* Aug. 3, 2011, http://www.thenation.com/blog/162543/great-hiroshima-cover.

See also Abé Mark Nornes, ed., "Production Materials from The Effects of the Atomic Bomb on Hiroshima and Nagasaki," at https://www.cjspubs.lsa .umich.edu/electronic/facultyseries/list/series/production.php. For the postwar debate over the consequences of atomic power, see Boyer, *By the Bomb's Early Light.*

2. The term is from McAlister, *Epic Encounters.*

3. Trouillot, *Silencing the Past.*

4. An online exhibit related to this film may be found at http://www.pcf.city .hiroshima.jp/virtual/VirtualMuseum_e/exhibit_e/exh0902_e/exh090215_e .html.

5. Serlin, *Replaceable You,* 57–110; Jacobs, "Reconstructing the Perpetrator's Soul by Reconstructing the Victim's Body."

6. Michael J. Hogan, "The Enola Gay Controversy," in Hogan, *Hiroshima in History and Memory,* 200–232; Kohn, "History at Risk."

7. On the horrors and cover-up of nuclear damage at Rocky Flats, Colorado, see Iversen, *Full Body Burden,* 301, 339. On health issues more broadly, see essays in Johnston, *Half-Lives and Half-Truths.* Some of the essays in Taylor, *Nuclear Legacies* explore the "discursive containment" of nuclear production. Broad cultural histories of the anxieties and occlusions afflicting atomic-age America include Henriksen, *Dr. Strangelove's America;* Gusterson, *People of the Bomb;* Rotter, *Hiroshima.* Weiner, *How We Forgot the Cold War,* 253–62 charts the failed attempt to memorialize Rocky Flats and Hanford as sites of Cold War victory.

8. See Jacobson and González, *What Have They Built You to Do?;* Marks, *The Search for the "Manchurian Candidate";* Weinstein, *Psychiatry and the* CIA.

9. Alfred W. McCoy, "Impunity at Home, Rendition Abroad," History News Network, Oct. 20, 2012, http://hnn.us/articles/impunity-home-rendition- abroad. His extended analysis is in McCoy, *Torture and Impunity.*

10. Marks, *The Search for the "Manchurian Candidate,"* is based on documents from MKUltra that had not been destroyed. See also U.S. Senate, *Joint Hearing before the Select Committee on Intelligence and the Subcommittee on Health and Scientific Research of the Committee on Human Resources,* 95th Cong., 1st Sess., Aug. 3, 1977, http://www.druglibrary.org/schaffer/history/e1950/mkultra/index.htm; Weinstein, *Psychiatry and the* CIA. For a broad perspective, see McCoy, *A Question of Torture* and *Torture and Impunity.*

11. Grandin, *The Last Colonial Massacre;* Rabe, *The Killing Zone,* 36–58.

12. "Kubark Counterintelligence Interrogation," July 1963, George Washington University, National Security Archive, at http://www.gwu.edu/~nsarchiv/ NSAEBB/NSAEBB27/01–01.htm, 6 (quote).

13. See especially the memo from Viron Vaky, Mar. 29, 1968, George Washington University, National Security Archive, http://www.gwu.edu/~ns archiv/NSAEBB/NSAEBB32/08–01.htm.

14. Rabe, *The Killing Zone,* 172–74. Large collections of declassified material on U.S.-Guatemalan relations and documentation on U.S. knowledge of the extensive human rights abuses committed, especially during the 1980s, may

be found on the website of the National Security Archive, http://www.gwu
.edu/ffinsarchiv/search.html, under the search term *Guatemala*.

15. Westad, *The Global Cold War.*

16. Rabe, *The Killing Zone*, 96.

17. See Turse, *Kill Anything That Moves* and Marilyn Young's article in this
volume. Four decades after the destruction of Agent Orange, the United
States finally began to take some limited responsibility for its clean-up. See
Thomas Fuller, "4 Decades On: U.S. Begins Clean-up of Agent Orange in Vietnam," *New York Times*, Aug. 10, 2012. On the manuals devised for inflicting
bodily harm, see McCoy, *Torture and Impunity*, 98–103; Moreno, *Mind Wars*, 64.
An important theoretical perspective is presented in Cavarero, *Horrorism.*

18. Simpson, *Economists with Guns*; Rabe, *The Killing Zone*, 114–43; Gill, *The
School of the Americas*; McCoy, *Torture and Impunity*, 114–50.

19. Rabe, *The Killing Zone*, 144–74; Grandin, *Empire's Workshop*; Coll, *Ghost
Wars.*

20. The Guatemalan report is at Human Rights Data Analysis Group,
https://hrdag.org/wp-content/uploads/2013/01/CEHreport-english.pdf. On El
Salvador, see Arnson, *El Salvador, Accountability and Human Rights.* On Honduras, see "Secret CIA Report Admits: 'Honduran Military Committed Hundreds
of Human Rights Abuses' and 'Inaccurate' Reporting to Congress," Oct. 23,
1998, George Washington University, National Security Archive, http://www
.gwu.edu/ffinsarchiv/news/19981023.htm, and the commission's report, Leo
Valladares Lanza and Susan C. Peacock, "In Search of Hidden Truths: An
Interim Report on Declassification by the National Commissioner for Human Rights in Honduras," http://www.gwu.edu/~nsarchiv/latin_america/
honduras/hidden_truths/hidden.htm.

21. Scarry, *The Body in Pain*, 60–62. Rejali, *Torture and Democracy* provides a
broad historical and topical survey of torture.

22. Examples, in addition to citations above, include contributions to
"Part I: The Dirty War's Declassified Documents: A New Perspective on Bilateral Relations" in Arnson, *Argentine–United States Bilateral Relations*, and Stern,
Battling for Hearts and Minds. The National Security Archive contains much
documentation on individual countries from these years that may be found
through their search engine.

23. Quoted in Rabe, *The Killing Zone*, 187.

24. McCoy, *Torture and Impunity*, 216–68 examines and documents aspects
of the "public forgetting."

25. Scarry, *The Body in Pain*, 60.

26. Mark Danner, "Now That We've Tortured: Image, Guilt, Conse-
quence," http://www.markdanner.com/articles/print/159. Danner references
"a great number of investigations since 2004, a dozen or so" that provide such
a concurrent record. The texts of many of the major early investigations are in
Danner, *Torture and Truth*, and in his collection of columns in *Stripping Bare the
Body.* The point is also made in Pitt, *Bodies, Nation, and Narrative in the Americas*,
173–76.

27. On rendition and torture generally, see Human Rights Watch, "Getting Away with Torture," July 12, 2011, http://www.hrw.org/reports/2011/07/12/getting-away-torture; Jane Mayer, "Outsourcing Torture: Annals of Justice," *New Yorker*, Feb. 14, 2005, 106–9. On rendition to Libya in particular, see Human Rights Watch, "Delivered into Enemy Hands," Sept. 5, 2012, http://www.hrw.org/reports/2012/09/05/delivered-enemy-hands.

28. Draft memorandum from John Yoo, deputy assistant attorney general, Office of Legal Counsel, to William J. Haynes II, general counsel Department of Defense, regarding "Application of Treaties and Laws to al Qaeda and Taliban Detainees," Jan. 9, 2002, http://www.torturingdemocracy.org/documents/20020109.pdf; Memorandum from White House Counsel Alberto Gonzales to President George W. Bush, "Decision Re Application of the Geneva Convention on Prisoners of War to the Conflict with Al Qaeda and the Taliban," Jan. 25, 2002, http://www.gwu.edu/ffinsarchiv/NSAEBB/NSAEBB127/02.01.25.pdf. See Mayer, *The Dark Side*.

29. See Horton, *"Kriegsraison or Military Necessity?"*; Sikkink, "Bush Administration Noncompliance with the Prohibition on Torture and Cruel and Degrading Treatment."

30. Danner, *Stripping Bare the Body*, 499.

31. "From El Salvador to Iraq: Washington's Man behind Brutal Police Squads," *Guardian*, Mar. 6, 2013, http://www.guardian.co.uk/world/2013/mar/06/el-salvador-iraq-police-squads-washington; "Revealed: Pentagon's Link to Iraqi Torture Centres," *Guardian*, Mar. 6, 2013, http://www.guardian.co.uk/world/2013/mar/06/pentagon-iraqi-torture-centres-link?CMP=twt_gu.

32. For details on available document and reports, and of official responses, see Sikkink, "Bush Administration Noncompliance with the Prohibition on Torture and Cruel and Degrading Treatment"; Danner, *Stripping Bare the Body*, 392–563; McCoy, *Torture and Impunity*. Siems, *The Torture Report* presents a large cache of documents released through the Freedom of Information Act and reports by victims, perpetrators, dissenters, and investigators.

33. Takacs, *Terrorism TV*, 85–96, and see her abundant citations as well. McCoy, *Torture and Impunity*, 151–87 explores the acceptance of torture in the interrelationship between political culture and mass culture. An outpouring of scholarly and popular books, some cited in this essay, show that Americans did debate and grapple with questions of which wars and which tactics should be deemed just and necessary; Takacs suggests, however, that popular visual mass media trended away from such complicated questions.

34. For a theoretical discussion, see the introduction to Debrix and Barder, *Beyond Biopolitics*. Influential interpretations of image, war, and bodies include Sontag, *Regarding the Pain of Others*; Butler, *Frames of War*.

35. See Susan C. Carruthers, "Zero Dark Thirty," *Cineaste* 38 (spring 2013): 50.

36. Singer, *Wired for War* provides a history, looks to the future, and weighs new questions raised by robotic techniques. The numbers here are from Department of Defense sources as reported in Nick Turse, "A Drone-Eat-Drone

World," *Huffington Post*, May 31, 2012, http://www.huffingtonpost.com/nick-turse/obama-drones_b_1558965.html?ref=world&ir=World. See also Turse and Engelhardt, *Terminator Planet*. For the military planning document on the expansion of drone technology, see U.S. Department of Defense, *2009–2034 Unmanned Systems Integrated Roadmap*; for congressional hearings from 2010 assessing the implications, see U.S. House of Representatives, *Rise of the Drones*.

37. Elisabeth Bumiller, "A Day Job Waiting for a Kill Shot a World Away," *New York Times*, July 30, 2012.

38. For some of the debate over drones, see, for example, Scott Shane, "The Moral Case for Drones," *New York Times*, July 15, 2012; Scott Shane, "Coming Soon: The Drone's Arms Race," *New York Times*, Oct 8, 2011; Daniel R. Brunstetter, "Can We Wage a Just Drone War?," *Atlantic*, July, 19, 2012, http://www.theatlantic.com/technology/archive/2012/07/can-we-wage-a-just-drone-war/260055/.

39. Singer, *Wired for War*.

40. A classic text on American media and American power is Schiller, *Mass Communication and American Empire*. Comparing Tunstall, *The Media Are American* and his follow-up work, *The Media Were American*, illustrates how changing technology and processes of economic globalization have contributed to transforming America's role in the global media market. Also see Boyd-Barrett, *Communications Media, Globalization, and Empire*.

41. The term *semiotic center* is borrowed from Rob Kroes, "American Empire and Cultural Imperialism," in Bender, *Rethinking American History in a Global Age*, 17, 297. On media multipolarity, see Artz and Kamalipour, *The Media Globe*.

42. Moreno, *Mind Wars*, 139–79.

43. The quote is from Massumi, "National Enterprise Emergency," 23. See also Debrix and Barder, *Beyond Biopolitics*. On the theoretical implications of how disease and national security threat come together within the realm of biopolitics, see Eugene Thacker, "Nomos, Nosos and Bios," *Culture Machine* 7 (2005), http://www.culturemachine.net/index.php/cm/article/view/25/32.

44. The classic formulation of the "state of exception" is Schmitt, *Political Theology*. Recent influential theoretical works on exception, sovereignty, and the body include Agamben, *State of Exception*; Ong, *Neoliberalism as Exception*.

bibliography

Abella, Alex. *Soldiers of Reason: The* RAND *Corporation and the Rise of the American Empire.* New York: Houghton Mifflin Harcourt, 2008.

Adams, Mark. *Mr. America: How Muscular Millionaire Bernarr Macfadden Transformed the Nation through Sex, Salad, and the Ultimate Starvation Diet.* New York: HarperCollins, 2009.

Adams, Rachel. *Sideshow USA: Freaks and the American Cultural Imagination.* Chicago: University of Chicago Press, 2002.

Agamben, Giorgio. *State of Exception.* Translated by Kevin Attell. Chicago: University of Chicago Press, 2005.

Aldrich, Robert F. *Colonialism and Homosexuality.* New York: Routledge, 2003.

Alexander, Michelle. *The New Jim Crow: Mass Incarceration in the Age of Colorblindness.* New York: New Press, 2012.

Allen, Michael. *Until the Last Man Comes Home:* POWS, MIAS, *and the Unending Vietnam War.* Chapel Hill: University of North Carolina Press, 2009.

Alter, Joseph. *Yoga in Modern India.* Princeton, NJ: Princeton University Press, 2004.

American Bureau of Shipping. *1905 Record of American and Foreign Shipping.* New York: American Bureau of Shipping, 1905.

Anderson, Benedict. *Imagined Communities.* Revised ed. London: Verso, 1999.

Anderson, Clare. *Legible Bodies: Race, Criminality, and Colonialism in South Asia.* Oxford: Berg, 2004.

Anderson, Sherwood. *Tar: A Midwest Childhood.* 1926. Cleveland, OH: Press of Case Western Reserve University, 1969.

Anderson, Warwick. *Colonial Pathologies: American Tropical Medicine, Race, and Hygiene in the Philippines.* Durham, NC: Duke University Press, 2006.

Appadurai, Arjun. *Modernity at Large: Cultural Dimensions of Globalization.* Minneapolis: University of Minnesota Press, 1996.

Arnold, Rebecca. *The American Look: Sportswear, Fashion and the Image of Women in 1930s and 1940s New York.* London: I. B. Tauris, 2008.

Arnold, Rebecca. "Looking American: Louise Dahl-Wolfe's Fashion Photographs of the 1930s and 1940s." *Fashion Theory: The Journal of Dress, Body and Culture* 6 (2002): 45–60.

Arnson, Cynthia J., ed. *Argentine–United States Bilateral Relations: An Historical Perspective and Future Challenges.* Washington, DC: Woodrow Wilson Center, 2003.

Arnson, Cynthia. El Salvador, Accountability and Human Rights: The Report of the United Nations Commission on the Truth for El Salvador. America's Watch, 1993.

Aronowitz, Stanley. *Choosing Sides: Playground and Street Life on the Lower East Side.* New York: Schocken Books, 1979.

Artz, Lee, and Yahya R. Kamalipour, eds. *The Media Globe: Trends in International Mass Media.* Lanham, MD: Rowman and Littlefield, 2007.

Babington, Anthony. *Shell-Shock: A History of the Changing Attitudes to War Neurosis.* London: Pen and Sword, 1997.

Bailey, Beth, and David Farber. *The First Strange Place: The Alchemy of Race and Sex in World War II Hawaii.* New York: Free Press, 1992.

Ballantyne, Tony, and Antoinette Burton, eds. *Bodies in Contact: Rethinking Colonial Encounters in World History.* Durham, NC: Duke University Press, 2005.

Barham, Peter. *Forgotten Lunatics of the Great War.* New Haven, CT: Yale University Press, 2004.

Barkan, Elazar, and Ronald Bush, eds. *Prehistories of the Future: The Primitivist Project and the Culture of Modernism.* Palo Alto, CA: Stanford University Press, 1995.

Bass, Amy. *Not the Triumph but the Struggle: The 1968 Olympics and the Making of the Black Athlete.* Minneapolis: University of Minnesota Press, 2002.

Baudrillard, Jean. *The Consumer Society: Myths and Structures.* 1970. London: Sage, 1998.

Baudrillard, Jean. *Symbolic Exchange and Death.* 1976. London: Sage, 1993.

Beard, George Miller. *American Nervousness, Its Causes and Consequences.* New York: G. P. Putnam's Sons, 1881.

Beckles, Hilary McD., and Brian Stoddart, eds. *Liberation Cricket: West Indies Cricket Culture.* New York: Manchester University Press, 1995.

Bederman, Gail. *Manliness and Civilization: A Cultural History of Gender and Race in the United States, 1880–1917.* Chicago: University of Chicago Press, 1995.

Belmonte, Laura. *Selling the American Way.* Philadelphia: University of Pennsylvania Press, 2010.

Belmonte, Laura A. *Selling the American Way: U.S. Propaganda and the Cold War.* Philadelphia: University of Pennsylvania Press, 2008.

Berezhkov, Valentin. *History in the Making: Memoirs of World War II Diplomacy.* Moscow: Progress, 1982.

Bergfelder, Tim. "Negotiating Exoticism: Hollywood, Film Europe and the Cultural Reception of Anna May Wong." In *"Film Europe" and "Film America": Cinema, Commerce and Cultural Exchange, 1920–1939,* edited by Andrew Higson and Richard Maltby, 302–24. Exeter, U.K.: University of Exeter Press, 1999.

Beria, Sergo. *Beria: My Father inside Stalin's Kremlin*. London: Duckworth, 2001.

Blakemore, Colin, and Sheila Jennett, eds. *The Oxford Companion to the Body*. New York: Oxford University Press, 2002.

Blight, David W. "In Retrospect: Nathan Irvin Huggins, the Art of History, and the Irony of the American Dream." *Reviews in American History* 22 (Mar. 1994): 174–90.

Bloom, Lisa. "Constructing Whiteness: Popular Science and *National Geographic* in the Age of Multiculturalism." *Configurations* 2, no. 1 (1994): 15–32.

Bohlen, Charles E. *Witness to History: 1929–1969*. New York: Norton, 1973.

Bordo, Susan. *Unbearable Weight: Feminism, Western Culture, and the Body*. Berkeley: University of California Press, 1993.

Borgwardt, Elizabeth. *A New Deal for the World*. Cambridge: Harvard University Press, 2005.

Bourke, Joanna. *Dismembering the Male*. Chicago: University of Chicago Press, 1996.

Boyd-Barrett, Oliver. *Communications Media, Globalization, and Empire*. Eastleigh, U.K.: J. Libbey, 2006.

Boydell, Tommy. *My Beloved Country*. Cape Town: Nasionale Boekhandel, 1959.

Boyer, Paul S. *By the Bomb's Early Light: American Thought and Culture at the Dawn of the Atomic Age*. New York: Pantheon, 1985.

Bradley, Mark. *Imagining Vietnam and America: The Making of Postcolonial Vietnam, 1919–1950*. Chapel Hill: University of North Carolina Press, 2000.

Briggs, Charles W. *The Progressing Philippines*. Philadelphia, PA: Griffith and Rowland Press, 1913.

Briggs, Laura. *Reproducing Empire: Race, Science, and U.S. Imperialism in Puerto Rico*. Berkeley: University of California Press, 2002.

Briggs, Laura, Gladys McCormick, and J. T. Way. "Transnationalism: A Category of Analysis." *American Quarterly* 60, no. 3 (2008): 625–48.

Brown, Judith. *Glamour in Six Dimensions: Modernism and the Radiance of Form*. Ithaca, NY: Cornell University Press, 2009.

Brown, Kathleen M. "The Anglo-Algonquian Gender Frontier." In *Negotiators of Change: Historical Perspectives on Native American Women*, edited by Nancy Shoemaker, 26–48. New York: Routledge, 1995.

Brown, Kathleen M. *Foul Bodies: Cleanliness in Early America*. New Haven, CT: Yale University Press, 2009.

Brownell, Susan. *Training the Body for China: Sports in the Moral Order of the People's Republic*. Chicago: University of Chicago Press, 1995.

Brunner, José. "Psychiatry, Psychoanalysis, and Politics during the First World War." *Journal of the History of the Behavioral Sciences* 27, no. 4 (1991): 352–65.

Buckland, Sandra Stansbery. "Promoting American Designers, 1940–44:

Building Our Own House." In *Twentieth-Century American Fashion*, edited by Linda Welters and Patricia A. Cunningham, 99–122. Oxford, U.K.: Berg, 2005.

Budd, Michael Anton. *The Sculpture Machine*. New York: NYU Press, 1997.

Burchell, Graham, Colin Gordon, and Peter Miller, eds. *The Foucault Effect: Studies in Governmentality*. Chicago: University of Chicago Press, 1991.

Burnham, John Chynoweth. "Psychiatry, Psychology and the Progressive Movement." *American Quarterly* 12, no. 4 (1960): 457–65.

Butler, Judith. *Bodies That Matter: On the Discursive Limits of "Sex."* New York: Routledge, 1993.

Butler, Judith. *Frames of War: When Is Life Grievable?* London: Verso, 2009.

Butler, Judith. *Gender Trouble: Feminism and the Subversion of Identity*. New York: Routledge, 1990.

Calavita, Kitty . *Inside the State: The Bracero Program, Immigration, and the I.N.S.* New York: Routledge, 1992.

Camagay, Maria Luisa. *Working Women of Manila in the 19th Century*. Manila: University of the Philippines Press, Center for Women's Studies, 1995.

Campbell, James T., Matthew P. Guterl, and Robert G. Lee. *Race, Nation, and Empire in American History*. Chapel Hill: University of North Carolina Press, 2007.

Campbell, Patricia Warner. *When the Girls Came Out to Play: The Birth of American Sportswear*. Amherst: University of Massachusetts Press, 2006.

Canzler, Weertz, Vincent Kaufmann, and Sven Kesselring, eds. *Tracing Mobilities: Towards a Cosmopolitan Perspective*. Burlington, VT: Ashgate, 2008.

Casper, Monica, and Lisa Jean Moore, *Missing Bodies: The Politics of Visibility*. New York: NYU Press, 2009.

Castillo, Greg. *Cold War on the Home Front: The Soft Power of Midcentury Design*. Minneapolis: University of Minnesota Press, 2010.

Cather, Willa. *O Pioneers!* 1913. Lincoln: University of Nebraska Press, 1992.

Cavallo, Dominick. *Muscles and Morals: Organized Playgrounds and Urban Reform, 1880–1920*. Philadelphia: University of Pennsylvania Press, 1981.

Cavarero, Adriana. *Horrorism: Naming Contemporary Violence*. New York: Columbia University Press, 2007.

Chan, Anthony C. *Perpetually Cool: The Many Lives of Anna May Wong, 1905–1961*. New York: Rowman and Littlefield, 2003.

Chan, Sucheng. *Asian Americans: An Interpretive History*. Boston, MA: Twayne, 1991.

Chapman, David. *Sandow the Magnificent*. Champaign: University of Illinois Press, 1994.

Charap, Lawrence. "Teaching the Globalization of American Popular Culture in the Twentieth Century." In *America on the World Stage*, edited by Gary W. Reichard and Ted Dickson. Urbana: University of Illinois Press, 2008.

Chauncey, George. *Gay New York: Gender, Urban Culture, and the Making of the Gay Male World, 1890–1940*. New York: Basic Books, 1995.

Chavez, Leo R. *The Latino Threat: Constructing Immigrants, Citizens, and the Nation*. Stanford, CA: Stanford University Press, 2008.

Cherniavsky, Eva. *Incorporations: Race, Nation, and the Body Politics of Capital*. Minneapolis: University of Minnesota Press, 2006.

Chun, Gloria H. "'Go West . . . to China': Chinese American Identity in the 1930s." In *Claiming America: Constructing Chinese American Identities in the Exclusion Era*, edited by K. Scott Wong and Sucheng Chan, 165–90. Philadelphia, PA: Temple University Press, 1998.

Clough, Patricia Ticineto, and Craig Willse, eds. *Beyond Biopolitics: Essays on the Governance of Life and Death*. Durham, NC: Duke University Press, 2011.

Coe, Andrew. *Chop Suey: A Cultural History of Chinese Food in the United States*. New York: Oxford University Press, 2009.

Cohen, Deborah. "Masculine Sweat, Stoop-Labor Modernity: Gender, Race, and Nation in Mid-Twentieth Century Mexico and the U.S." PhD diss., University of Chicago, 2001.

Cohen, Warren I., and Nancy Bernkopf Tucker. "America in Asian Eyes." *American Historical Review* III, no. 4 (2006): 1092–119.

Coll, Steven. *Ghost Wars: The Secret History of the CIA, Afghanistan, and Bin Laden, from the Soviet Invasion to September 10, 2001*. New York: Penguin, 2004.

Colville, John R. *The Fringes of Power*. New York: Norton, 1985.

Connelly, Matthew. *Fatal Misconception: The Struggle to Control World Population*. Cambridge, MA: Harvard University Press, 2008.

Conor, Liz. *The Spectacular Modern Women: Feminine Visibility in the 1920s*. Bloomington: Indiana University Press, 2004.

Costigliola, Frank. *Roosevelt's Lost Alliances: How Personal Politics Helped Start the Cold War*. Princeton, NJ: Princeton University Press, 2012.

Creak, Simon. "Cold War Rhetoric and the Body: Physical Cultures in Early Socialist Laos." In *Cultures at War: The Cold War and Cultural Expression in Southeast Asia*, edited by Tony Day and Maya H. T. Liem, 103–30. Ithaca, NY: Cornell Southeast Asia Program Publications, 2010.

Creswell, Tim. *On the Move: Mobility in the Modern Western World*. New York: Routledge, 2006.

Cripps, Thomas. *Slow Fade to Black: The Negro in American Film*. New York: Oxford University Press, 1977.

Crombie, Isobel. *Body Culture: Max DuPain, Photography, and Australian Culture, 1919–1939*. Mulgrave, VIC: Images, 2004.

Cull, Nicholas. *The Cold War and the United States Information Agency*. Cambridge: Cambridge University Press, 2009.

Cullather, Nick. *The Hungry World: America's Cold War Battle against Poverty in Asia*. Cambridge, MA: Harvard University Press, 2010.

Cuordileone, K. A. *Manhood and American Political Culture in the Cold War*. New York: Routledge, 2005.

Curell, Susan, and Christina Cogdell. *Popular Eugenics: National Efficiency and American Mass Culture in the 1930s*. Athens: Ohio University Press, 2006.

Daddis, Gregory A. *No Sure Victory: Measuring U.S. Army Effectiveness and Progress in the Vietnam War*. New York: Oxford University Press, 2011.

Daley, Caroline. *Leisure and Pleasure: Reshaping and Revealing the New Zealand Body*. Auckland: Auckland University Press, 2003.

Daley, Caroline. "The Strongman of Eugenics, Eugen Sandow." *Australian Historical Studies* 33, no. 120 (2002): 233–48.

Danchev, Alex, and Daniel Todman, eds. *War Diaries, 1939–1945: Field Marshal Lord Alanbrooke*. Berkeley: University of California Press, 2001.

Danner, Mark. *Stripping Bare the Body: Politics, Violence, War*. New York: Nation Books, 2009.

Danner, Mark. *Torture and Truth: America, Abu Ghraib, and the War on Terror*. New York: New York Review Books, 2004.

Darian-Smith, Kate, and Paula Hamilton, eds. *Memory and History in Twentieth Century Australia*. Melbourne: Oxford University Press, 1994.

Davis, Janet M. *The Circus Age: Culture and Society under the American Big Top*. Chapel Hill: University of North Carolina Press, 2002.

Davis, Janet M. "The Circus Americanized." In *The American Circus*, edited by Susan Weber, Kenneth L. Ames, and Matthew Wittmann, 22–53. New York: Bard Graduate Center and Yale University Press, 2012.

Davis, Lennard, ed. *The Disability Studies Reader*. New York: Routledge, 1997.

Day, Tony, and Maya H. T. Liem, eds. *Cultures at War: The Cold War and Cultural Expression in Southeast Asia*. Ithaca, NY: Cornell Southeast Asia Program Publications, 2010.

Deacon, Desley. "World English? How an Australian Invented 'Good American Speech.'" In *Talking and Listening in the Age of Modernity: Essays on the History of Sound*, edited by Joy Darnousi and Desley Deacon, 73–82. Canberra: ANU e-press, 2007.

Dean, Robert D. *Imperial Brotherhood: Gender and the Making of Cold War Foreign Policy*. Amherst: University of Massachusetts Press, 2001.

Deane, John R. *The Strange Alliance: The Story of Our Efforts at Wartime Cooperation with Russia*. New York: Viking, 1947.

de Baecque, Antoine. *The Body Politic: Corporeal Metaphor in Revolutionary France, 1770–1800*. Translated by Charlotte Mandell. Palo Alto, CA: Stanford University Press, 1997.

De Bevoise, Ken. *Agents of Apocalypse: Epidemic Disease in the Colonial Philippines*. Princeton: Princeton University Press, 1995.

Debrix, François, and Alexander D. Barder, eds. *Beyond Biopolitics: Theory, Violence, and Horror in World Politics*. New York: Routledge, 2011.

Defty, Andrew. *Britain, America, and Anti-Communist Propaganda, 1945–53*. London: Routledge, 2004.

de Grazia, Victoria. *Irresistible Empire: America's Advance through Twentieth Century Europe*. Cambridge, MA: Belknap Press of Harvard University, 2006.

Dery, Luis C. "Prostitution in Colonial Manila." *Philippine Studies* 39 (1991): 475–89.

Dilks, David, ed. *The Diaries of Sir Alexander Cadogan: 1938–1945.* London: Cassell, 1971.

Dillon, Michael, and Julian Reid. *The Liberal Way of War: Killing to Make Life Live.* London: Routledge, 2009.

Diprose, Rosalyn, and Robyn Ferrell, eds. *Cartographies: Poststructuralism and the Mapping of Bodies and Spaces.* Sydney: Allen and Unwin, 1991.

Doane, Mary Ann. *Femme Fatales: Feminism, Film Theory, and Psychoanalysis.* London: Routledge, 1991.

Donnell, John C. "National Renovation Campaigns in Vietnam." *Pacific Affairs* 32, no. 1 (1959): 73–88.

Dow, Mark. *American Gulag: Inside U.S. Immigration Prisons.* Berkeley: University of California Press, 2005.

Driscoll, Barbara A. *The Tracks North: The Railroad Bracero Program of World War II.* Austin: Center for Mexican American Studies, University of Texas at Austin, 1999.

Dubois, Laurent. *Soccer Empire: The World Cup and the Future of France.* Berkeley: University of California Press, 2011.

Dudziak, Mary L. "Josephine Baker, Racial Protest, and the Cold War." *Journal of American History*, September 1994, 543–70.

Dulaney, Willie, Raymond Jones, and Joseph D. Lewis. *Black Police in America.* Bloomington: Indiana University Press, 1996.

Dunn, Timothy J. *The Militarization of the U.S.-Mexico Border, 1978–1992.* Austin: University of Texas Press, 1996.

Dunnigan, Alice. *A Black Woman's Experience—From Schoolhouse to White House.* Philadelphia, PA: Dorrance, 1974.

During, Simon. "Popular Culture on a Global Scale: A Challenge for Cultural Studies?" *Critical Inquiry* 23 (Summer 1997): 808–33.

Eisen, George, and David K. Wiggins, eds. *Ethnicity and Sport in North American History and Culture.* Westport, CT: Greenwood Press, 1994.

Eisenstein, Sergei. "A Dialectical Approach to Film Form." In *Film Form: Essays in Film Form,* edited and translated by Jay Leyda, 101–122. New York: Harcourt, Brace and World, 1949.

Eissler, Kurt R. *Freud as an Expert Witness: The Discussion of War Neuroses between Freud and Wagner-Jauregg.* New York: International Universities Press, 1986.

Ellinghaus, Katherine, Jane Carey, and Leigh Boucher, eds. *Re-orienting Whiteness.* New York: Palgrave Macmillan, 2009.

Elliott, Mai V. RAND *in Southeast Asia: A History of the Vietnam War Era.* Arlington, VA: RAND, 2010.

Engs, Ruth C. *Clean Living Movements.* Westport, CT: Praeger, 2000.

Engstrom, David W. *Presidential Decision Making Adrift: The Carter Administration and the Mariel Boatlift.* Lanham, MD: Rowman and Littlefield, 1997.

Enloe, Cynthia. *Bananas, Beaches, and Bases: Making Feminist Sense of International Politics.* Berkeley: University of California Press, 1990.

Enloe, Cynthia. *The Morning After: Sexual Politics at the End of the Cold War.* Berkeley: University of California Press, 1993.

Ernst, Robert. *Weakness Is a Crime: The Life of Bernarr Macfadden.* Syracuse, NY: Syracuse University Press, 1991.

España-Maram, Linda. *Creating Masculinity in Los Angeles's Little Manila: Working-Class Filipinos and Popular Culture, 1920s–1950s.* New York: Columbia University Press, 2006.

Fabian, Ann. *The Unvarnished Truth: Personal Narratives in Nineteenth-Century America.* Berkeley: University of California Press, 2000.

Fabian, Johannes. *Time and the Other: How Anthropology Makes Its Object.* New York: Columbia University Press, 1983.

Fairchild, Amy L. *Science at the Borders: Immigrant Medical Inspection and the Shaping of the Modern Industrial Labor Force.* Baltimore, MD: Johns Hopkins University Press, 2003.

Falk, Andrew J. *Upstaging the Cold War.* Amherst: University of Massachusetts Press, 2010.

Farrell-Beck, Jane, and Jean Parsons. *20th Century Dress in the United States.* Ames, IA: Fairchild, 2007.

Farwell, Byron. *Over There: The United States in the Great War, 1917–1918.* New York: Norton, 1999.

Fausto-Sterling, Anne. *Sexing the Body: Gender Politics and the Construction of Sexuality.* New York: Basic Books, 2000.

Featherstone, Mike, Mike Hepworth, and Bryan S. Turner, eds. *The Body: Social Process and Cultural Theory.* London: Sage, 1991.

Fehrenbach, Heide. *Race after Hitler: Black Occupation Children in Postwar Germany and America.* Princeton, NJ: Princeton University Press, 2005.

Fernández, Gastón A. *The Mariel Exodus: Twenty Years Later. A Study on the Politics of Stigma and a Research Bibliography.* Miami, FL: Ediciones Universal, 2002.

Finkelstein, Lawrence S. "U.S. at Impasse in Southeast Asia." *Far Eastern Survey* 19, no. 16 (1950): 165–72.

Finnane, Mark. "'In the Same Bed Dreaming Differently': Tsai Wenyen and the Art of Diplomacy in Australia, 1936–1944." In *Australia's Asia: From Yellow Peril to Asian Century,* edited by David Walker and Agnieszka Sobocinska, 223–244. Perth: University of Western Australia Press, 2012.

Fitzpatrick, Shanon. "Pulp Empire: Macfadden Publications, Transnational America, and the Global Popular." PhD diss., University of California, Irvine, 2013.

Foucault, Michel. *Discipline and Punish.* New York: Pantheon, 1977.

Foucault, Michel. *The History of Sexuality.* New York: Pantheon, 1978.

Foucault, Michel. "Technologies of the Self." In *Technologies of the Self,* edited by Luther H. Martin et al., 16–49. Amherst: University of Massachusetts Press, 1988.

Fraser, Miriam, and Monica Greco, eds. *The Body: A Reader*. New York: Routledge, 2005.

Fraser, Nancy. "From Discipline to Flexibilization? Rereading Foucault in the Shadow of Globalization." *Constellations* 10, no. 2 (2003): 160–71.

Freidel, Frank. *Franklin D. Roosevelt: The Ordeal*. Boston, MA: Little, Brown, 1954.

Freidel, Frank. *Franklin D. Roosevelt: The Triumph*. Boston, MA: Little, Brown, 1956.

Freud, Sigmund. *The Standard Edition of the Complete Psychological Works of Sigmund Freud*, edited by James Strachey. London: Hogarth Press, 1953–74.

Frevert, Ute. *Women in German History: From Bourgeois Emancipation to Sexual Liberation*. Oxford: Berg, 1989.

Fussell, Paul. *The Great War and Modern Memory*. New York: Oxford University Press, 2000.

Gabaccia, Donna R. *Foreign Relations: American Immigration in Global Perspective*. Princeton, NJ: Princeton University Press, 2012.

Gabaccia, Donna R., and Vicky Ruiz, eds. *American Dreaming, Global Realities: Rethinking U.S. Immigration History*. Champaign: University of Illinois Press, 2006.

García, Maria Christina. *Havana USA: Cuban Exiles and Cuban Americans in South Florida, 1959–1994*. Berkeley: University of California Press, 1996.

Garland, Hamlin. *A Son of the Middle Border*. 1923. New York: Penguin, 1995.

Gartner, Scott Sigmund, and Marissa Edson Myers. "Body Counts and 'Success' in the Vietnam and Korean Wars." *Journal of Interdisciplinary History* 25, no. 3 (1995): 377–95.

George, Clare. *Berlin Days: 1946–1947*. London: Macmillan, 1989.

Gertz, Nolen. "Censorship, Propaganda, and the Production of 'Shell Shock' in World War I." *Journal of Contemporary History* 35, no. 1 (2000): 141–50.

Gijswijt-Hofstra, Marijke, and Roy Porter, eds. *Cultures of Neurasthenia from Beard to the First World War*. New York: Rodopi, 2001.

Gill, Lesley. *The School of the Americas: Military Training and Political Violence in the Americas*. Durham, NC: Duke University Press, 2004.

Glantz, Mary E. *FDR and the Soviet Union*. Lawrence: University Press of Kansas, 2005.

Go, Julian, and Anne L. Foster, eds. *The American Colonial State in the Philippines: Global Perspectives*. Durham, NC: Duke University Press, 2003.

Goedde, Petra. "From Villains to Victims: Fraternization and the Feminization of Germany, 1945–1947." *Diplomatic History* 23 (Winter 1999): 1–20.

Gonzalez-Pando, Miguel. *The Cuban Americans*. Westport, CT: Greenwood Press, 1998.

Goodall, Jane. *Performance and Evolution in the Age of Darwin*. New York: Routledge, 2002.

Goodman, Alan H., Deborah Heath, and M. Susan Lindee, eds. *Genetic*

Nature/Culture: Anthropology and Science beyond the Two-Culture Divide. Berkeley: University of California Press, 2003.

Grandin, Greg. *Empire's Workshop: Latin America, the United States, and the Rise of the New Imperialism*. New York: Metropolitan Books, 2006.

Grandin, Greg. *The Last Colonial Massacre: Latin America in the Cold War*. Chicago: University of Chicago Press, 2004.

Green, Harvey. *Fit for America*. London: Johns Hopkins University Press, 1988.

Greene, Julie. *The Canal Builders: Making America's Empire at the Panama Canal*. New York: Penguin Books, 2010.

Griffen-Foley, Bridget. "From Tit-Bits to *Big Brother*: A Century of Audience Participation in the Media." *Media, Culture and Society* 26, no. 4 (2004): 533–48.

Gross, Ariela Julie. *What Blood Won't Tell: A History of Race on Trial in America*. Cambridge, MA: Harvard University Press, 2010.

Gusterson, Hugh. *People of the Bomb: Portraits of America's Nuclear Complex*. Minneapolis: University of Minnesota Press, 2004.

Guthrie-Shimizu, Sayuri. *Transpacific Field of Dreams: How Baseball Linked the United States and Japan in Peace and War*. Chapel Hill: University of North Carolina Press, 2012.

Haddow, Robert H. *Pavilions of Plenty: Exhibiting American Culture Abroad in the 1950s*. Washington, DC: Smithsonian Institution Press, 1997.

Hale, Nathan G. *The Rise and Crisis of Psychoanalysis in the United States*. New York: Oxford University Press, 1995.

Haley, Bruce. *The Healthy Body in Victorian Culture*. Cambridge: Harvard University Press, 1978.

Hamlin, Kimberly A. "The 'Case of a Bearded Woman': Hypertrichosis and the Construction of Gender in the Age of Darwin." *American Quarterly* 63, no. 4 (2011): 955–81.

Hamm, Mark S. *The Abandoned Ones: The Imprisonment and Uprising of the Mariel Boat People*. Boston, MA: Northeastern University Press, 1995.

Hansen, Thomas Blom, and Finn Stepputat, eds. *Sovereign Bodies: Citizens, Migrants, and States in the Postcolonial World*. Princeton, NJ: Princeton University Press, 2005.

Harrington, Oliver W. *Why I Left America and Other Essays*. Jackson: University Press of Mississippi, 1993.

Hawkins, Stephanie L. *American Iconographic*. Charlottesville: University of Virginia Press, 2010.

Heilbrun, Carolyn. *Toward a Recognition of Androgyny*. New York: Knopf, 1973.

Henriksen, Margot A. *Dr. Strangelove's America: Society and Culture in the Atomic Age*. Berkeley: University of California Press, 1997.

Hershfield, Joanne. *Imagining La Chica Moderna*. Durham, NC: Duke University Press, 2008.

Hixson, Walter L. *Parting the Curtain: Propaganda, Culture, and the Cold War, 1945–1961*. New York: St. Martin's Press, 1997.

Hodges, Graham. *Anna May Wong*. New York: Palgrave, 2004.

Hofer, Hans-Georg. "War Neurosis and Viennese Psychiatry in World War One." In *Uncovered Fields: Perspectives in First World War Studies*, edited by Jenny Macleod and Pierre Purseigle, 243–260. Boston, MA: Brill, 2004.

Hoffman, Annette R., ed. *Turnen and Sport: Transatlantic Transfers*. Munich: Waxman, 2004.

Hogan, Michael J., ed. *Hiroshima in History and Memory*. New York: Cambridge University Press, 1996.

Hoganson, Kristin L. "'As Bad Off as the Filipinos': U.S. Women Suffragists and the Imperial Issue at the Turn of the Twentieth Century." *Journal of Women's History* 13, no. 2 (2001): 9–33.

Hoganson, Kristin L. *Consumers' Imperium: The Global Production of American Domesticity, 1865–1920*. Chapel Hill: University of North Carolina Press, 2007.

Hoganson, Kristin L. *Fighting for American Manhood: How Gender Politics Provoked the Spanish-American and Philippine-American Wars*. New Haven, CT: Yale University Press, 1998.

Höhn, Maria. "Frau im Haus und Girl im *Spiegel*: Discourse on Women in the Interregnum Period of 1945–1949 and the Question of German Identity." *Central European History* 26 (1993): 57–91.

Höhn, Maria. "'We Will Never Go Back to the Old Way Again': Germany in the African-American Debate on Civil Rights." *Central European History* 41 (2008): 628–34.

Höhn, Maria. "GIS, Veronikas and Lucky Strikes: German Reactions to the American Presence in the Rhineland-Palatinate during the 1950s." PhD diss., University of Pennsylvania, 1995.

Höhn, Maria, and Martin Klimke. *A Breath of Freedom: The Civil Rights Struggle, African American GIS, and Germany*. New York: Palgrave Macmillan, 2010.

Höhn, Maria, and Seungsook Moon, eds. *Over There: Living with the U.S. Military Empire from World War Two to the Present*. Durham, NC: Duke University Press, 2010.

Hondagneu-Sotelo, Pierrette. "Women and Children First: New Directions in Anti-Immigrant Politics." *Socialist Review* 25, no. 1 (1995): 169–90.

Horsman, Reginald. *Race and Manifest Destiny: The Origins of American Racial Anglo-Saxonism*. Cambridge, MA: Harvard University Press, 1981.

Horton, Scott. "Kriegsraison or Military Necessity? The Bush Administration's Wilhelmine Attitude towards the Conduct of War." *Fordham International Law Journal* 30 (2006), http://ir.lawnet.fordham.edu/ilj/vol30/iss3/7.

Houck, David W., and Amos Kiewe. *FDR's Body Politics: The Rhetoric of Disability*. College Station: Texas A&M University Press, 2003.

Hufker, Brian, and Gray Cavender. "From Freedom Flotilla to America's Burden: The Social Construction of the Mariel Immigrants." *Sociological Quarterly* 31, no. 2 (1990): 321–35.

Hügel-Marshall, Ika. *Invisible Woman: Growing Up Black in Germany*. New York: Peter Lang, 2008.

Inda, Jonathan Xavier. *Targeting Immigrants: Government, Technology, and Ethics.* Malden, MA: Blackwell, 2006.

Iversen, Kristen. *Full Body Burden: Growing Up in the Nuclear Shadow of Rocky Flats.* New York: Crown, 2012.

Jacob, Wilson Chacko. *Working Out Egypt: Effendi Masculinity and Subject Formation in Colonial Modernity, 1870–1940.* Durham, NC: Duke University Press, 2011.

Jacobs, Margaret D. *Engendered Encounters: Feminism and Pueblo Cultures, 1879–1934.* Lincoln: University of Nebraska Press, 1999.

Jacobs, Margaret D. *White Mother to a Dark Race: Settler Colonialism, Maternalism, and the Removal of Indigenous Children in the American West and Australia, 1880–1940.* Lincoln: University of Nebraska Press, 2009.

Jacobs, Robert. "Reconstructing the Perpetrator's Soul by Reconstructing the Victim's Body: The Portrayal of the 'Hiroshima Maidens' by the Mainstream Media in the United States." *Intersections: Gender and Security in Asia and the Pacific* 24 (June 2010), http://intersections.anu.edu.au/issue24/intro.htm.

Jacobs, Seth. *America's Miracle Man in Vietnam: Ngo Dinh Diem, Religion, Race, and the U.S. Intervention in Southeast Asia.* Durham, NC: Duke University Press, 2005.

Jacobson, Matthew Frye. *Barbarian Virtues: The United States Encounters Foreign Peoples at Home and Abroad, 1876–1917.* New York: Hill and Wang, 2000.

Jacobson, Matthew Frye, and Gaspar González. *What Have They Built You to Do? The Manchurian Candidate and Cold War America.* Minneapolis: University of Minnesota Press, 2006.

James, C. L. R. *Beyond a Boundary.* Durham, NC: Duke University Press, 1993.

Jameson, Fredric. *Postmodernism, or The Cultural Logic of Late Capitalism.* Durham, NC: Duke University Press, 1991.

Jayasuirya, Laksiri, and Kee Pookong. *The Asianization of Australia? Some Facts about the Myths.* Melbourne: Melbourne University Press, 1999.

Jennings, Eric T. "From Indochine to Indochic: The Lang Bain/Dalat Palace Hotel and French Colonial Leisure, Power and Culture." *Modern Asian Studies* 37, no. 1 (2003): 159–94.

Johnston, Jessica R. *The American Body in Context: An Anthology.* Wilmington, DE: Scholarly Resources, 2001.

Johnston, Rose, ed. *Half-Lives and Half-Truths: Confronting the Radioactive Legacies of the Cold War.* Santa Fe, NM: School for Advanced Research Press, 2007.

Jones, Colin, and Roy Porter, eds. *Reassessing Foucault: Power, Knowledge, and the Body.* London: Routledge, 1994.

Jones, Edgar, and Simon Wessely. "Psychiatric Battle Casualties: An Intra- and Interwar Comparison." *British Journal of Psychiatry* 178 (2001): 242–47.

Kaplan, Amy. *The Anarchy of Empire in the Making of U.S. Culture.* Cambridge: Harvard University Press, 2005.

Kaplan, E. Ann. *Looking for the Other: Feminism, Film, and the Imperial Gaze*. New York: Routledge, 1997.

Karlin, Wayne. *Wandering Souls: Journeys with the Dead and the Living in Vietnam*. New York: Nation Books, 2009.

Kasson, John F. *Houdini, Tarzan, and the Perfect Man*. New York: Hill and Wang, 2001.

Kats, John. *The Will to Civilization: An Inquiry into the Principles of Historic Change*. London: Secker and Warburg, 1938.

Kelly, John. "Exclusionary America: Jackie Robinson, Decolonization and Baseball Not Black and White." In *Sport and American Society: Exceptionalism, Insularity, and "Imperialism,"* edited by Mark Dyreson and J. A. Mangan, 91–114. New York: Routledge, 2007.

Kelly, M. G. E. "International Biopolitics: Foucault, Globalisation and Imperialism." *Theoria* 57, no. 123 (2010): 1–26.

Kershner, R. B., Jr. "Degeneration: The Explanatory Nightmare." *Georgia Review* 40 (Summer 1986): 416–44.

Kestling, Robert W. "Blacks under the Swastika: A Research Note." *Journal of Negro History* 83 (Winter 1998): 84–99.

Keys, Barbara. *Globalizing Sport: National Rivalry and International Community in the 1930s*. Cambridge: Harvard University Press, 2006.

Kimball, Warren F., ed. *Churchill and Roosevelt: The Complete Correspondence*. Vol. 3. Princeton, NJ: Princeton University Press, 1987.

Kimball, Warren F. *Forged in War: Roosevelt, Churchill, and the Second World War*. New York: William Morrow, 1997.

Kimmel, Michael. *Manhood in America: A Cultural History*. New York: Oxford University Press, 2011.

Kinnard, Douglas. *The War Managers*. Hanover, NH: University Press of New England, 1977.

Kirchfeld, Friedhelm, and Wade Boyle. *Nature Doctors: Pioneers in Naturopathic Medicine*. Portland, OR: Medicina Biologica, 1994.

Kitamura, Hiroshi. *Screening Enlightenment: Hollywood and the Cultural Reconstruction of Defeated Japan*. Ithaca, NY: Cornell University Press, 2010.

Klein, Christina. "Family Ties and Political Obligation: The Discourse of Adoption and the Cold War Commitment to Asia." In *Cold War Constructions: The Political Culture of United States Imperialism, 1945–1966*, edited by Christian Appy, 35–66. Amherst: University of Massachusetts Press, 2000.

Kline, Tiny. *Circus Queen and Tinker Bell: The Life of Tiny Kline*, edited by Janet M. Davis. Urbana: University of Illinois Press, 2008.

Kohn, Richard H. "History at Risk: The Case of the Enola Gay." In *History Wars: The Enola Gay and Other Battles for the American Past*, edited by Edward Linenthal and Tom Engelhardt, 140–70. New York: Metropolitan, 1996.

Krafft-Ebing, R. *Psychopathia sexualis: Mit besonderer Berucksichtigung der contraren sexualempfindung. Eine klinisch-forensische Studie*. Stuttgart: Verlag F. Enke, 1892.

Kramer, Paul A. *The Blood of Government: Race, Empire, the United States, and the Philippines.* Chapel Hill: University of North Carolina Press, 2006.

Kramer, Paul A. "Historias Transimperiales: Raíces Espanoles del Estado Colonial Estadounidense en Filipinas." In *Filipinas: Un País Entre Dos Imperios,* edited by María Dolores Elizalde and Josep Ma. Delgado, 125–41. Barcelona: CSIC, 2011.

Kramer, Paul A. "Power and Connection: Imperial Histories of the United States in the World," *American Historical Review* 116, no. 5 (December 2011): 1–44.

Kramer, Paul A. "Reflex Actions: Colonialism, Corruption and the Politics of Technocracy in the Early 20th Century United States." In *Challenging U.S. Foreign Policy: America and the World in the Long Twentieth Century,* edited by Bevan Sewell and Scott Lucas, 14–35. New York: Palgrave Macmillan, 2011.

Kraut, Alan M. *Germs, Genes, and the "Immigrant Menace."* New York: Basic Books, 1994.

Kroes, Rob. "American Empire and Cultural Imperialism." In *Rethinking American History in a Global Age,* edited by Thomas Bender, 295–313. Berkeley: University of California Press, 1993.

Kudlick, Catherine J. "Disability History: Why We Need Another 'Other.'" *American Historical Review* 108 (June 2003): 763–93.

Kuleshov, Lev. *Kuleshov on Film: Writings,* edited and translated by Ronald Levaco. Berkeley: University of California Press, 1974.

Kwon, Heonik. *The Ghosts of War in Vietnam.* Cambridge: Cambridge University Press, 2008.

LaFeber, Walter. *Michael Jordan and the New Global Capitalism.* New York: Norton, 1999.

Lake, Marilyn, and Henry Reynolds. *Drawing the Global Colour Line: White Men's Countries and the International Challenge of Racial Equality.* New York: Cambridge University Press, 2008.

Lam, Quang Thi. *The Twenty-five Year Century: A South Vietnamese General Remembers the Indochina War to the Fall of Saigon.* Denton: University of Texas Press, 2001.

Larzelere, Alex. *The 1980 Cuban Boatlift: Castro's Ploy—America's Dilemma.* Washington, DC: National Defense University Press, 1988.

Latham, Michael E. *The Right Kind of Revolution: Modernization, Development, and U.S. Foreign Policy from the Cold War to the Present.* Ithaca, NY: Cornell University Press, 2011.

Laville, Helen. "'Our Country Endangered by Underwear': Fashion, Femininity, and the Seduction Narrative in *Ninotchka* and *Silk Stockings.*" *Diplomatic History* 30 (Sept. 2006): 623–44.

Lears, Jackson. *Fables of Abundance: A Cultural History of Advertising in America.* New York: Basic Books, 1994.

Lears, Jackson. *Rebirth of a Nation: The Making of Modern America, 1877–1920.* New York: HarperCollins, 2009.

Le Bon, Gustave. *The Psychology of the Great War.* New York: Macmillan, 1916.

Lee, Erika. *At America's Gates: Chinese Immigration During the Exclusion Era, 1882–1943.* Chapel Hill: University of North Carolina Press, 2003.

Lee, Robert G. *Orientals: Asian Americans in Popular Culture.* Philadelphia, PA: Temple University Press, 1999.

Leed, Eric. "Fateful Memories: Industrialized War and Traumatic Neuroses." *Journal of Contemporary History* 25, no. 1 (2000): 85–100.

Leed, Eric J. *No Man's Land: Combat and Identity in World War I.* Cambridge: Cambridge University Press, 1979.

Leese, Peter. *Shell Shock: Traumatic Neurosis and the British Soldiers of the First World War.* New York: Palgrave, 2002.

Leffler, Melvyn P., and Odd Arne Westad, eds. *The Cambridge History of the Cold War.* Vol. 3. Cambridge: Cambridge University Press, 2010.

Lehman, Jeffrey, ed. *Gale Encyclopedia of Multicultural America.* 2nd edition. New York: Gale Group, 2000.

Leibfried, Philip, and Chei Mi Lane. *Anna May Wong: A Complete Guide to Her Film, Stage, Radio, and Television Work.* New York: McFarland, 2003.

Leong, Karen. *China Mystique: Pearl S. Buck, Anna May Wong, Mayling Soong, and the Transformation of American Orientalism.* Berkeley: University of California Press, 2005.

Leong, Karen J., and Judy Tzu-Chun Wu. "Filling the Rice Bowls of China: Staging Humanitarian Relief during the Sino-Japanese War." In *Chinese Americans and the Politics of Race and Culture,* edited by Sucheng Chan and Madeline Hsu, 132–148. Philadelphia, PA: Temple University Press, 2008.

Lerner, Paul. *Hysterical Men: War, Psychiatry, and the Politics of Trauma in Germany, 1890–1930.* Ithaca: Cornell University Press, 2003.

Levine, Philippa. *Prostitution, Race and Politics: Policing Venereal Disease in the British Empire.* New York: Routledge, 2003.

Lifton, Robert Jay, and Greg Mitchell. *Hiroshima in America.* New York: Harper's Sons, 1995.

Lim, Shirley Jennifer. *A Feeling of Belonging: Asian American Women's Public Culture.* New York: New York University Press, 2006.

Lipman, Jana K. *Guantánamo: A Working-Class History between Empire and Revolution.* Berkeley: University of California Press, 2009.

Llanes, José. *Cuban Americans: Masters of Survival.* Cambridge, Mass.: Abt Books, 1982.

Lomazow, Steven, and Eric Fettmann. *FDR's Deadly Secret.* New York: Public Affairs, 2009.

Long, Austin. "Doctrine of Eternal Recurrence: The U.S. Military and Counterinsurgency Doctrine, 1960–1970 and 2003–2006." RAND Counterinsurgency Study, Paper 6, prepared for the Office of the Secretary of Defense. Santa Monica, CA: RAND Corporation, 2008.

Longmore, Paul K., and Lauri Umansky, eds. *The New Disability History: American Perspectives.* New York: New York University Press, 2001.

Loosbrock, Richard D. "Mal Whitfield." In *African Americans in Sports*, edited by David K. Wiggins. Armonk, NY: Sharpe Reference, 2004.

Lowe, Lisa. *Immigrant Acts: On Asian American Cultural Politics*. Durham, NC: Duke University Press, 1996.

Lusane, Clarence. *Hitler's Black Victims: The Historical Experiences of Afro-Germans, European Blacks, Africans, and African Americans in the Nazi Era*. New York: Routledge, 2002.

MacCurdy, John. *War Neuroses*. Cambridge: Cambridge University Press, 1918.

Macfadden, Mary, and Emile Gauvreau. *Dumbbells and Carrot Strips*. New York: Holt, 1953.

Mangan, J. A., ed. *Superman Supreme: Fascist Body as Political Icon—Global Fascism*. London: Frank Cass, 2000.

Marchand, Roland. *Advertising the American Dream: Making Way for Modernity, 1920–1940*. Berkeley: University of California Press, 1986.

Markel, Howard, and Alexandra Minna Stern. "Which Face? Whose Nation? Immigration, Public Health, and the Construction of Disease at America's Ports and Borders, 1891–1928." *American Behavioral Scientist* 42, no. 9 (1999): 1314–31.

Marks, John. *The Search for the "Manchurian Candidate."* New York: Norton, 1979.

Marks, Sally. "Black Watch on the Rhine: A Study in Propaganda, Prejudice, and Prurience." *European Studies Review* 13 (1983): 297–333.

Markus, Andrew. "Chinese Immigration under the 'White Australia Policy.'" In *Histories of the Chinese in Australasia and the South Pacific*, edited by P. Macgregor, 354–360. Melbourne: Museum of Chinese Australian History, 1995.

Marr, David. *Vietnam 1945: The Quest for Power*. Berkeley: University of California Press, 1995.

Martin, Charles D. *The White African American Body: A Cultural and Literary Exploration*. New Brunswick, NJ: Rutgers University Press, 2002.

Massumi, Brian. "National Enterprise Emergency: Steps toward an Ecology of Powers." In *Beyond Biopolitics: Essays on the Governance of Life and Death*, edited by Patricia Ticineto Clough and Craig Willse, 25–65. Durham, NC: Duke University Press, 2011.

Matthews, George R. *America's First Olympics: The St. Louis Games of 1904*. St. Louis: University of Missouri Press, 2005.

Matthews, Jill Julius. "Building the Body Beautiful." *Australian Feminist Studies* 2, no. 5 (1987): 17–34.

May, Elaine Tyler. *Homeward Bound: American Families in the Cold War Era*. New York: Basic Books, 1988.

Mayer, Jane. *The Dark Side: The Inside Story of How the War on Terror Turned into a War on American Ideals*. New York: Doubleday, 2008.

McAlister, Melani. *Epic Encounters: Culture, Media, and U.S. Interests in the Middle East, 1945–2000*. Berkeley: University of California Press, 2001.

McCoy, Alfred W. *A Question of Torture: CIA Interrogation from the Cold War to the War on Terror*. New York: Holt, 2006.

McCoy, Alfred W. *Torture and Impunity: The U.S. Doctrine of Coercive Interrogations*. Madison: University of Wisconsin Press, 2012.

McCoy, Alfred W., and Francisco A. Scarano. *The Colonial Crucible: Empire in the Making of the Modern American State*. Madison: University of Wisconsin Press, 2009.

McEuen, Melissa A. *Making War, Making Women: Femininity and Duty on the American Home Front, 1941–1945*. Athens: University of George Press, 2011.

McKiernan-Gonzalez, J. "Fevered Measures: Race, Contagious Disease and Community Formation on the Texas-Mexico Border, 1880–1923." PhD diss., University of Michigan, 2002.

Melossi, Dario. "Michel Foucault and the Obsolescent State: Between the American Century and the Dawn of the European Union." In *Michel Foucault and Power Today: International Multidisciplinary Studies in the History of the Present*, edited by Alain Beaulieu and David Gabbard, 3–12. Oxford: Lexington Books, 2006.

Metcalf, Eugene W. "Circus Toys in the Gilded Age." In *The American Circus*, edited by Susan Weber, Kenneth L. Ames, and Matthew Wittmann, 358–381. New York: Bard Graduate Center and Yale University Press, 2012.

Metzger, Sean. "Patterns of Resistance? Anna May Wong and the Fabrication of China in American Cinema of the Late 30s." *Quarterly Review of Film and Video* 23 (2006): 1–11.

Micale, Mark S., and Paul Frederick Lerner, eds. *Traumatic Pasts: History, Psychiatry, and Trauma in the Modern Age, 1870–1930*. New York: Cambridge University Press, 2001.

Miller, Jake C. *The Plight of Haitian Refugees*. New York: Praeger, 1984.

Miller, Toby, et al. *Global Hollywood: No. 2*. London: British Film Institute, 2008.

Mills, James H., ed. *Subaltern Sports: Politics and Sport in South Asia*. London: Anthem Press, 2005.

Mitchell, Greg. *Atomic Cover-up: Two U.S. Soldiers, Hiroshima and Nagasaki, and the Greatest Movie Never Made*. New York: Sinclair, 2011.

Mitchell, Timothy. *Rule of Experts: Egypt, Techno-politics, Modernity*. Berkeley: University of California Press, 2002.

Mizruchi, Susan L. *The Rise of Multicultural America: Economy and Print Culture, 1865–1915*. Chapel Hill: University of North Carolina Press, 2008.

Molina, Natalia. *Fit to Be Citizens? Public Health and Race in Los Angeles, 1879–1939*. Berkeley: University of California Press, 2006.

Moran, Lord. *Churchill at War, 1940–1945*. New York: Carroll and Graf, 2002.

Moreno, Jonathan D. *Mind Wars: Brain Research and National Defense*. New York: Dana Press, 2006.

Morgan, Jennifer. *Laboring Women: Reproduction and Gender in New World Slavery*. Philadelphia: University of Pennsylvania Press, 2004.

Mormino, Gary Ross. "The Playing Fields of St. Louis: Italian Immigrants and Sport." *Journal of Sport History* 9, no. 2 (1982): 5–16.

Morris, Andrew D. *Colonial Project, National Game: A History of Baseball in Taiwan.* Berkeley: University of California Press, 2010.

Morris, Andrew D. *Marrow of the Nation: A History of Sport and Physical Culture in Republican China.* Berkeley: University of California Press, 2004.

Morris, Andrew D. "Native Songs and Dances: Southeast Asia in a Greater Chinese Sporting Community, 1920–1948." *Journal of Southeast Asian Studies* 31, no. 1 (2000): 48–69.

Morton, H. V. *Atlantic Meeting.* London: Methuen, 1943.

Mosse, George L. *The Image of Man: The Creation of Modern Masculinity.* New York: Oxford University Press, 1998.

Mosse, George L. "Shell-Shock as a Social Disease." *Journal of Contemporary History* 35, no. 1 (January 2000): 101–8.

Nagel, Joane. "Masculinities and Nations." In *Handbook of Studies on Men and Masculinities,* edited by Michael S. Kimmel, Jeff Hearn, and Robert W. Connell, 397–413. London: Sage, 2004.

Nalty, Bernard C., and Morris J. MacGregor. *Blacks in the Military: Essential Documents.* Wilmington, DE: Scholarly Resources, 1981.

Nandy, Ashish. *The Tao of Cricket: On Games of Destiny and the Destiny of Games.* New York: Viking, 1989.

Nelson, Keith L. "The Black Horror on the Rhine: Race as a Factor in Post–World War I Diplomacy." *Journal of Modern History* 42 (Apr. 1970): 606–27.

Nenno, Nancy, Tim Bergfelder, Erica Carter, and Deniz Goturk, eds. *The German Cinema Book.* London: BFI, 2003.

Ngai, Mae M. *Impossible Subjects: Illegal Aliens and the Making of Modern America.* Princeton, NJ: Princeton University Press, 2004.

Nichols, Lee. *Breakthrough on the Color Front.* 2nd edition. Colorado Springs: Three Continents Press, 1993.

Nielsen, Kim E. *A Disability History of the United States.* New York: Beacon, 2012.

Nomura, Gail. "Beyond a Level Playing Field: The Significance of Pre–World War II Japanese American Baseball in the Yakima Valley." In *Bearing Dreams, Shaping Visions: Asian Pacific American Perspectives,* edited by Linda Revilla et al., 15–31. Pullman: Washington State University Press, 1993.

Obermeier, Karin. "Afro-German Women: Recording Their Own History." *New German Critique* 46 (Winter 1989): 172–80.

Oguntoye, Katharina, and May Opitz. "Showing Our Colours: The Testimony of Two Afro German Women." In *Invisible Europeans? Black People in the "New Europe,"* edited by Les Back and Anoop Nayak, 94–119. Birmingham, U.K.: AFFOR, 1993.

Oguntoye, Katharina, May Opitz, and Dagmar Schultz, eds. *Showing Our Colors: Afro-German Women Speak Out.* Amherst: University of Massachusetts Press, 1992.

Omi, Michael, and Howard Winant. *Racial Formation in the United States*. 2nd edition. New York: Routledge, 1994.

Ong, Aihwa. *Neoliberalism as Exception: Mutations in Citizenship and Sovereignty.* Durham, NC: Duke University Press, 2006.

Ong, Aihwa, and Michael G. Peletz, eds. *Bewitching Women, Pious Men: Gender and Body Politics in Southeast Asia.* Berkeley: University of California Press, 1995.

Osgood, Kenneth. *Total Cold War and the United States and Public Diplomacy.* Lawrence: University Press of Kansas, 2006.

Ottosson, A. "The First Historical Movements of Kinesiology." *International Journal of the History of Sport* 27, no. 11 (2010): 1892–919.

Paisley, Fiona. "'Unnecessary Crimes and Tragedies': Race, Gender and Sexuality in Australian Policies of Aboriginal Child Removal." In *Gender, Sexuality and Colonial Modernities*, edited by Antoinette Burton, 134–147. London: Routledge, 1999.

Parascandola, John. "Quarantining Women: Venereal Disease Rapid Treatment Centers in World War II America." *Bulletin of the History of Medicine* 83 (Fall 2009): 431–59.

Park, Lisa Sun-Hee. "Perpetuation of Poverty through Public Charge." *Denver University Law Review* 78 (2001): 1161–77.

Pelley, Patricia. "'Barbarians' and 'Younger Brothers': The Remaking of Race in Postcolonial Vietnam." *Journal of Southeast Asian Studies* 29, no. 2 (1988): 374–91.

Pelley, Patricia. *Postcolonial Vietnam: New Histories of the National Past.* Durham, NC: Duke University Press, 2002.

Pells, Richard H. *Modernist America: Art, Music, Movies, and the Globalization of American Culture.* New Haven, CT: Yale University Press, 2011.

Pence, Katherine. "The 'Fräuleins' Meet the 'Amis': Americanization of German Women in the Reconstruction of the West German State." *Michigan Feminist Studies* 7 (1992–93): 83–108.

Pendar, Kenneth. *Adventure in Diplomacy.* New York: Dodd, Mead, 1945.

Perez, Louis A., Jr. "Between Baseball and Bullfighting: The Quest for Nationality in Cuba, 1868–1898." *Journal of American History* 81, no. 2 (1994): 493–517.

Pick, Daniel. *Faces of Degeneration: A European Disorder, 1848–1918.* Cambridge: Cambridge University Press, 1993.

Pine, Lisa. *Education in Nazi Germany.* Oxford, UK: Berg, 2010.

Pitt, Kristen E. *Body, Nation, and Narrative in the Americas.* New York: Palgrave Macmillan, 2010.

Playne, Caroline E. *Neuroses of the Nations.* London: G. Allen and Unwin, 1925.

Playne, Caroline E. *The Prewar Mind in Britain: An Historical Review.* London: Allen and Unwin, 1928.

Plokhy, S. M., *Yalta: The Price of Peace.* New York: Viking, 2010.

Plummer, Brenda Gayle. ed. *Window on Freedom: Race, Civil Rights, and Foreign Affairs, 1945–1988*. Chapel Hill: University of North Carolina Press, 2003.

Pommerin, Reiner. "The Fate of the Mixed Blood Children in Germany." *German Studies Review* 5, no. 3 (1982): 315–23.

Pratt, Mary Louise. *Imperial Eyes: Travel Writing and Transculturation*. New York: Routledge, 1992.

Pratt, Mary Louise. *Imperial Eyes: Travel Writing and Transculturation*, 2nd edition. New York: Routledge, 2007.

Prevots, Naima. *Dance for Export*. Middletown, CT: Wesleyan University Press, 1999.

Putney, Clifford. *Muscular Christianity: Manhood and Sports in Protestant America, 1880–1920*. Cambridge: Harvard University Press, 2001.

Putzi, Jennifer. *Identifying Marks: Race, Gender, and the Marked Body in Nineteenth-Century America*. Athens: University of Georgia Press, 2006.

Rabe, Stephen G. *The Killing Zone: The United States Wages Cold War in Latin America*. New York: Oxford, 2012.

Rafael, Vicente. "White Love: Surveillance and National Resistance in the U.S. Colonization of the Philippines." In *Cultures of United States Imperialism*, edited by Amy Kaplan and Donald E. Pease, 185–218. Durham, NC: Duke University Press, 1993.

Rail, Geneviéve, and Jean Harvey. "Body at Work: Michel Foucault and the Sociology of Sport." *Sociology of Sport Journal* 12, no. 2 (1995): 164–79.

Reagan, Ronald. "First Inaugural Address, Tuesday, January 20, 1981." In *Inaugural Addresses of the Presidents of the United States*. Washington, DC: U.S. Government Printing Office, 1989.

Reagan, Ronald. *The Reagan Diaries*, edited by Douglas Brinkley. New York: HarperCollins, 2007.

Reeves-Ellington, Barbara, Kathryn Kish-Sklar, and Connie Shemo, eds. *Competing Kingdoms: Women, Mission, Nation and the American Protestant Empire, 1812–1960*. Durham, NC: Duke University Press, 2010.

Reich, Jacqueline. "The World's Most Perfectly Developed Man." *Men and Masculinities* 12, no. 4 (2010): 444–61.

Reilly, Michael F. *Reilly of the White House*. New York: Simon and Schuster, 1947.

Reisler, Mark. *By the Sweat of Their Brow: Mexican Immigrant Labor in the United States, 1900–1940*. Westport, CT: Greenwood Press, 1976.

Rejali, Darius M. *Torture and Democracy*. Princeton: Princeton University Press, 2007.

Renda, Mary A. *Taking Haiti: Military Occupation and the Culture of U.S. Imperialism, 1915–1940*. Chapel Hill: University of North Carolina Press, 2001.

Richardson, Charles. *From Churchill's Secret Circle to the BBC*. Washington, DC: Brassey's, 1991.

Rigdon, William M. *White House Sailor*. New York: Doubleday, 1962.

Rivera, Mario Antonio. *Decision and Structure: U.S. Refugee Policy in the Mariel Crisis.* Lanham, Md.: University Press of America, 1991.

Robinson, Rebecca J. "American Sportswear: A Study of the Origins and Women Designers from the 1930's to the 1960's." MDes thesis, University of Cincinnati.

Robison, Mark A. "Recreation in World War I and the Practice of Play in *One of Ours.*" *Cather Studies* 6 (2006): 160–83.

Rodgers, Daniel T. *Atlantic Crossings: Social Politics in a Progressive Age.* Cambridge: Belknap Press of Harvard University Press, 2000.

Rogin, Michael. *Blackface, White Noise: Jewish Immigrants in the Hollywood Melting Pot.* Berkeley: University of California Press, 1996.

Roosevelt, Eliott. *As He Saw It.* New York: Duell, Sloan and Pearce, 1946.

Rosas, Ana Elizabeth. "Flexible Families: Bracero Families' Lives across Cultures, Communities, and Countries, 1942–1964." PhD diss., University of Southern California, 2006.

Rose, Sonya O. "Sex, Citizenship, and the Nation in World War II Britain." *American Historical Review* 103 (Oct. 1998): 1147–76.

Rosenberg, Emily S. "Consumer Capitalism and the End of the Cold War." In *The Cambridge History of the Cold War,* vol. 3, edited by Melvyn P. Leffler and Odd Arne Westad, 913–56. Cambridge: Cambridge University Press, 2010.

Rosenberg, Emily S. "'Foreign Affairs' after World War II: Connecting Sexual and International Politics." *Diplomatic History* 18 (Jan. 1994): 59–70.

Rosenberg, Emily S. *Spreading the American Dream.* New York: Hill and Wang, 1982.

Ross, Chad. *Naked Germany: Health, Race and the Nation.* Oxford: Berg, 2005.

Ross, Stephen J. *Working-Class Hollywood: Silent Film and the Shaping of Class in America.* Princeton: Princeton University Press, 1998.

Rothfels, Nigel. *Savages and Beasts: The Birth of the Modern Zoo.* Baltimore, MD: Johns Hopkins University Press, 2002.

Rothman, David J. *Conscience and Convenience: The Asylum and Its Alternatives in Progressive America.* New York: Aldine de Gruyter, 2002.

Rotter, Andrew J. *Hiroshima: The World's Bomb.* New York: Oxford University Press, 2009.

Rotundo, E. Anthony. *American Manhood: Transformations in Masculinity from the Revolution to the Modern Era.* New York: Basic Books, 1994.

Runstedtler, Theresa. "Visible Men: African American Boxers, the New Negro, and the Global Color Line." *Radical History Review* 103 (Winter 2009): 59–81.

Rydell, Robert. *All the World's a Fair: Visions of Empire at American International Expositions, 1876–1916.* Chicago: University of Chicago Press, 1987.

Rydell, Robert W., and Rob Kroes. *Buffalo Bill in Bologna: The Americanization of the World, 1869–1922.* Chicago: University of Chicago Press, 2005.

Salazar, James. *Bodies of Reform.* New York: New York University Press, 2010.

Sandburg, Carl. *Always the Young Strangers*. New York: Harcourt, Brace, 1952.

Saunders, Frances. *The Cultural Cold War*. New York: New Press, 2000.

Sawyer, Frederic H. *The Inhabitants of the Philippines*. New York: C. Scribner's Sons, 1900.

Scarry, Elaine. *The Body in Pain: The Making and Unmaking of the World*. New York: Oxford University Press, 1985.

Schiller, Herbert I. *Mass Communication and American Empire*. 1969. 2nd edition. Boulder, CO: Westview Press, 1992.

Schlesinger, Andrew, and Stephen Schlesinger. *Journals 1952–2000: Arthur M. Schlesinger, Jr.* New York: Penguin, 2007.

Schmitt, Carl. *Political Theology: Four Chapters on the Concept of Sovereignty*, edited by George Schwab, translated by Tracy Strong. Chicago: University of Chicago Press, 2006.

Schroer, Timothy L. *Recasting Race after World War II: Germans and African Americans in American-Occupied Germany*. Boulder: University Press of Colorado, 2007.

Schweitzer, Marlis. "American Fashions for American Women: The Rise and Fall of Fashion Nationalism." In *Producing Fashion: Commerce, Culture, and Consumers*, edited by Regina Lee Blaszczyk, 130–49. Philadelphia: University of Pennsylvania Press, 2007.

Scott, James C. *Seeing Like a State: How Certain Schemes to Improve the Human Condition Have Failed*. New Haven, CT: Yale University Press, 1998.

Scott, Joan W. "Experience." In *Feminists Theorize the Political*, edited by Judith Butler and Joan W. Scott, 22–40. New York: Routledge, 1992.

Sedgwick, Eve Kosofsky. *Between Men*. New York: Columbia University Press, 1985.

Serlin, David. *Replaceable You: Engineering the Body in Postwar America*. Chicago: University of Chicago Press, 2004.

Shah, Nayan. *Contagious Divides: Epidemics and Race in San Francisco's Chinatown*. Berkeley: University of California Press, 2001.

Sheehan, Neil. "Prisoners of the Past." *New Yorker*, May 24, 1993, 46–51.

Sherwood, Robert Emmet. *Roosevelt and Hopkins: An Intimate History*. New York: Enigma Books, 2008.

Shibusawa, Naoko. *America's Geisha Ally: Reimagining the Japanese Enemy*. Cambridge: Harvard University Press, 2006.

Shimizu, Celine Parrenas. *The Hypersexuality of Race: Performing Asian/American Women on Screen and Scene*. Durham, NC: Duke University Press, 2007.

Shock, Myra. "Healing the Patient, Serving the State: Medical Ethics and the British Medical Profession in the Great War." PhD diss., University of California, Berkeley, 2000.

Shukert, Elfrieda Berthiaume, and Barbara Smith Scibetta. *War Brides of World War II*. Novato, CA: Presidio, 1988.

Siems, Larry. *The Torture Report: What the Documents Say about America's Post-9/11 Torture Program*. New York: OR Books, 2011.

Sikkink, Katheryn. "Bush Administration Noncompliance with the Prohibition on Torture and Cruel and Degrading Treatment." In *Bringing Human Rights Home: From Civil Rights to Human Rights*, vol. 2, edited by Cynthia Soohoo, Catherine Albisa, and Martha F. Davis, 187–208. Westport, CT: Praeger, 2008.

Silverberg, Miriam. *Erotic Grotesque Nonsense: The Mass Culture of Japanese Modern Times.* Berkeley: University of California Press, 2006.

Simpson, Bradley R. *Economists with Guns: Authoritarian Development and U.S.-Indonesian Relations, 1960–1968.* Palo Alto, CA: Stanford University Press, 2008.

Singer, Peter W. *Wired for War: The Robotics Revolution and Conflict in the 21st Century.* New York: Penguin, 2009.

Singleton, Mark. *Yoga Body.* Oxford: Oxford University Press, 2010.

Smith, Graham. *When Jim Crow Met John Bull: Black American Soldiers in World War II Britain.* New York: St. Martin's Press, 1987.

Smith, Jean Edward. *FDR.* New York: Random House, 2007.

Smulyan, Susan. *Popular Ideologies: Mass Culture at Mid-Century.* Philadelphia: University of Pennsylvania Press, 2007.

Solis, Hilda. "Foreword to Disparities Special Issue." *American Journal of Industrial Medicine* 53, no. 2 (2010): 81.

Sollinger, Rickie. "Race and 'Value': Black and White Illegitimate Babies in the U.S.A., 1945–1965." *Gender and History* 4 (Autumn 1992): 348–50.

Sollinger, Rickie. *Wake Up Little Susie: Single Pregnancy and Race before Roe v. Wade.* New York: Routledge, 1992.

Sontag, Susan. *Regarding the Pain of Others.* New York: Picador, 2004.

Staiger, Janet. *Media Reception Studies.* New York: New York University Press, 2001.

Stansell, Christine. *American Moderns.* Princeton: Princeton University Press, 2009.

Statler, Kathryn C. *Replacing France: The Origins of American Intervention in Vietnam.* Lexington: University Press of Kentucky, 2007.

Stern, Alexandra Minna. "Buildings, Boundaries, and Blood: Medicalization and Nation-Building on the U.S.-Mexican Border, 1910–1930." *Hispanic American Historical Review* 79, no. 1 (1999): 41–81.

Stern, Alexandra Minna. *Eugenic Nation: Faults and Frontiers of Better Breeding in Modern America.* Berkeley: University of California Press, 2005.

Stern, Steve J. *Battling for Hearts and Minds: Memory Struggles in Pinochet's Chile, 1973–1988.* Durham, NC: Duke University Press, 2006.

Sternheimer, Karen. *Celebrity Culture and the American Dream: Stardom and Social Mobility.* New York: Routledge, 2011.

Stibbe, Matthew. "Women and the Nazi State." *History Today* 43 (Nov. 1993): 35–40.

Stokes, Melvin, and Richard Maltby, eds. *Hollywood Abroad: Audiences and Cultural Exchange.* London: British Film Institute, 2008.

Stoler, Ann Laura. *Haunted by Empire: Geographies of Intimacy in North American History.* Durham, NC: Duke University Press, 2004.

Stoler, Ann Laura. *Race and the Education of Desire: Foucault's History of Sexuality and the Colonial Order of Things.* Durham, NC: Duke University Press, 1995.

Sweet, John Wood. *Bodies Politic: Negotiating Race in the American North, 1730–1830.* Baltimore: Johns Hopkins University Press, 2003.

Takacs, Stacy. *Terrorism TV: Popular Entertainment in Post-9/11 America.* Lawrence: University Press of Kansas, 2012.

Taylor, Bryan C., ed. *Nuclear Legacies: Communication, Controversy, and the U.S. Nuclear Weapons Complex.* Lanham, MD.: Lexington Books, 2007.

Terami-Wada, Motoe. "Karayuki-San of Manila: 1890–1920." *Philippine Studies* 34 (1986).

Thacker, Andrew. *Moving through Modernity: Space and Geography in Modernism.* Manchester, UK: Manchester University Press, 2003.

Thacker, Eugene. "Nomos, Nosos and Bios." *Culture Machine* 7 (2005).

Thayer, Stuart. "The Anti-Circus Laws in Connecticut, 1773–1840." *Bandwagon: The Journal of the Circus Historical Society* 20 (Jan.–Feb. 1976): 18–20.

Thayer, Stuart. "Legislating the Shows: Vermont, 1824–1933." *Bandwagon* 25 (July–Aug. 1981): 20–22.

Thomas, Damion. "'The Good Negroes': African-American Athletes and the Cultural Cold War, 1945–1968." PhD diss., University of California, Los Angeles, 2002.

Thomas, Damion. "Playing the 'Race Card': U.S. Foreign Policy and the Integration of Sports." In *East Plays West: Sport and the Cold War,* edited by Stephen Wagg and David L. Andrews, 207–21. New York: Routledge, 2007.

Thomas, Gregory M. *Treating the Trauma of the Great War: Soldiers, Civilians, and Psychiatry in France, 1914–1940.* Baton Rouge: Louisiana State University Press, 2009.

Thompson, Holland, ed. *The Book of History: The World's Greatest War,* Vol. 3: *The Events of 1918: The Armistice and the Peace Treaties.* New York: Grolier Society, 1921.

Thomson, Rosemarie Garland. *Extraordinary Bodies.* New York: Columbia University Press, 1997.

Todd, Jan. "Bernarr Macfadden: Reformer of the Feminine Form." *Journal of Sport History* 14, no. 1 (1987): 61–75.

Trachtenberg, Alan. *The Incorporation of America: Culture and Society in the Gilded Age.* New York: Hill and Wang, 1982.

Tröger, Anne-Marie. "Between Rape and Prostitution: Survival Strategies and Chances of Emancipation for Berlin Women after World War II." In *Women in Culture and Politics,* edited by Judith Friedlander, Blanche Wiesen Cook, Alice Kesler-Harris, and Carroll Smith-Rosenberg, 97–120. Bloomington: University of Indiana Press, 1986.

Trouillot, Michel-Rolph. *Silencing the Past: Power and the Production of History.* Boston, MA: Beacon Press, 1995.

Tunstall, Jeremy. *The Media Are American: Anglo-American Media in the World.* New York: Columbia University Press, 1977. Tunstall, Jeremy. *The Media Were American: U.S. Mass Media in Decline.* New York: Oxford University Press, 2007.

Turse, Nick. *Kill Anything That Moves: The Real American War in Vietnam.* New York: Metropolitan Books, 2013.

Turse, Nick, and Tom Engelhardt. *Terminator Planet: The First History of Drone Warfare, 2001–2050.* Createspace, http://dispatchbooks.tumblr.com/, 2012.

Tyrrell, Ian R. *Reforming the World: The Creation of America's Moral Empire.* Princeton, NJ: Princeton University Press, 2010.

Tyrrell, Ian R. *Transnational Nation: United States History in Global Perspective since 1789.* New York: Palgrave Macmillan, 2007.

Tyrrell, Ian R. *Woman's World/Woman's Empire: The Woman's Christian Temperance Union in International Perspective.* Chapel Hill: University of North Carolina Press, 1991.

U.S. Department of Defense. *2009–2034 Unmanned Systems Integrated Roadmap—Unmanned Aircraft (UAS), Unmanned Aerial Vehicle (UAV), UGV Ground Vehicles, UMS Maritime Systems, Drones, Technologies, Current and Future Programs.* Los Angeles, CA: Progressive Management, 2010.

U.S. Department of State. *Cuban Refugees.* Washington, DC: U.S. Government Printing Office, 1980.

U.S. Department of State. *Foreign Relations of the United States (FRUS): The Conferences at Cairo and Tehran.* Washington, DC: U.S. Government Printing Office, 1943.

U.S. Department of State. *Foreign Relations of the United States (FRUS): The Conferences at Washington, 1941–1942, and Casablanca, 1943.* Washington, DC: U.S. Government Printing Office, 1941–43.

U.S. Department of State. *Foreign Relations of the United States (FRUS), 1952–1954: National Security Affairs (in two parts).* Washington, DC: U.S. Government Printing Office, 1952–54.

U.S. House of Representatives. *Rise of the Drones: Unmanned Systems and the Future of War.* Ann Arbor, MI: Nimble Books, 2010.

Utley, Freda. *The High Cost of Vengeance.* Chicago: Henry Regnery, 1949.

Vaizey, Heather. *Surviving Hitler's War: Family Life in Germany, 1939–48.* New York: Palgrave Macmillan, 2010.

Valiani, Arafaat A. *Militant Publics in India.* New York: Palgrave Macmillan, 2011.

Von Eschen, Penny M. *Race against Empire: Black Americans and Anticolonialism, 1937–1957.* Ithaca, NY: Cornell University Press, 1997.

Von Eschen, Penny M. *Satchmo Blows Up the World: Jazz Ambassadors Play the Cold War.* Cambridge: Harvard University Press, 2006.

Wagg, Stephen, and David L. Andrews, eds. *East Plays West: Sport and the Cold War.* London: Routledge, 2007.

Walker, David. "Shooting Mabel: Warrior Masculinity and Asian Invasion." *History Australia* 2, no. 3 (2005): 89.1–89.11.

Walker, David, and Agnieszka Sobocinska, eds. *Australia's Asia: Reviewing Australia's Asian Pasts*. Perth: University of Western Australia Press, 2012.

Wang, Yiman. "The Art of Screen Passing: Anna May Wong's Yellow Yellowface Performance in the Art Deco Era." *Camera Obscura* 60 (2005): 159–91.

Ward, Geoffrey, ed. *Closest Companion: The Unknown Story of the Friendship between Franklin Roosevelt and Margaret Suckley*. New York: Houghton Mifflin, 1995.

Ward, Geoffrey C. *A First Class Temperament: The Emergence of Franklin D. Roosevelt*. New York: Harper and Row, 1989.

Warner, Patricia Campbell. "The Americanization of Fashion: Sportswear, the Movies and the 1930s." In *Twentieth-Century American Fashion*, edited by Linda Welters and Patricia A. Cunningham, 79–98. Oxford: Berg, 2005.

Warren, Louis. *Buffalo Bill's America: William Cody and the Wild West Show*. New York: Vintage, 2005.

Washburn, Patrick. *A Question of Sedition: The Federal Government's Investigation of the Black Press during World War II*. New York: Oxford University Press, 1986.

Waugh, Thomas. *Hard to Imagine: Gay Male Eroticism in Photography and Film*. New York: Columbia University Press, 1996.

Webber-Hanchett, Tiffany. "Dorothy Shaver: Promoter of 'The American Look.'" *Dress* 30 (2003): 80–90.

Webber-Hanchett, Tiffany M. "Dorothy Shaver: Promoter of the American Look." M.S. thesis, University of Rhode Island, 2003.

Weber, Susan, Kenneth Ames, and Matthew Wittmann, eds. *The American Circus*. New Haven, CT: Bard Graduate Center and Yale University Press, 2012.

Weil, Kari. *Androgyny and the Denial of Difference*. Charlottesville: University of Virginia Press, 1992.

Weinbaum, Alys Eve, Lynn M. Thomas, Priti Ramamurthy, Uta G. Poiger, Madeline Yue Dong, and Toni E. Barlow, eds. *The Modern Girl around the World: Consumption, Modernity, and Globalization*. Durham, NC: Duke University Press, 2008.

Weindling, Paul J. *Epidemics and Genocide in Eastern Europe*. Oxford: Oxford University Press, 2000.

Weiner, Jon. *How We Forgot the Cold War: A Historical Journey across America*. Berkeley: University of California Press, 2012.

Weinstein, Harvey. *Psychiatry and the CIA: Victims of Mind Control*. Washington, DC: American Psychiatric Press, 1990.

Welters, Linda, and Patricia A. Cunningham, eds. *Twentieth-Century American Fashion*. Oxford: Berg, 2005.

Westad, Odd Arne. *The Global Cold War: Third World Interventions and the Making of Our Times*. Cambridge, U.K.: Cambridge University Press, 2006.

Wexler, Laura. *Tender Violence: Domestic Visions in an Age of U.S. Imperialism.* Chapel Hill: University of North Carolina Press, 2000.

Whorton, James C. *Crusaders for Fitness.* Princeton: Princeton University Press, 1984.

Wiens, Gerhard. "Hunger." *Books Abroad* 22 (Winter 1948): 5–10.

Wilcox, Fred A. "'Dead Forests, Dying People': Agent Orange and Chemical Warfare in Vietnam." *Asia-Pacific Journal* 9, issue 50, no. 3 (2011), http://www.japanfocus.org/-Fred_A_-Wilcox/3662.

Williams, Michael. "'Would This Not Help Your Federation.'" *Otherland Literary Journal* 9 (2004): 217–36.

Winter, Jay. "Shell Shock and the Cultural History of the Great War." *Journal of Contemporary History* 35, no. 1 (2000): 7–11.

Wister, Owen. *The Pentecost of Calamity.* New York: Macmillan, 1915.

Wister, Owen. *A Straight Deal or The Ancient Grudge.* New York: Macmillan, 1921.

Wong, K. Scott, and Sucheng Chan, eds. *Claiming America: Constructing Chinese American Identities During the Exclusion Era.* Philadelphia, PA: Temple University Press, 1998.

Wong, Sau-ling Cynthia. *Reading Asian American Literature: From Necessity to Extravagance.* Princeton, NJ: Princeton University Press, 1993.

Wood, Clement. *Bernarr Macfadden: A Study in Success.* New York: Lewis Copeland, 1929.

Woollacott, Angela. "Rose Quong Becomes Chinese: An Australian in London and New York." *Australian Historical Studies* 129 (2007): 16–31.

Wu, Judy Tzu-Chun. *Dr. Mom Chung of the Fair-Haired Bastards: The Life of a Wartime Celebrity.* Berkeley: University of California Press, 2005.

Wyman, Mark. *Round-trip to America: The Immigrants Return to Europe, 1880–1930.* Ithaca, NY: Cornell University Press, 1993.

Yarrow, Andrew L. "Selling a New Vision of America to the World: Changing Messages in Early U.S. Cold War Print Propaganda." *Journal of Cold War Studies* 11 (Fall 2009): 3–45.

Yellin, Emily. *Our Mothers' War: American Women at Home and at the Front During World War II.* New York: Free Press, 2005.

Yep, Kathleen. *Outside the Paint: When Basketball Ruled at the Chinese Playground.* Philadelphia, PA: Temple University Press, 2009.

Yohannan, Kohle, and Nancy Nolf. *Claire McCardell: Redefining Modernism.* New York: Harry Abrams, 1998.

Young, Marilyn B. *The Vietnam Wars, 1945–1990.* New York: HarperCollins, 1991.

Young, Marilyn B., John J. Fitzgerald, and A. Tom Grunfeld, eds. *The Vietnam War: A History in Documents.* New York: Oxford University Press, 2002.

Young, Robert. *Colonial Desire: Hybridity in Theory, Culture, and Race.* New York: Routledge, 1995.

Yu, Henry. *Thinking Orientals: Migration, Contact, and Exoticism in Modern America*. New York: Oxford University Press, 2001.

Zaretsky, Natasha. *No Direction Home: The American Family and the Fear of National Decline, 1968–1980*. Chapel Hill: University of North Carolina Press, 2007.

Zeiger, Susan. *Entangling Alliances: Foreign War Brides and American Soldiers in the Twentieth Century*. New York: New York University Press, 2010.

Ziemke, Earl F. *The U.S. Army in the Occupation of Germany*. Washington, DC: Center of Military History, U.S. Army 1975.

Zimmerman, Jonathan. *Innocents Abroad: American Teachers in the American Century*. Cambridge: Harvard University Press, 2008.

Zolberg, Aristide R. *A Nation by Design: Immigration Policy in the Fashioning of America*. Cambridge: Harvard University Press, 2006.

contributors

FRANK COSTIGLIOLA is a professor of history at the University of Connecticut. He is the author of *Roosevelt's Lost Alliances: How Personal Politics Helped Start the Cold War* (2012); *France and the United States: The Cold Alliance Since World War II* (1992); and *Awkward Dominion: American Political, Economic, and Cultural Relations with Europe, 1919–1933* (1984). He is currently editing the diaries of George F. Kennan.

JANET M. DAVIS is an associate professor of American studies and history at the University of Texas at Austin. She is the author of *The Circus Age: Culture and Society under the American Big Top* (2002) and the editor of *Tiny Kline, Circus Queen and Tinker Bell: The Life of Tiny Kline* (2008). She is also the author of *The Gospel of Kindness: Animal Welfare and the Making of Modern America* (forthcoming).

SHANON FITZPATRICK is a faculty lecturer in the Department of History at McGill University. Her current project, *Pulp Empire*, explores transnational America's globalized, nonelite print media in the twentieth century. Other research interests include the histories of eugenics, physical culture, modernity, and consumption.

PAUL A. KRAMER is an associate professor of history at Vanderbilt University and coeditor of Cornell University Press's United States in the World series. He is the author of *The Blood of Government: Race, Empire, the United States and the Philippines* (2006) and numerous articles, including "Power and Connection: Imperial Histories of the United States in the World" (*American Historical Review* 2011).

SHIRLEY JENNIFER LIM is an associate professor of history and affiliate faculty in cultural analysis and theory and Africana studies at SUNY Stony Brook. She is the author of *A Feeling of Belonging: Asian American Women's Public*

Culture, 1930–1960 (2005) and is completing the book *Performing the Modern: Anna May Wong and Josephine Baker.*

MARY TING YI LUI is a professor of American studies and history at Yale University. She is the author of *The Chinatown Trunk Mystery: Murder, Miscegenation, and Other Dangerous Encounters in Turn-of-the-Century New York City* (2005), the 2007 cowinner of the best book prize for history from the Association of Asian American Studies. Her current book project, *Making Model Minorities: Asian Americans, Race, and Citizenship in Cold War America at Home and Abroad,* examines the history of Asian American and U.S. cultural diplomacy in Asia in the early years of the cold war.

NATALIA MOLINA is the associate dean for faculty equity, Division of Arts and Humanities, and an associate professor in the Department of History and Urban Studies Program at the University of California, San Diego. She is the author of *Fit to be Citizens? Public Health and Race in Los Angeles, 1879–1939* (2006) and *How Race Is Made in America: Immigration, Citizenship, and the Historical Power of Racial Scripts* (2013).

BRENDA GAYLE PLUMMER is a professor in the Department of History at the University of Wisconsin, Madison. She is the author of *Rising Wind: Black Americans and U.S. Foreign Affairs, 1935–1960* (1996); *Haiti and the United States* (1992); and *Haiti and the Great Powers, 1902–1915* (1988).

EMILY S. ROSENBERG, professor and chair of history at the University of California, Irvine, specializes in the history of the United States and the World in the twentieth century. She is author of *Transnational Currents in a Shrinking World, 1870–1945* (2014) and editor of *A World Connecting: 1870–1945* (2012). Other books include *Spreading the American Dream: American Economic and Cultural Expansion, 1890–1945* (1982); *Financial Missionaries to the World: The Politics and Culture of Dollar Diplomacy, 1900–1930* (1999); and *A Date Which Will Live: Pearl Harbor in American Memory* (2003).

KRISTINA SHULL is a doctoral candidate in history at the University of California, Irvine. She has also worked as a researcher for the Detention Watch Network and published essays on the War on Drugs, the War on Terror, and anti-immigrant movements in the United States.

ANNESSA C. STAGNER is a doctoral candidate in the Department of History at the University of California, Irvine. Her publications include "Healing a Soldier, Restoring the Nation: Representations of Shell Shock in the United States during and after the First World War" (*Journal of Contemporary History*

2014). She is a recipient of the Humanities and Medicine Andrew V. White University of California Scholarship and the PEO International Scholar Award.

MARILYN B. YOUNG is a professor of history at NYU and director of the Tamiment Center for the Study of the Cold War. She is the coeditor with Yuki Tanaka of *Bombing Civilians* (2009) and the author of *The Vietnam Wars, 1945–1990* (1991).

index